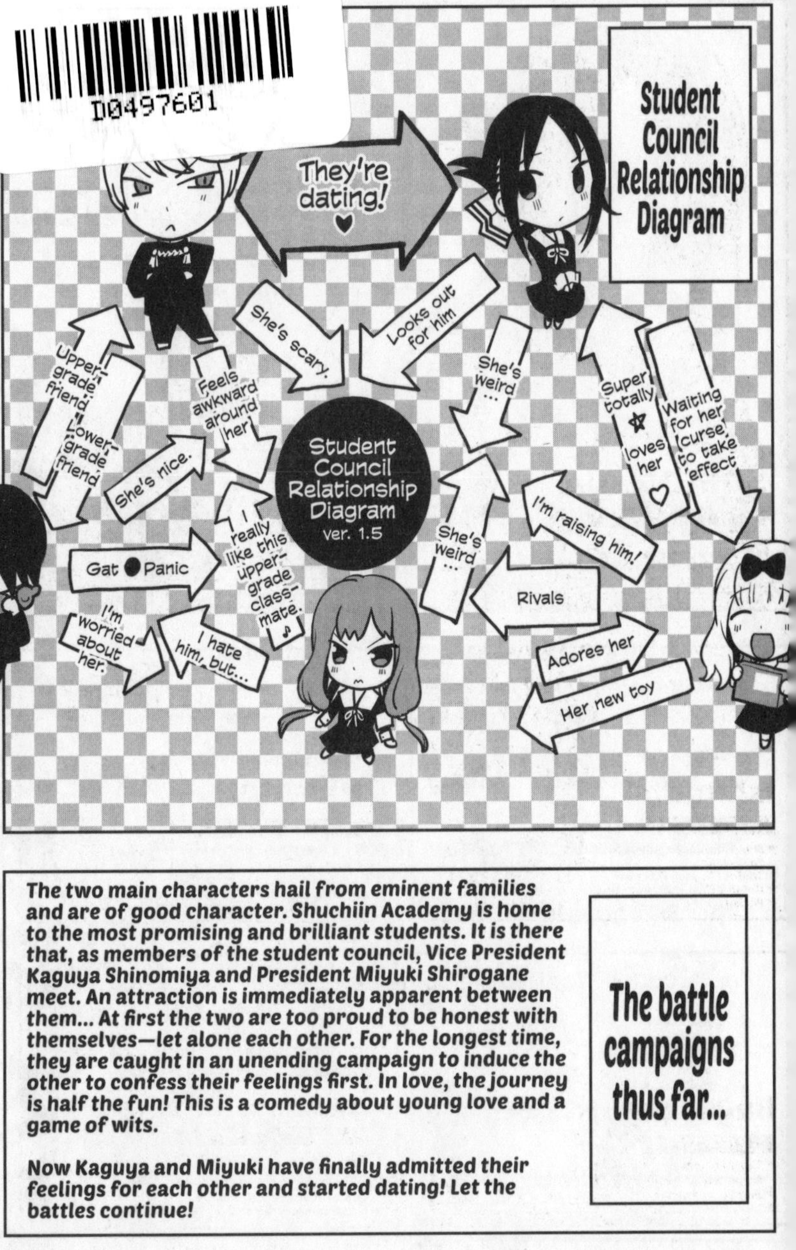
Student Council Relationship Diagram
They're dating! ♥
She's scary.
Looks out for him
She's weird...
Super totally ☆ loves her ♡
Waiting for her [curse] to take effect
Upper-grade friend
Lower-grade friend
Feels awkward around her
She's nice.
Student Council Relationship Diagram ver. 1.5
I really like this upper-grade classmate. ♪
She's weird...
I'm raising him!
Gat ● Panic
Rivals
I'm worried about her.
I hate him, but...
Adores her
Her new toy

The two main characters hail from eminent families and are of good character. Shuchiin Academy is home to the most promising and brilliant students. It is there that, as members of the student council, Vice President Kaguya Shinomiya and President Miyuki Shirogane meet. An attraction is immediately apparent between them... At first the two are too proud to be honest with themselves—let alone each other. For the longest time, they are caught in an unending campaign to induce the other to confess their feelings first. In love, the journey is half the fun! This is a comedy about young love and a game of wits.

Now Kaguya and Miyuki have finally admitted their feelings for each other and started dating! Let the battles continue!

The battle campaigns thus far...

KAGUYA-SAMA LOVE IS WAR

BATTLE CAMPAIGNS

21

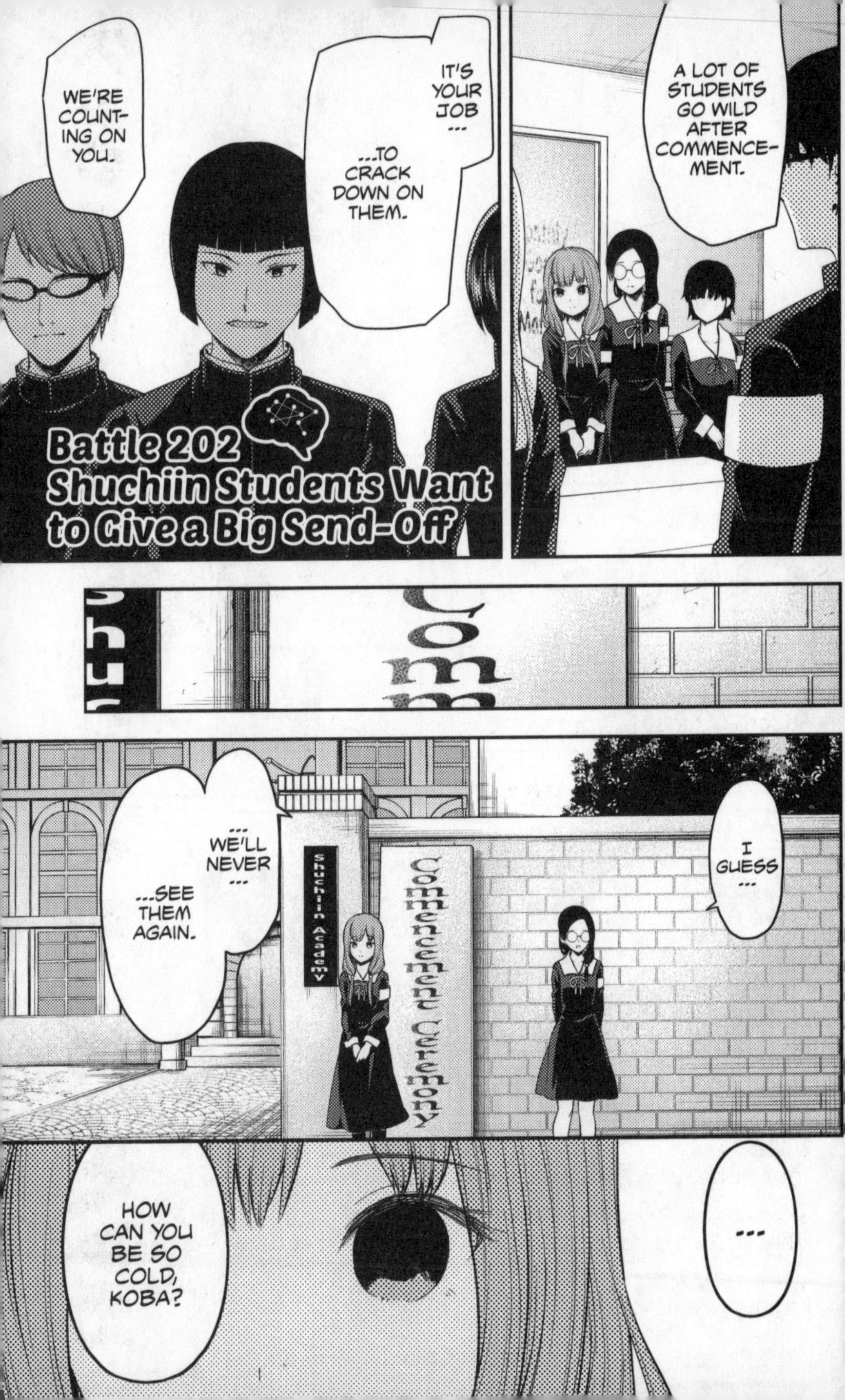
A LOT OF STUDENTS GO WILD AFTER COMMENCEMENT.
IT'S YOUR JOB ...
...TO CRACK DOWN ON THEM.
WE'RE COUNTING ON YOU.
Battle 202 Shuchiin Students Want to Give a Big Send-Off
I GUESS ...
... WE'LL NEVER ...
...SEE THEM AGAIN.
Shuchiin Academy
Commencement Ceremony
...
HOW CAN YOU BE SO COLD, KOBA?

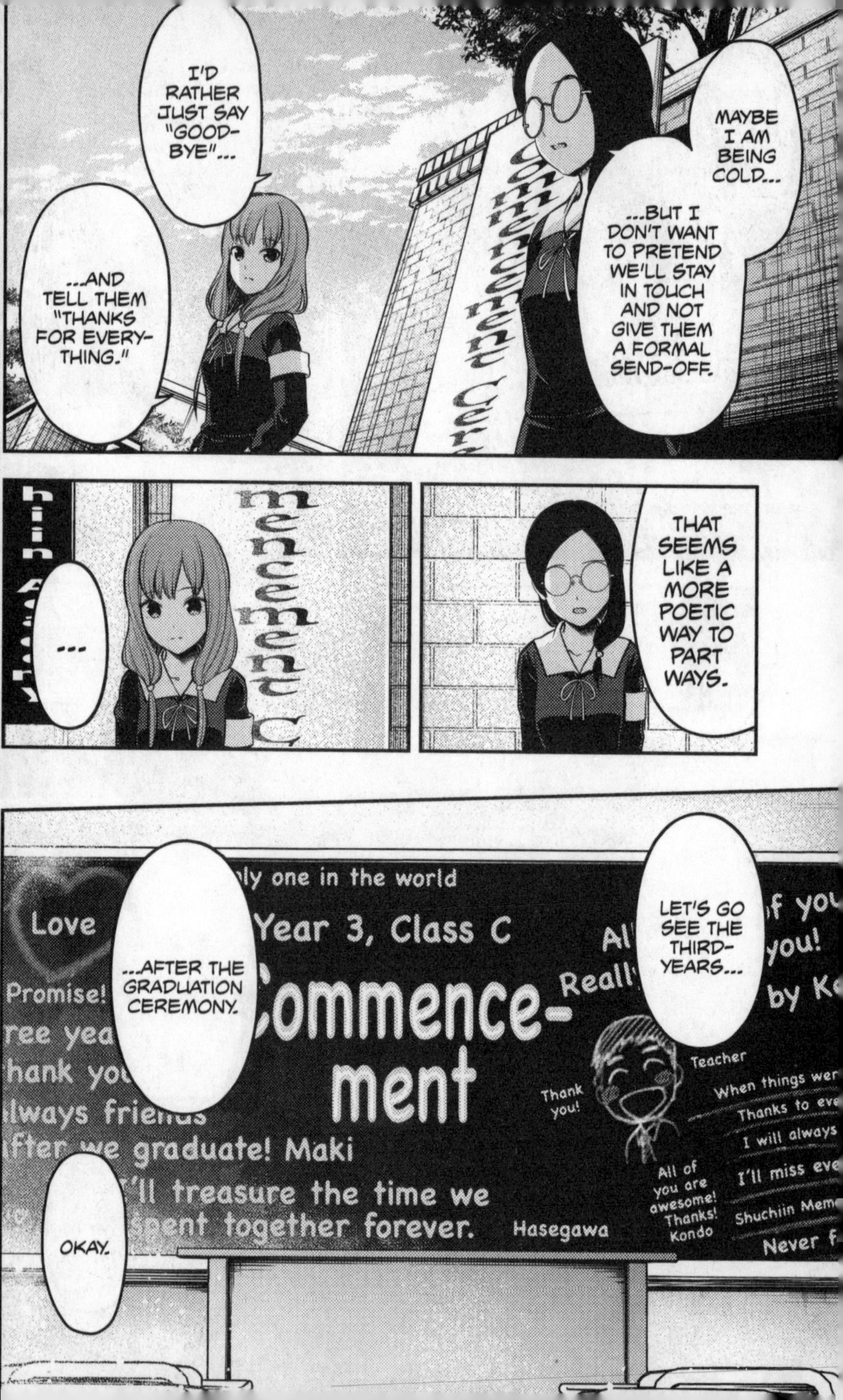
MAYBE I AM BEING COLD...
...BUT I DON'T WANT TO PRETEND WE'LL STAY IN TOUCH AND NOT GIVE THEM A FORMAL SEND-OFF.
I'D RATHER JUST SAY "GOOD-BYE"...
...AND TELL THEM "THANKS FOR EVERY-THING."
THAT SEEMS LIKE A MORE POETIC WAY TO PART WAYS.
...
LET'S GO SEE THE THIRD-YEARS...
...AFTER THE GRADUATION CEREMONY.
OKAY.
Year 3, Class C
Commence-ment
Love
Promise!
Teacher
Thank you!
All of you are awesome! Thanks! Kondo
Hasegawa

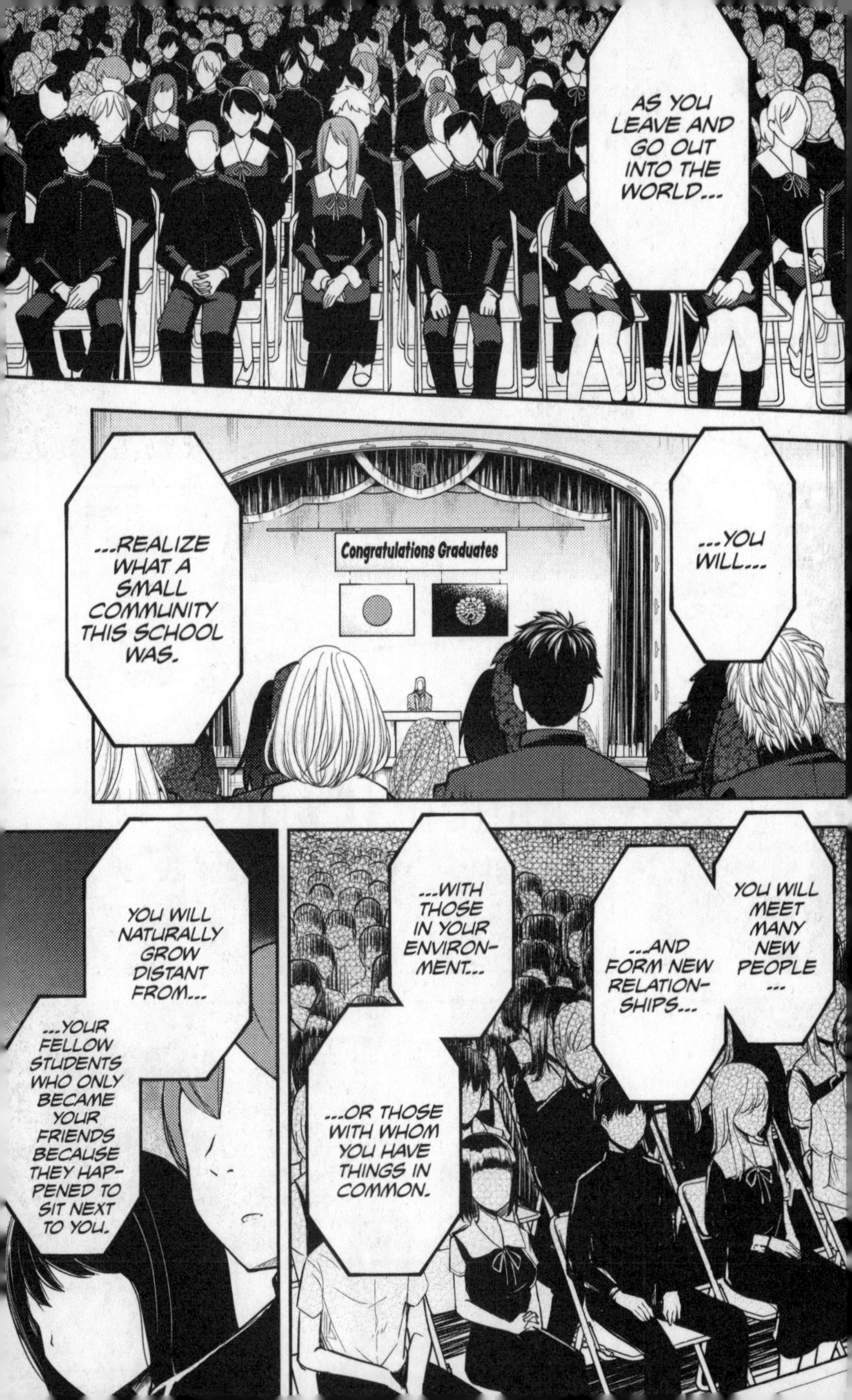
AS YOU LEAVE AND GO OUT INTO THE WORLD...
...YOU WILL...
...REALIZE WHAT A SMALL COMMUNITY THIS SCHOOL WAS.
Congratulations Graduates
YOU WILL MEET MANY NEW PEOPLE ...
...AND FORM NEW RELATIONSHIPS...
...WITH THOSE IN YOUR ENVIRONMENT...
...OR THOSE WITH WHOM YOU HAVE THINGS IN COMMON.
YOU WILL NATURALLY GROW DISTANT FROM...
...YOUR FELLOW STUDENTS WHO ONLY BECAME YOUR FRIENDS BECAUSE THEY HAPPENED TO SIT NEXT TO YOU.

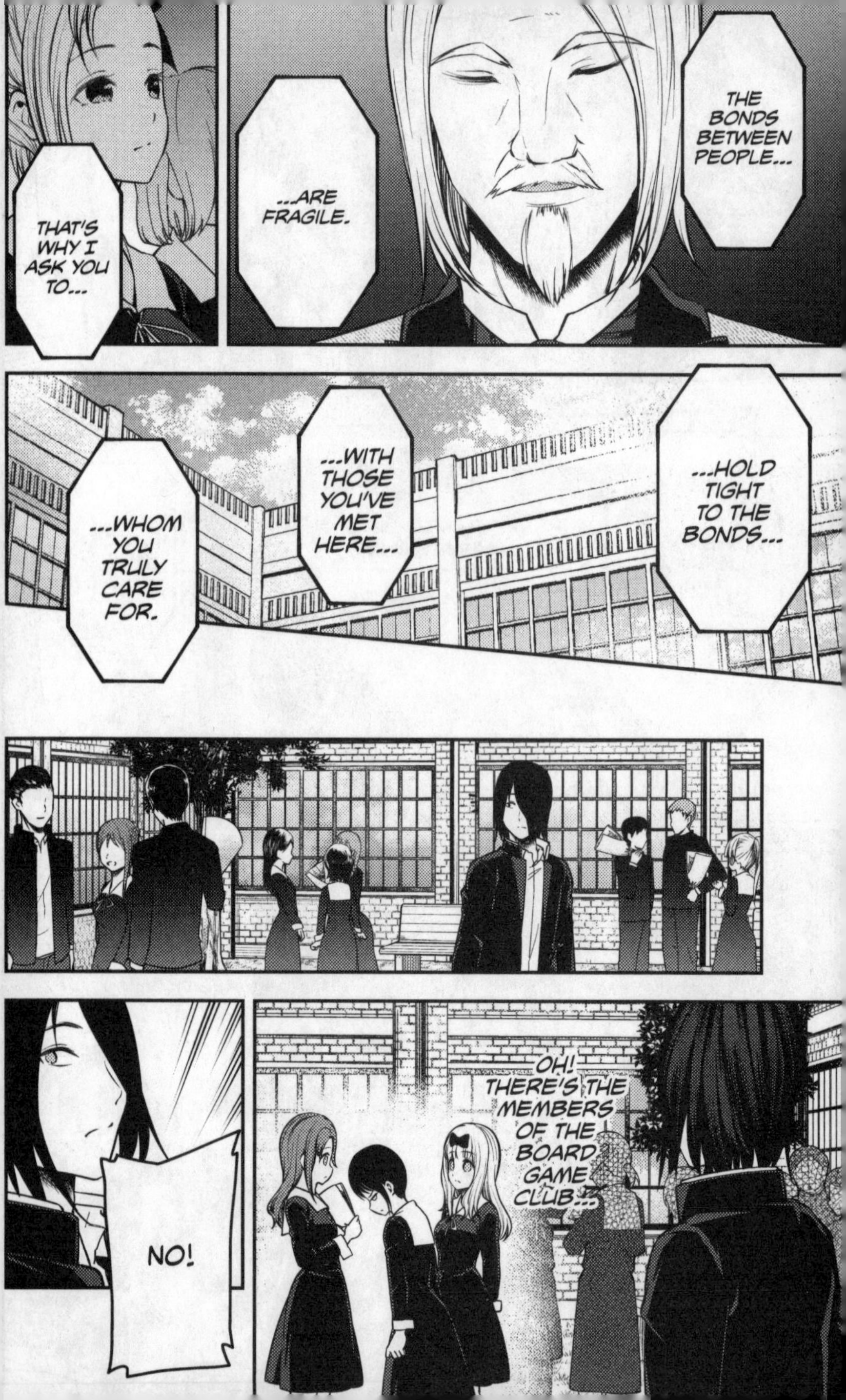
THE BONDS BETWEEN PEOPLE...
...ARE FRAGILE.
THAT'S WHY I ASK YOU TO...
...HOLD TIGHT TO THE BONDS...
...WITH THOSE YOU'VE MET HERE...
...WHOM YOU TRULY CARE FOR.
OH! THERE'S THE MEMBERS OF THE BOARD GAME CLUB...!
NO!

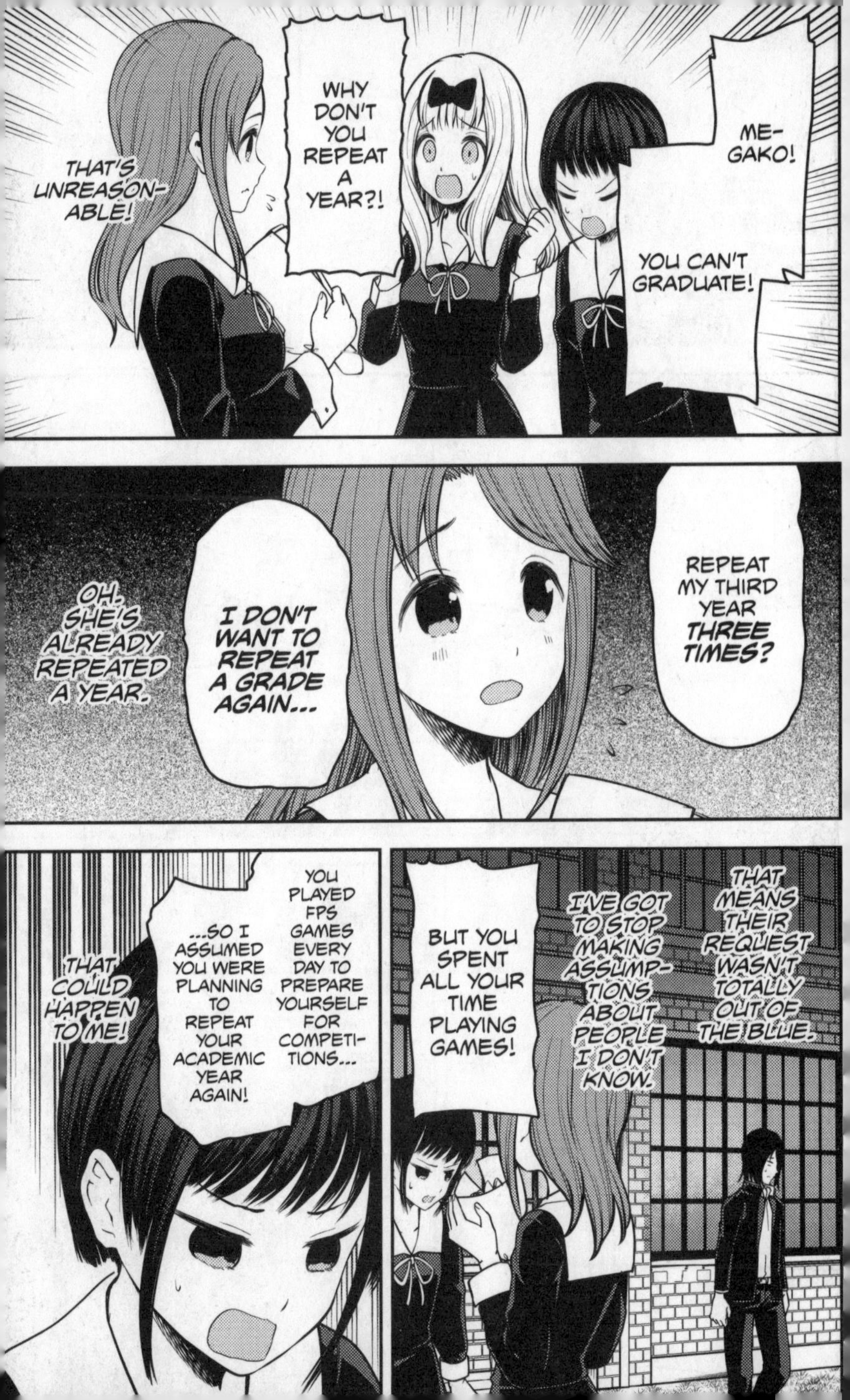

ME-GAKO!
YOU CAN'T GRADUATE!
WHY DON'T YOU REPEAT A YEAR?!
THAT'S UNREASON-ABLE!
REPEAT MY THIRD YEAR THREE TIMES?
I DON'T WANT TO REPEAT A GRADE AGAIN...
OH. SHE'S ALREADY REPEATED A YEAR.
YOU PLAYED FPS GAMES EVERY DAY TO PREPARE YOURSELF FOR COMPETI-TIONS...
...SO I ASSUMED YOU WERE PLANNING TO REPEAT YOUR ACADEMIC YEAR AGAIN!
THAT COULD HAPPEN TO ME!
THAT MEANS THEIR REQUEST WASN'T TOTALLY OUT OF THE BLUE.
I'VE GOT TO STOP MAKING ASSUMP-TIONS ABOUT PEOPLE I DON'T KNOW.
BUT YOU SPENT ALL YOUR TIME PLAYING GAMES!

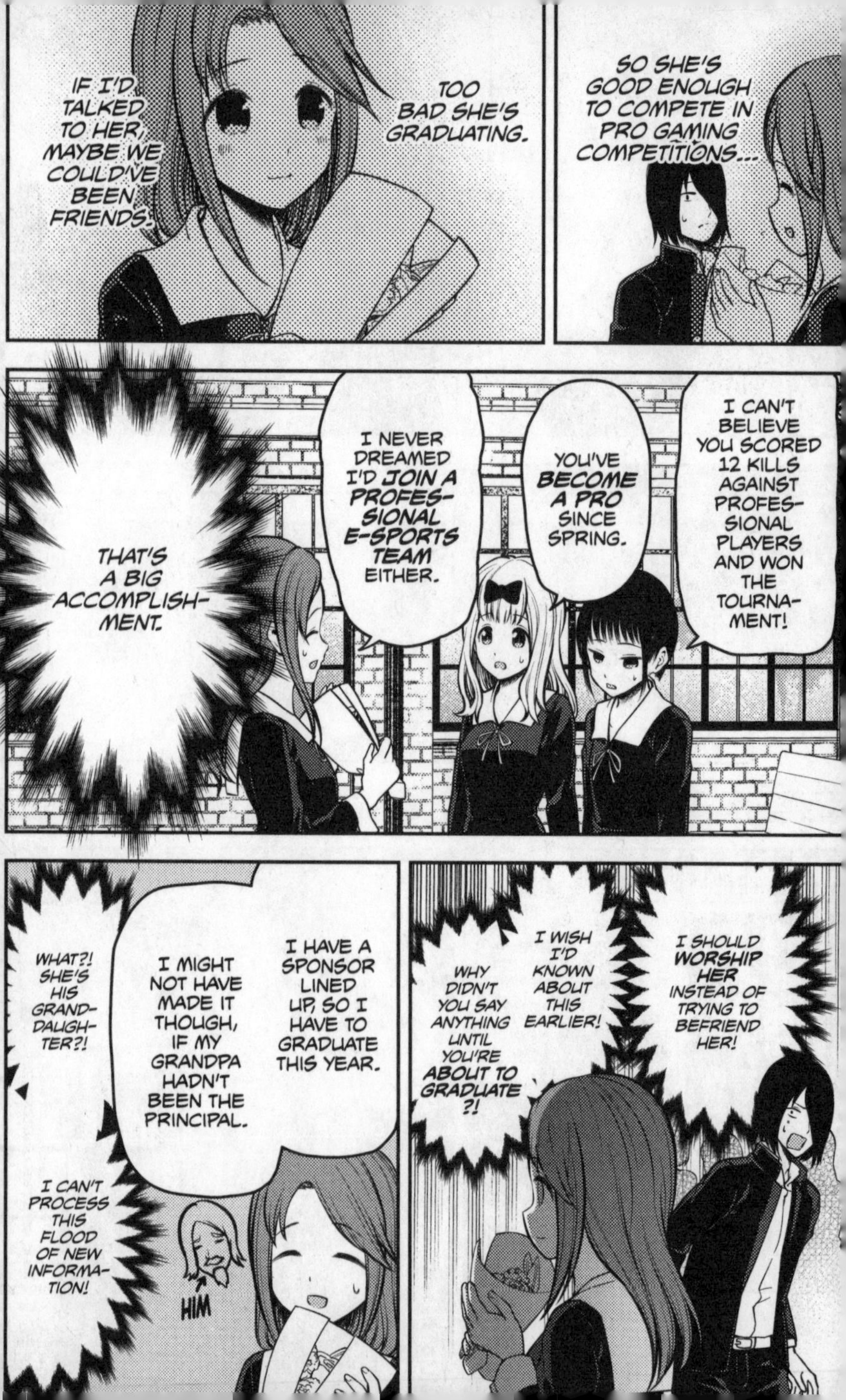

SO SHE'S GOOD ENOUGH TO COMPETE IN PRO GAMING COMPETITIONS...
TOO BAD SHE'S GRADUATING.
IF I'D TALKED TO HER, MAYBE WE COULD'VE BEEN FRIENDS.
I CAN'T BELIEVE YOU SCORED 12 KILLS AGAINST PROFES-SIONAL PLAYERS AND WON THE TOURNA-MENT!
YOU'VE BECOME A PRO SINCE SPRING.
I NEVER DREAMED I'D JOIN A PROFES-SIONAL E-SPORTS TEAM EITHER.
THAT'S A BIG ACCOMPLISH-MENT.
I SHOULD WORSHIP HER INSTEAD OF TRYING TO BEFRIEND HER!
I WISH I'D KNOWN ABOUT THIS EARLIER!
WHY DIDN'T YOU SAY ANYTHING UNTIL YOU'RE ABOUT TO GRADUATE?!
I HAVE A SPONSOR LINED UP, SO I HAVE TO GRADUATE THIS YEAR.
I MIGHT NOT HAVE MADE IT THOUGH, IF MY GRANDPA HADN'T BEEN THE PRINCIPAL.
WHAT?! SHE'S HIS GRAND-DAUGH-TER?!
I CAN'T PROCESS THIS FLOOD OF NEW INFORMA-TION!
HIM

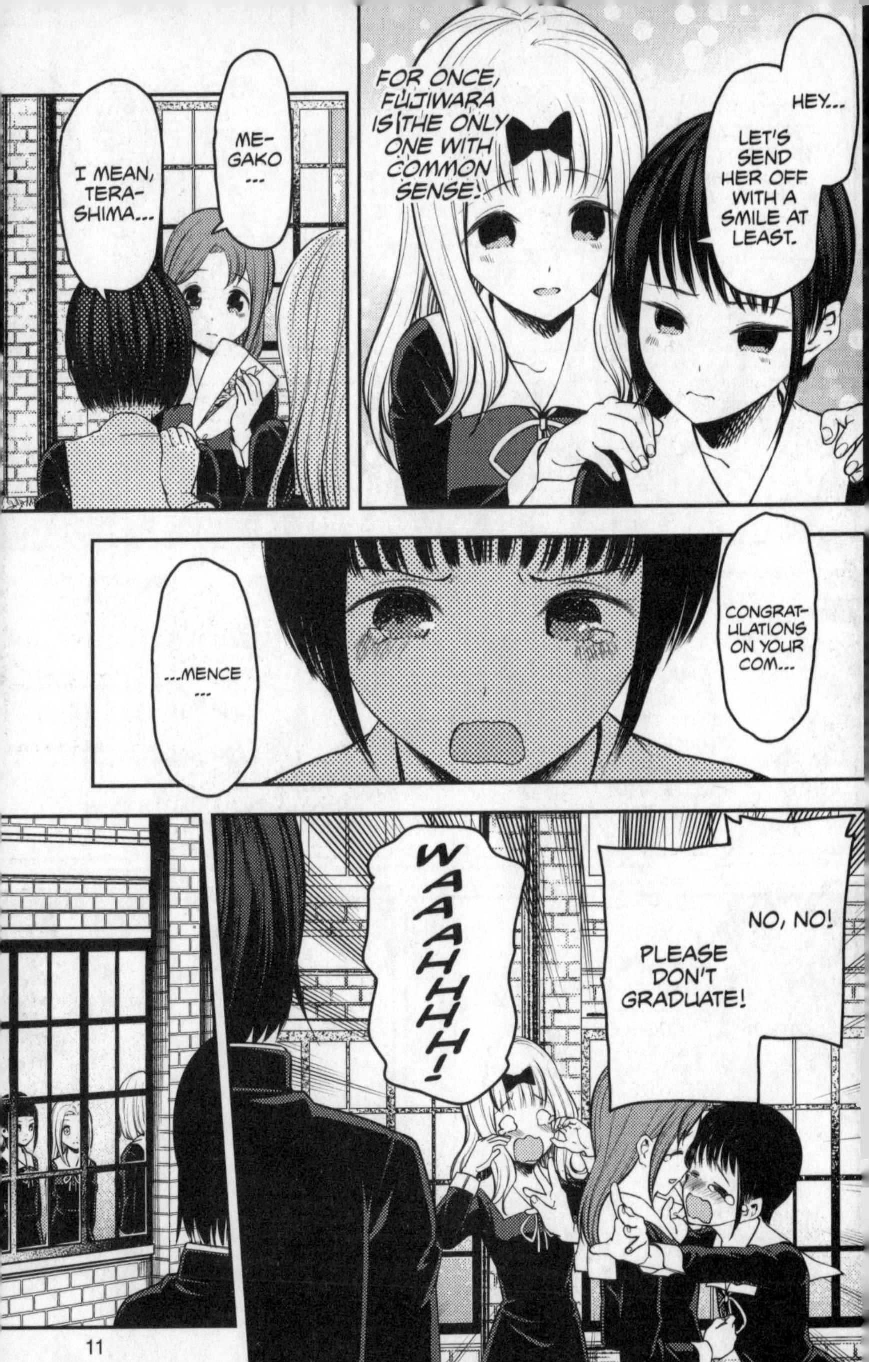
HEY... LET'S SEND HER OFF WITH A SMILE AT LEAST.
FOR ONCE, FUJIWARA IS THE ONLY ONE WITH COMMON SENSE!
ME-GAKO...
I MEAN, TERA-SHIMA...
CONGRAT-ULATIONS ON YOUR COM...
...MENCE...
NO, NO! PLEASE DON'T GRADUATE!
WAAAHHHH!

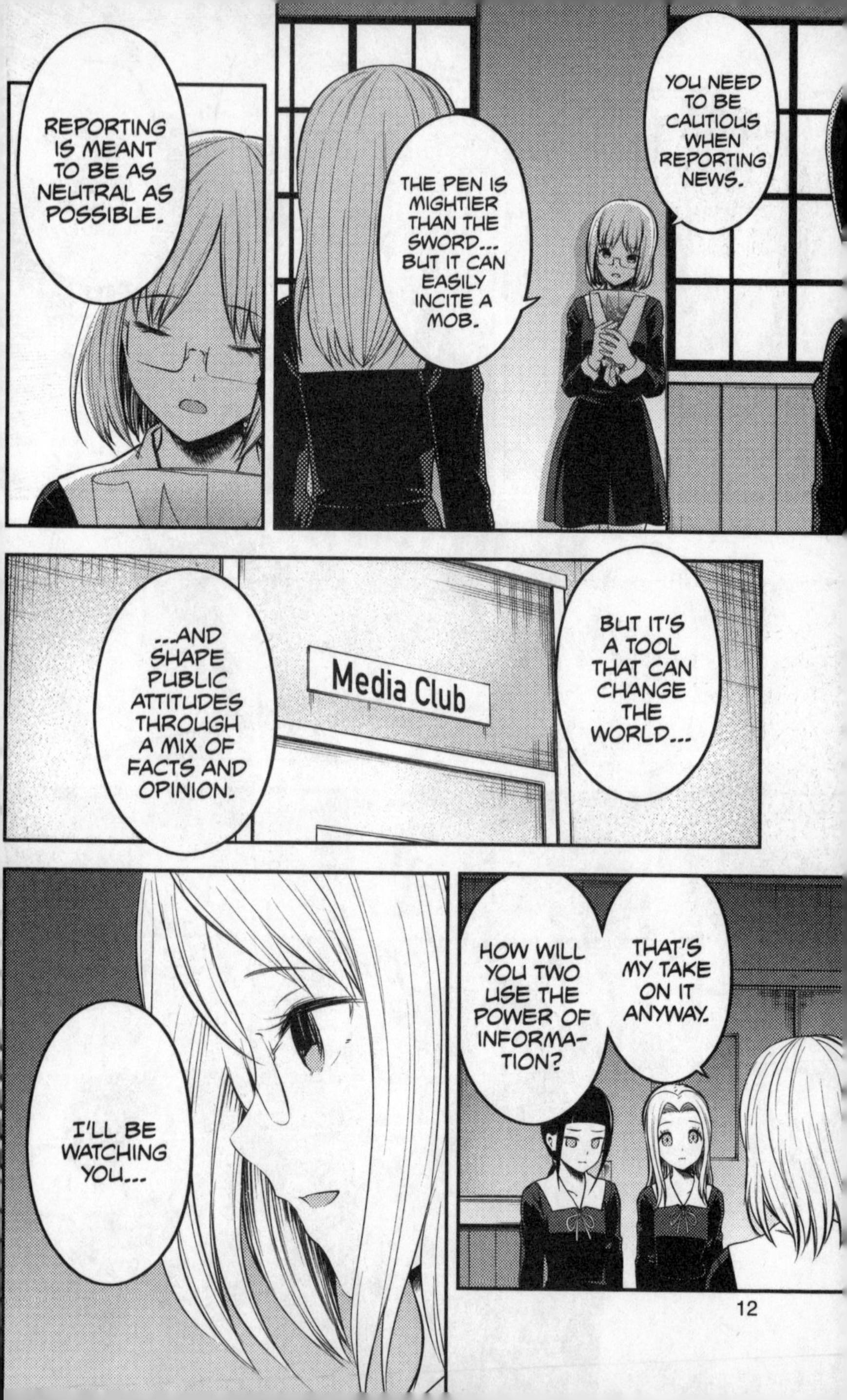
YOU NEED TO BE CAUTIOUS WHEN REPORTING NEWS.
THE PEN IS MIGHTIER THAN THE SWORD... BUT IT CAN EASILY INCITE A MOB.
REPORTING IS MEANT TO BE AS NEUTRAL AS POSSIBLE.
BUT IT'S A TOOL THAT CAN CHANGE THE WORLD...
Media Club
...AND SHAPE PUBLIC ATTITUDES THROUGH A MIX OF FACTS AND OPINION.
THAT'S MY TAKE ON IT ANYWAY.
HOW WILL YOU TWO USE THE POWER OF INFORMA-TION?
I'LL BE WATCHING YOU...

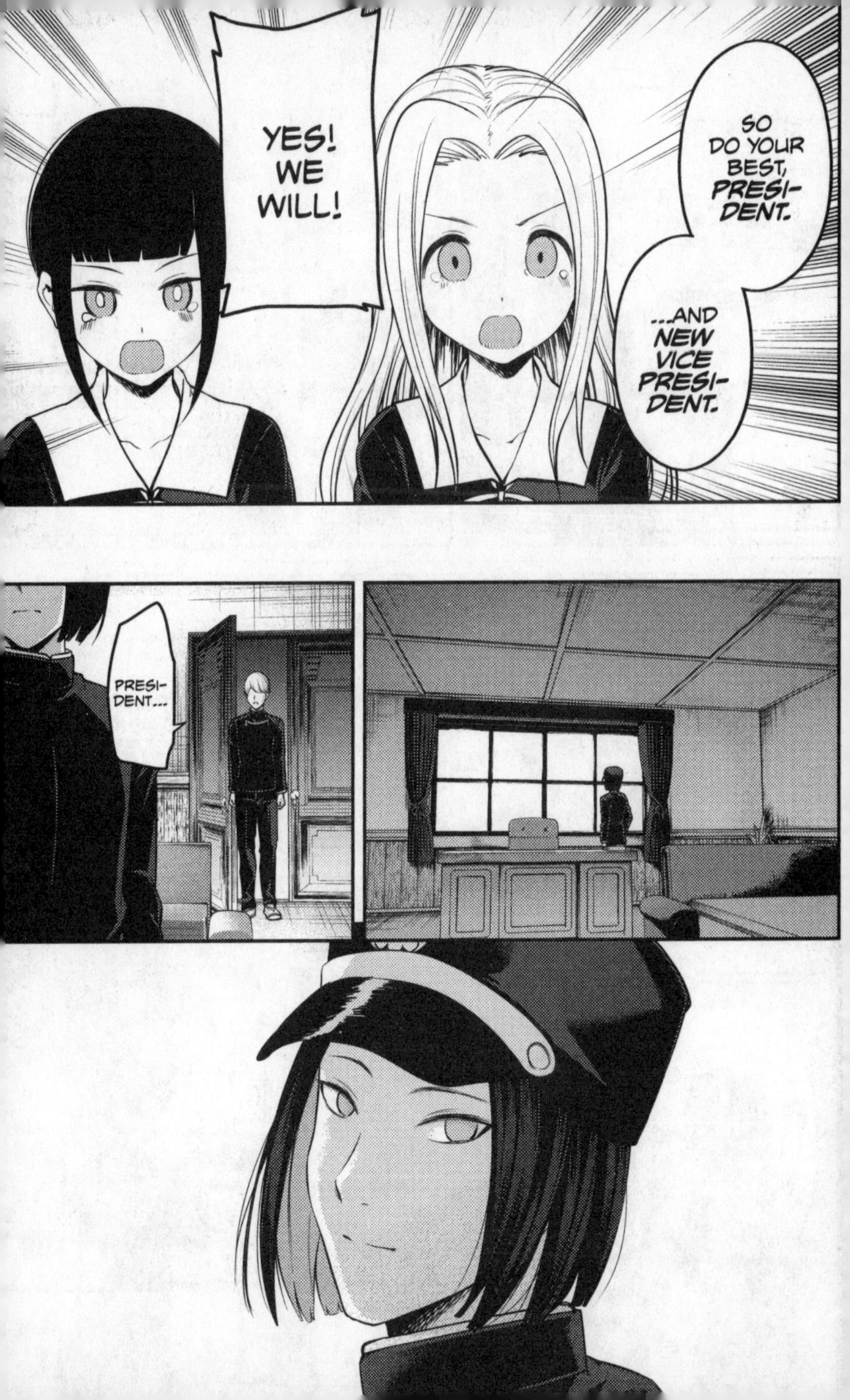
SO DO YOUR BEST, PRESIDENT.
...AND NEW VICE PRESIDENT.
YES! WE WILL!
PRESIDENT...

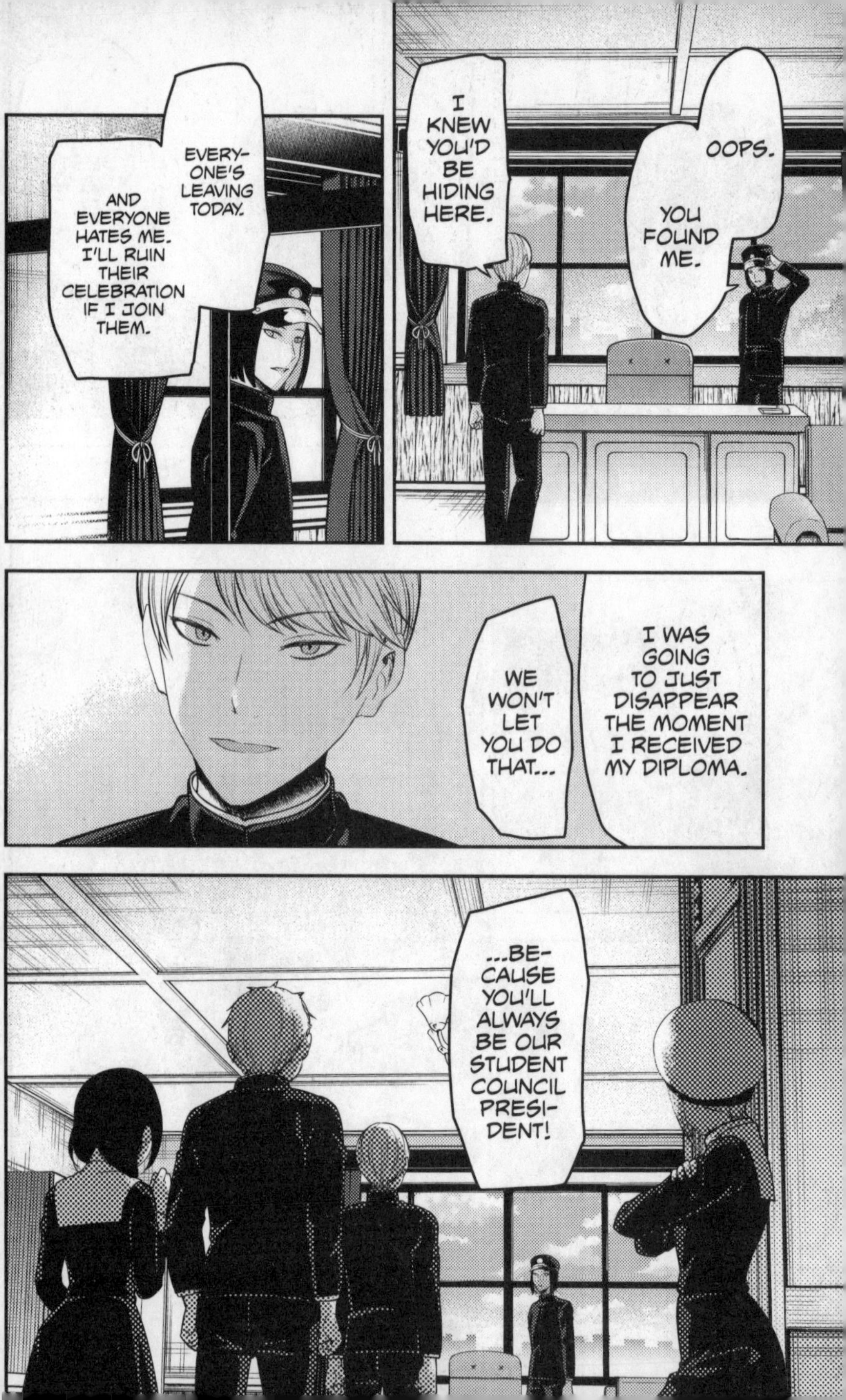
I KNEW YOU'D BE HIDING HERE.
OOPS.
YOU FOUND ME.
EVERY-ONE'S LEAVING TODAY.
AND EVERYONE HATES ME. I'LL RUIN THEIR CELEBRATION IF I JOIN THEM.
I WAS GOING TO JUST DISAPPEAR THE MOMENT I RECEIVED MY DIPLOMA.
WE WON'T LET YOU DO THAT...
...BE-CAUSE YOU'LL ALWAYS BE OUR STUDENT COUNCIL PRESI-DENT!

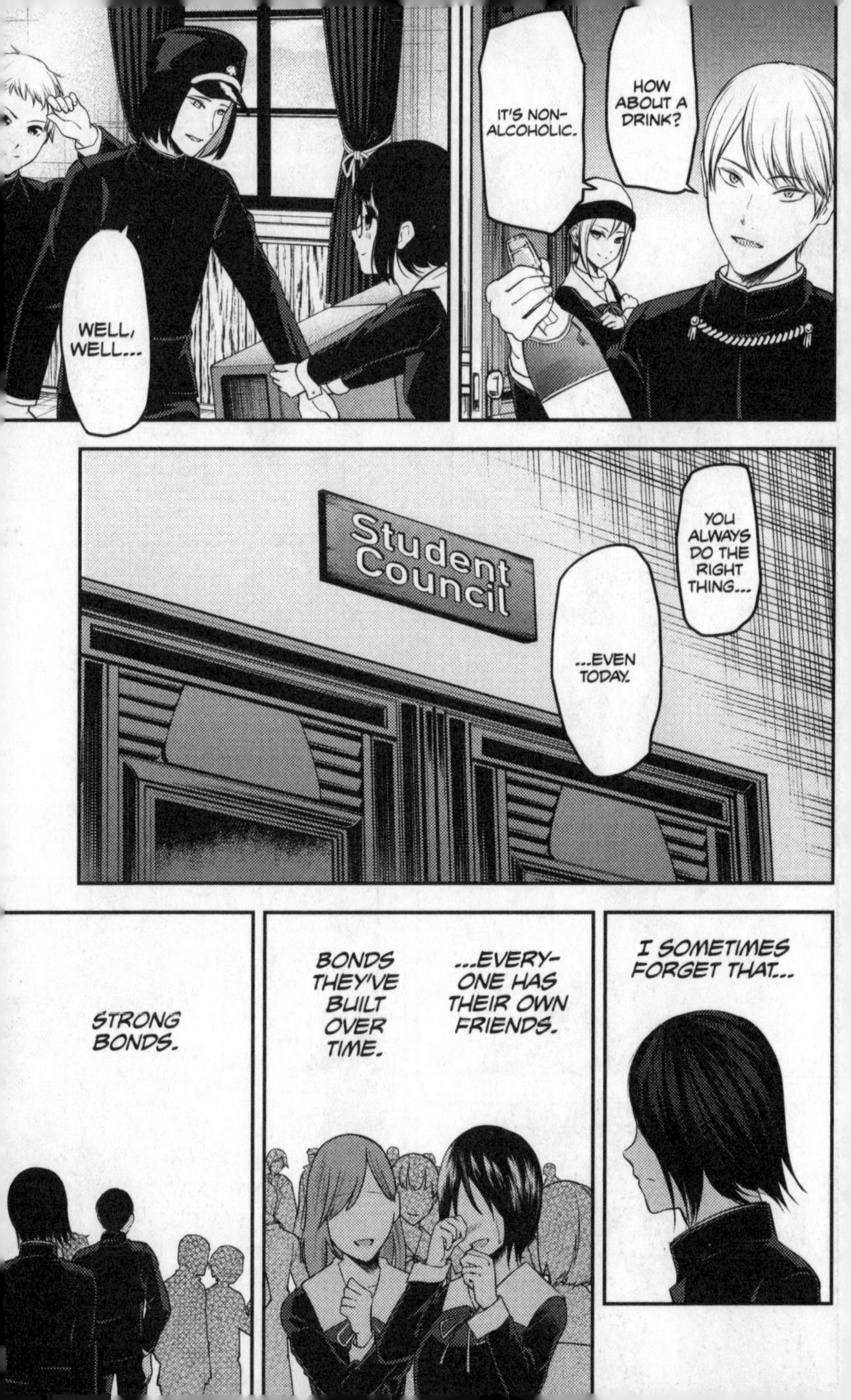
HOW ABOUT A DRINK?
IT'S NON-ALCOHOLIC.
WELL, WELL...
Student Council
YOU ALWAYS DO THE RIGHT THING...
...EVEN TODAY.
I SOMETIMES FORGET THAT...
...EVERYONE HAS THEIR OWN FRIENDS.
BONDS THEY'VE BUILT OVER TIME.
STRONG BONDS.

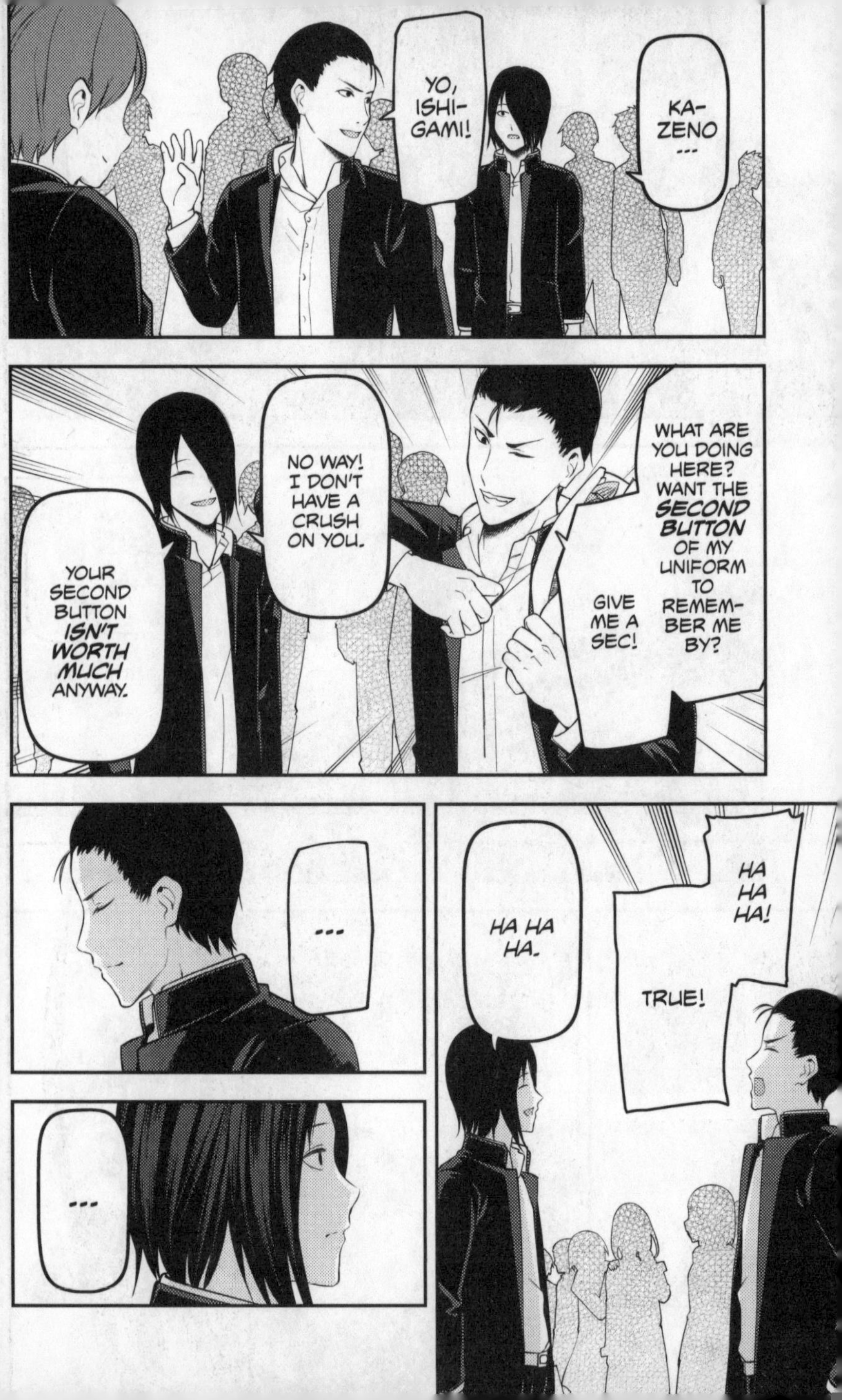
KA-ZENO ...
YO, ISHI-GAMI!
WHAT ARE YOU DOING HERE? WANT THE ***SECOND BUTTON*** OF MY UNIFORM TO REMEMBER ME BY?
GIVE ME A SEC!
NO WAY! I DON'T HAVE A CRUSH ON YOU.
YOUR SECOND BUTTON ***ISN'T WORTH MUCH*** ANYWAY.
HA HA HA!
TRUE!
HA HA HA.
...
...

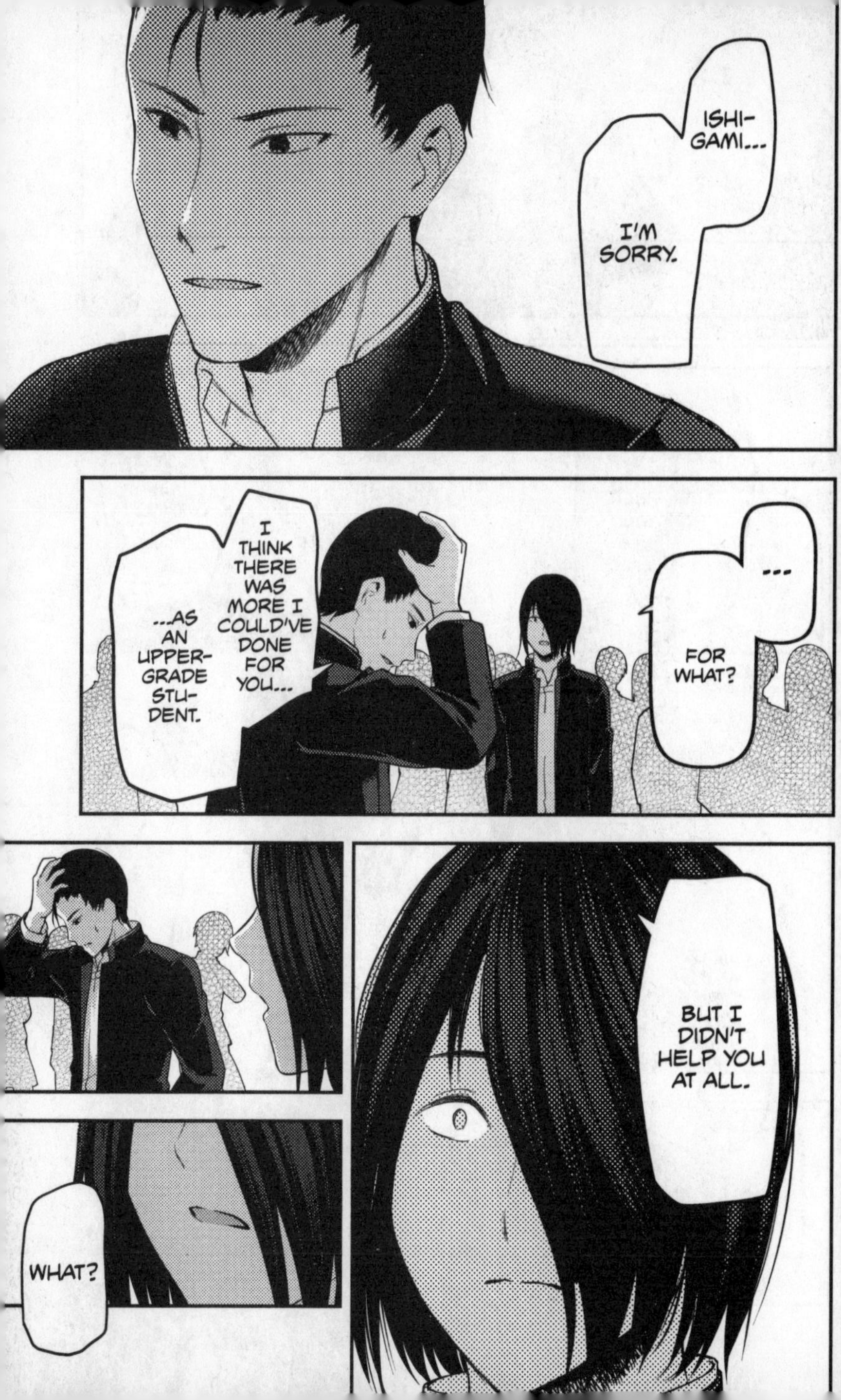
ISHI-GAMI...
I'M SORRY.
... FOR WHAT?
I THINK THERE WAS MORE I COULD'VE DONE FOR YOU...
...AS AN UPPER-GRADE STU-DENT.
BUT I DIDN'T HELP YOU AT ALL.
WHAT?

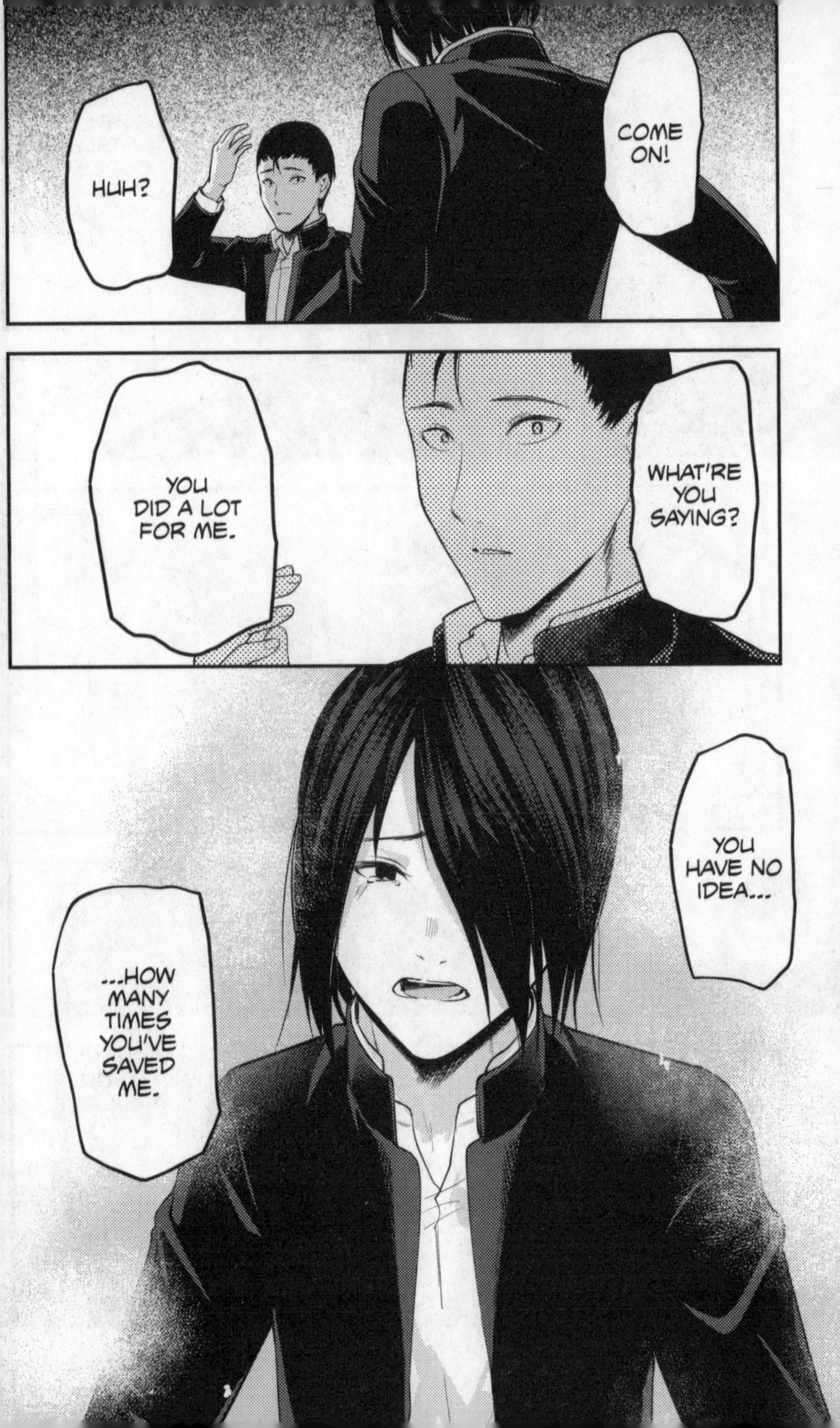
COME ON!
HUH?
WHAT'RE YOU SAYING?
YOU DID A LOT FOR ME.
YOU HAVE NO IDEA...
...HOW MANY TIMES YOU'VE SAVED ME.

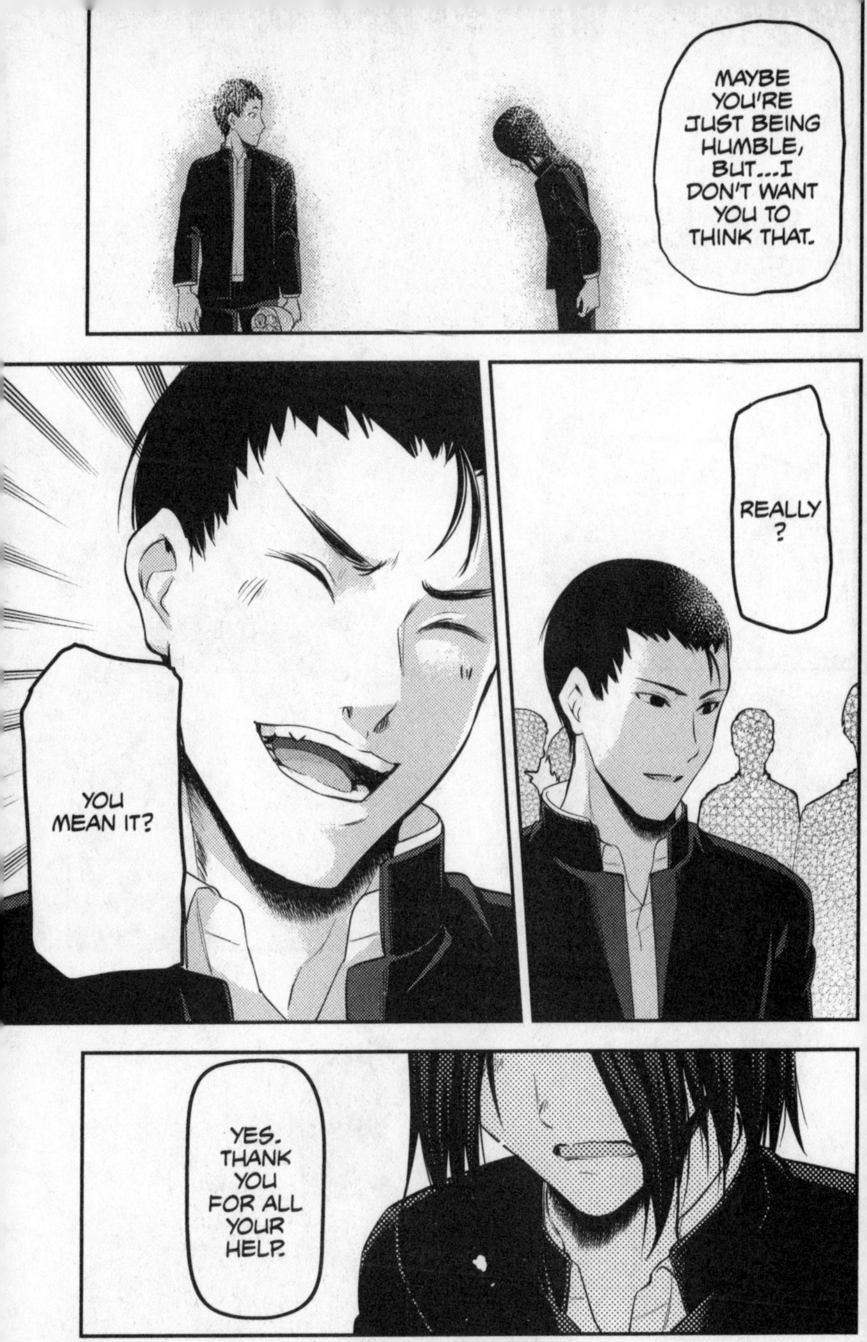
MAYBE YOU'RE JUST BEING HUMBLE, BUT...I DON'T WANT YOU TO THINK THAT.
REALLY?
YOU MEAN IT?
YES. THANK YOU FOR ALL YOUR HELP.

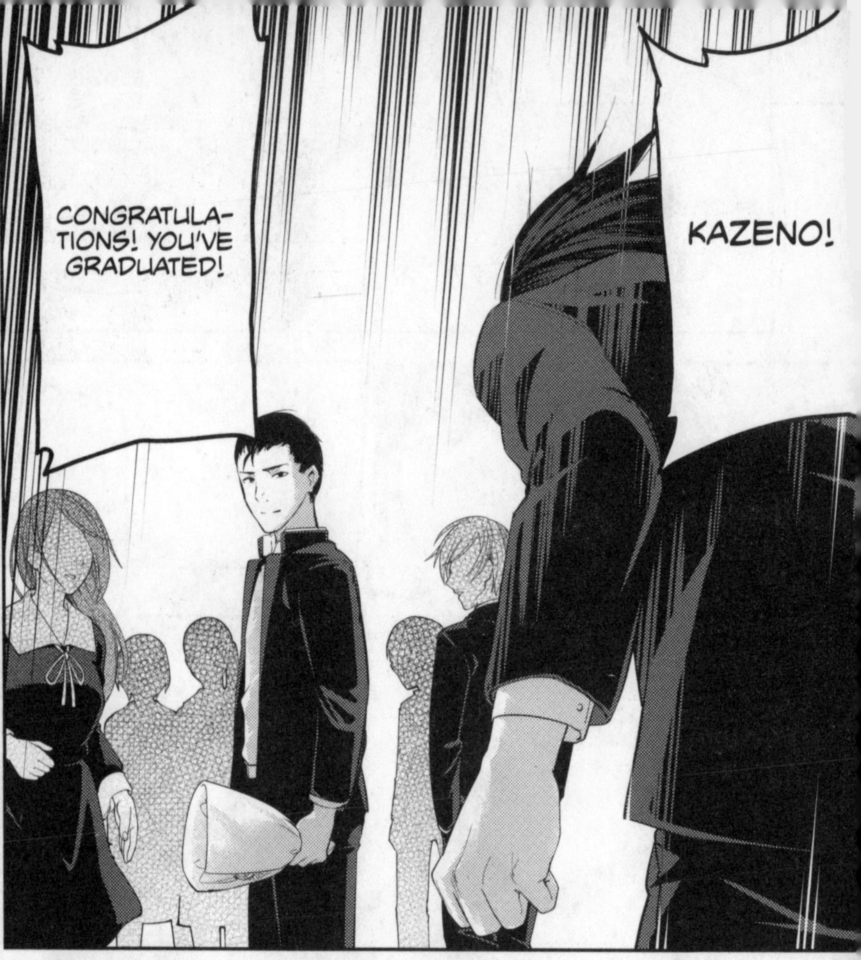
KAZENO!
CONGRATULA-TIONS! YOU'VE GRADUATED!
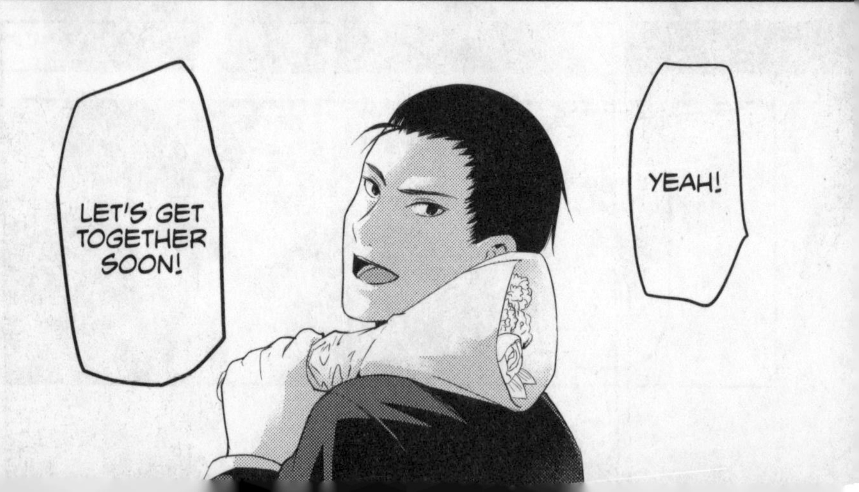
YEAH!
LET'S GET TOGETHER SOON!

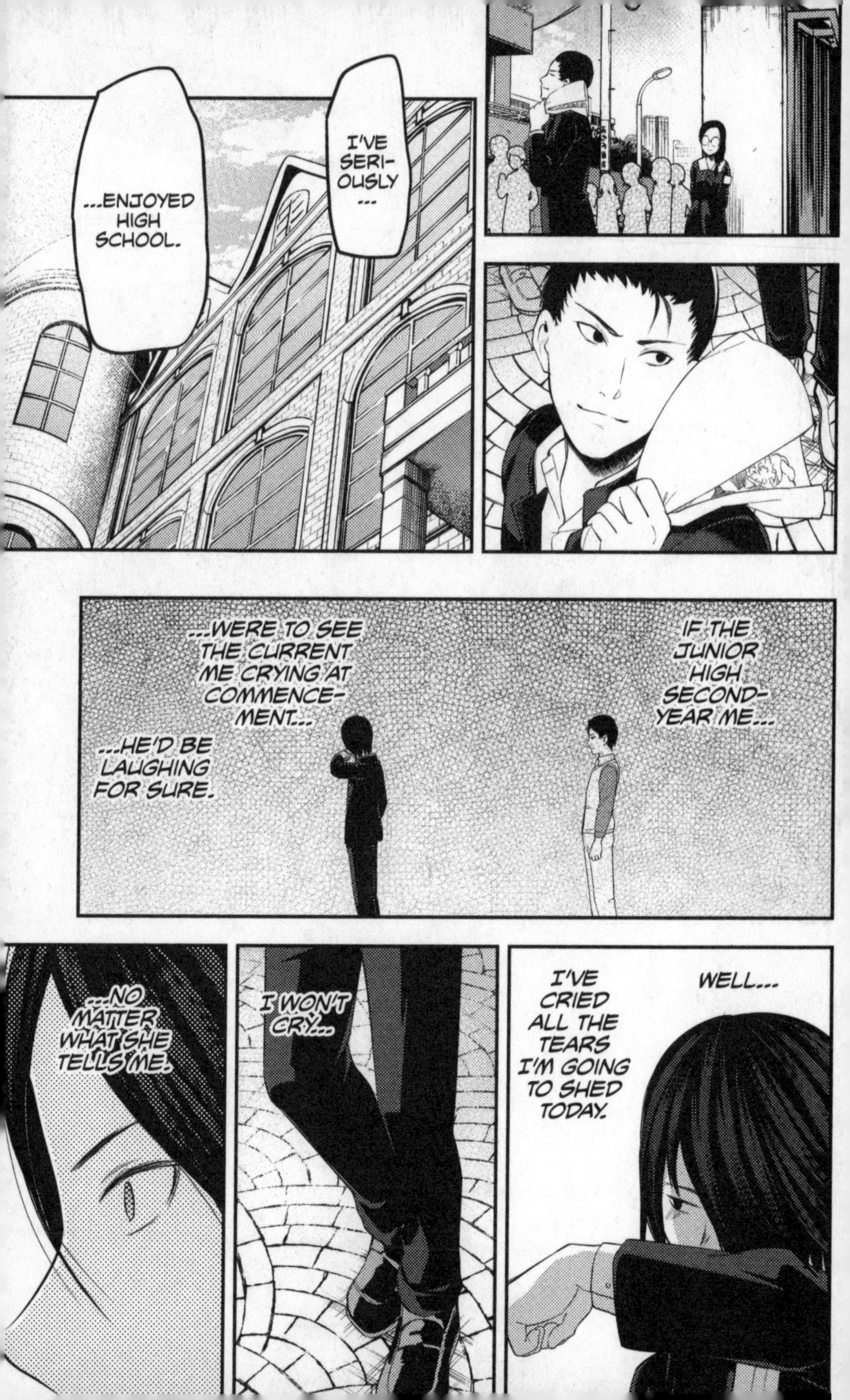
I'VE SERI-OUSLY ...
...ENJOYED HIGH SCHOOL.
IF THE JUNIOR HIGH SECOND-YEAR ME...
...WERE TO SEE THE CURRENT ME CRYING AT COMMENCE-MENT...
...HE'D BE LAUGHING FOR SURE.
WELL...
I'VE CRIED ALL THE TEARS I'M GOING TO SHED TODAY.
I WON'T CRY...
...NO MATTER WHAT SHE TELLS ME.

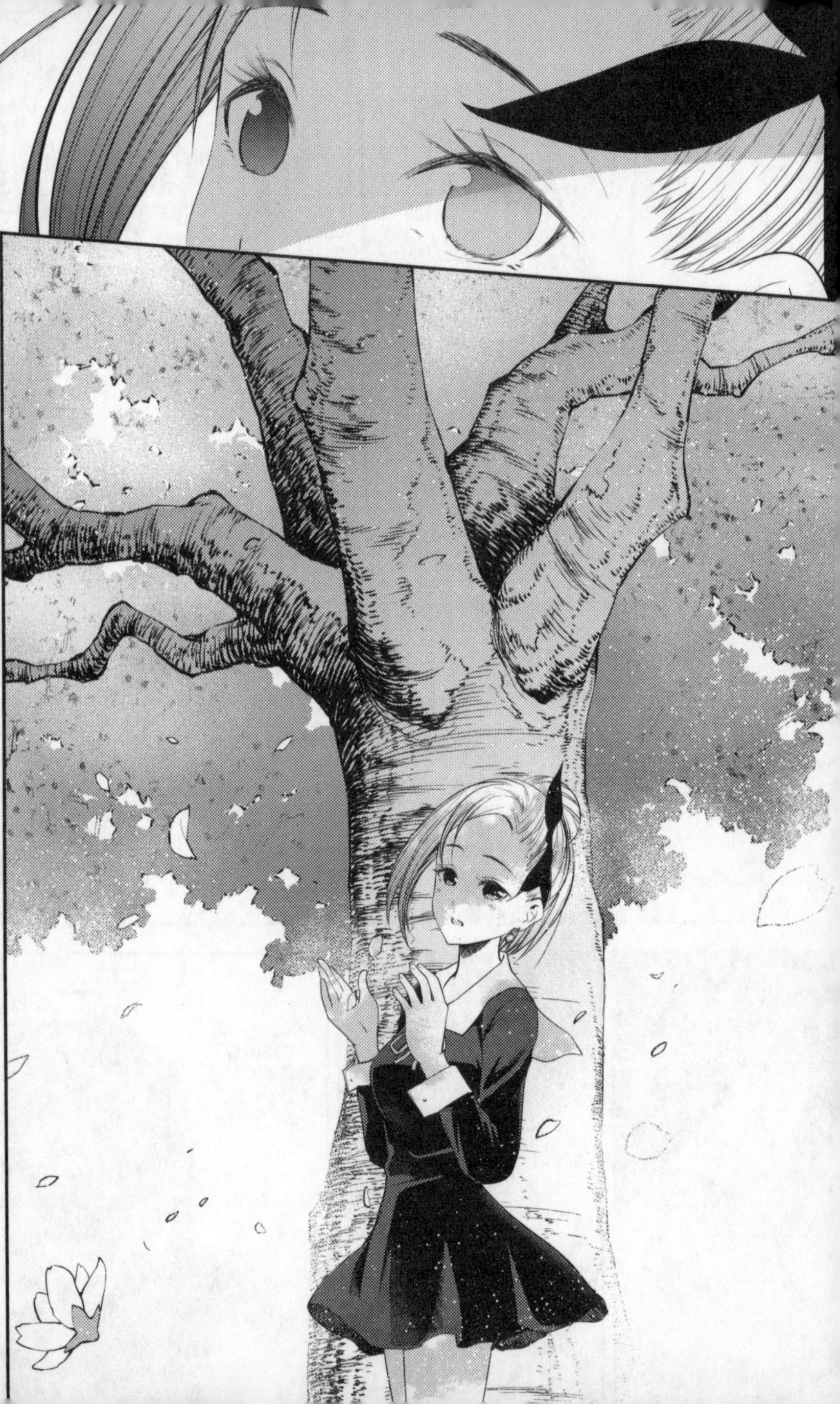

KAGUYA-SAMA

LOVE IS WAR

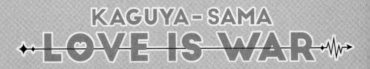

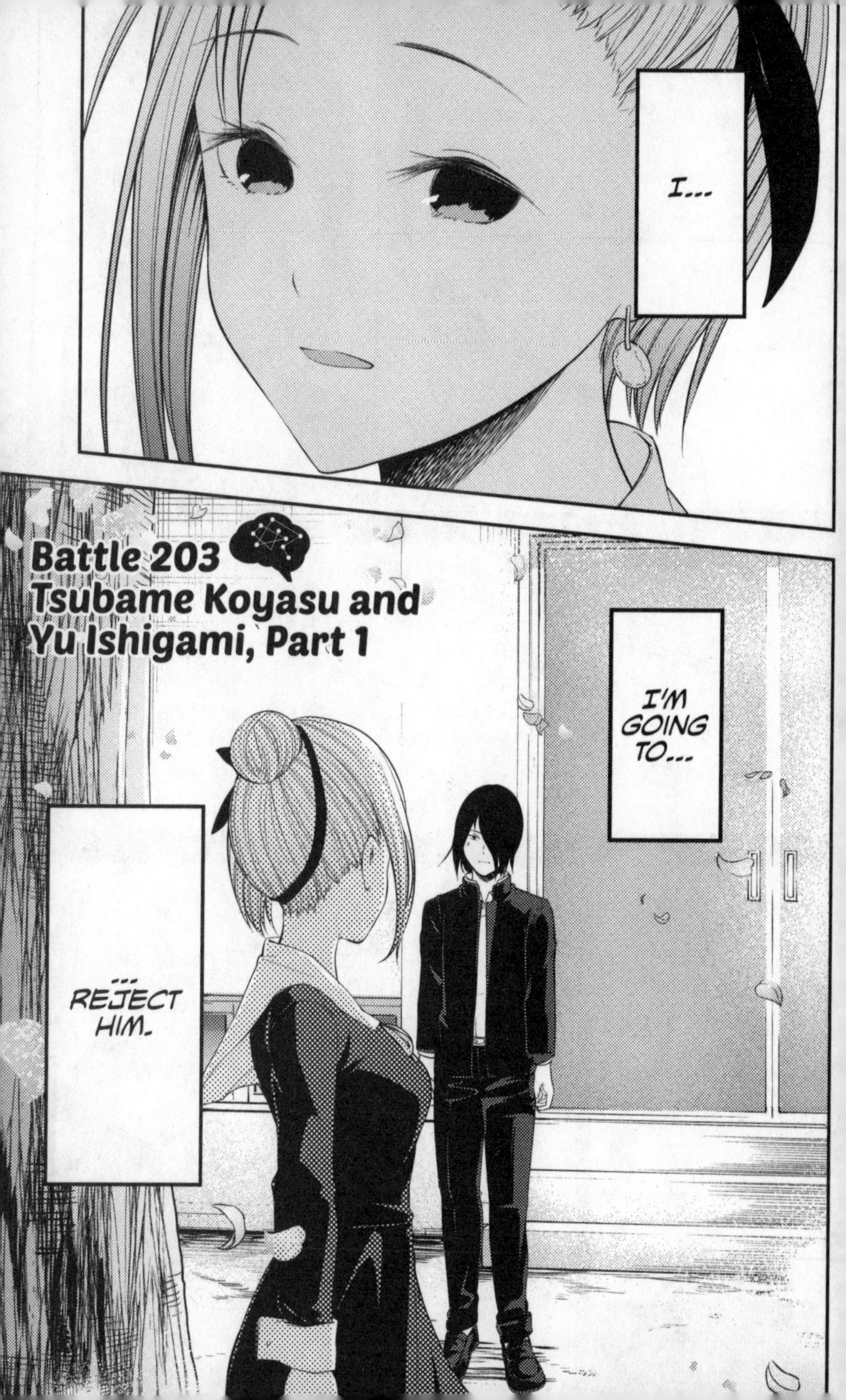
I...
Battle 203
Tsubame Koyasu and Yu Ishigami, Part 1
I'M GOING TO...
...REJECT HIM.

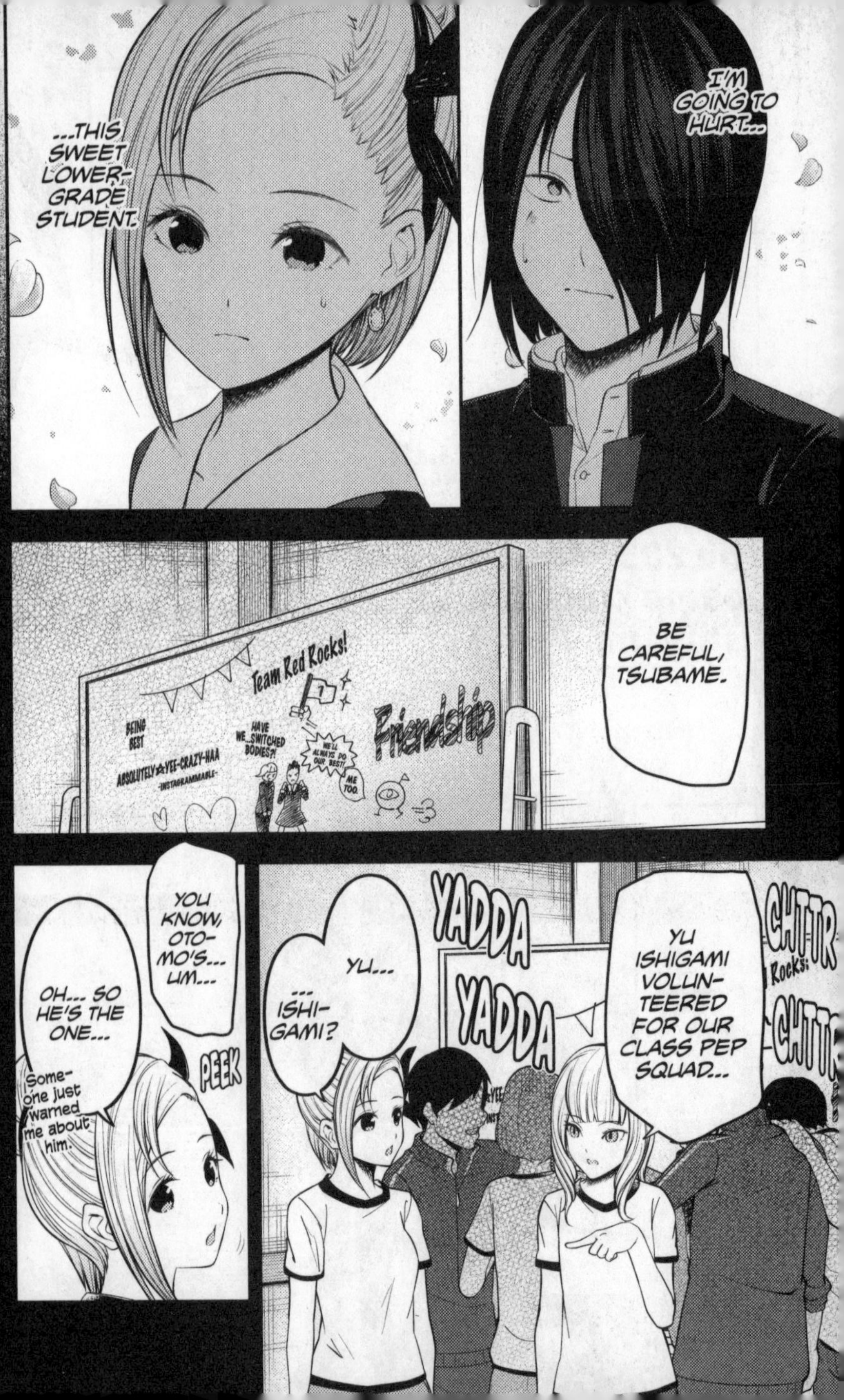
I'M GOING TO HURT...
...THIS SWEET LOWER-GRADE STUDENT.
BE CAREFUL, TSUBAME.
Team Red Rocks!
Friendship
BEING BEST
HAVE WE...SWITCHED BODIES?!
WE'LL ALWAYS DO OUR BEST!
ME TOO.
ABSOLUTELY☆YEE-CRAZY-HAA
-INSTAGRAMMABLE-
CHTTR
CHTTR
YADDA
YADDA
YU ISHIGAMI VOLUNTEERED FOR OUR CLASS PEP SQUAD...
YU... ...ISHIGAMI?
YOU KNOW, OTOMO'S... UM...
OH... SO HE'S THE ONE...
PEEK
Someone just warned me about him.

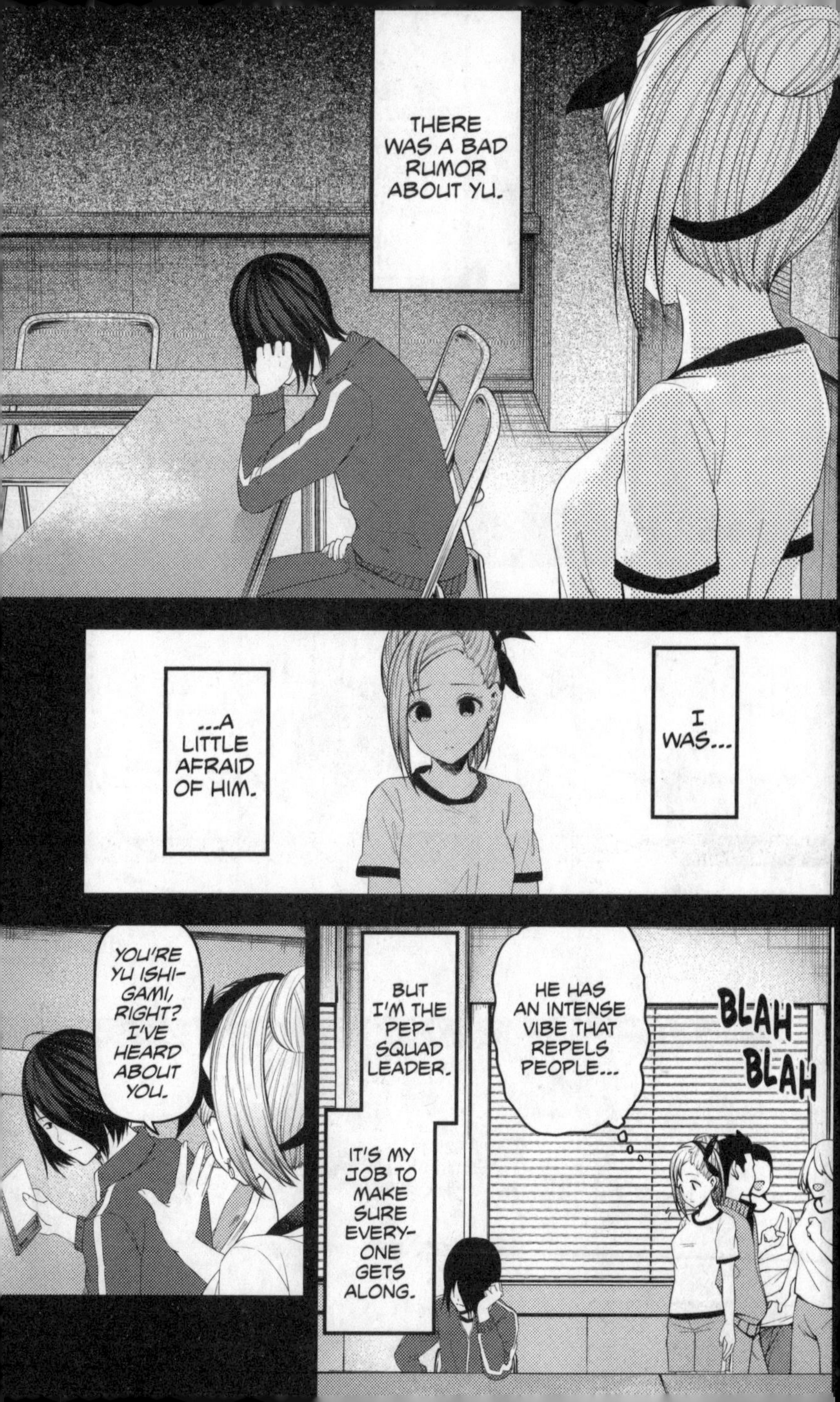
THERE WAS A BAD RUMOR ABOUT YU.
I WAS...
...A LITTLE AFRAID OF HIM.
BLAH BLAH
HE HAS AN INTENSE VIBE THAT REPELS PEOPLE...
BUT I'M THE PEP-SQUAD LEADER.
IT'S MY JOB TO MAKE SURE EVERY-ONE GETS ALONG.
YOU'RE YU ISHI-GAMI, RIGHT? I'VE HEARD ABOUT YOU.

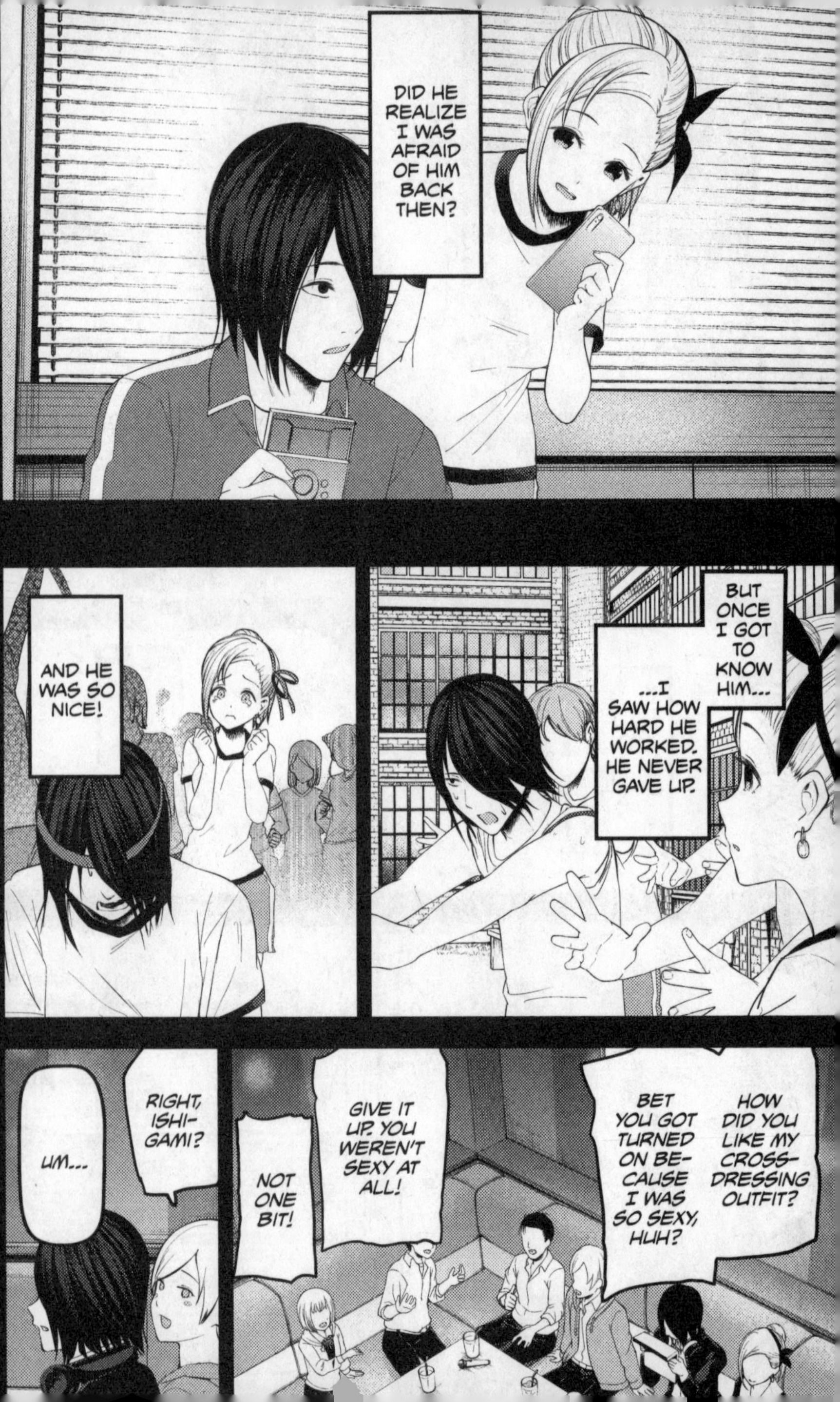
DID HE REALIZE I WAS AFRAID OF HIM BACK THEN?
BUT ONCE I GOT TO KNOW HIM...
...I SAW HOW HARD HE WORKED. HE NEVER GAVE UP.
AND HE WAS SO NICE!
HOW DID YOU LIKE MY CROSS-DRESSING OUTFIT?
BET YOU GOT TURNED ON BE-CAUSE I WAS SO SEXY, HUH?
GIVE IT UP. YOU WEREN'T SEXY AT ALL!
NOT ONE BIT!
RIGHT, ISHI-GAMI?
UM...

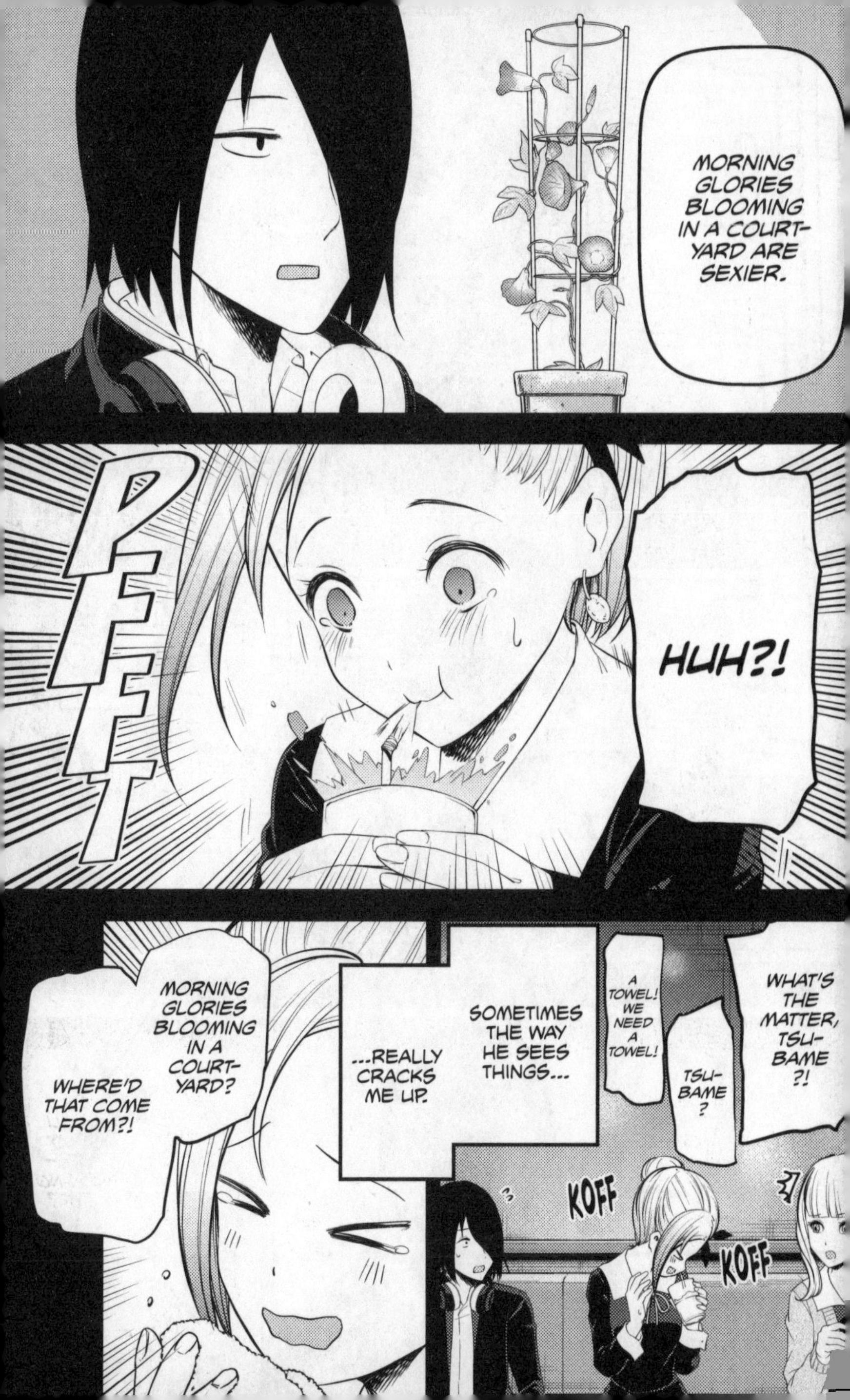
MORNING GLORIES BLOOMING IN A COURT-YARD ARE SEXIER.
HUH?!
PFFT
WHAT'S THE MATTER, TSU-BAME?!
TSU-BAME?
A TOWEL! WE NEED A TOWEL!
KOFF
KOFF
SOMETIMES THE WAY HE SEES THINGS...
...REALLY CRACKS ME UP.
MORNING GLORIES BLOOMING IN A COURT-YARD?
WHERE'D THAT COME FROM?!

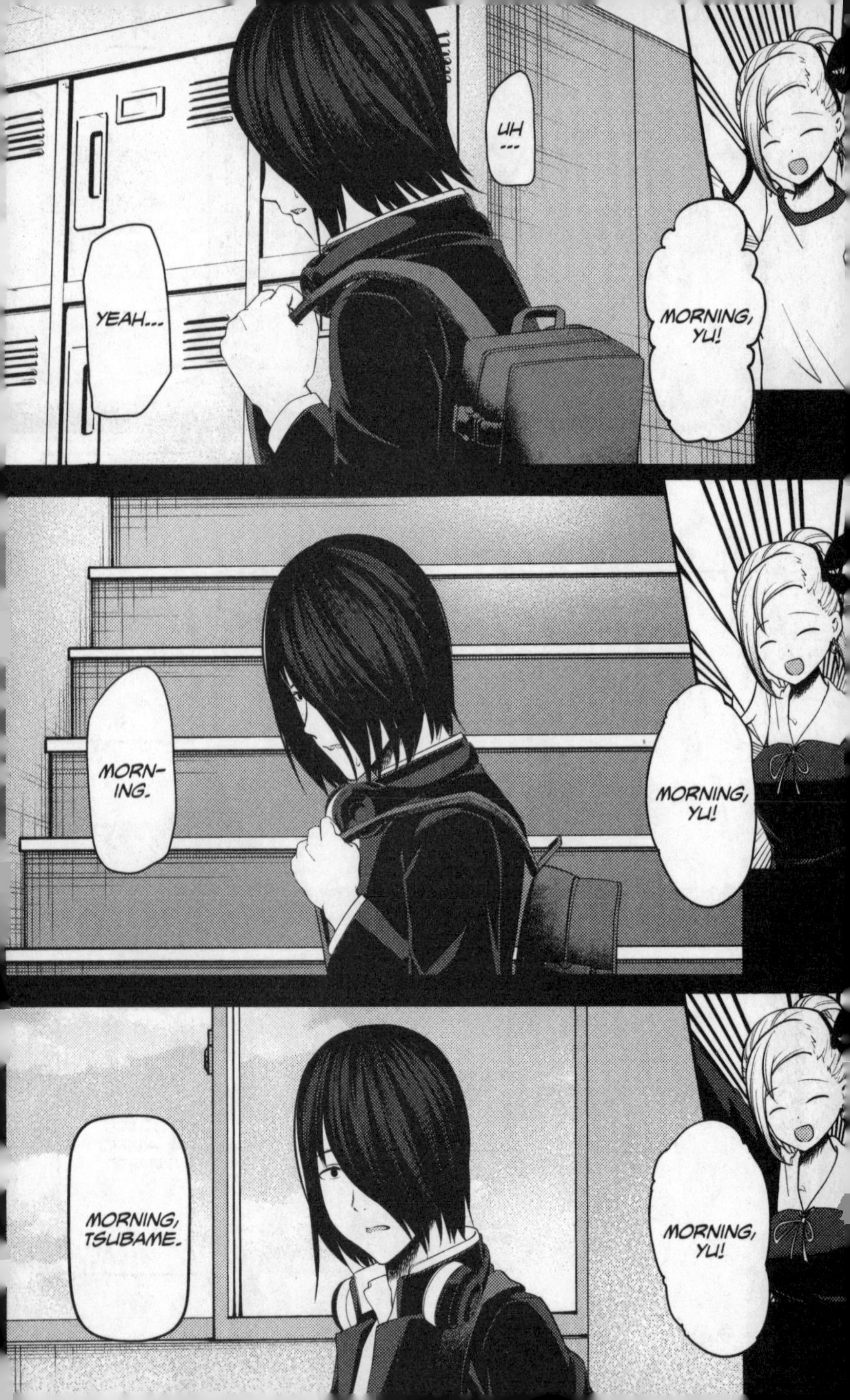
MORNING, YU!
UH ---
YEAH...
MORNING, YU!
MORN-ING.
MORNING, YU!
MORNING, TSUBAME.

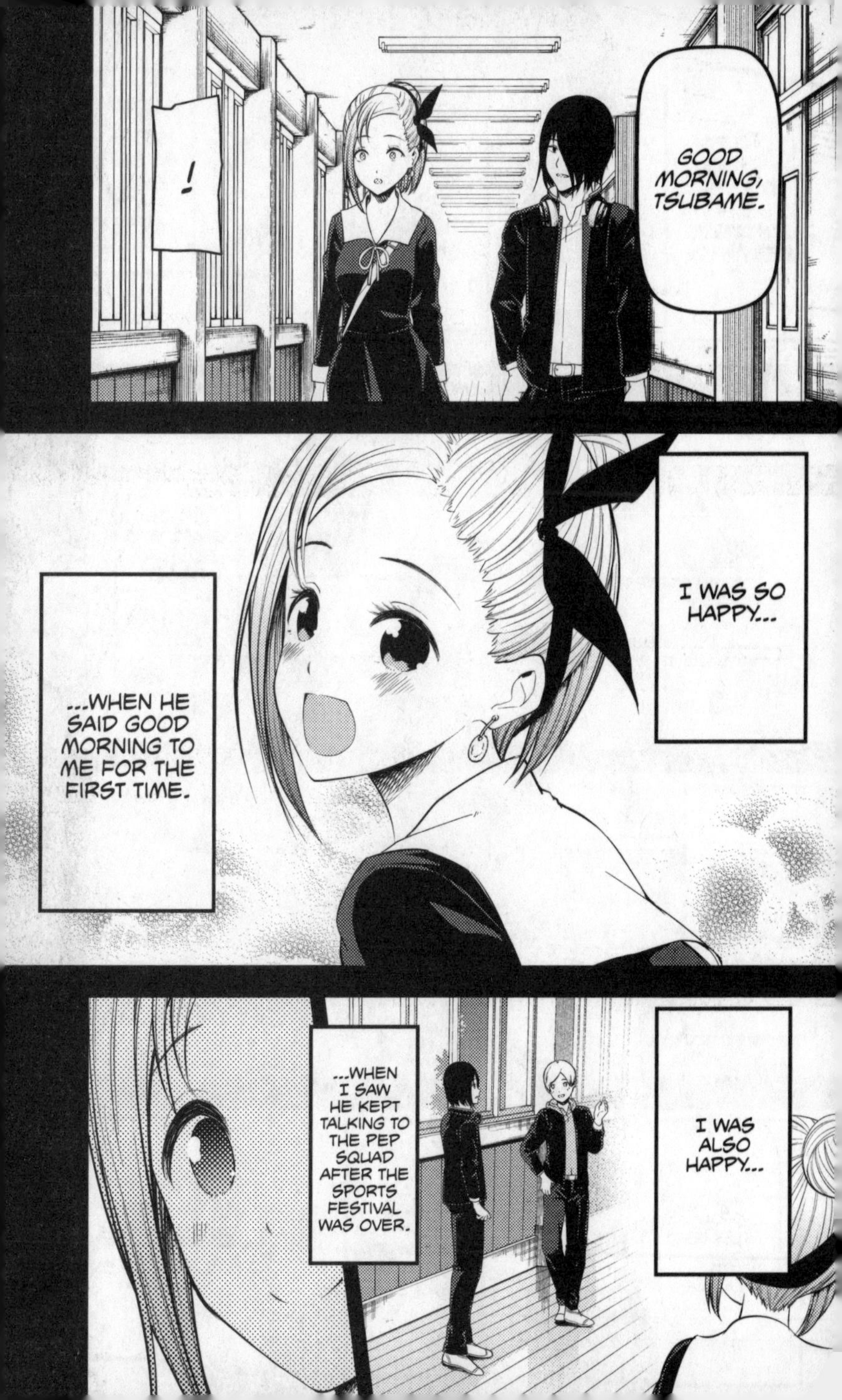
GOOD MORNING, TSUBAME.
!
I WAS SO HAPPY...
...WHEN HE SAID GOOD MORNING TO ME FOR THE FIRST TIME.
I WAS ALSO HAPPY...
...WHEN I SAW HE KEPT TALKING TO THE PEP SQUAD AFTER THE SPORTS FESTIVAL WAS OVER.

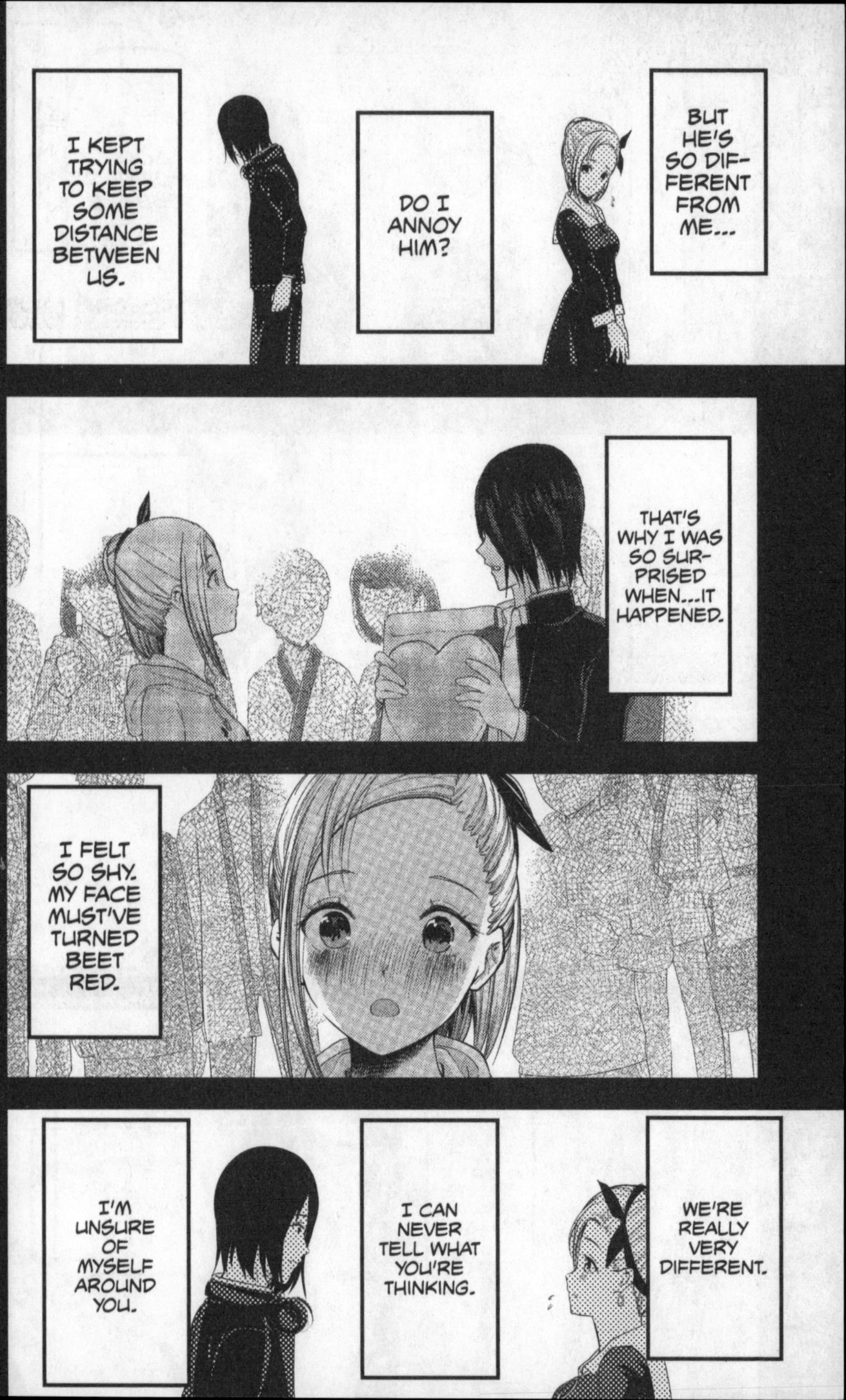
BUT HE'S SO DIFFERENT FROM ME...
DO I ANNOY HIM?
I KEPT TRYING TO KEEP SOME DISTANCE BETWEEN US.
THAT'S WHY I WAS SO SURPRISED WHEN...IT HAPPENED.
I FELT SO SHY. MY FACE MUST'VE TURNED BEET RED.
WE'RE REALLY VERY DIFFERENT.
I CAN NEVER TELL WHAT YOU'RE THINKING.
I'M UNSURE OF MYSELF AROUND YOU.

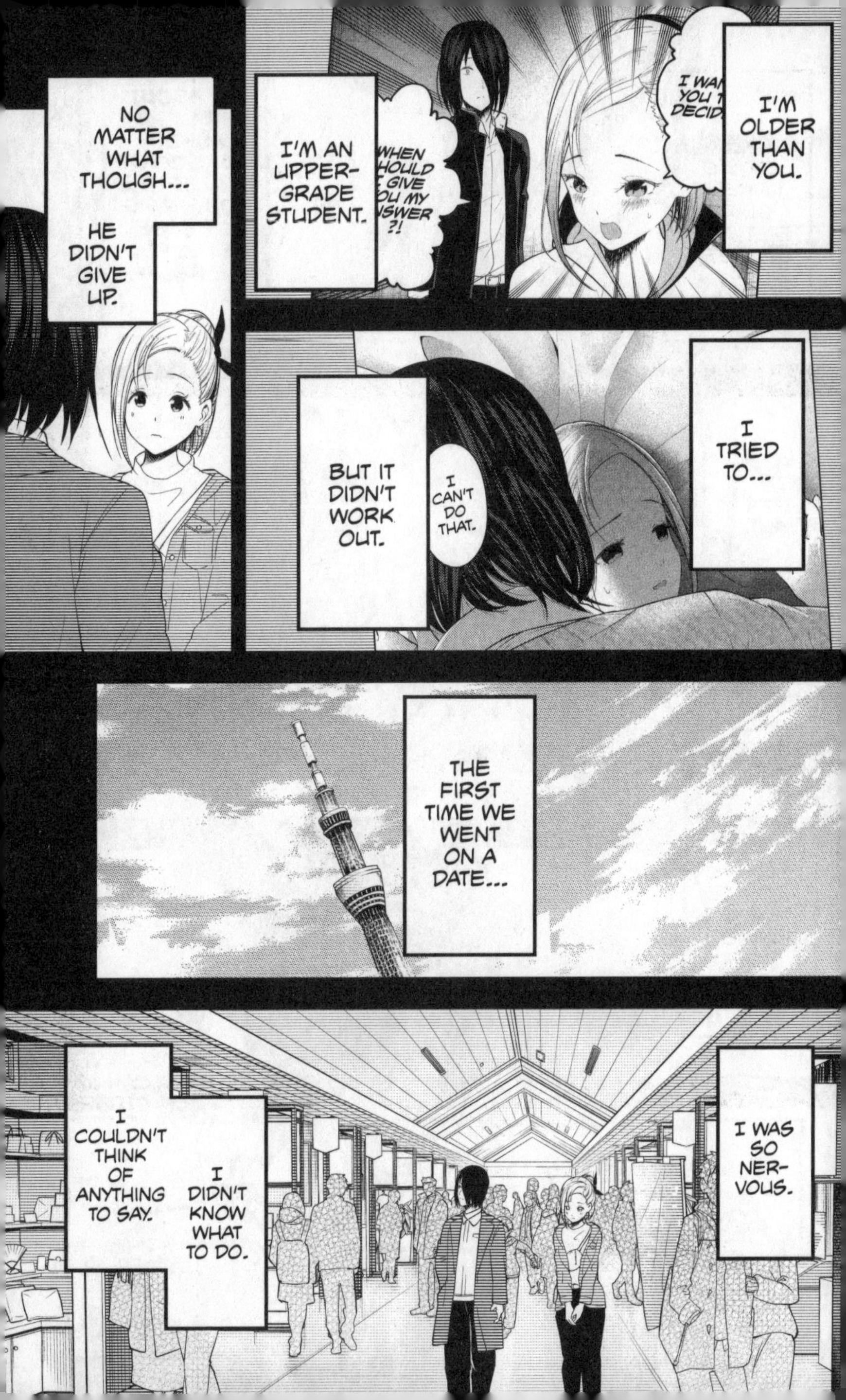
I'M OLDER THAN YOU.
I WAN YOU T DECID
I'M AN UPPER-GRADE STUDENT.
WHEN HOULD E GIVE OU MY NSWER ?!
NO MATTER WHAT THOUGH...
HE DIDN'T GIVE UP.
I TRIED TO...
I CAN'T DO THAT.
BUT IT DIDN'T WORK OUT.
THE FIRST TIME WE WENT ON A DATE...
I WAS SO NERVOUS.
I DIDN'T KNOW WHAT TO DO.
I COULDN'T THINK OF ANYTHING TO SAY.

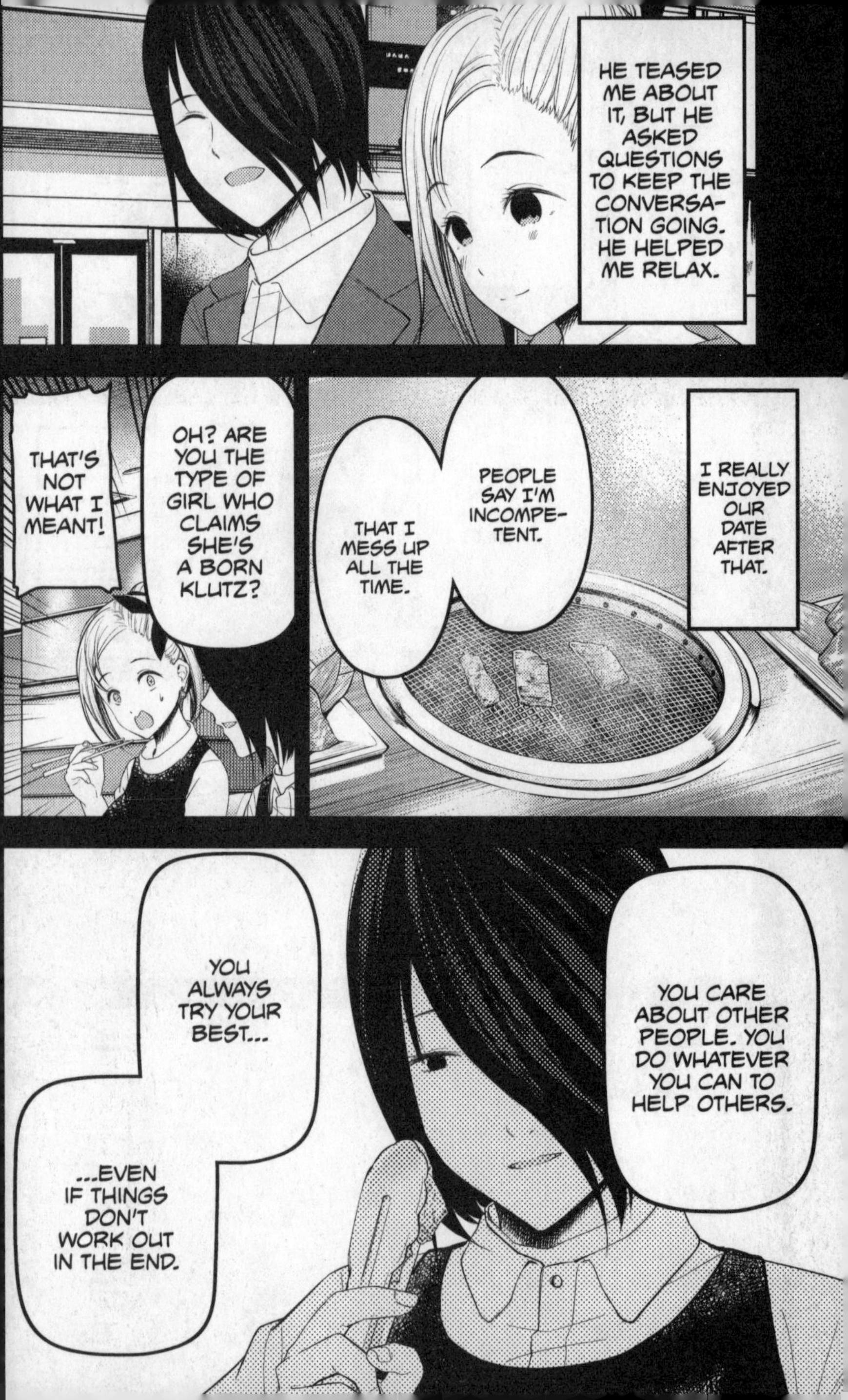
HE TEASED ME ABOUT IT, BUT HE ASKED QUESTIONS TO KEEP THE CONVERSATION GOING. HE HELPED ME RELAX.
I REALLY ENJOYED OUR DATE AFTER THAT.
PEOPLE SAY I'M INCOMPETENT.
THAT I MESS UP ALL THE TIME.
OH? ARE YOU THE TYPE OF GIRL WHO CLAIMS SHE'S A BORN KLUTZ?
THAT'S NOT WHAT I MEANT!
YOU CARE ABOUT OTHER PEOPLE. YOU DO WHATEVER YOU CAN TO HELP OTHERS.
YOU ALWAYS TRY YOUR BEST...
...EVEN IF THINGS DON'T WORK OUT IN THE END.

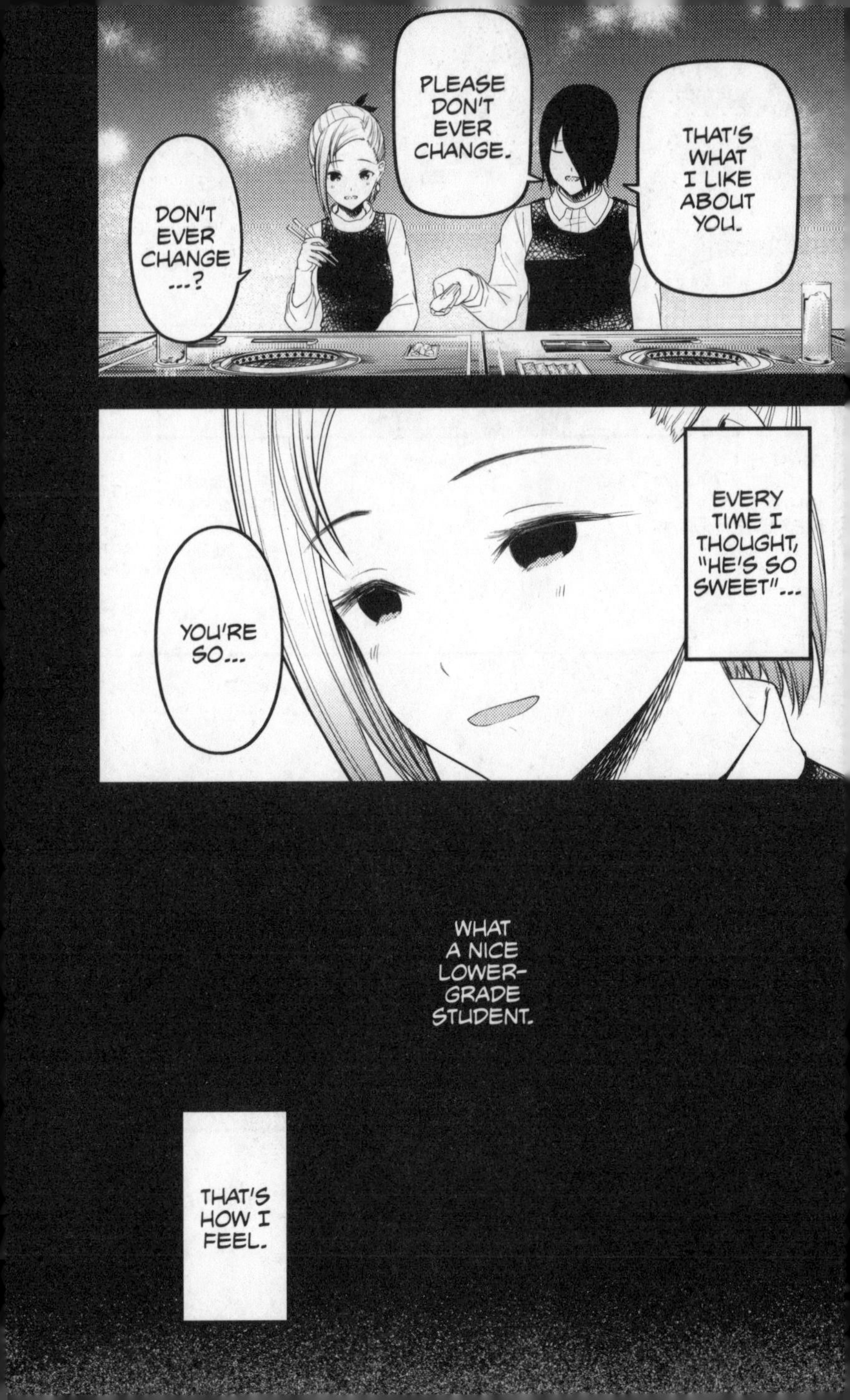
THAT'S WHAT I LIKE ABOUT YOU.
PLEASE DON'T EVER CHANGE.
DON'T EVER CHANGE ...?
EVERY TIME I THOUGHT, "HE'S SO SWEET"...
YOU'RE SO...
WHAT A NICE LOWER-GRADE STUDENT.
THAT'S HOW I FEEL.

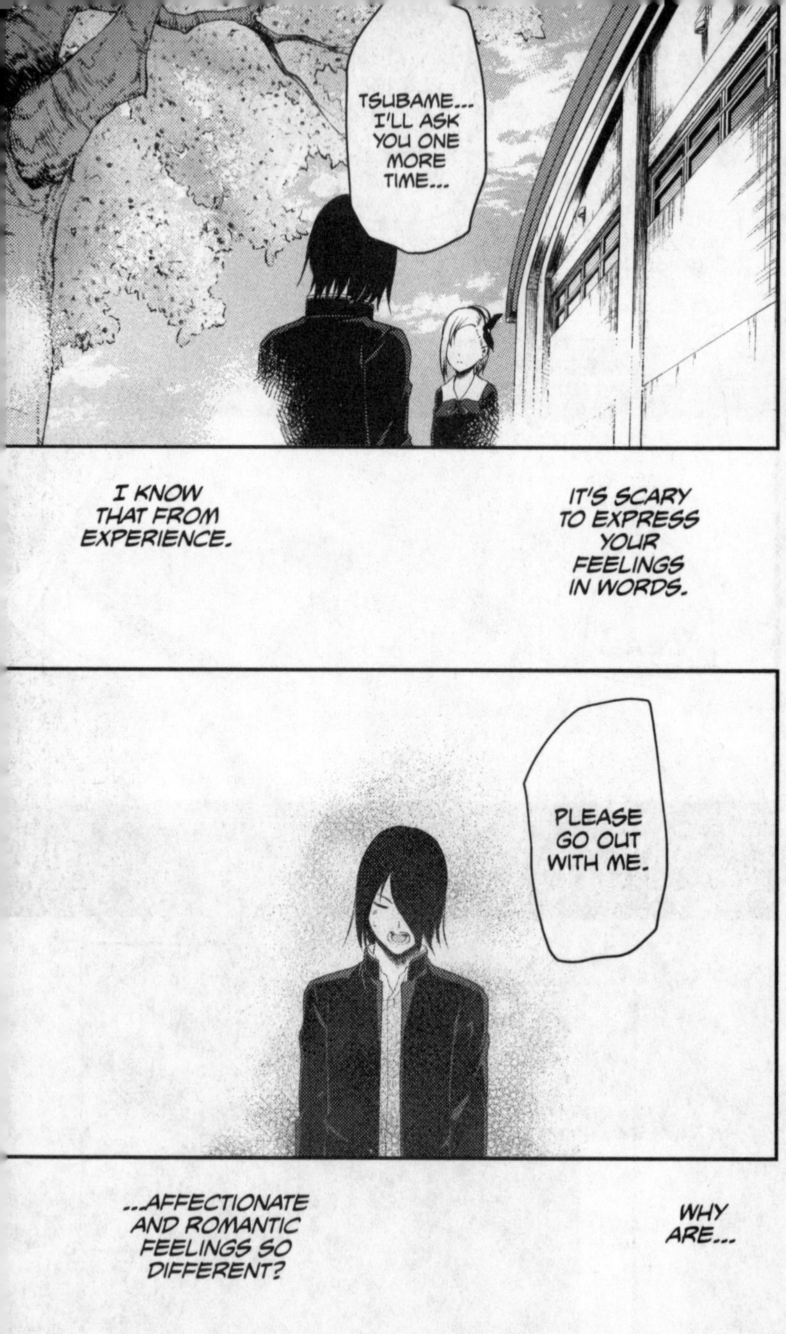
TSUBAME... I'LL ASK YOU ONE MORE TIME...
IT'S SCARY TO EXPRESS YOUR FEELINGS IN WORDS.
I KNOW THAT FROM EXPERIENCE.
PLEASE GO OUT WITH ME.
WHY ARE...
...AFFECTIONATE AND ROMANTIC FEELINGS SO DIFFERENT?

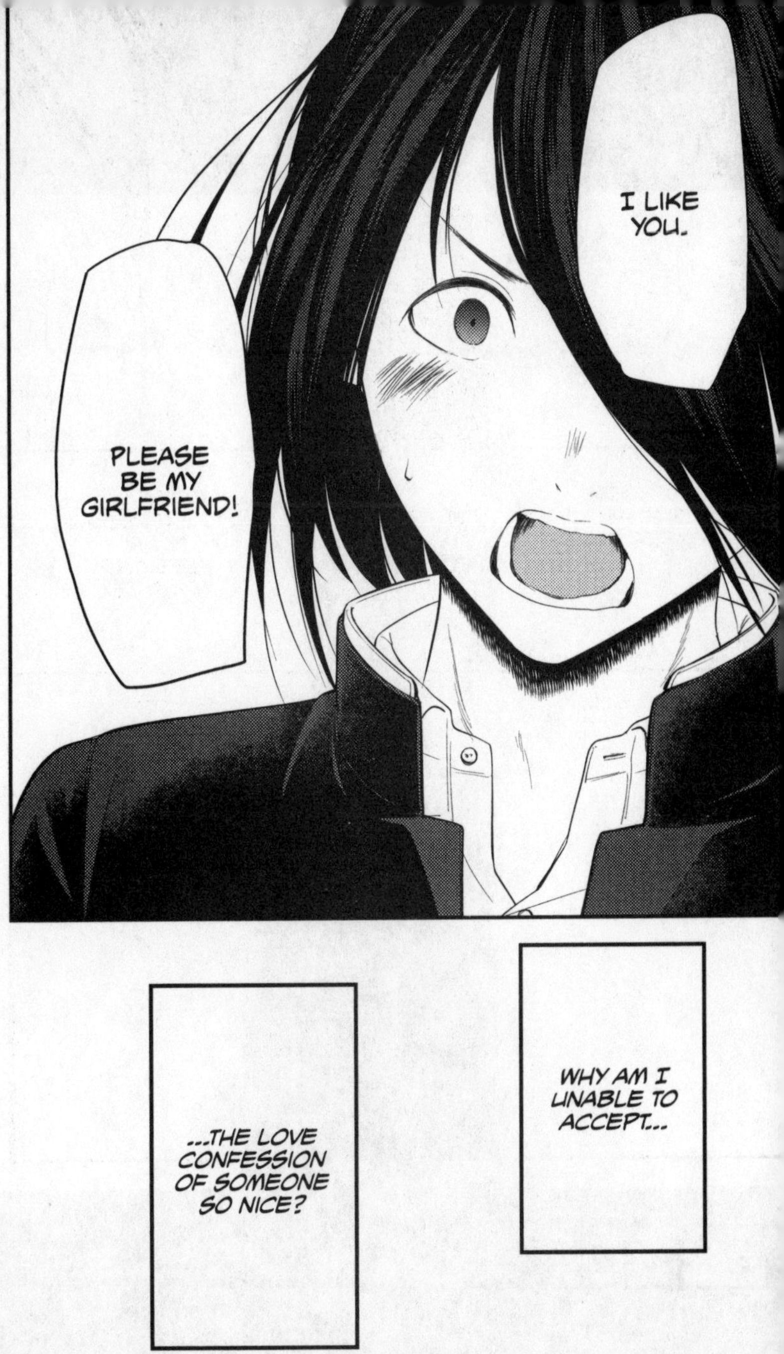
I LIKE YOU.
PLEASE BE MY GIRLFRIEND!
WHY AM I UNABLE TO ACCEPT...
...THE LOVE CONFESSION OF SOMEONE SO NICE?

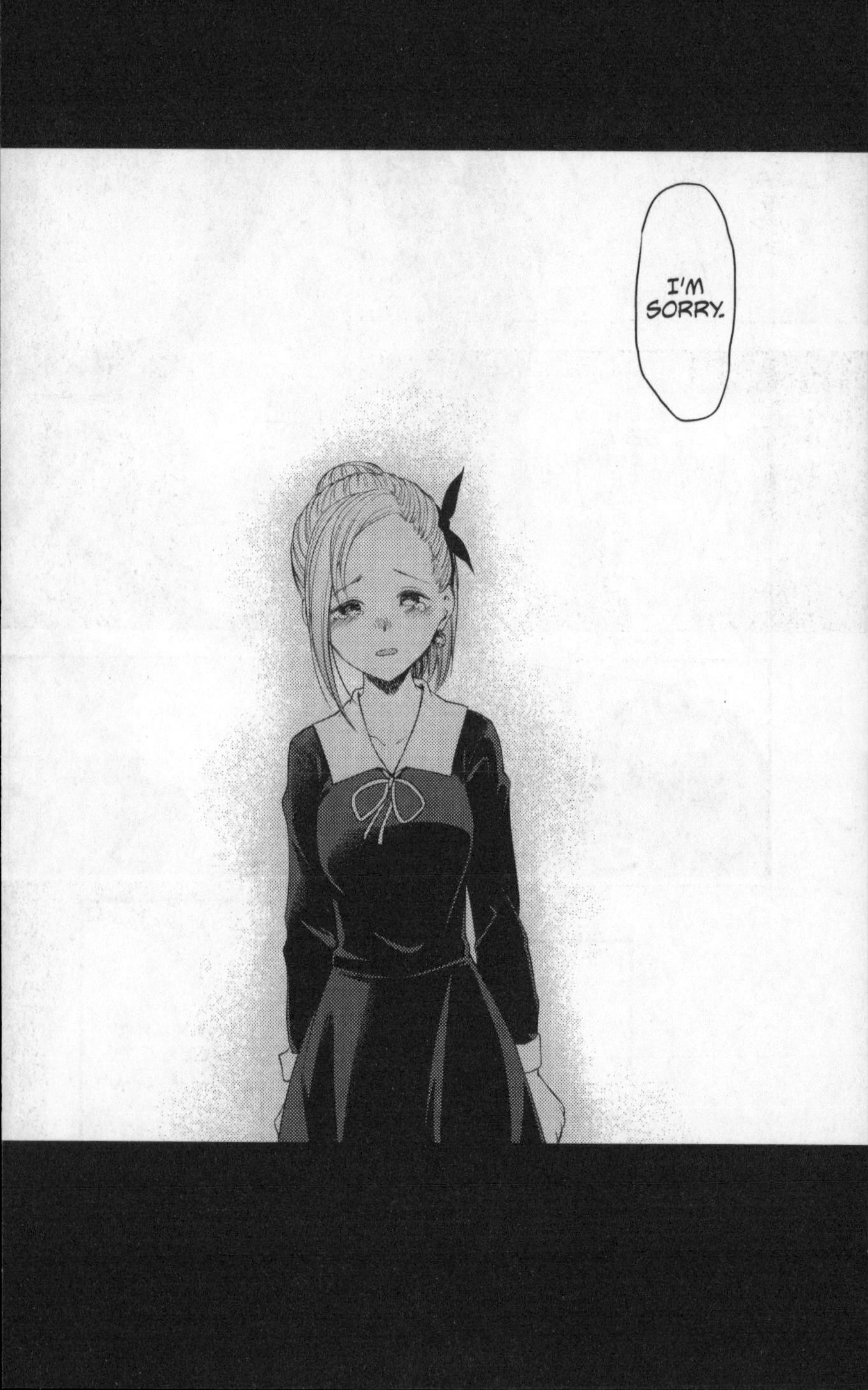
I'M SORRY.

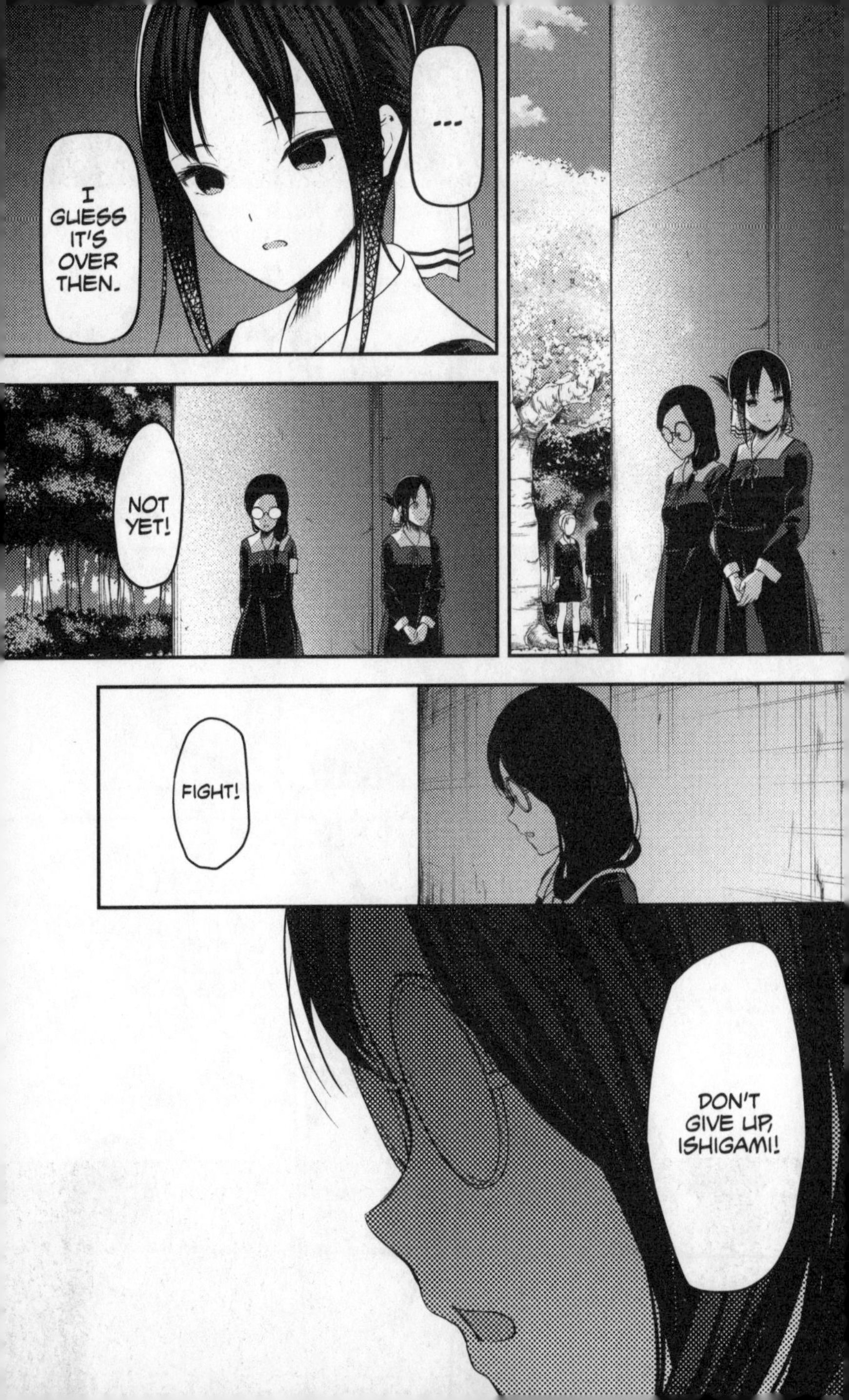
...
I GUESS IT'S OVER THEN.
NOT YET!
FIGHT!
DON'T GIVE UP, ISHIGAMI!

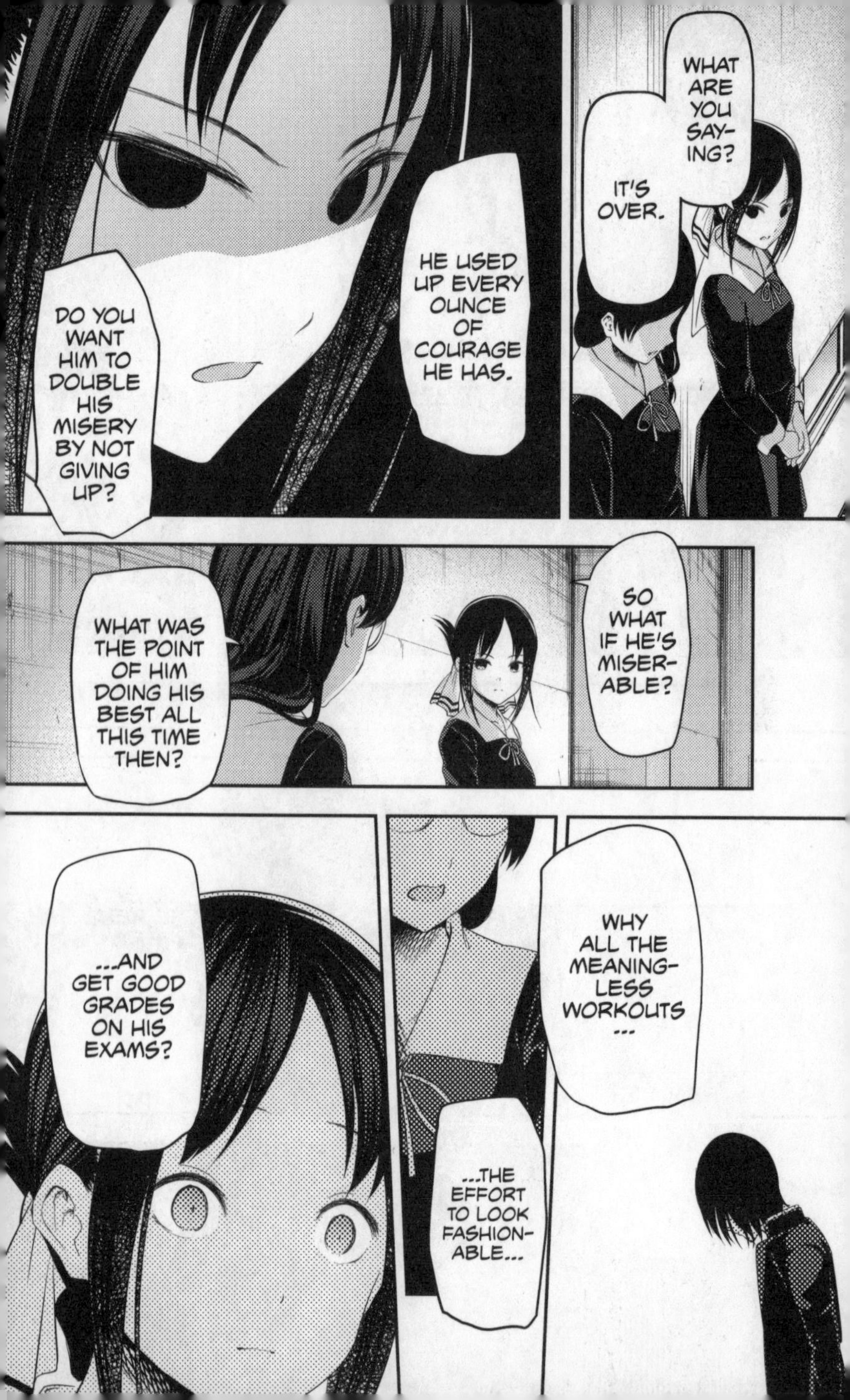
WHAT ARE YOU SAYING?
IT'S OVER.
HE USED UP EVERY OUNCE OF COURAGE HE HAS.
DO YOU WANT HIM TO DOUBLE HIS MISERY BY NOT GIVING UP?
SO WHAT IF HE'S MISERABLE?
WHAT WAS THE POINT OF HIM DOING HIS BEST ALL THIS TIME THEN?
WHY ALL THE MEANINGLESS WORKOUTS...
...THE EFFORT TO LOOK FASHIONABLE...
...AND GET GOOD GRADES ON HIS EXAMS?

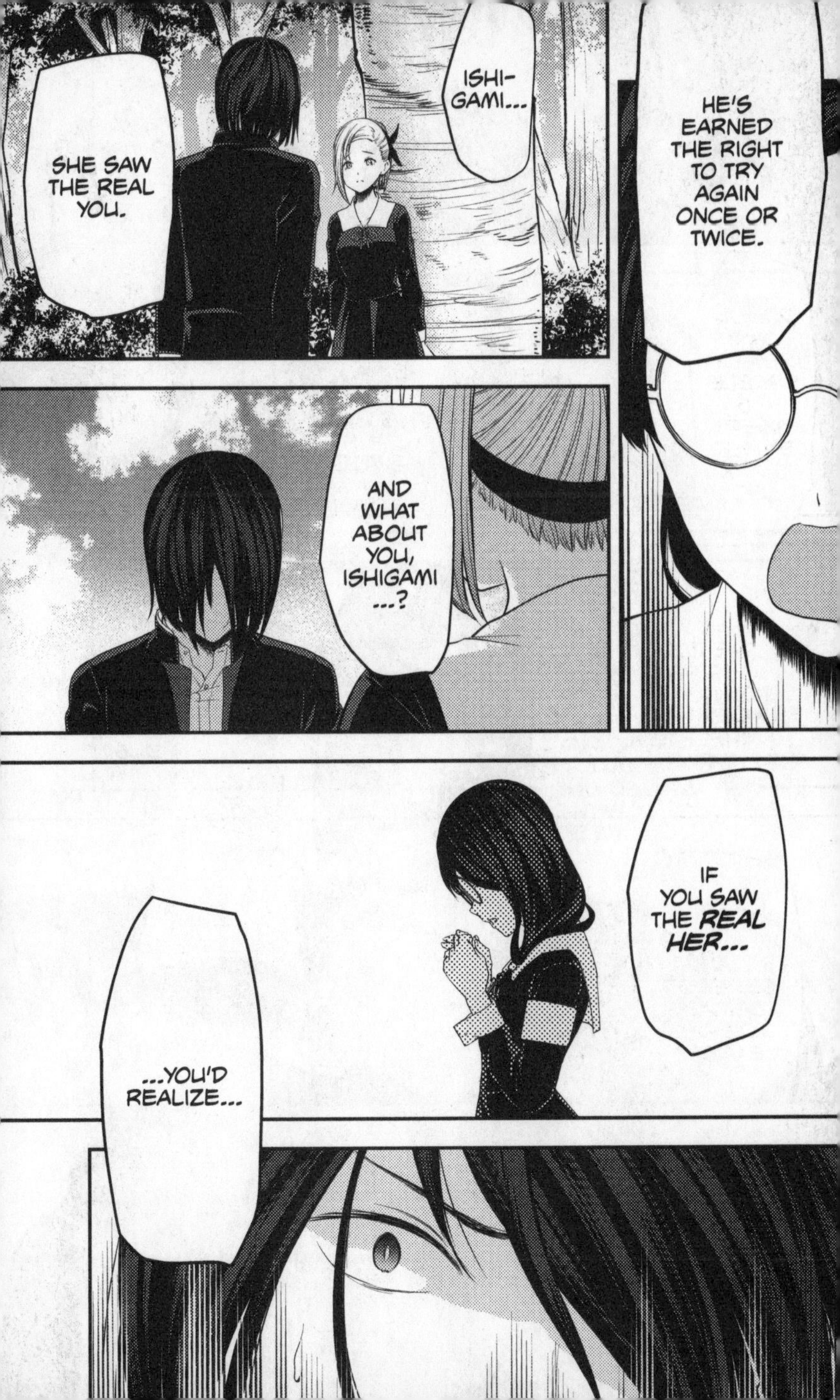
HE'S EARNED THE RIGHT TO TRY AGAIN ONCE OR TWICE.
ISHI-GAMI...
SHE SAW THE REAL YOU.
AND WHAT ABOUT YOU, ISHIGAMI ...?
IF YOU SAW THE *REAL HER*...
...YOU'D REALIZE...

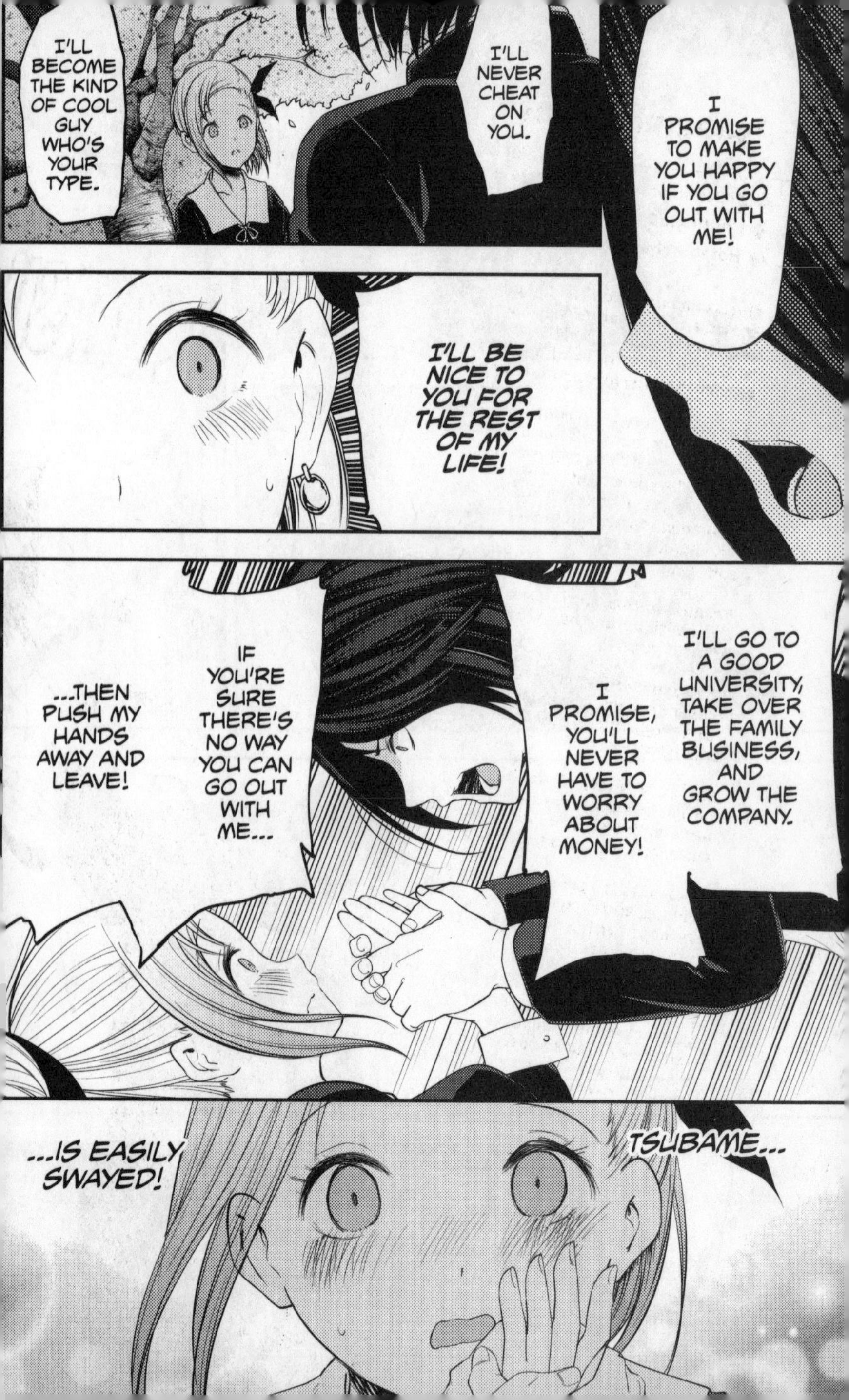
I PROMISE TO MAKE YOU HAPPY IF YOU GO OUT WITH ME!
I'LL NEVER CHEAT ON YOU.
I'LL BECOME THE KIND OF COOL GUY WHO'S YOUR TYPE.
I'LL BE NICE TO YOU FOR THE REST OF MY LIFE!
I'LL GO TO A GOOD UNIVERSITY, TAKE OVER THE FAMILY BUSINESS, AND GROW THE COMPANY.
I PROMISE, YOU'LL NEVER HAVE TO WORRY ABOUT MONEY!
IF YOU'RE SURE THERE'S NO WAY YOU CAN GO OUT WITH ME...
...THEN PUSH MY HANDS AWAY AND LEAVE!
TSUBAME...
...IS EASILY SWAYED!

Tsubame Koyasu

- Shuchiin Academy High School Third-Year
- Rhythmic Gymnastics Club Vice President
- Notable characteristics: belle of Shuchiin

She is considered one of the popular crowd and has many friends and acquaintances. She has had her heart broken in romantic relationships earlier than the average teenage girl.

She performs well in rhythmic gymnastics, but she's naturally a bit clumsy. She's been pursued as a trophy by some boys, as well as by stalkers and gropers. Women have been mean to her out of jealousy. Her beauty has caused her a lot of suffering.

Because of this, she is quite wary and cautious, and has a low opinion of most guys.

She hasn't entirely lost her natural trust of others, however. She is a supportive friend and mentor to those who need her.

Some of her friends say Tsubame can be a pain, but others sympathize with her and think it's a miracle she hasn't suffered a mental breakdown.

She makes it a priority to help her friends, and they in turn help her. She has healthy, mutually supportive relationships.

According to Miyuki Shirogane, "If you don't ask other people for help, you lack communication skills." Tsubame has asked other people for help. She wins people's trust with her generosity of spirit.

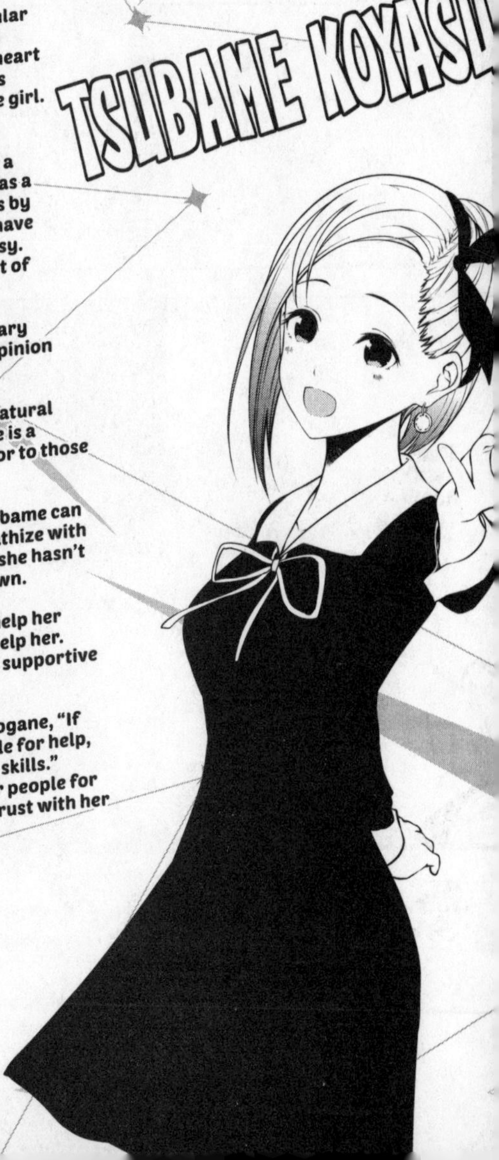
TSUBAME KOYASU

KAGUYA-SAMA
LOVE IS WAR

I LIKE TSUBAME.

Battle 204
Tsubame Koyasu and Yu Ishigami, Part 2

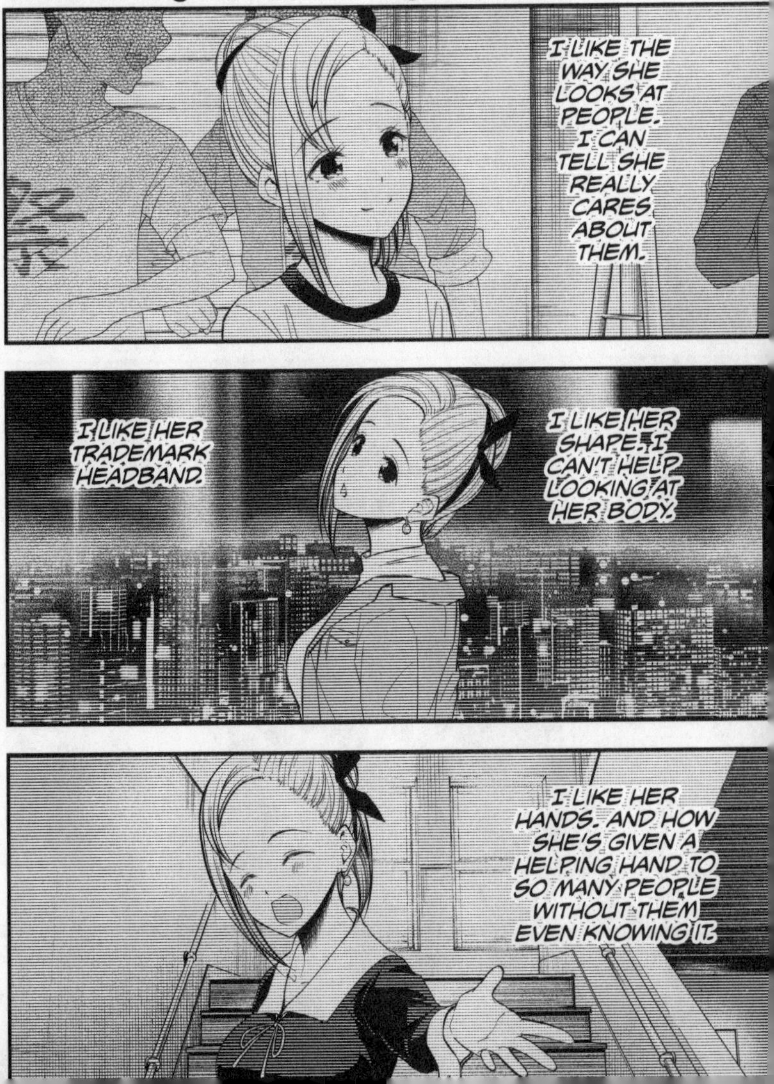
I LIKE THE WAY SHE LOOKS AT PEOPLE. I CAN TELL SHE REALLY CARES ABOUT THEM.
I LIKE HER SHAPE. I CAN'T HELP LOOKING AT HER BODY.
I LIKE HER TRADEMARK HEADBAND.
I LIKE HER HANDS. AND HOW SHE'S GIVEN A HELPING HAND TO SO MANY PEOPLE WITHOUT THEM EVEN KNOWING IT.

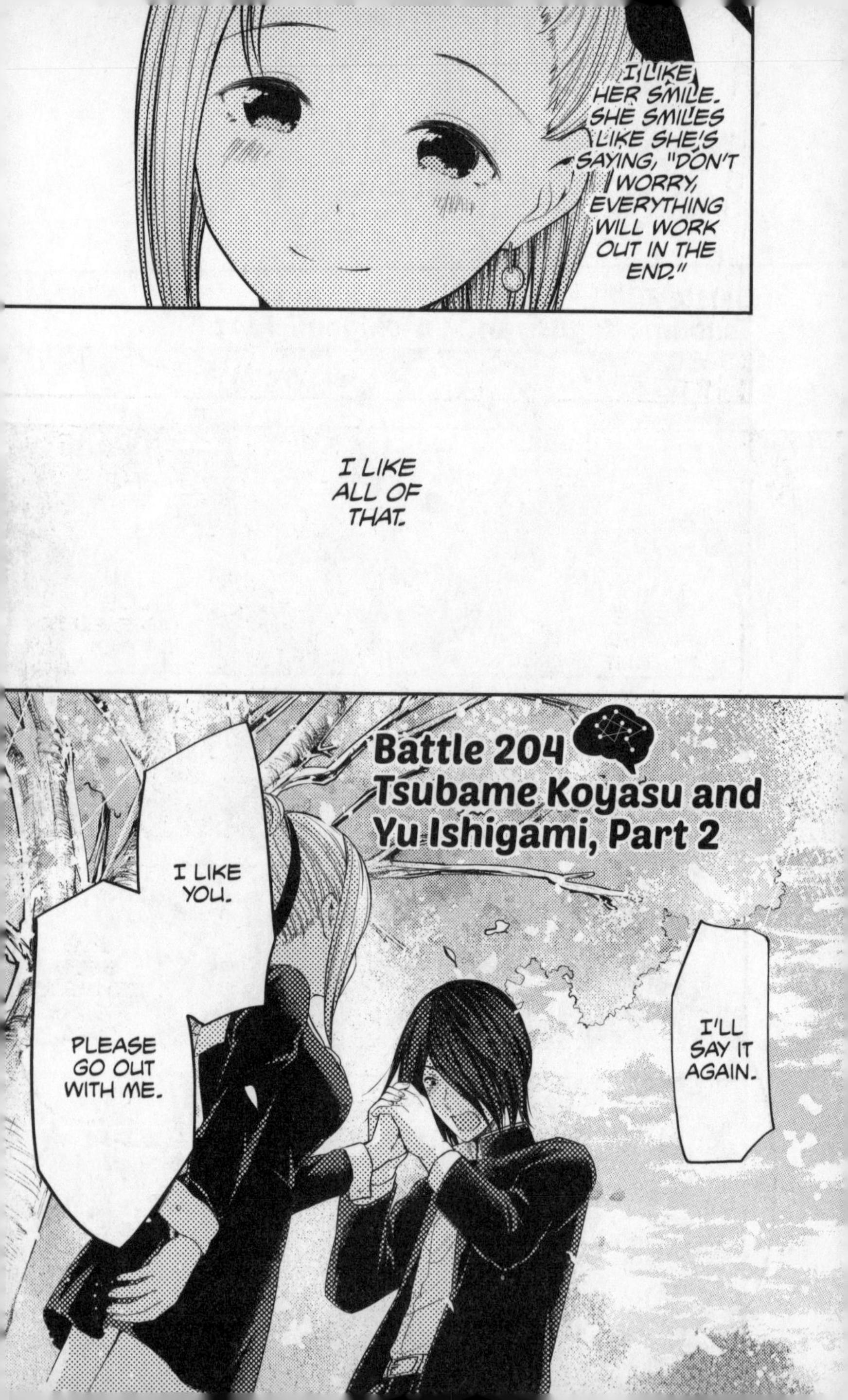
I LIKE HER SMILE. SHE SMILES LIKE SHE'S SAYING, "DON'T WORRY, EVERYTHING WILL WORK OUT IN THE END."
I LIKE ALL OF THAT.
I'LL SAY IT AGAIN.
Battle 204 Tsubame Koyasu and Yu Ishigami, Part 2
I LIKE YOU.
PLEASE GO OUT WITH ME.

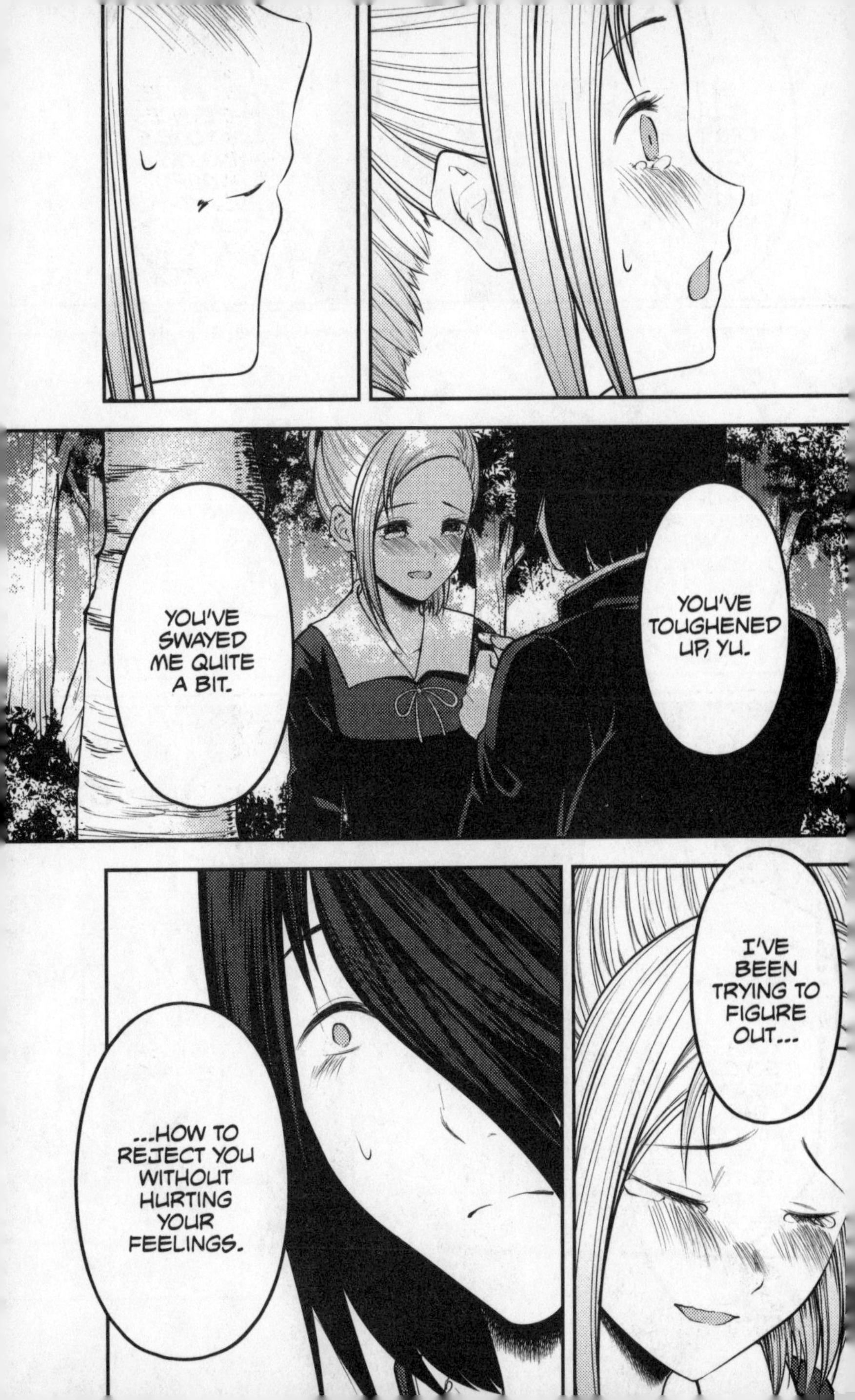
YOU'VE TOUGHENED UP, YU.
YOU'VE SWAYED ME QUITE A BIT.
I'VE BEEN TRYING TO FIGURE OUT...
...HOW TO REJECT YOU WITHOUT HURTING YOUR FEELINGS.

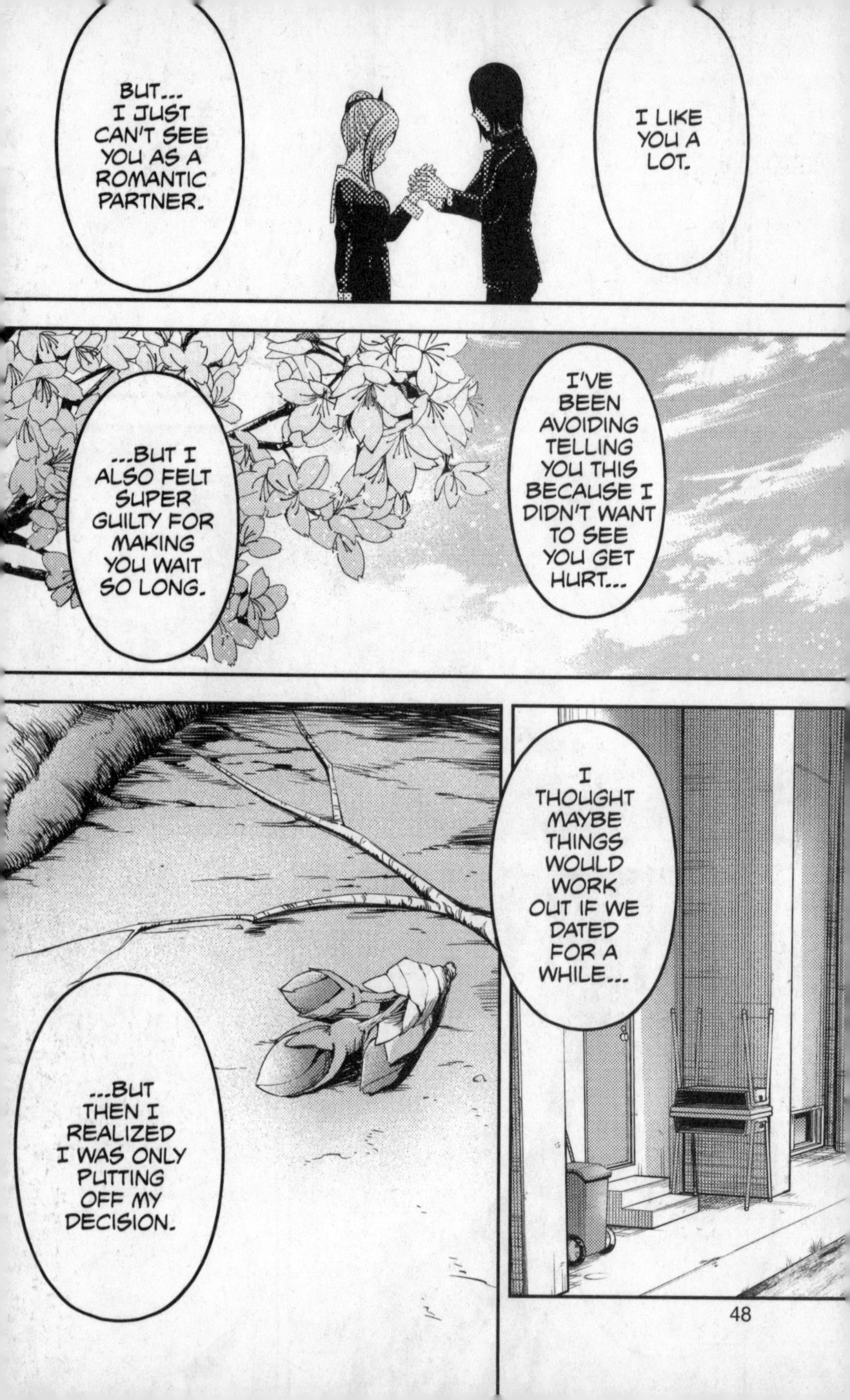
I LIKE YOU A LOT.
BUT... I JUST CAN'T SEE YOU AS A ROMANTIC PARTNER.
I'VE BEEN AVOIDING TELLING YOU THIS BECAUSE I DIDN'T WANT TO SEE YOU GET HURT...
...BUT I ALSO FELT SUPER GUILTY FOR MAKING YOU WAIT SO LONG.
I THOUGHT MAYBE THINGS WOULD WORK OUT IF WE DATED FOR A WHILE...
...BUT THEN I REALIZED I WAS ONLY PUTTING OFF MY DECISION.

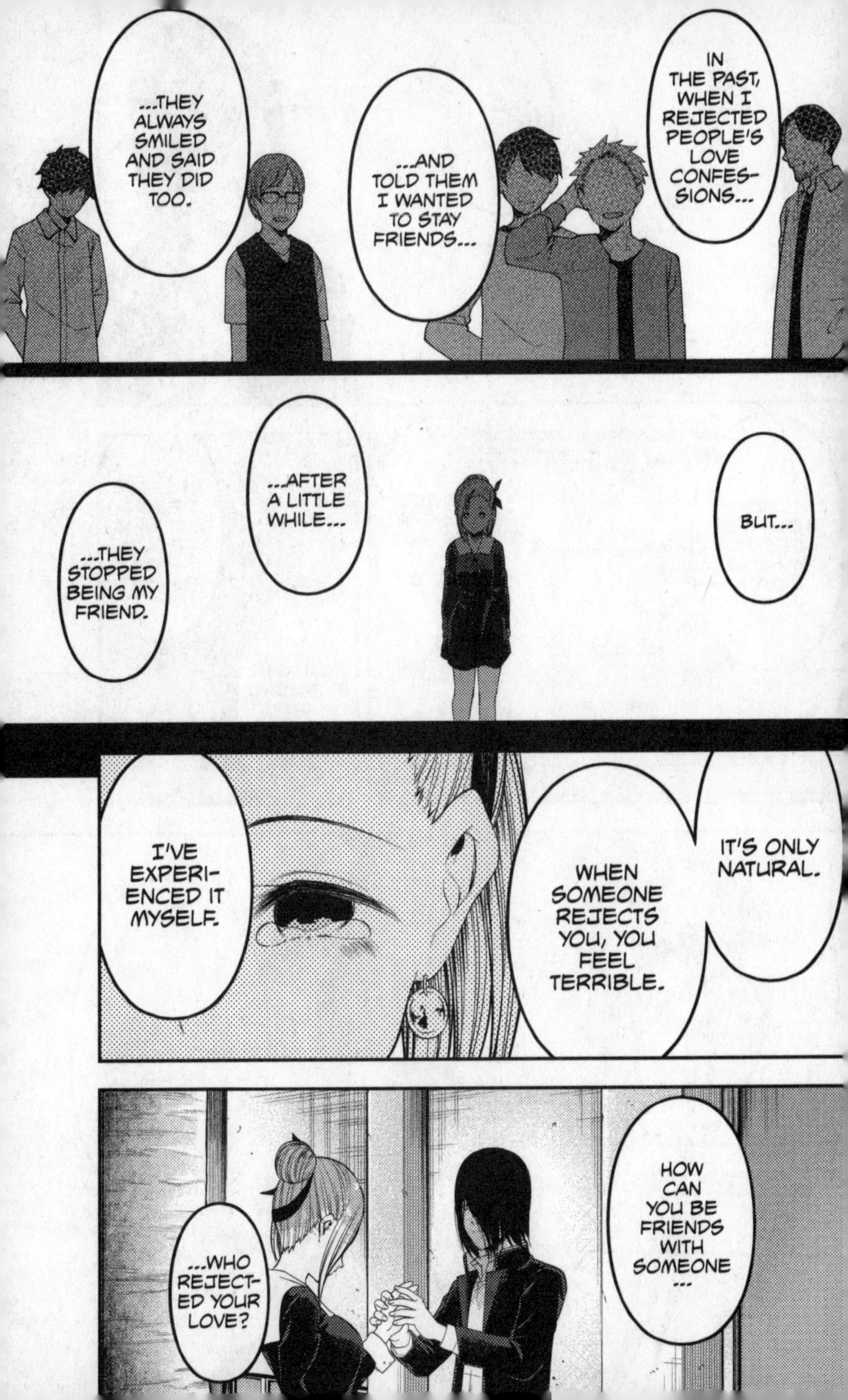
IN THE PAST, WHEN I REJECTED PEOPLE'S LOVE CONFESSIONS...
...AND TOLD THEM I WANTED TO STAY FRIENDS...
...THEY ALWAYS SMILED AND SAID THEY DID TOO.
BUT...
...AFTER A LITTLE WHILE...
...THEY STOPPED BEING MY FRIEND.
IT'S ONLY NATURAL.
WHEN SOMEONE REJECTS YOU, YOU FEEL TERRIBLE.
I'VE EXPERIENCED IT MYSELF.
HOW CAN YOU BE FRIENDS WITH SOMEONE ...
...WHO REJECTED YOUR LOVE?

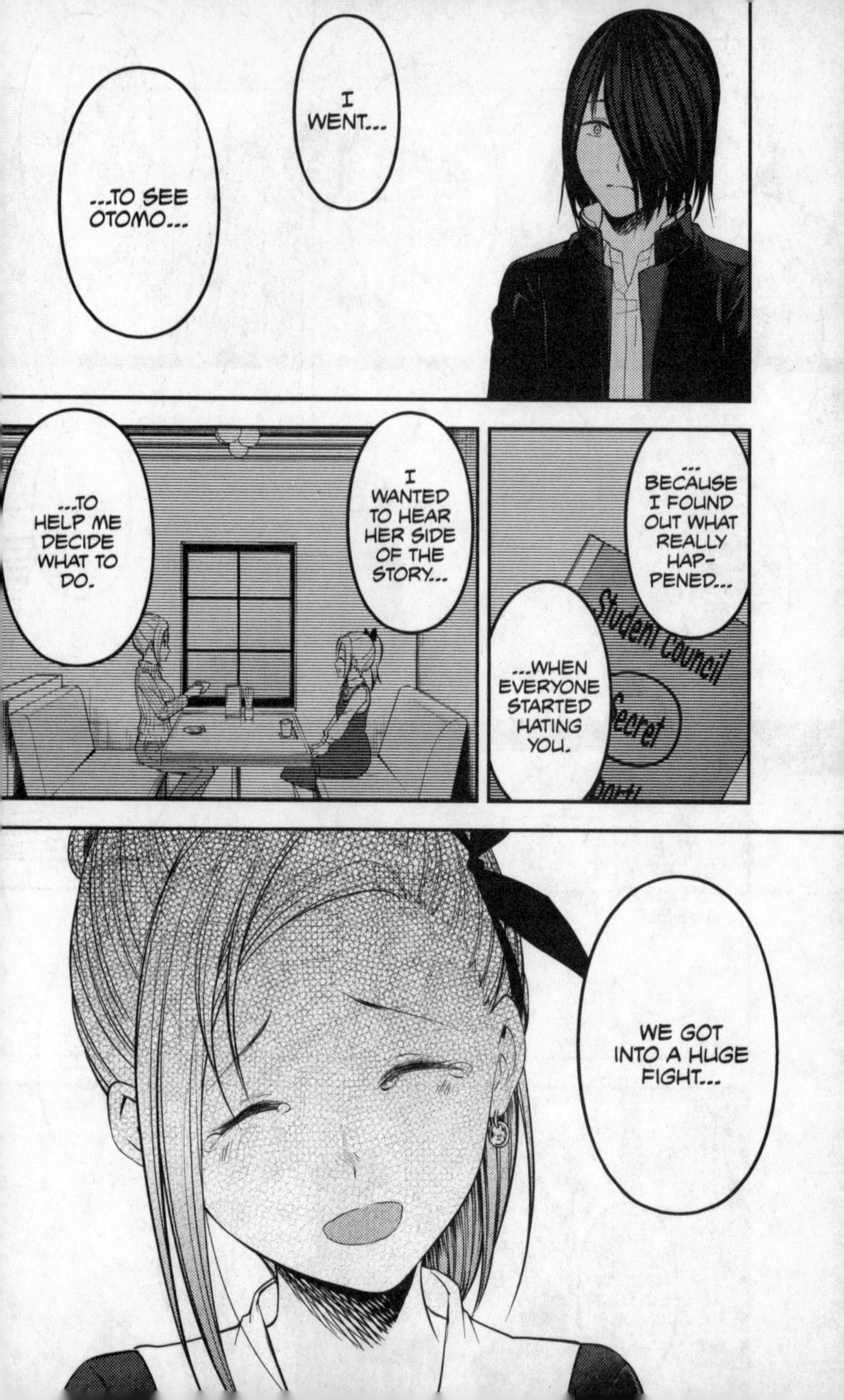
I WENT...
...TO SEE OTOMO...
... BECAUSE I FOUND OUT WHAT REALLY HAPPENED...
Student Council
Secret
...WHEN EVERYONE STARTED HATING YOU.
I WANTED TO HEAR HER SIDE OF THE STORY...
...TO HELP ME DECIDE WHAT TO DO.
WE GOT INTO A HUGE FIGHT...

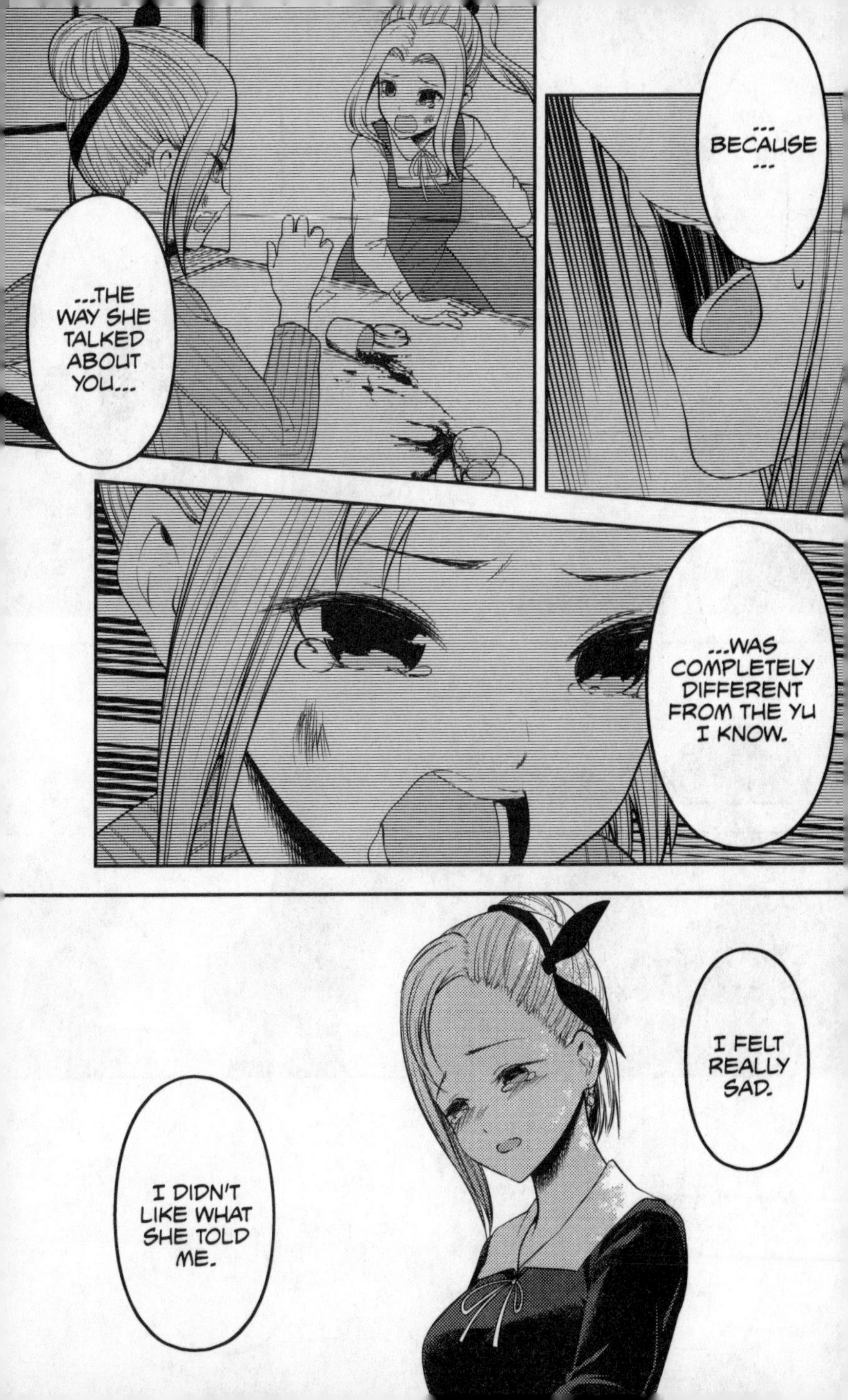

...BECAUSE...
...THE WAY SHE TALKED ABOUT YOU...
...WAS COMPLETELY DIFFERENT FROM THE YU I KNOW.
I FELT REALLY SAD.
I DIDN'T LIKE WHAT SHE TOLD ME.

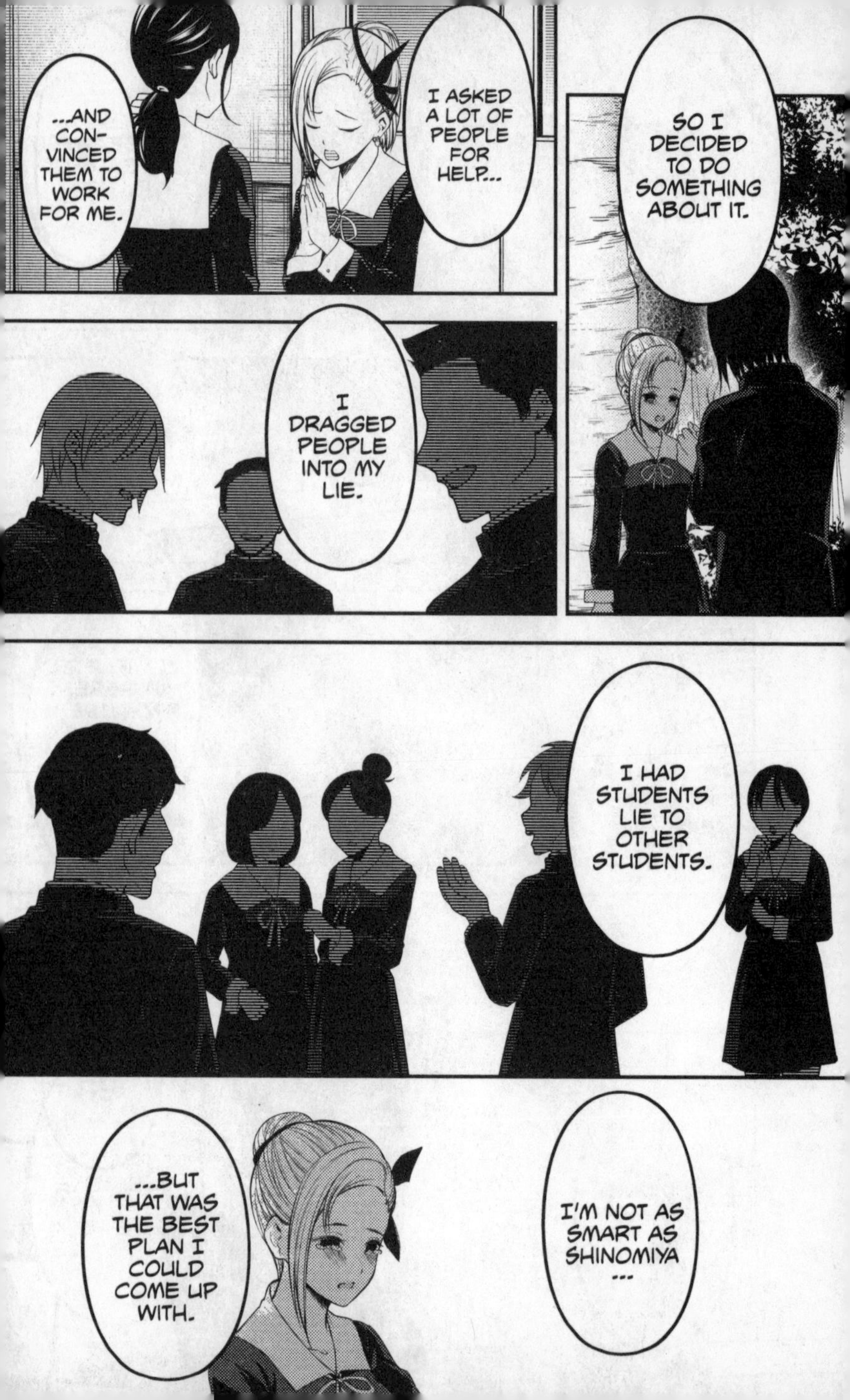
SO I DECIDED TO DO SOMETHING ABOUT IT.
I ASKED A LOT OF PEOPLE FOR HELP...
...AND CON-VINCED THEM TO WORK FOR ME.
I DRAGGED PEOPLE INTO MY LIE.
I HAD STUDENTS LIE TO OTHER STUDENTS.
I'M NOT AS SMART AS SHINOMIYA...
...BUT THAT WAS THE BEST PLAN I COULD COME UP WITH.

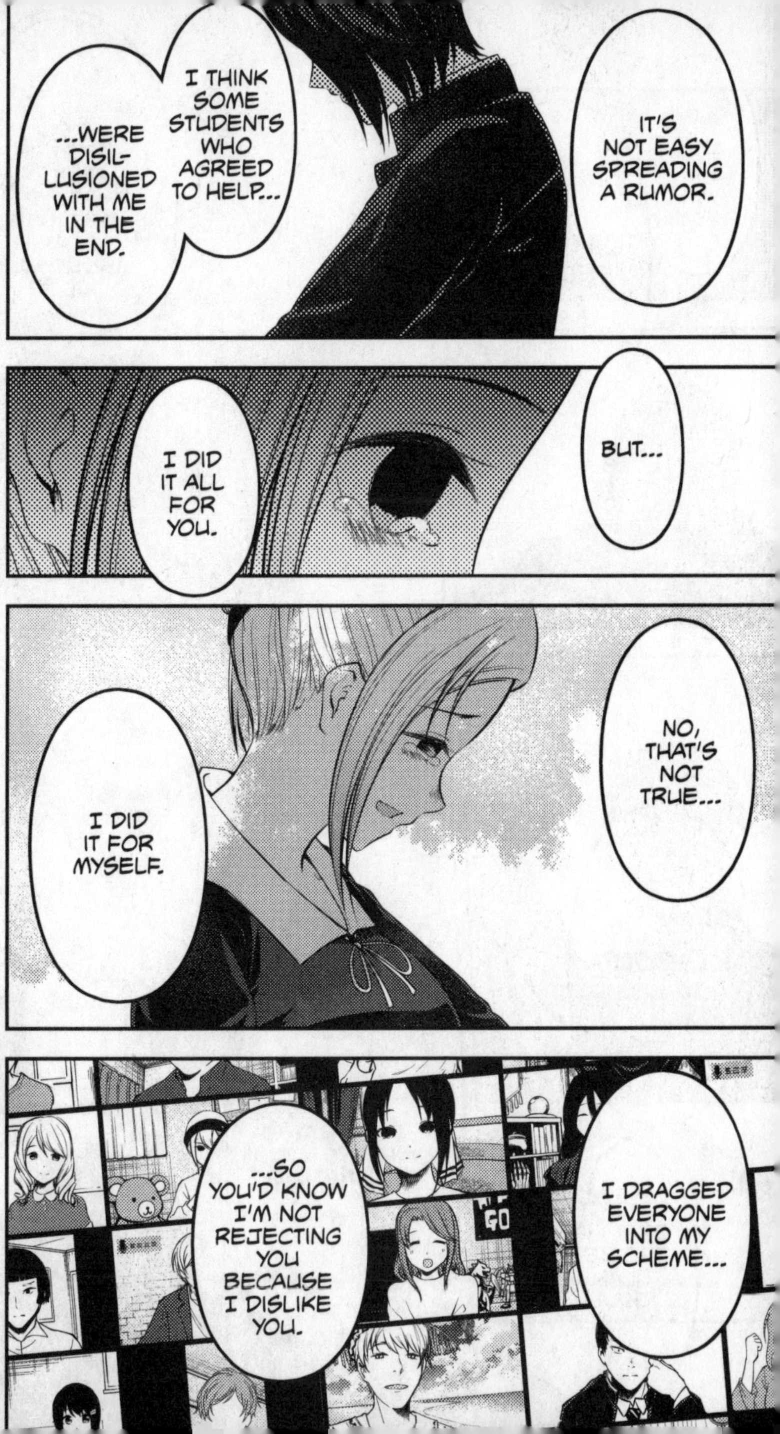
IT'S NOT EASY SPREADING A RUMOR.
I THINK SOME STUDENTS WHO AGREED TO HELP...
...WERE DISIL-LUSIONED WITH ME IN THE END.
BUT...
I DID IT ALL FOR YOU.
NO, THAT'S NOT TRUE...
I DID IT FOR MYSELF.
I DRAGGED EVERYONE INTO MY SCHEME...
...SO YOU'D KNOW I'M NOT REJECTING YOU BECAUSE I DISLIKE YOU.

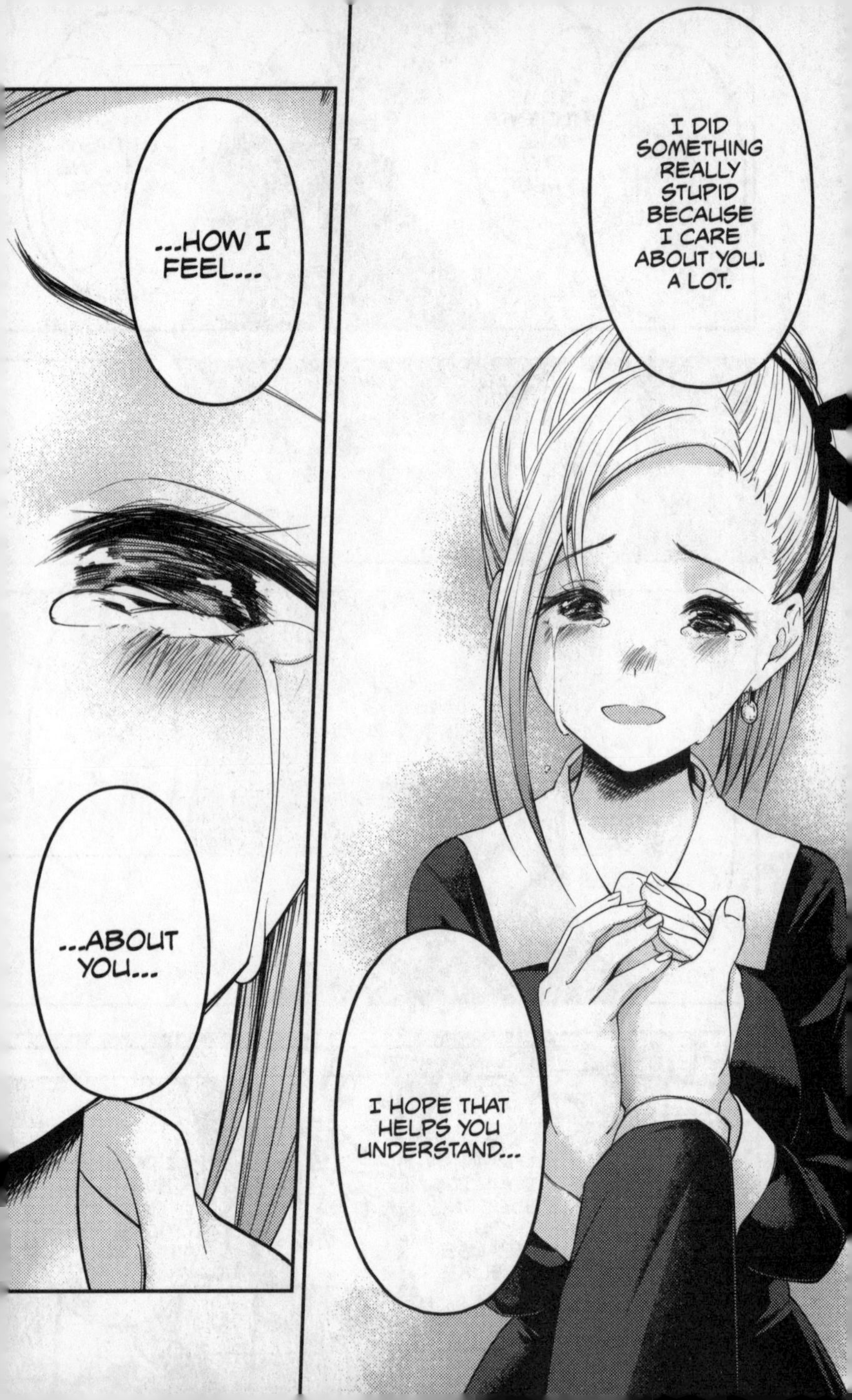
I DID SOMETHING REALLY STUPID BECAUSE I CARE ABOUT YOU. A LOT.
I HOPE THAT HELPS YOU UNDERSTAND...
...HOW I FEEL...
...ABOUT YOU...

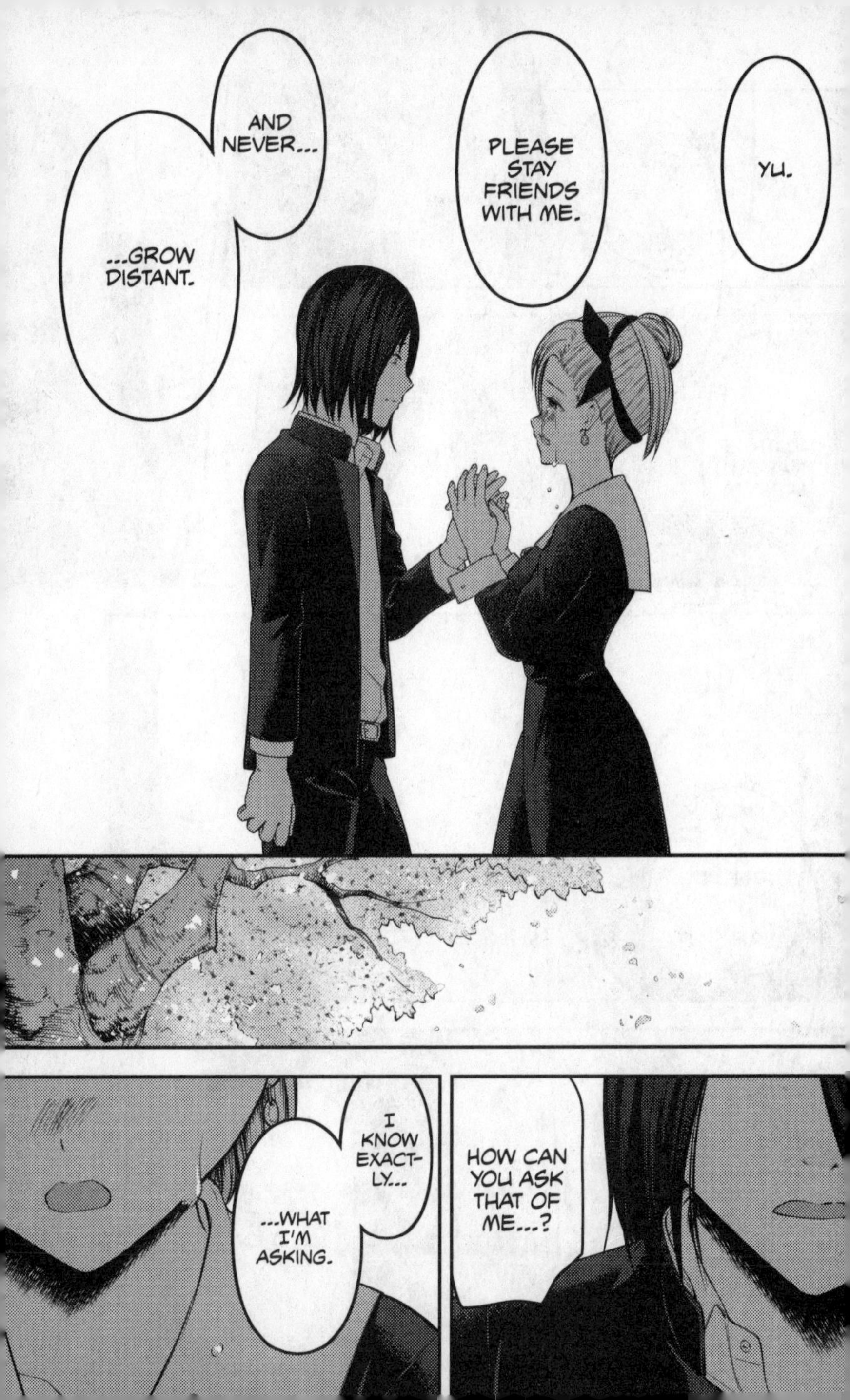
YU.
PLEASE STAY FRIENDS WITH ME.
AND NEVER...
...GROW DISTANT.
HOW CAN YOU ASK THAT OF ME...?
I KNOW EXACTLY...
...WHAT I'M ASKING.

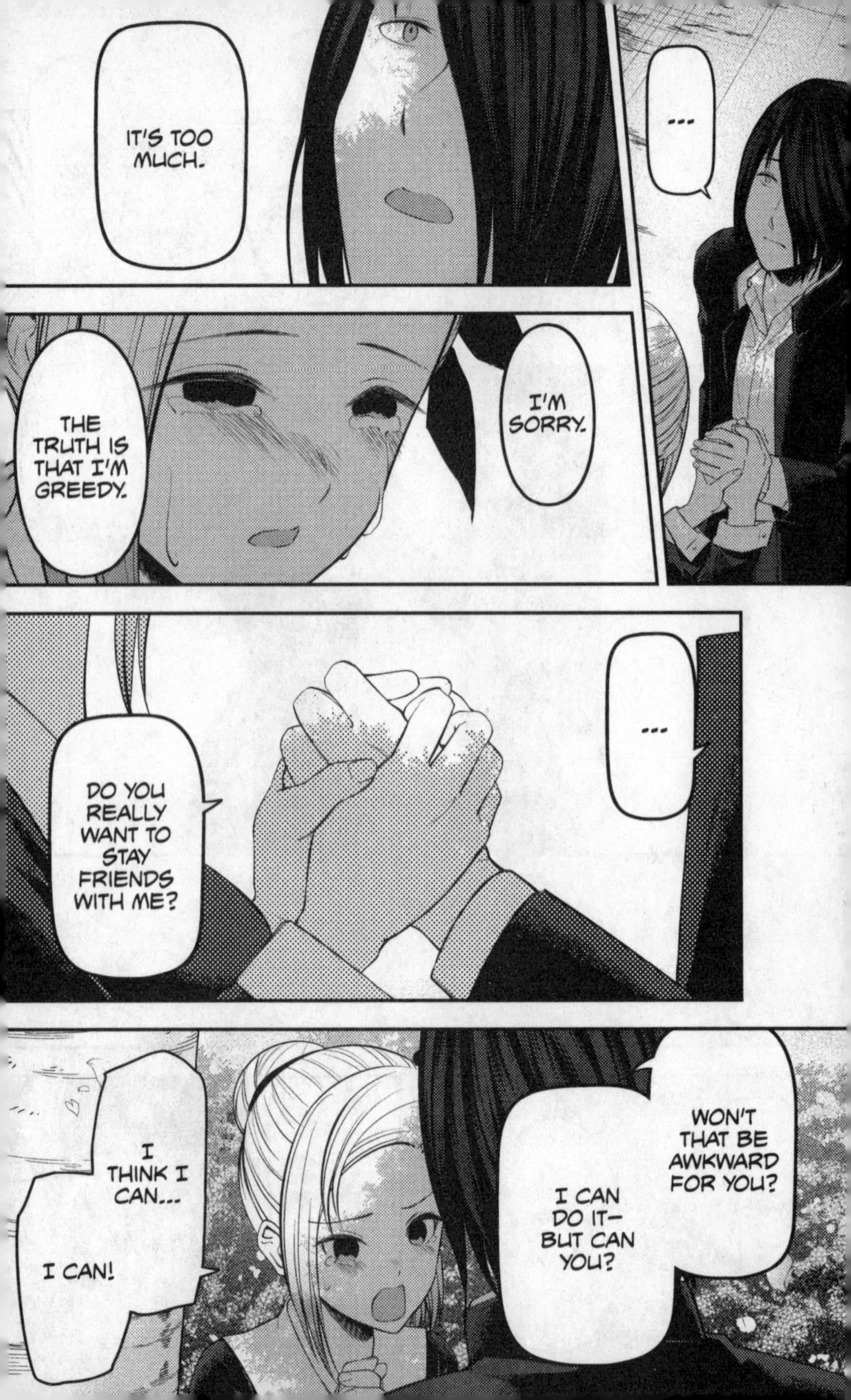
...
IT'S TOO MUCH.
I'M SORRY.
THE TRUTH IS THAT I'M GREEDY.
...
DO YOU REALLY WANT TO STAY FRIENDS WITH ME?
WON'T THAT BE AWKWARD FOR YOU?
I CAN DO IT— BUT CAN YOU?
I THINK I CAN...
I CAN!

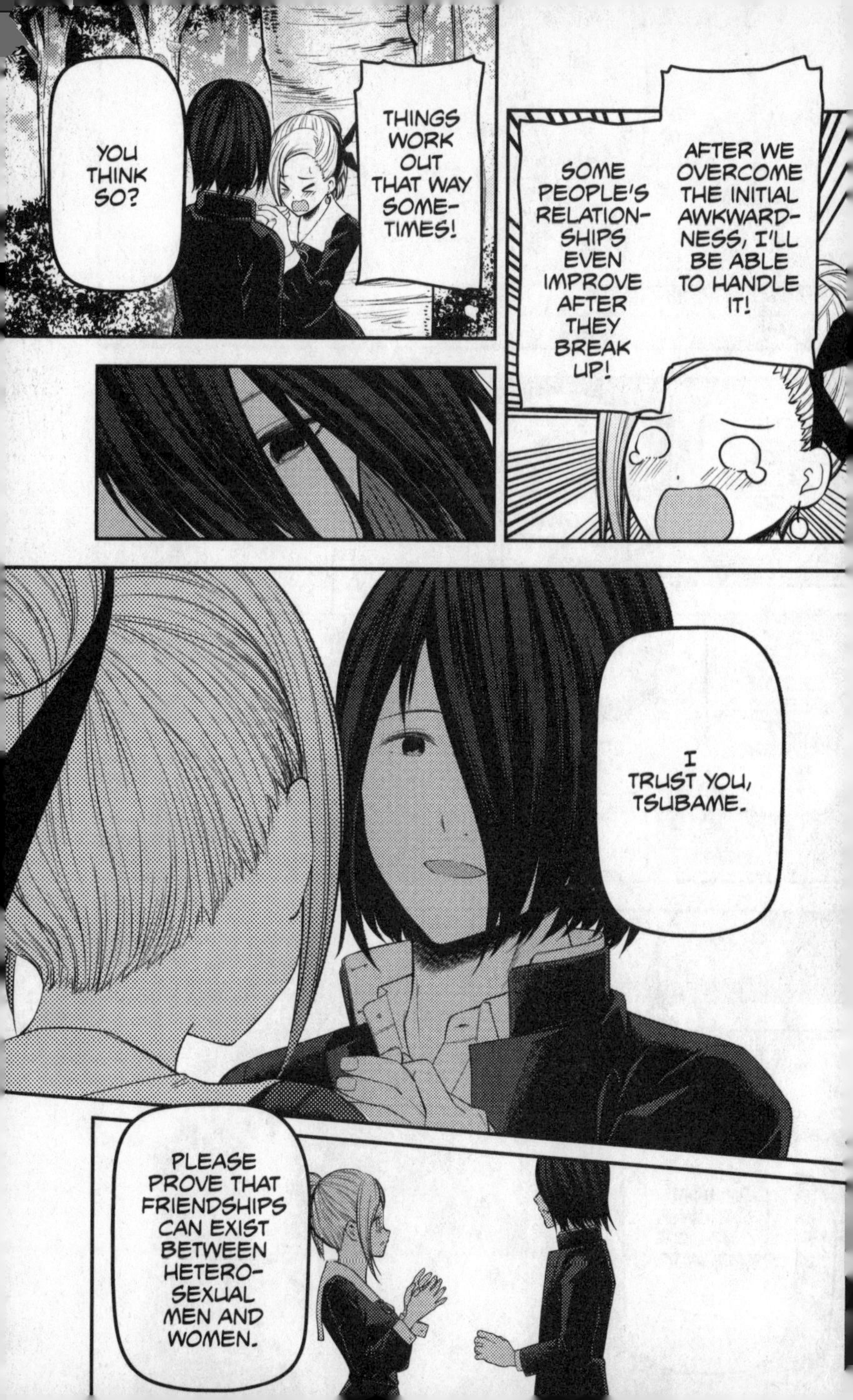
THINGS WORK OUT THAT WAY SOME-TIMES!
YOU THINK SO?
SOME PEOPLE'S RELATION-SHIPS EVEN IMPROVE AFTER THEY BREAK UP!
AFTER WE OVERCOME THE INITIAL AWKWARD-NESS, I'LL BE ABLE TO HANDLE IT!
I TRUST YOU, TSUBAME.
PLEASE PROVE THAT FRIENDSHIPS CAN EXIST BETWEEN HETERO-SEXUAL MEN AND WOMEN.

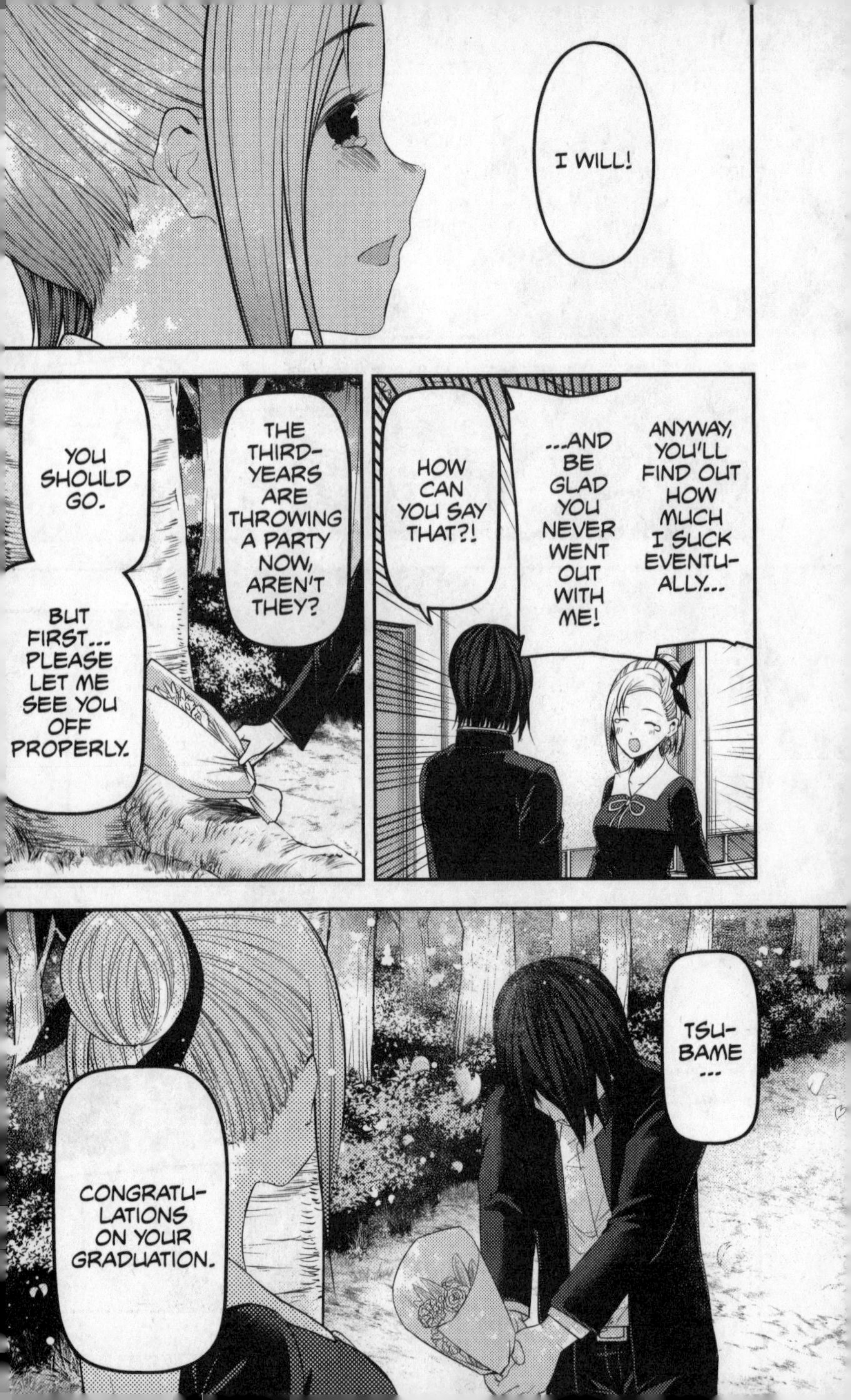
I WILL!
ANYWAY, YOU'LL FIND OUT HOW MUCH I SUCK EVENTUALLY...
...AND BE GLAD YOU NEVER WENT OUT WITH ME!
HOW CAN YOU SAY THAT?!
THE THIRD-YEARS ARE THROWING A PARTY NOW, AREN'T THEY?
YOU SHOULD GO.
BUT FIRST... PLEASE LET ME SEE YOU OFF PROPERLY.
TSU-BAME...
CONGRATULATIONS ON YOUR GRADUATION.

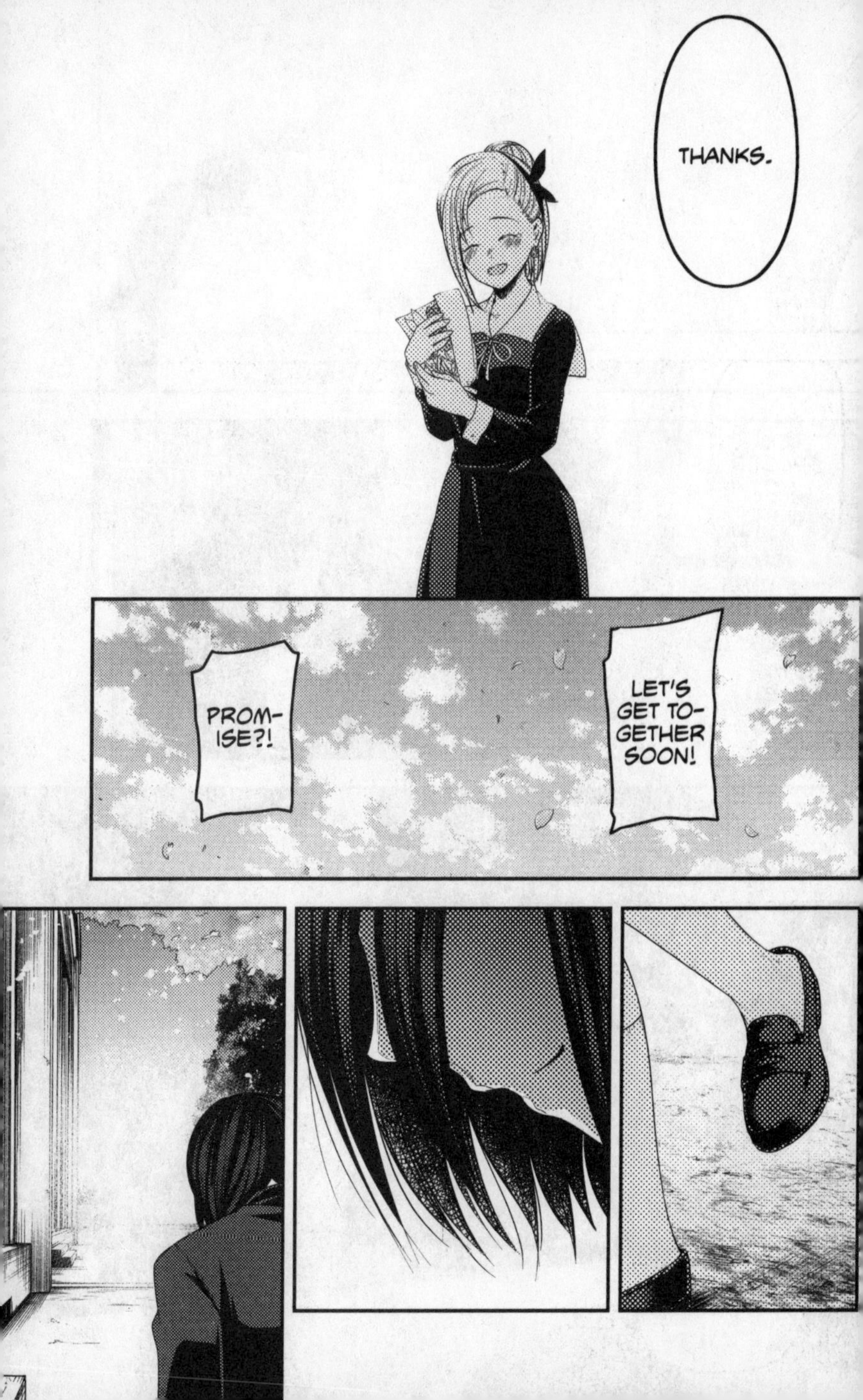
THANKS.
LET'S GET TO-GETHER SOON!
PROM-ISE?!

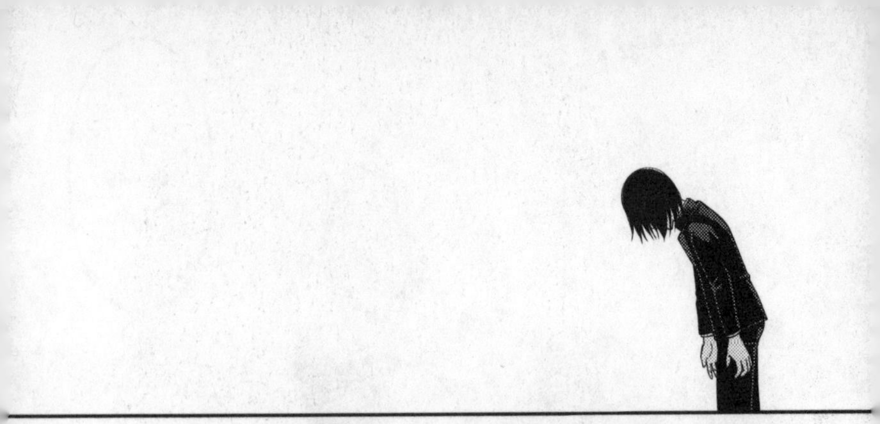

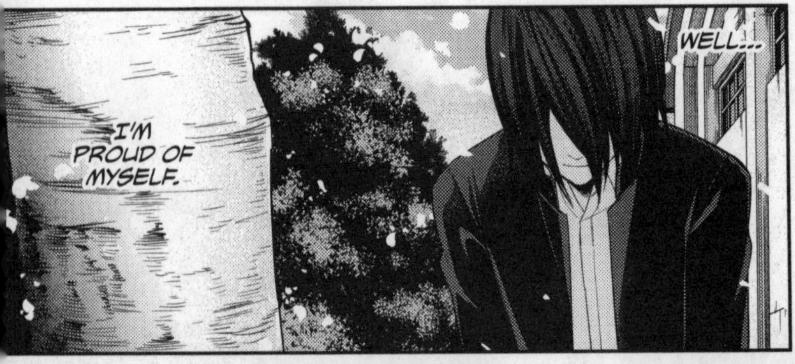
WELL...
I'M PROUD OF MYSELF.

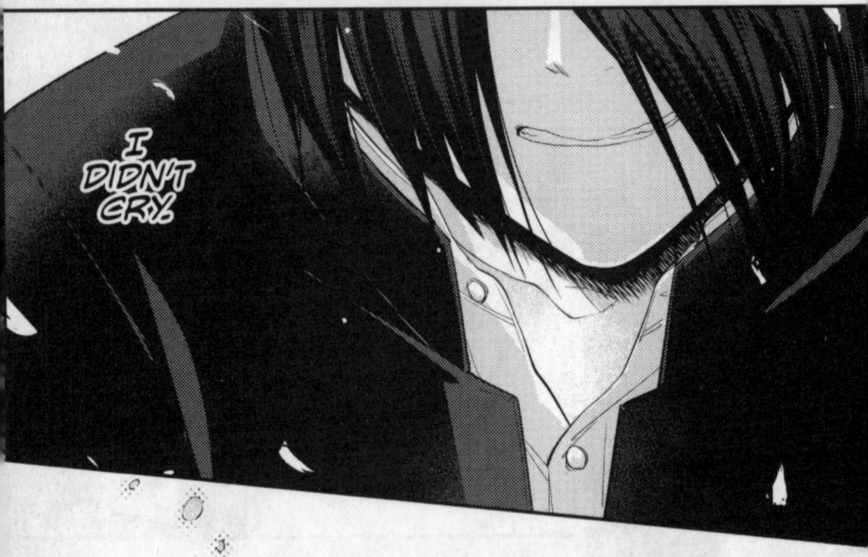
I DIDN'T CRY.

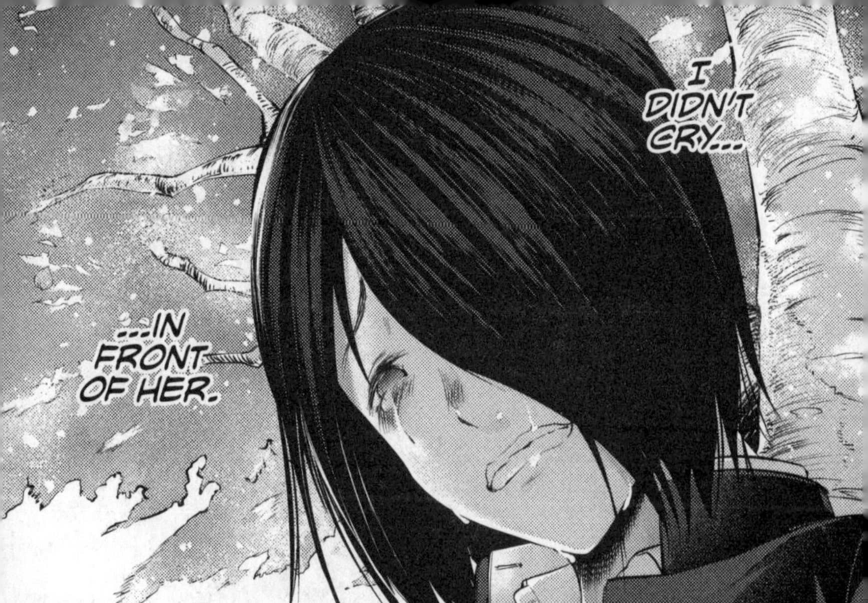
I DIDN'T CRY...
...IN FRONT OF HER.
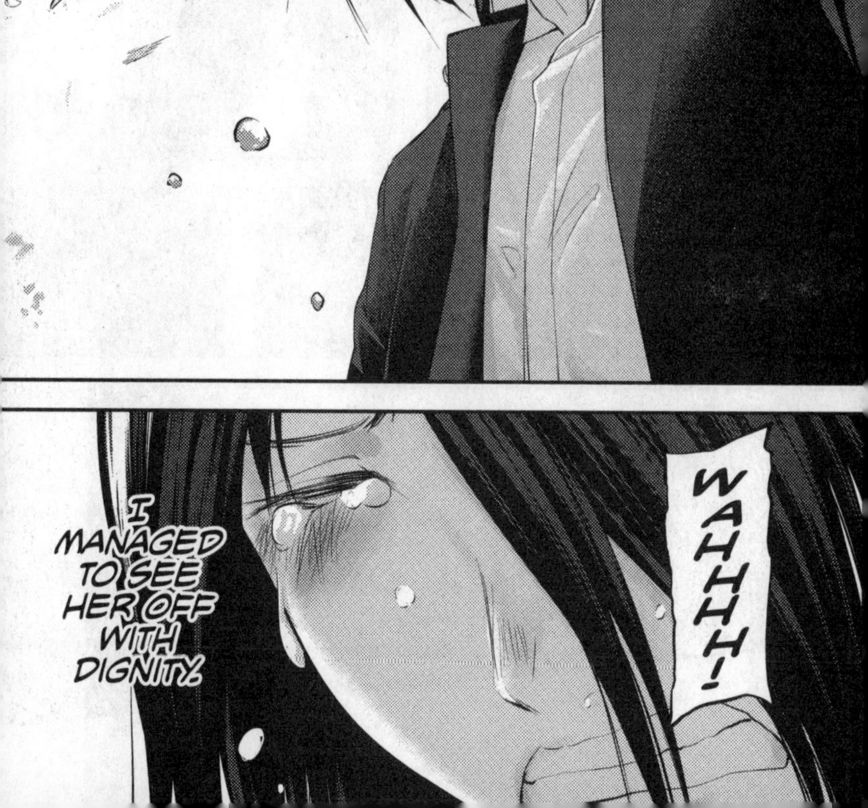
WAHHHH!
I MANAGED TO SEE HER OFF WITH DIGNITY.

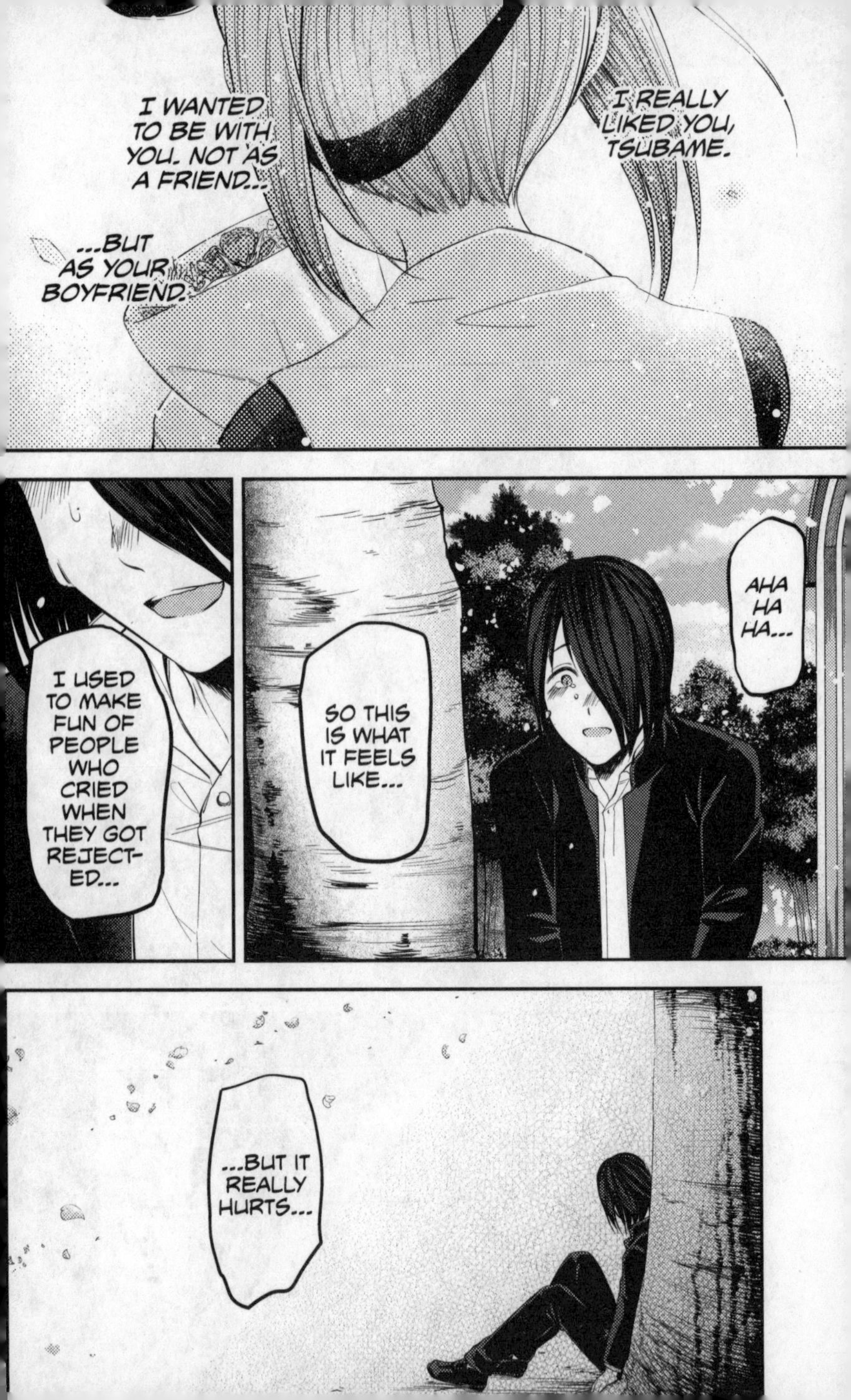
I REALLY LIKED YOU, TSUBAME.
I WANTED TO BE WITH YOU. NOT AS A FRIEND...
...BUT AS YOUR BOYFRIEND.
AHA HA HA...
SO THIS IS WHAT IT FEELS LIKE...
I USED TO MAKE FUN OF PEOPLE WHO CRIED WHEN THEY GOT REJECTED...
...BUT IT REALLY HURTS...

KAGUYA-SAMA
LOVE IS WAR

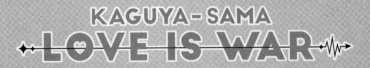

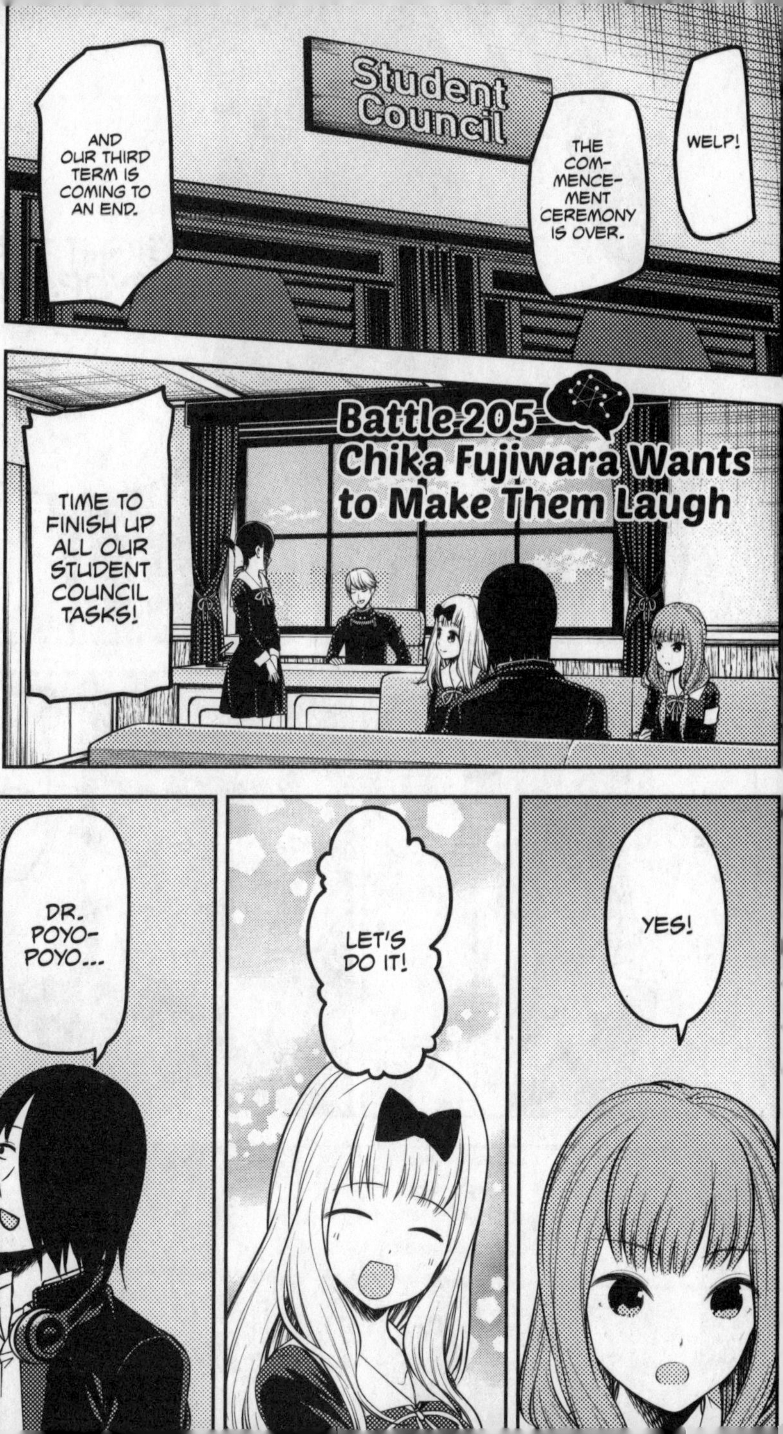
WELP!
THE COMMENCEMENT CEREMONY IS OVER.
Student Council
AND OUR THIRD TERM IS COMING TO AN END.
Battle 205 Chika Fujiwara Wants to Make Them Laugh
TIME TO FINISH UP ALL OUR STUDENT COUNCIL TASKS!
YES!
LET'S DO IT!
DR. POYO-POYO...

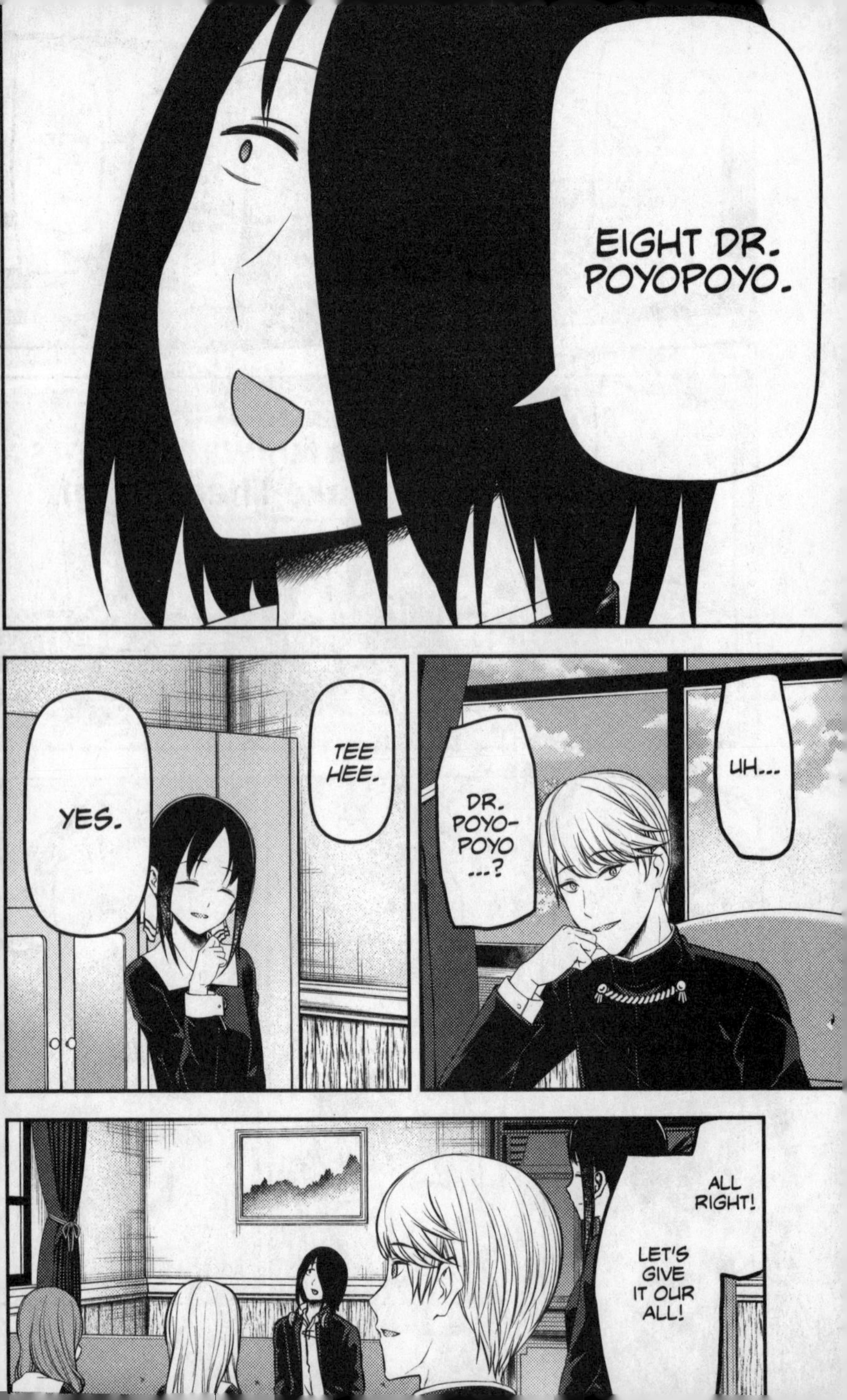
EIGHT DR. POYOPOYO.
UH...
DR. POYO-POYO ...?
TEE HEE.
YES.
ALL RIGHT!
LET'S GIVE IT OUR ALL!

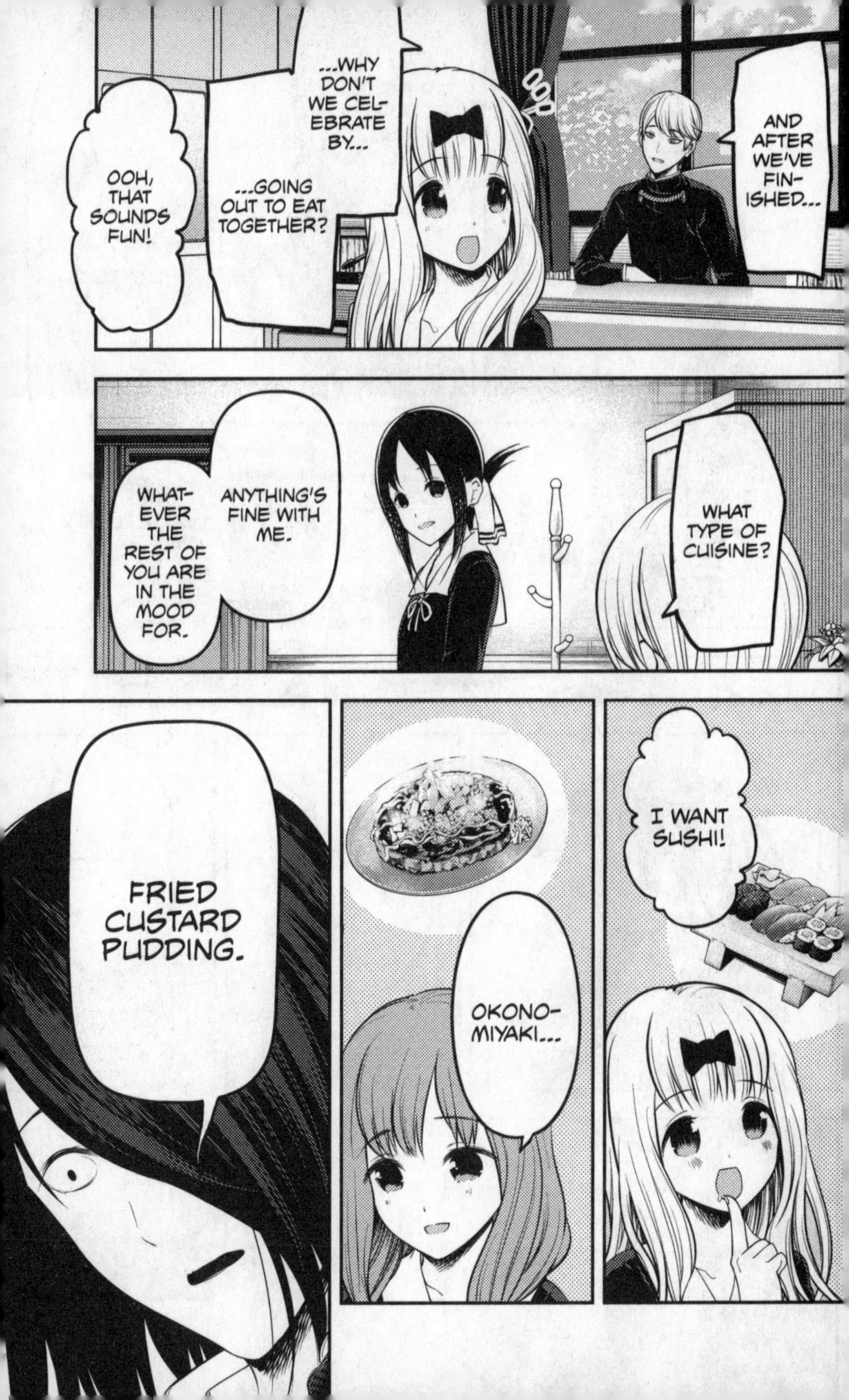
AND AFTER WE'VE FIN-ISHED...
...WHY DON'T WE CEL-EBRATE BY...
...GOING OUT TO EAT TOGETHER?
OOH, THAT SOUNDS FUN!
WHAT TYPE OF CUISINE?
ANYTHING'S FINE WITH ME.
WHAT-EVER THE REST OF YOU ARE IN THE MOOD FOR.
I WANT SUSHI!
OKONO-MIYAKI...
FRIED CUSTARD PUDDING.

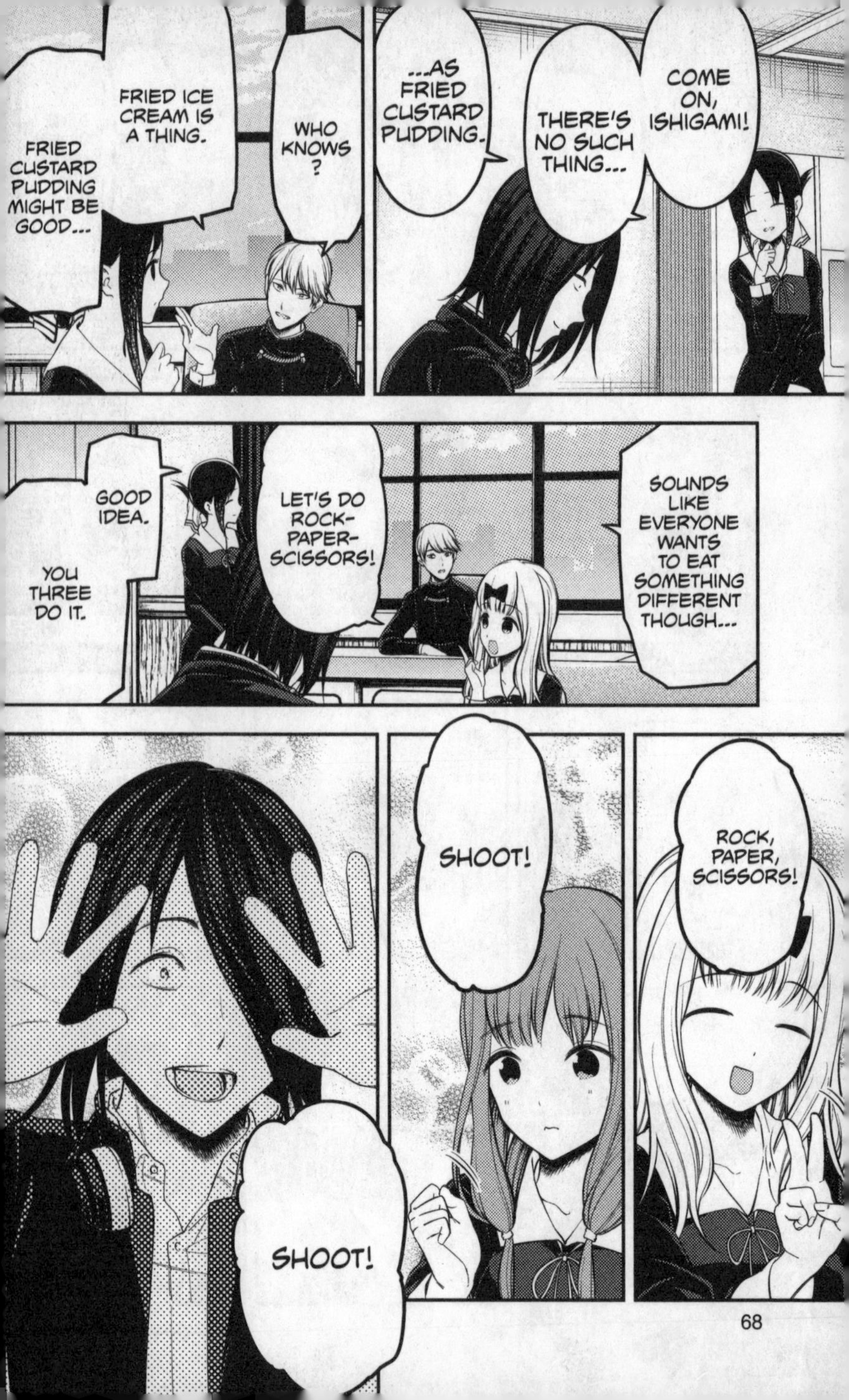
COME ON, ISHIGAMI!
THERE'S NO SUCH THING...
...AS FRIED CUSTARD PUDDING.
WHO KNOWS?
FRIED ICE CREAM IS A THING.
FRIED CUSTARD PUDDING MIGHT BE GOOD...
SOUNDS LIKE EVERYONE WANTS TO EAT SOMETHING DIFFERENT THOUGH...
LET'S DO ROCK-PAPER-SCISSORS!
GOOD IDEA.
YOU THREE DO IT.
ROCK, PAPER, SCISSORS!
SHOOT!
SHOOT!

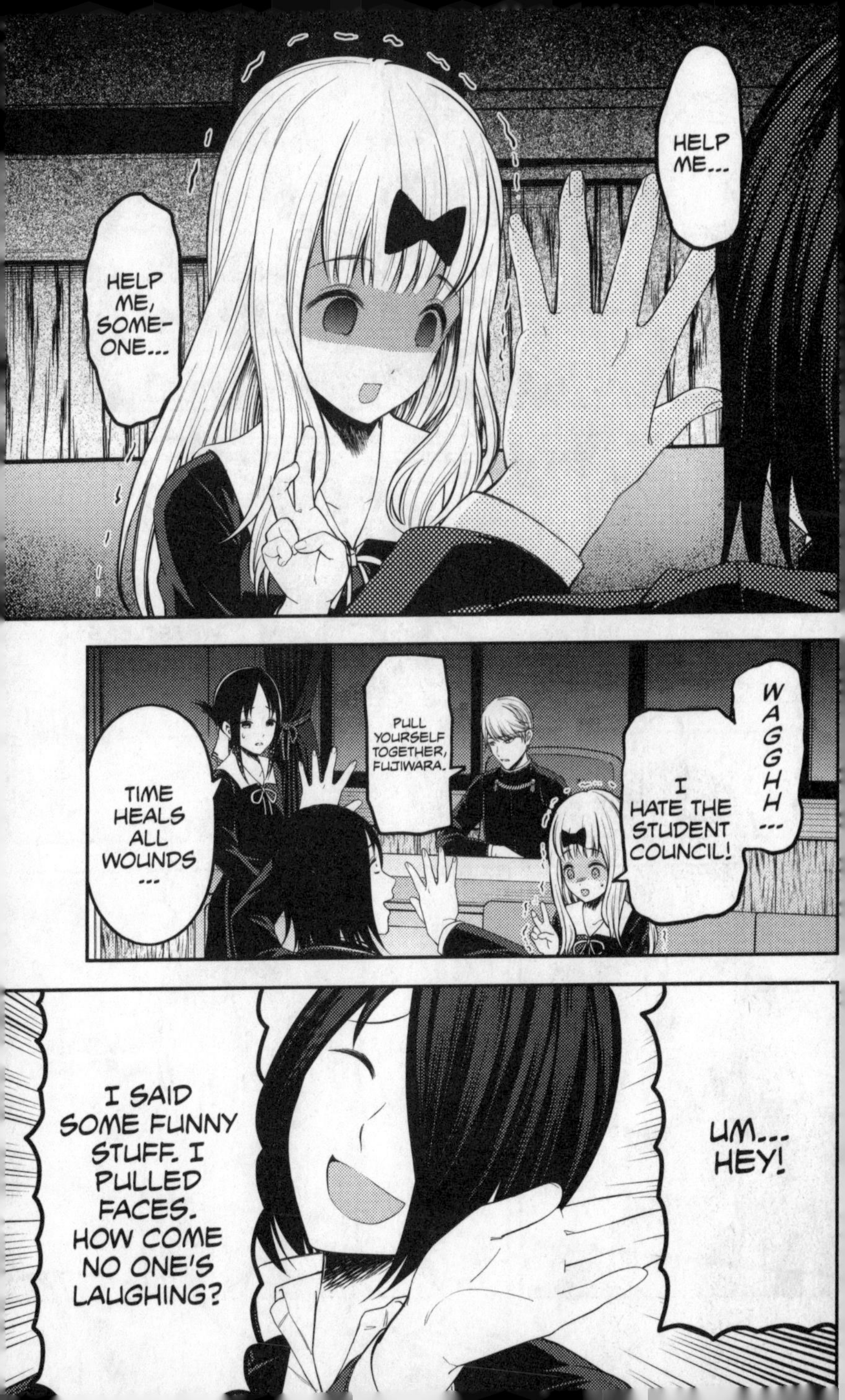
HELP ME...
HELP ME, SOME-ONE...
WAGGHH...
I HATE THE STUDENT COUNCIL!
PULL YOURSELF TOGETHER, FUJIWARA.
TIME HEALS ALL WOUNDS...
UM... HEY!
I SAID SOME FUNNY STUFF. I PULLED FACES. HOW COME NO ONE'S LAUGHING?

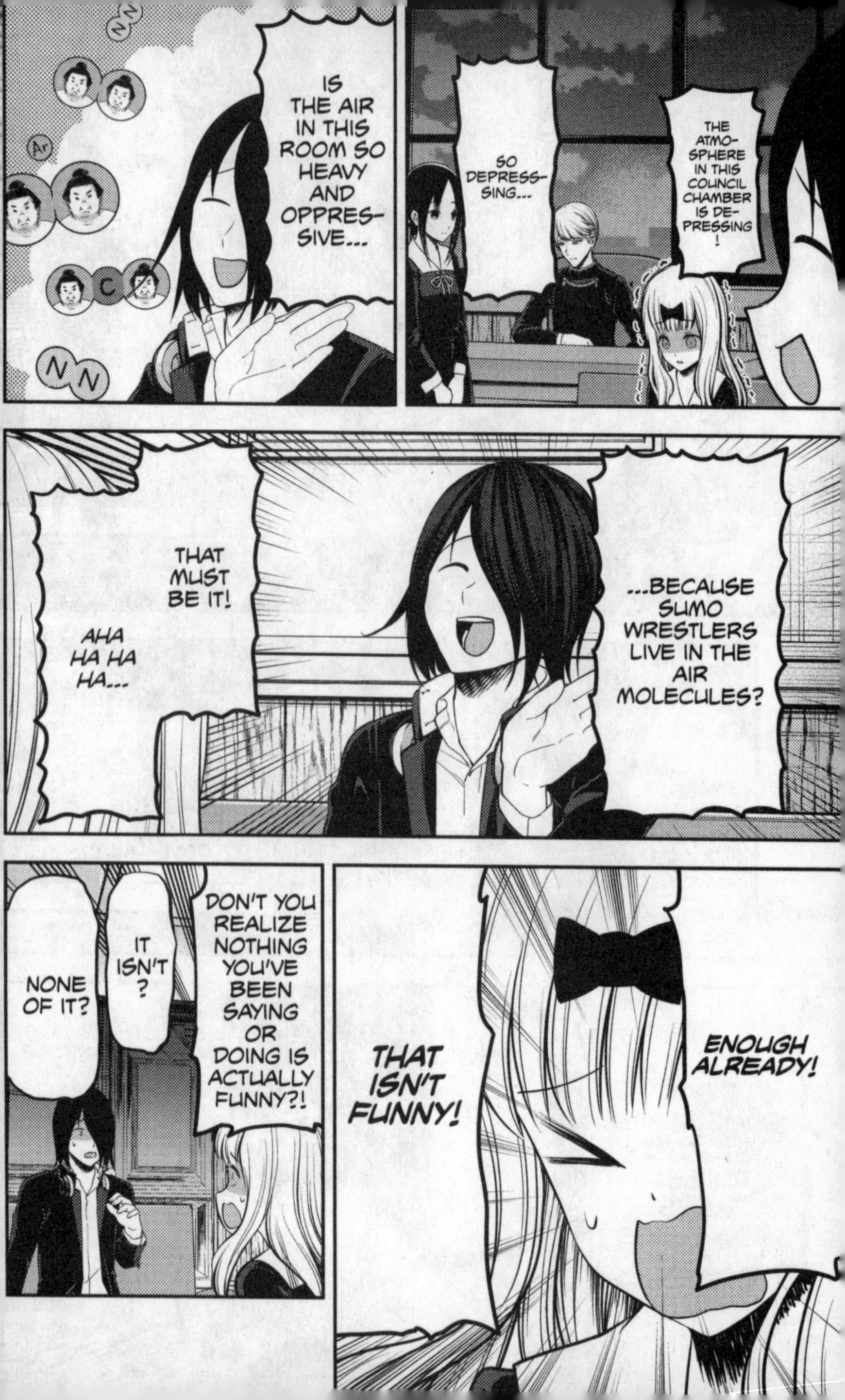
THE ATMOSPHERE IN THIS COUNCIL CHAMBER IS DEPRESSING!
SO DEPRESSING...
IS THE AIR IN THIS ROOM SO HEAVY AND OPPRESSIVE...
...BECAUSE SUMO WRESTLERS LIVE IN THE AIR MOLECULES?
THAT MUST BE IT!
AHA HA HA HA...
ENOUGH ALREADY!
THAT ISN'T FUNNY!
DON'T YOU REALIZE NOTHING YOU'VE BEEN SAYING OR DOING IS ACTUALLY FUNNY?!
IT ISN'T?
NONE OF IT?

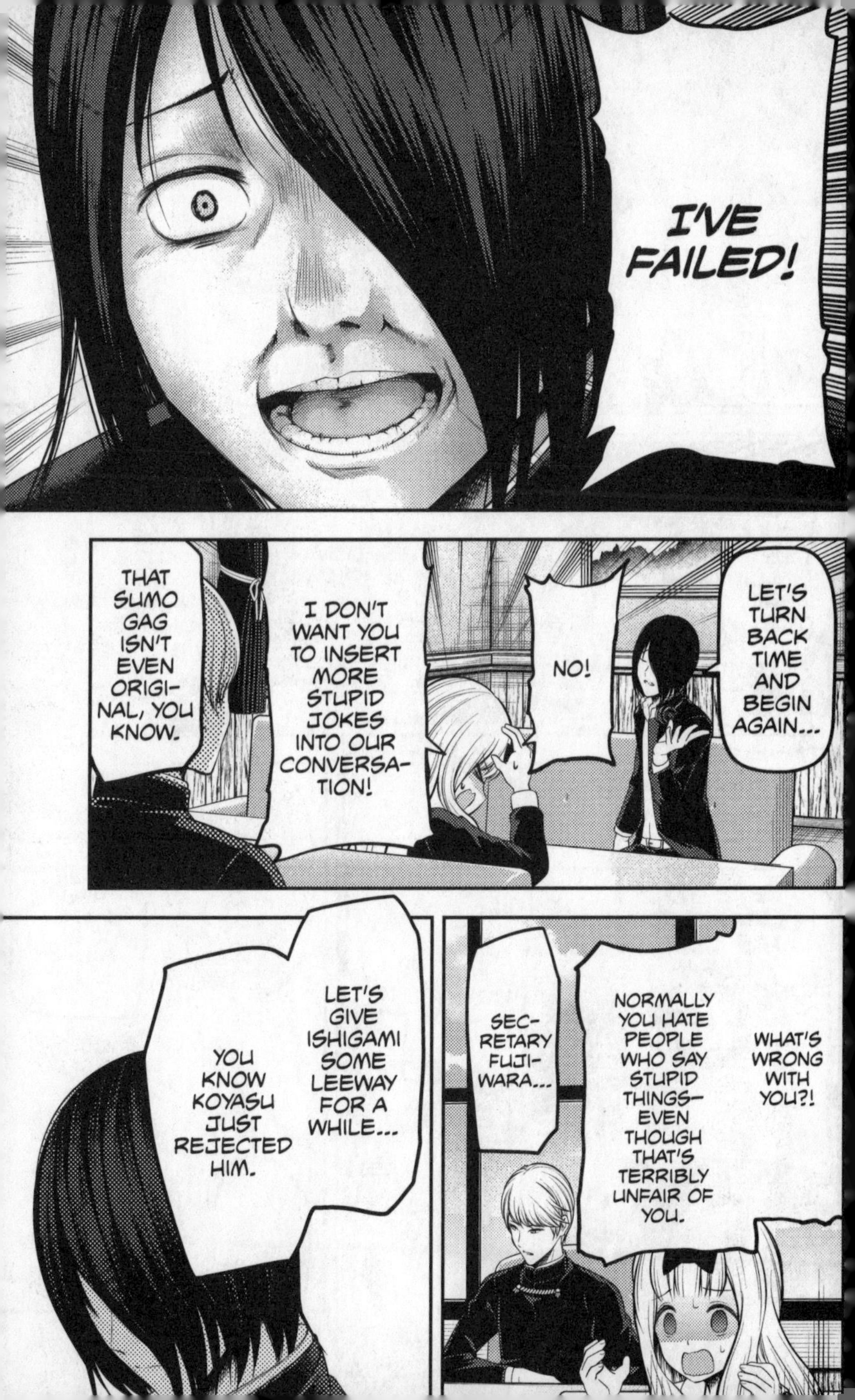
I'VE FAILED!
LET'S TURN BACK TIME AND BEGIN AGAIN...
NO!
I DON'T WANT YOU TO INSERT MORE STUPID JOKES INTO OUR CONVERSATION!
THAT SUMO GAG ISN'T EVEN ORIGINAL, YOU KNOW.
WHAT'S WRONG WITH YOU?!
NORMALLY YOU HATE PEOPLE WHO SAY STUPID THINGS—EVEN THOUGH THAT'S TERRIBLY UNFAIR OF YOU.
SECRETARY FUJIWARA...
LET'S GIVE ISHIGAMI SOME LEEWAY FOR A WHILE...
YOU KNOW KOYASU JUST REJECTED HIM.

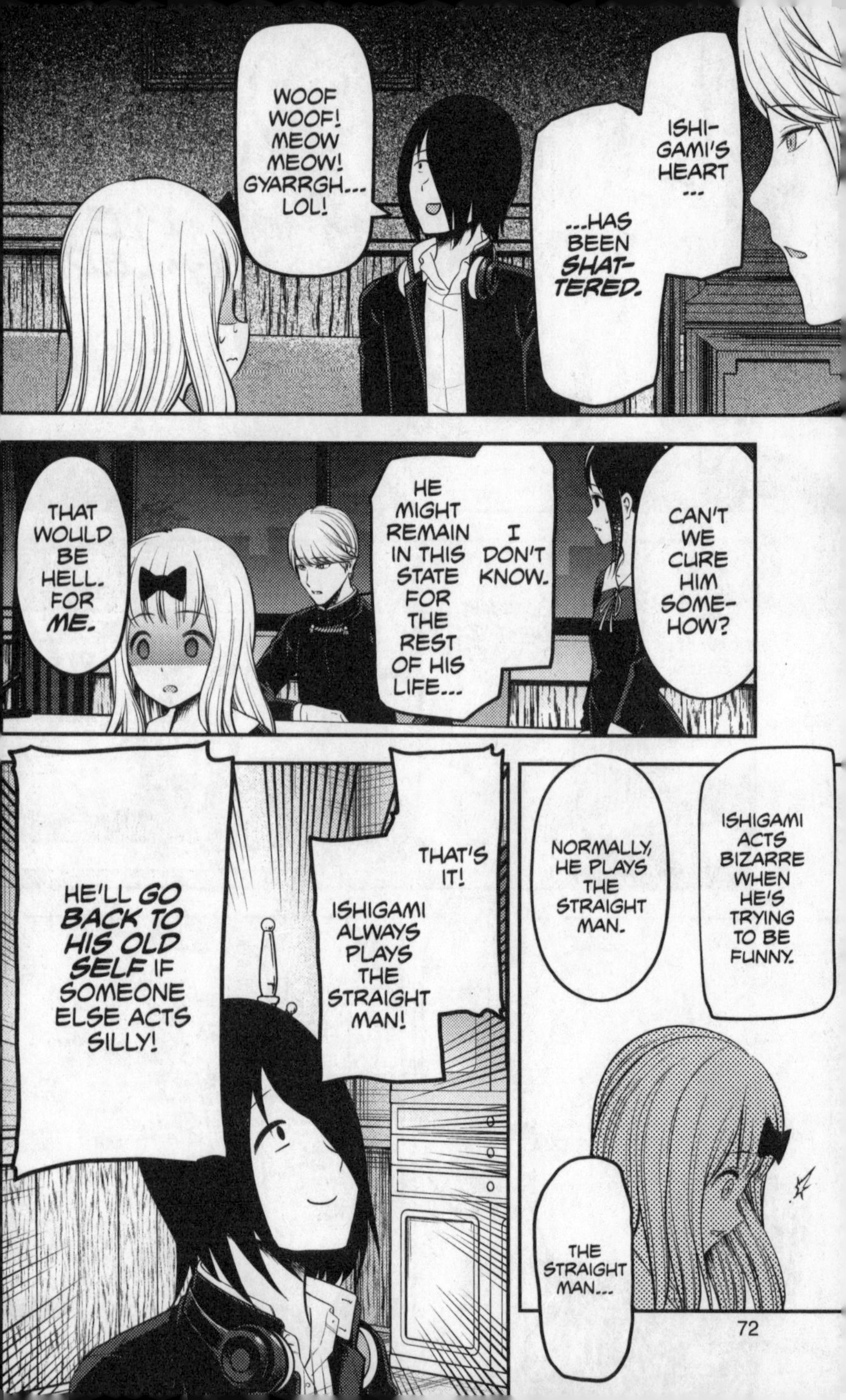
ISHIGAMI'S HEART...
...HAS BEEN SHATTERED.
WOOF WOOF! MEOW MEOW! GYARRGH... LOL!
CAN'T WE CURE HIM SOMEHOW?
I DON'T KNOW.
HE MIGHT REMAIN IN THIS STATE FOR THE REST OF HIS LIFE...
THAT WOULD BE HELL. FOR ME.
ISHIGAMI ACTS BIZARRE WHEN HE'S TRYING TO BE FUNNY.
NORMALLY, HE PLAYS THE STRAIGHT MAN.
THE STRAIGHT MAN...
THAT'S IT!
ISHIGAMI ALWAYS PLAYS THE STRAIGHT MAN!
HE'LL GO BACK TO HIS OLD SELF IF SOMEONE ELSE ACTS SILLY!

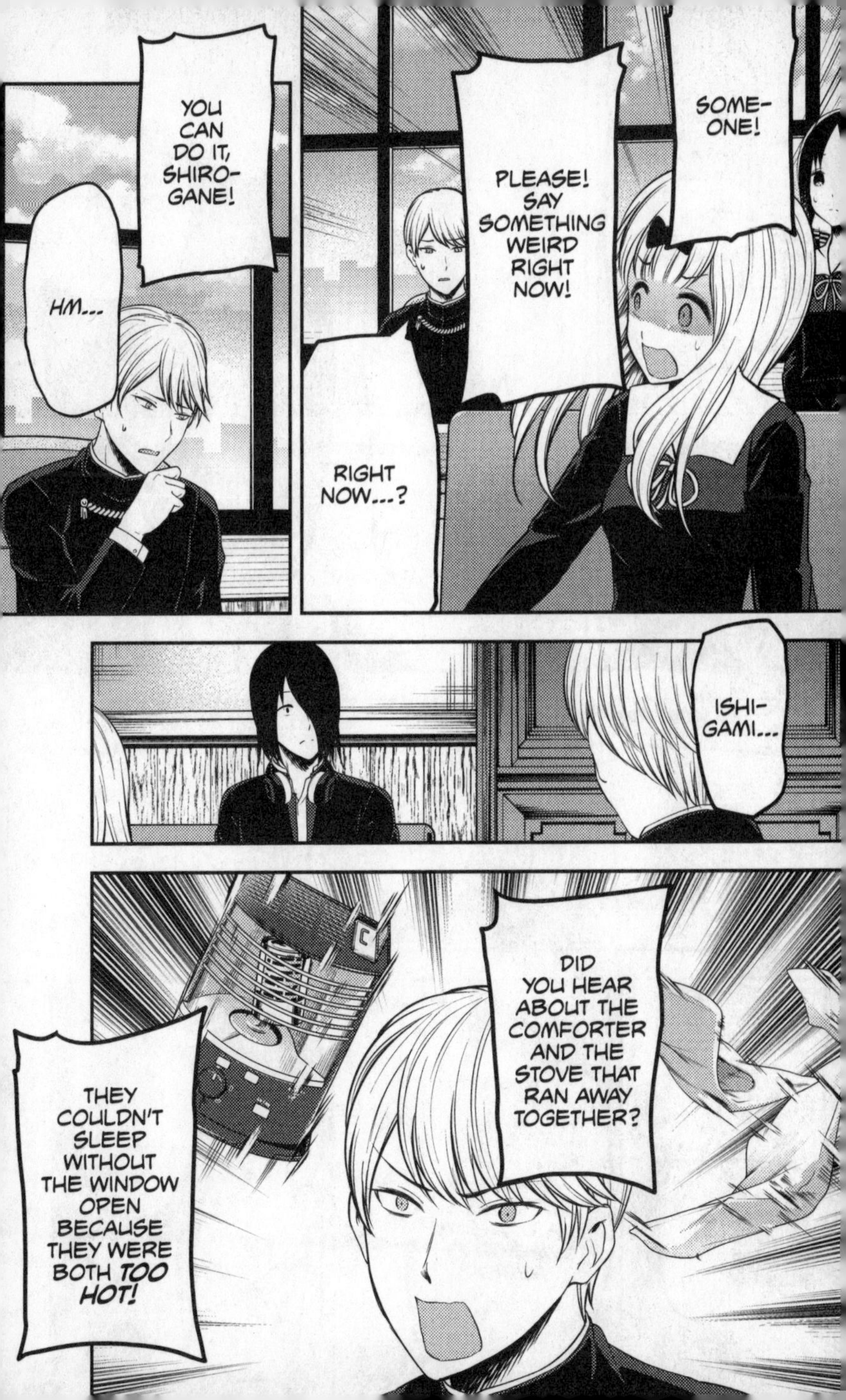
SOME-ONE!
PLEASE! SAY SOMETHING WEIRD RIGHT NOW!
RIGHT NOW...?
YOU CAN DO IT, SHIRO-GANE!
HM...
ISHI-GAMI...
DID YOU HEAR ABOUT THE COMFORTER AND THE STOVE THAT RAN AWAY TOGETHER?
THEY COULDN'T SLEEP WITHOUT THE WINDOW OPEN BECAUSE THEY WERE BOTH *TOO HOT!*

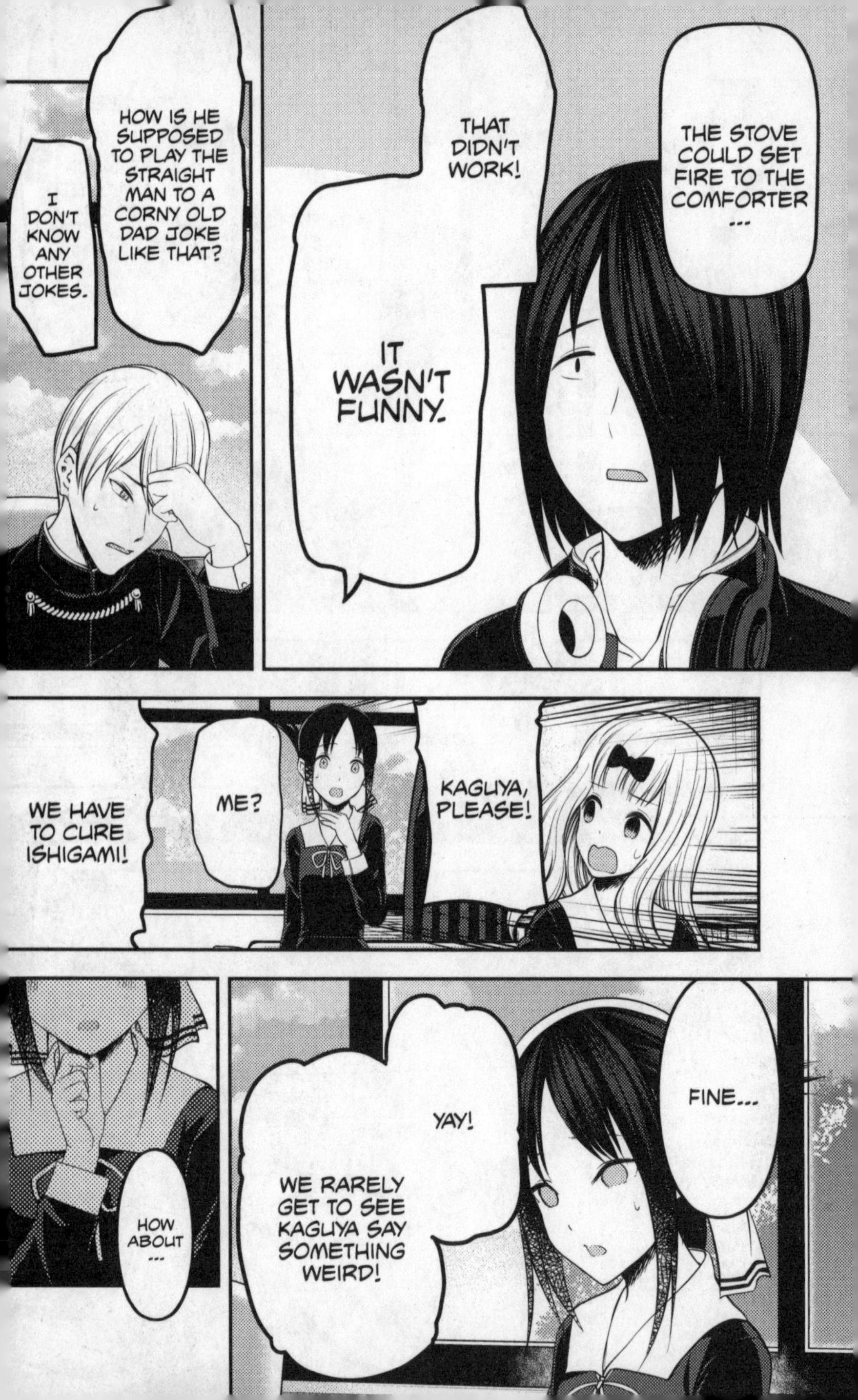
THE STOVE COULD SET FIRE TO THE COMFORTER ...
THAT DIDN'T WORK!
IT WASN'T FUNNY.
HOW IS HE SUPPOSED TO PLAY THE STRAIGHT MAN TO A CORNY OLD DAD JOKE LIKE THAT?
I DON'T KNOW ANY OTHER JOKES.
KAGUYA, PLEASE!
ME?
WE HAVE TO CURE ISHIGAMI!
FINE...
YAY!
WE RARELY GET TO SEE KAGUYA SAY SOMETHING WEIRD!
HOW ABOUT ...

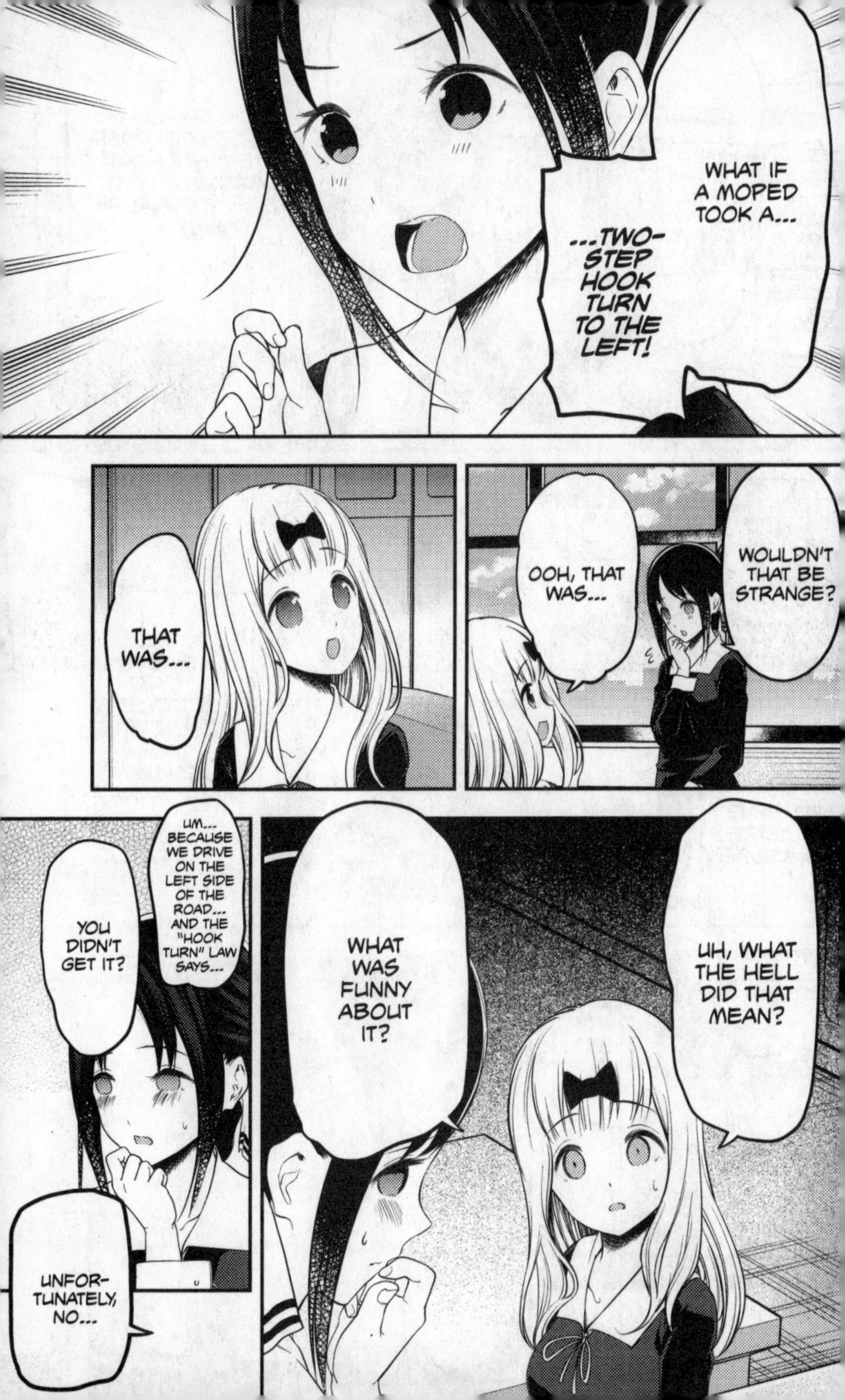
WHAT IF A MOPED TOOK A...
...TWO-STEP HOOK TURN TO THE LEFT!
WOULDN'T THAT BE STRANGE?
OOH, THAT WAS...
THAT WAS...
UH, WHAT THE HELL DID THAT MEAN?
WHAT WAS FUNNY ABOUT IT?
UM... BECAUSE WE DRIVE ON THE LEFT SIDE OF THE ROAD... AND THE "HOOK TURN" LAW SAYS...
YOU DIDN'T GET IT?
UNFOR-TUNATELY, NO...

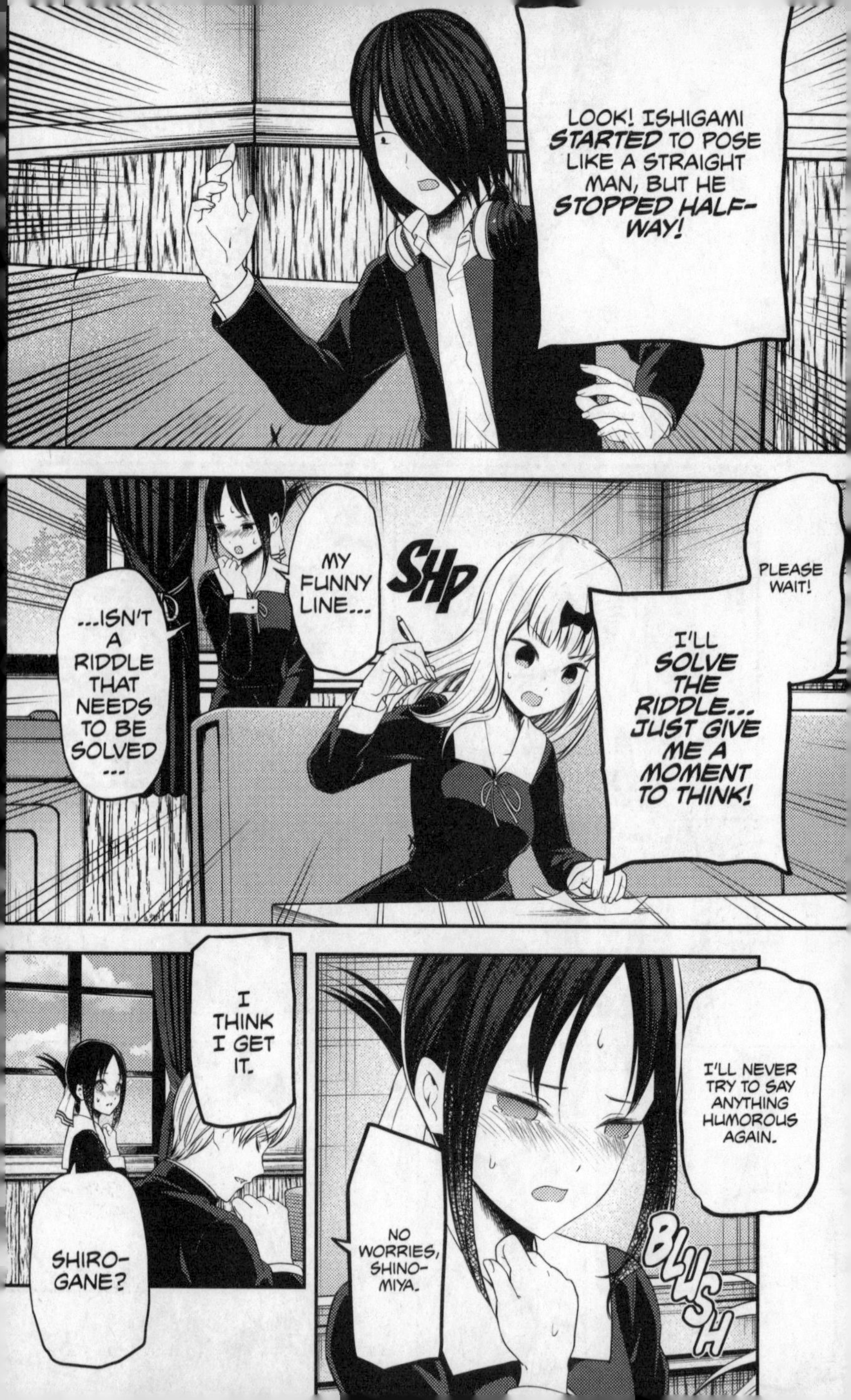
LOOK! ISHIGAMI STARTED TO POSE LIKE A STRAIGHT MAN, BUT HE STOPPED HALF-WAY!
PLEASE WAIT!
I'LL SOLVE THE RIDDLE... JUST GIVE ME A MOMENT TO THINK!
SHP
MY FUNNY LINE...
...ISN'T A RIDDLE THAT NEEDS TO BE SOLVED...
I'LL NEVER TRY TO SAY ANYTHING HUMOROUS AGAIN.
BLUSH
NO WORRIES, SHINO-MIYA.
I THINK I GET IT.
SHIRO-GANE?

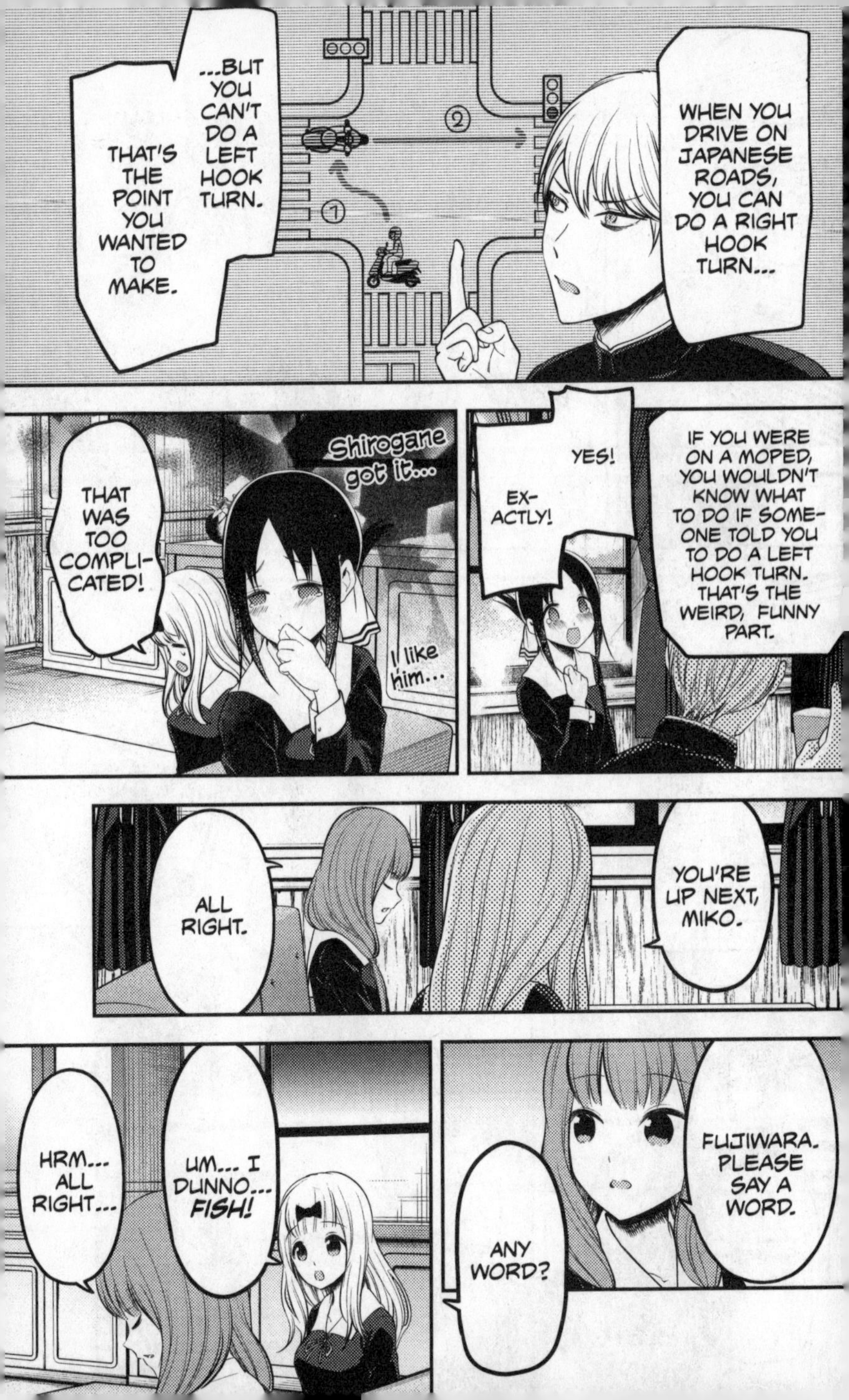
WHEN YOU DRIVE ON JAPANESE ROADS, YOU CAN DO A RIGHT HOOK TURN...
...BUT YOU CAN'T DO A LEFT HOOK TURN.
THAT'S THE POINT YOU WANTED TO MAKE.
IF YOU WERE ON A MOPED, YOU WOULDN'T KNOW WHAT TO DO IF SOME-ONE TOLD YOU TO DO A LEFT HOOK TURN. THAT'S THE WEIRD, FUNNY PART.
YES!
EX-ACTLY!
Shirogane got it...
THAT WAS TOO COMPLI-CATED!
I like him...
YOU'RE UP NEXT, MIKO.
ALL RIGHT.
FUJIWARA. PLEASE SAY A WORD.
ANY WORD?
UM... I DUNNO... *FISH!*
HRM... ALL RIGHT...

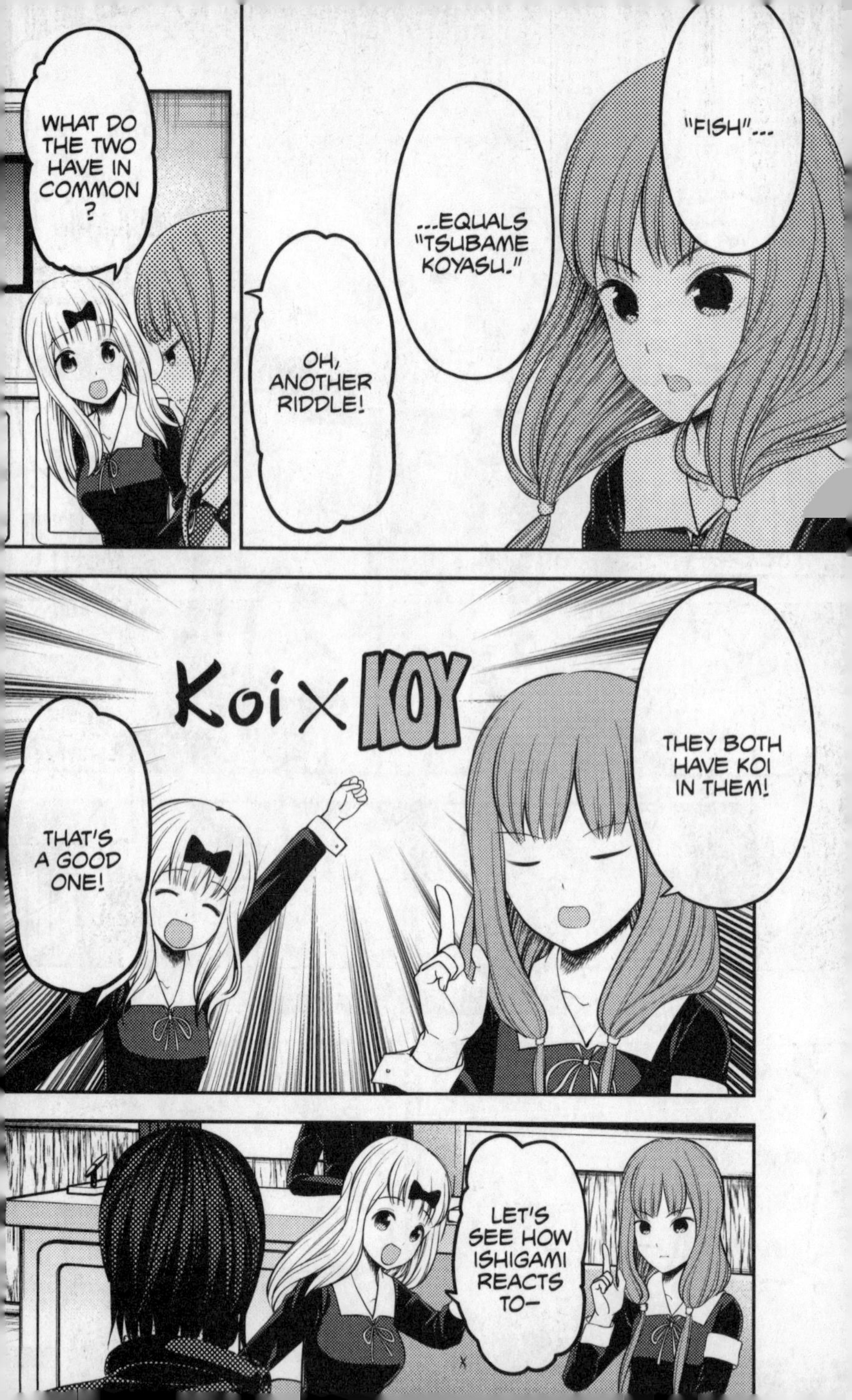
"FISH"...
...EQUALS "TSUBAME KOYASU."
OH, ANOTHER RIDDLE!
WHAT DO THE TWO HAVE IN COMMON?
THEY BOTH HAVE KOI IN THEM!
Koi × KOY
THAT'S A GOOD ONE!
LET'S SEE HOW ISHIGAMI REACTS TO—

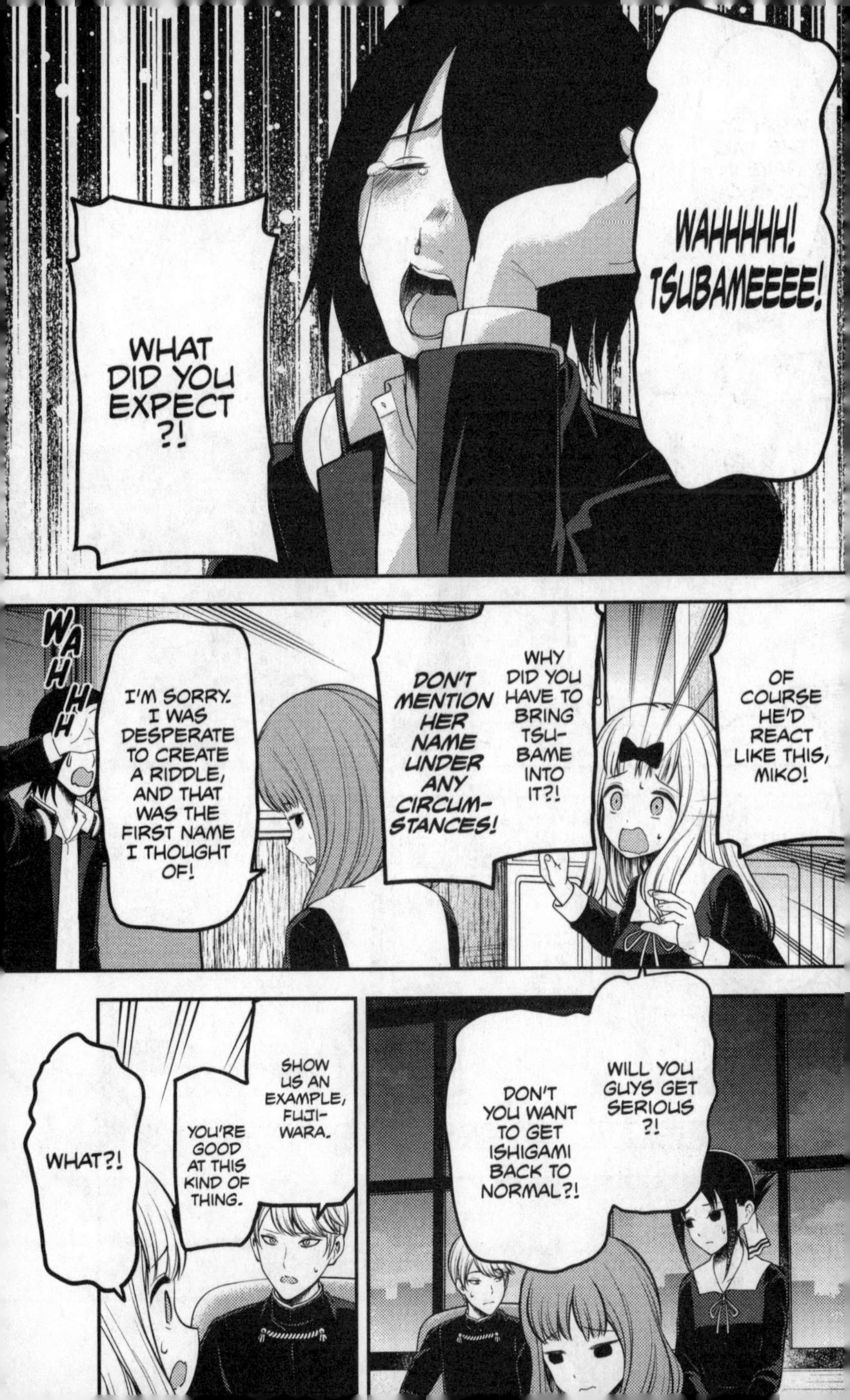
WAHHHHH! TSUBAMEEEEE!
WHAT DID YOU EXPECT?!
OF COURSE HE'D REACT LIKE THIS, MIKO!
WHY DID YOU HAVE TO BRING TSU-BAME INTO IT?!
DON'T MENTION HER NAME UNDER ANY CIRCUM-STANCES!
I'M SORRY. I WAS DESPERATE TO CREATE A RIDDLE, AND THAT WAS THE FIRST NAME I THOUGHT OF!
WAHHHH
WILL YOU GUYS GET SERIOUS?!
DON'T YOU WANT TO GET ISHIGAMI BACK TO NORMAL?!
SHOW US AN EXAMPLE, FUJI-WARA.
YOU'RE GOOD AT THIS KIND OF THING.
WHAT?!

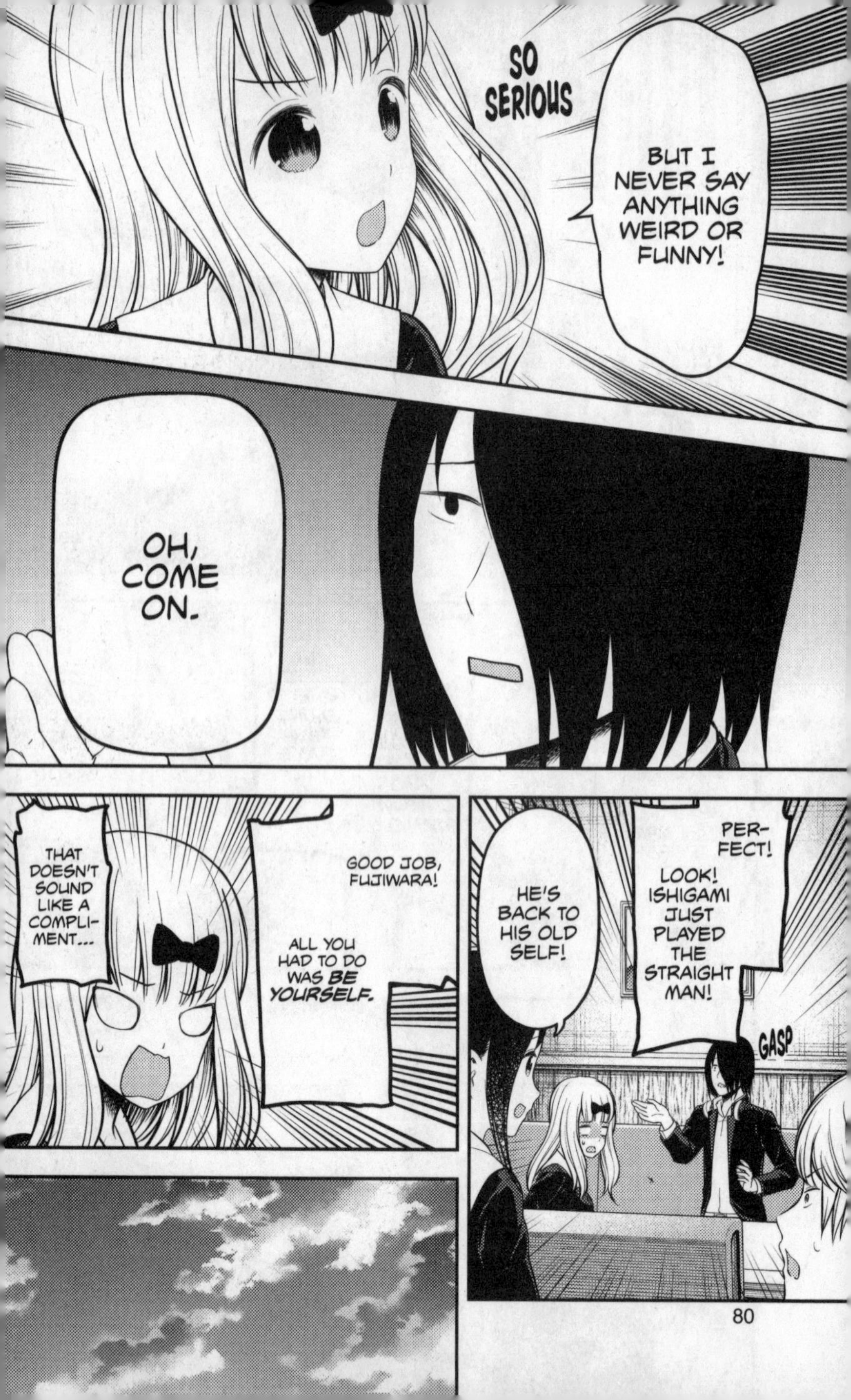
BUT I NEVER SAY ANYTHING WEIRD OR FUNNY!
SO SERIOUS
OH, COME ON.
PERFECT!
LOOK! ISHIGAMI JUST PLAYED THE STRAIGHT MAN!
HE'S BACK TO HIS OLD SELF!
GASP
GOOD JOB, FUJIWARA!
ALL YOU HAD TO DO WAS BE YOURSELF.
THAT DOESN'T SOUND LIKE A COMPLIMENT...

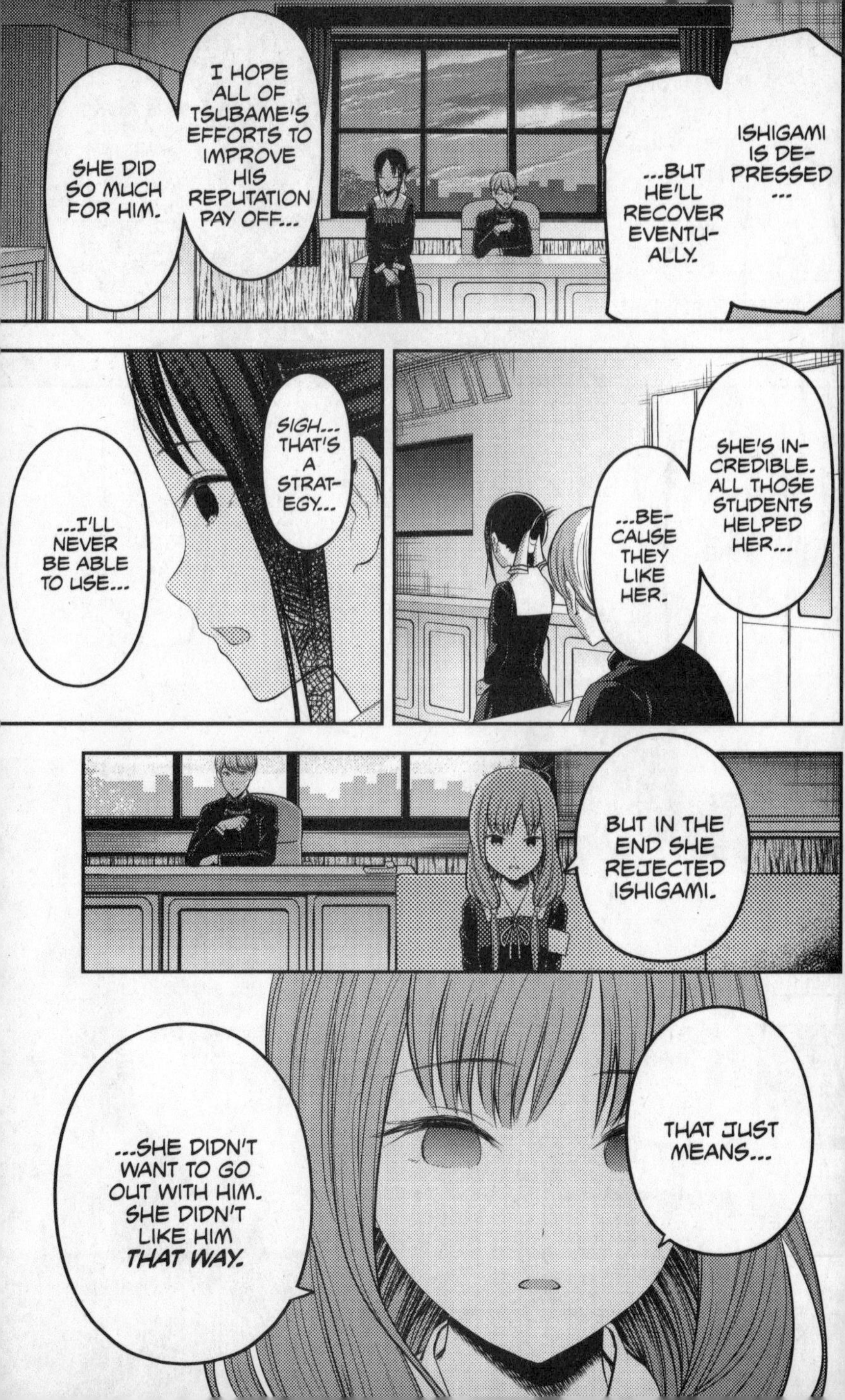
ISHIGAMI IS DE-PRESSED...
...BUT HE'LL RECOVER EVENTU-ALLY.
I HOPE ALL OF TSUBAME'S EFFORTS TO IMPROVE HIS REPUTATION PAY OFF...
SHE DID SO MUCH FOR HIM.
SHE'S IN-CREDIBLE. ALL THOSE STUDENTS HELPED HER...
...BE-CAUSE THEY LIKE HER.
SIGH... THAT'S A STRAT-EGY...
...I'LL NEVER BE ABLE TO USE...
BUT IN THE END SHE REJECTED ISHIGAMI.
THAT JUST MEANS...
...SHE DIDN'T WANT TO GO OUT WITH HIM. SHE DIDN'T LIKE HIM *THAT WAY.*

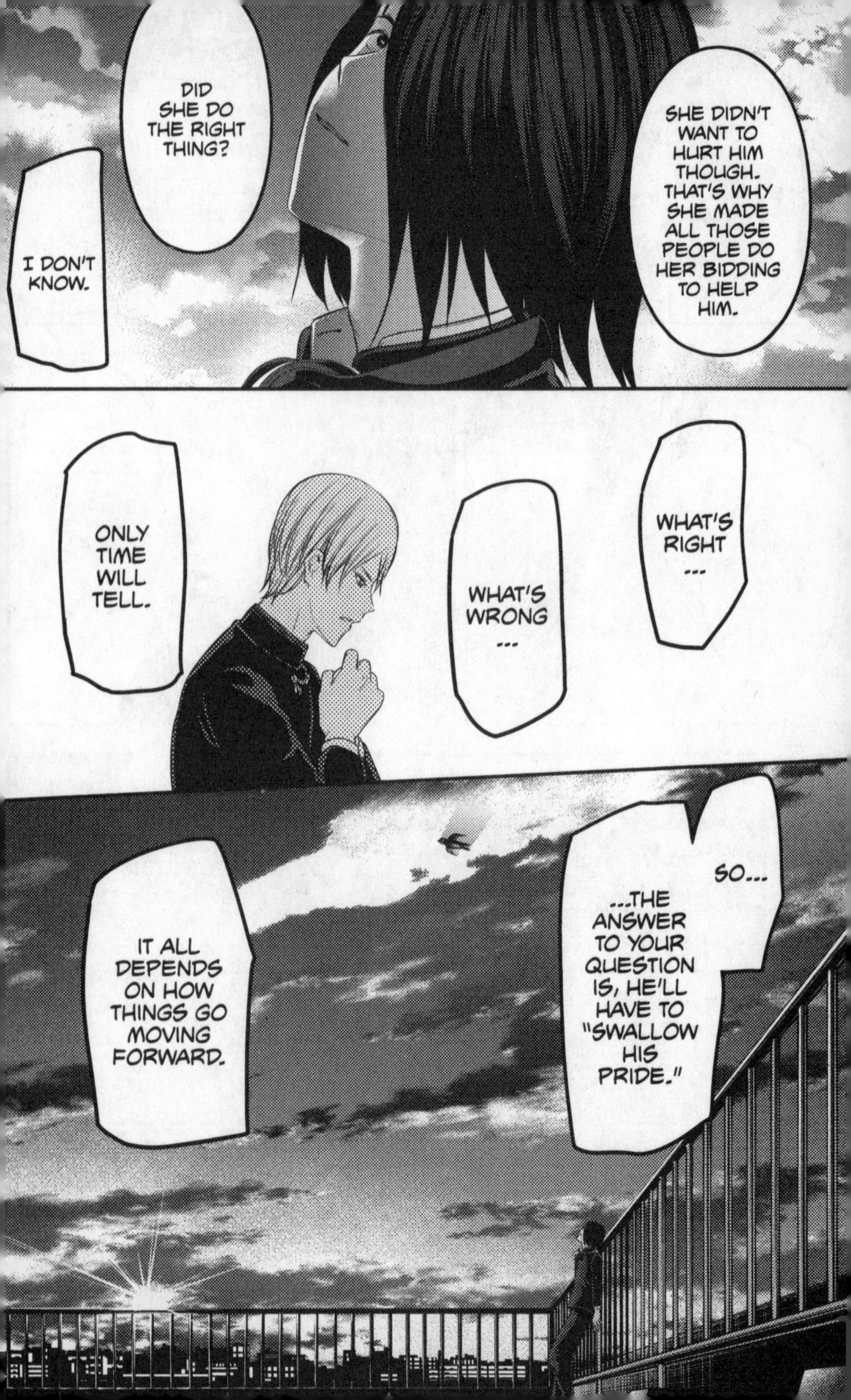
SHE DIDN'T WANT TO HURT HIM THOUGH. THAT'S WHY SHE MADE ALL THOSE PEOPLE DO HER BIDDING TO HELP HIM.
DID SHE DO THE RIGHT THING?
I DON'T KNOW.
WHAT'S RIGHT ...
WHAT'S WRONG ...
ONLY TIME WILL TELL.
SO...
...THE ANSWER TO YOUR QUESTION IS, HE'LL HAVE TO "SWALLOW HIS PRIDE."
IT ALL DEPENDS ON HOW THINGS GO MOVING FORWARD.

KAGUYA-SAMA
LOVE IS WAR

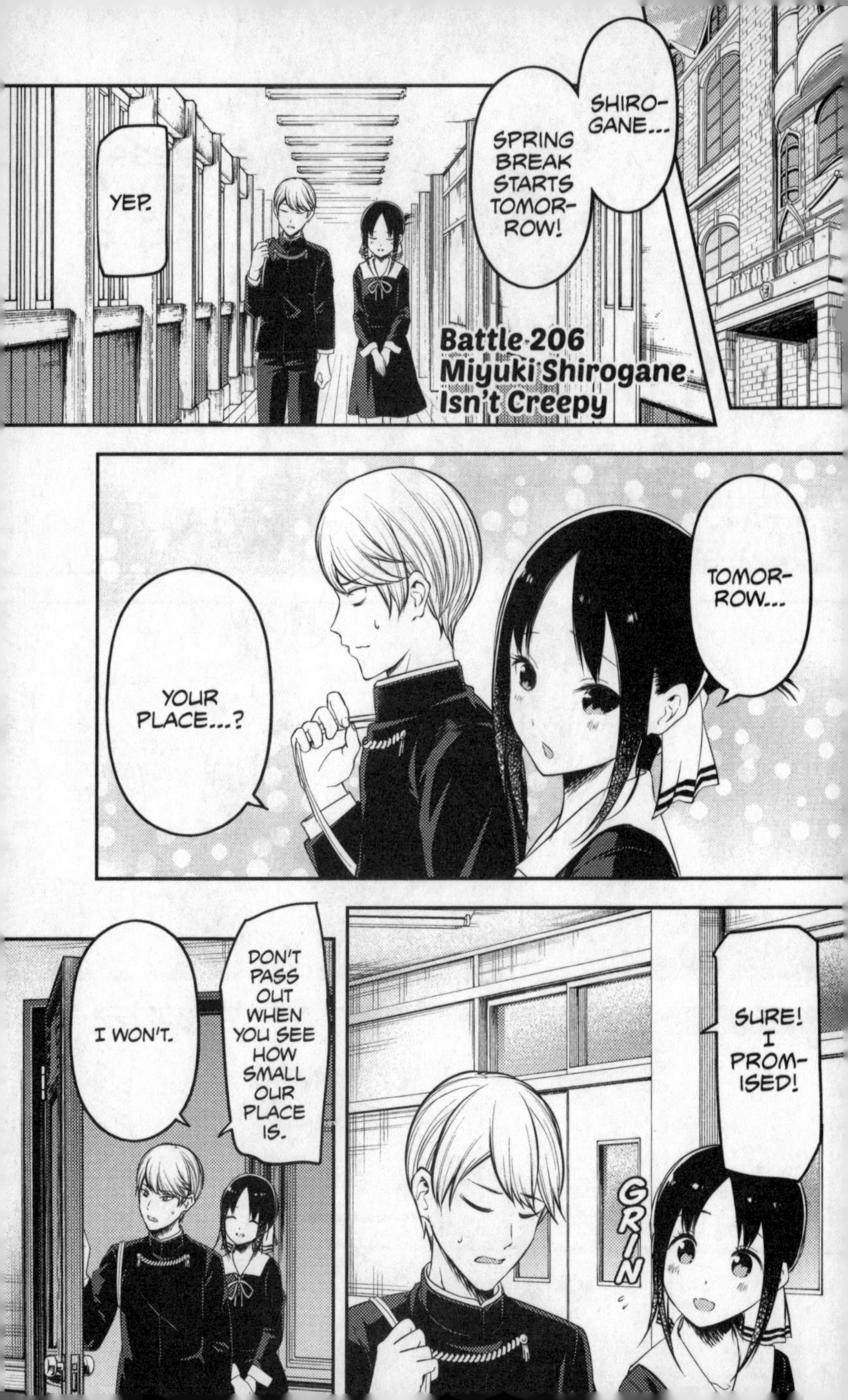
SHIRO-GANE...
SPRING BREAK STARTS TOMORROW!
YEP.
Battle 206 Miyuki Shirogane Isn't Creepy
TOMORROW...
YOUR PLACE...?
SURE! I PROMISED!
GRIN
DON'T PASS OUT WHEN YOU SEE HOW SMALL OUR PLACE IS.
I WON'T.

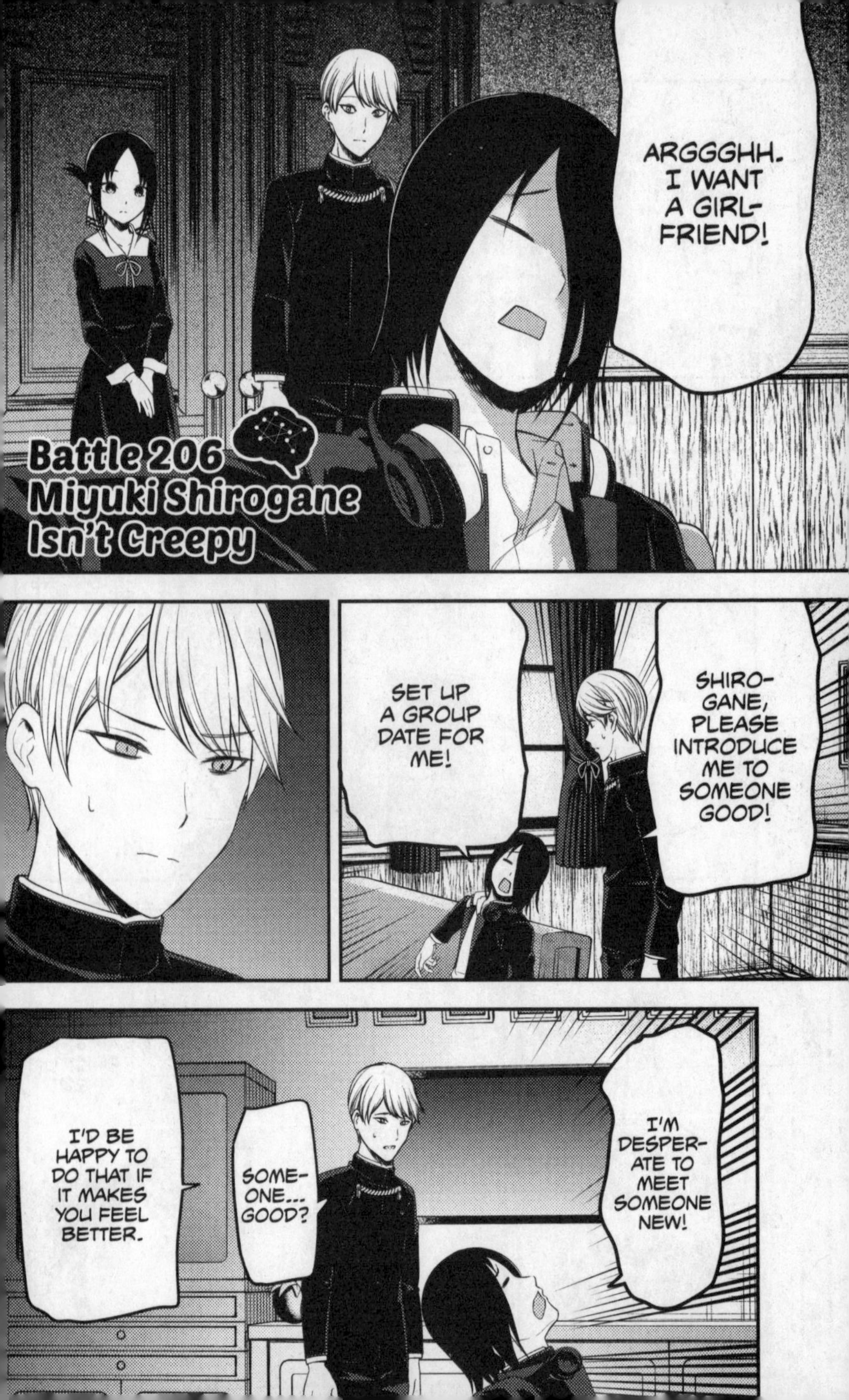
ARGGGHH. I WANT A GIRL-FRIEND!
Battle 206 Miyuki Shirogane Isn't Creepy
SHIRO-GANE, PLEASE INTRODUCE ME TO SOMEONE GOOD!
SET UP A GROUP DATE FOR ME!
I'M DESPER-ATE TO MEET SOMEONE NEW!
SOME-ONE... GOOD?
I'D BE HAPPY TO DO THAT IF IT MAKES YOU FEEL BETTER.

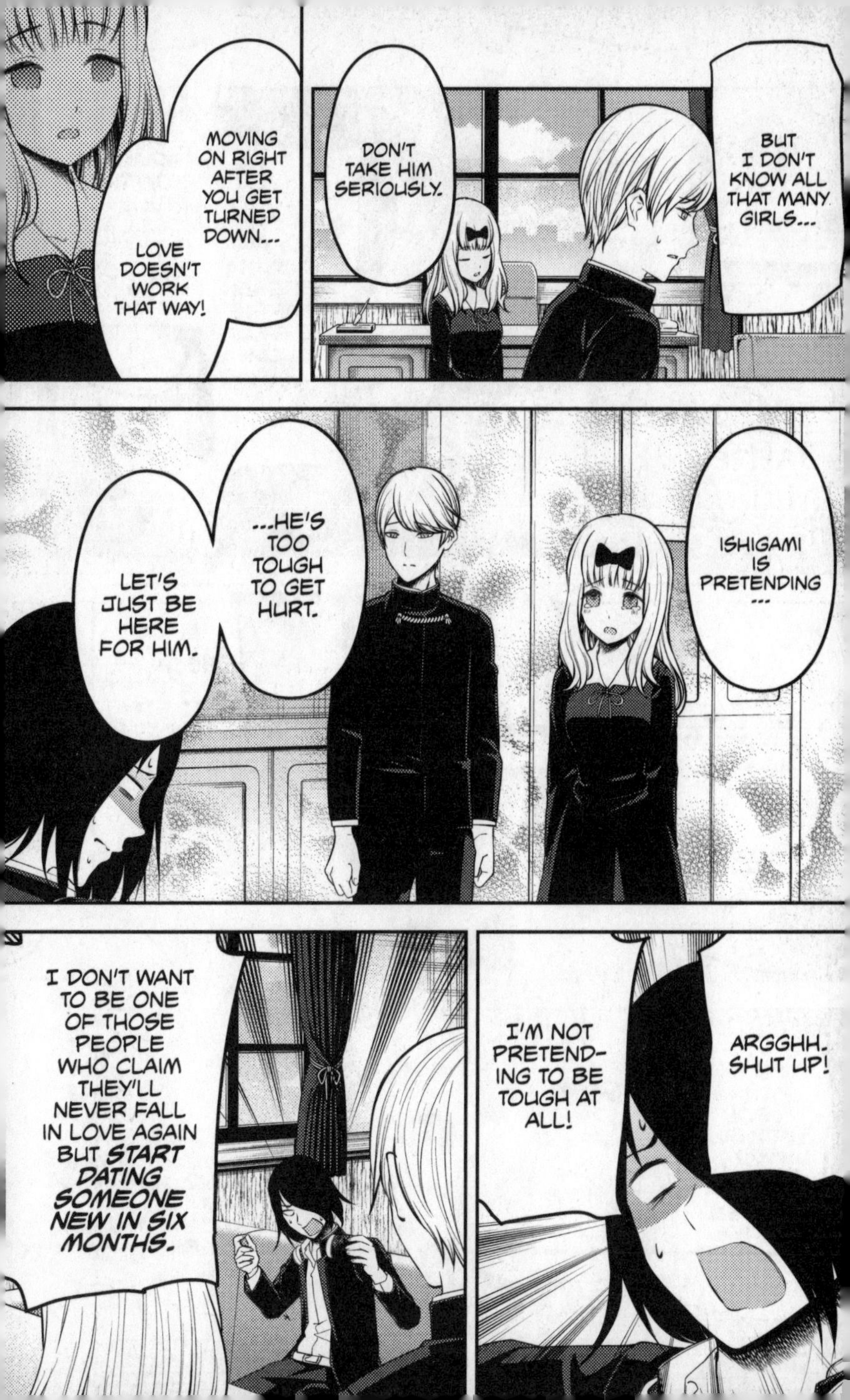
BUT I DON'T KNOW ALL THAT MANY GIRLS...
DON'T TAKE HIM SERIOUSLY.
MOVING ON RIGHT AFTER YOU GET TURNED DOWN...
LOVE DOESN'T WORK THAT WAY!
ISHIGAMI IS PRETENDING...
...HE'S TOO TOUGH TO GET HURT.
LET'S JUST BE HERE FOR HIM.
ARGGHH. SHUT UP!
I'M NOT PRETENDING TO BE TOUGH AT ALL!
I DON'T WANT TO BE ONE OF THOSE PEOPLE WHO CLAIM THEY'LL NEVER FALL IN LOVE AGAIN BUT ***START DATING SOMEONE NEW IN SIX MONTHS.***

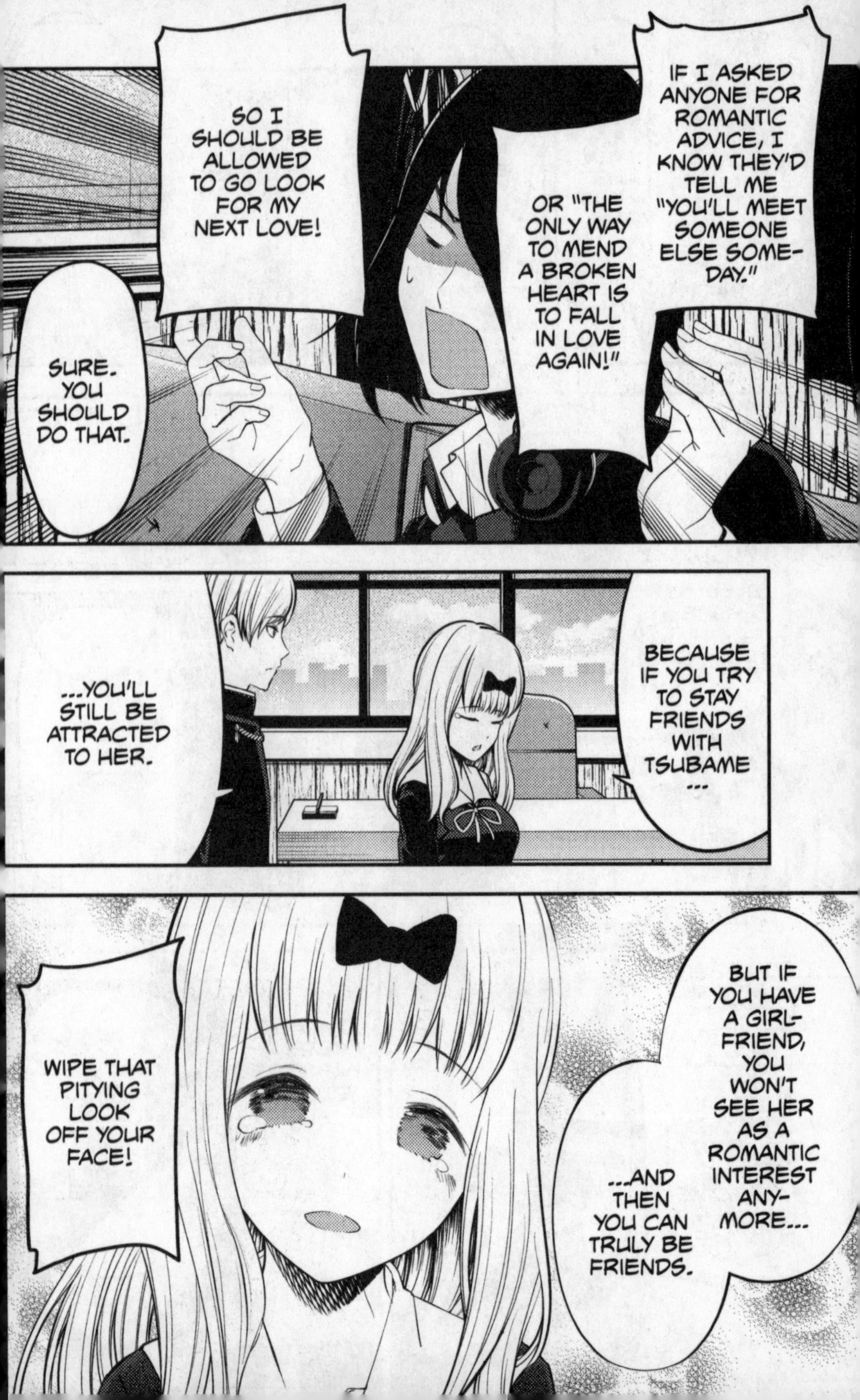
IF I ASKED ANYONE FOR ROMANTIC ADVICE, I KNOW THEY'D TELL ME "YOU'LL MEET SOMEONE ELSE SOME-DAY."
OR "THE ONLY WAY TO MEND A BROKEN HEART IS TO FALL IN LOVE AGAIN!"
SO I SHOULD BE ALLOWED TO GO LOOK FOR MY NEXT LOVE!
SURE. YOU SHOULD DO THAT.
BECAUSE IF YOU TRY TO STAY FRIENDS WITH TSUBAME...
...YOU'LL STILL BE ATTRACTED TO HER.
BUT IF YOU HAVE A GIRL-FRIEND, YOU WON'T SEE HER AS A ROMANTIC INTEREST ANY-MORE...
...AND THEN YOU CAN TRULY BE FRIENDS.
WIPE THAT PITYING LOOK OFF YOUR FACE!

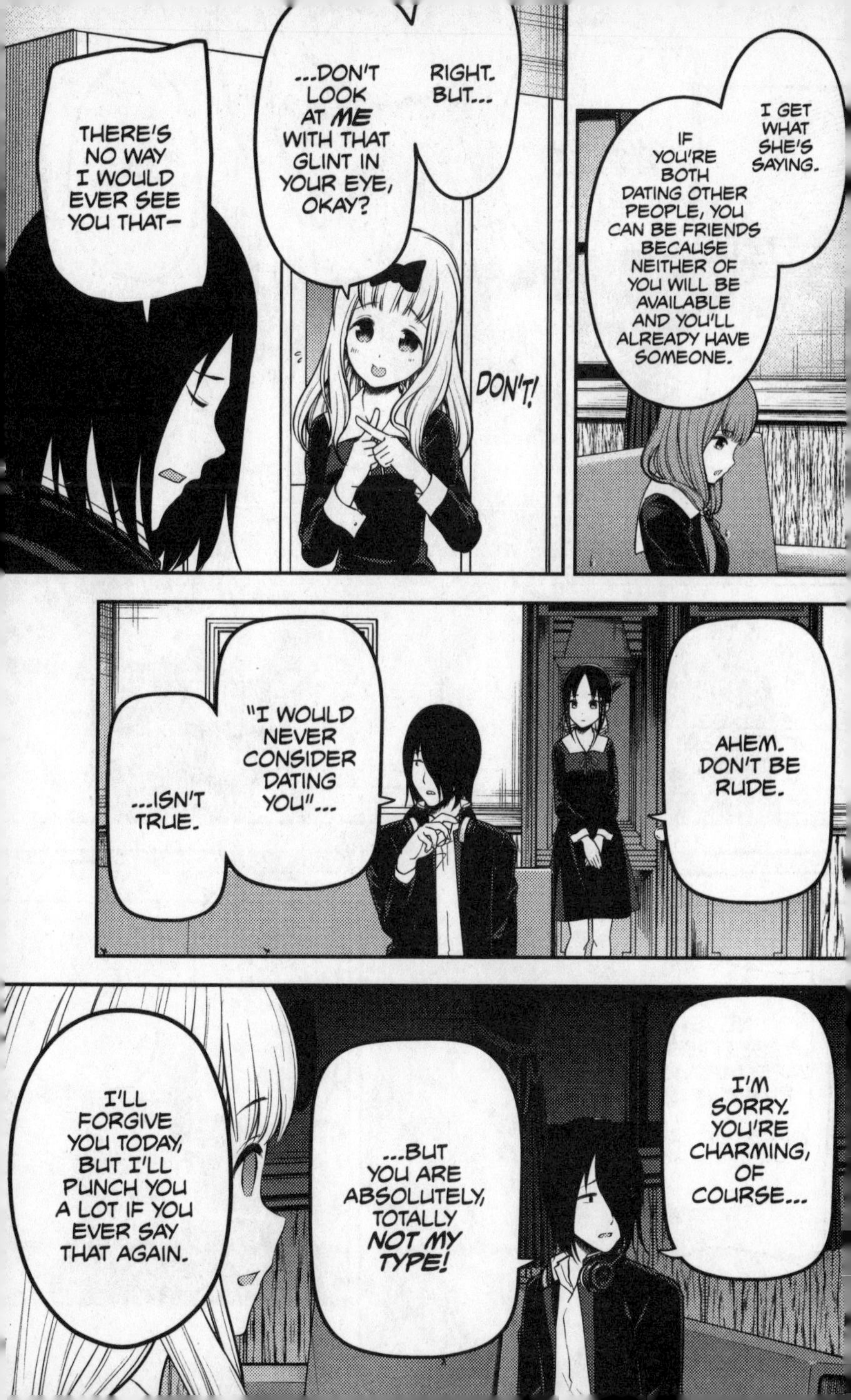
I GET WHAT SHE'S SAYING.
IF YOU'RE BOTH DATING OTHER PEOPLE, YOU CAN BE FRIENDS BECAUSE NEITHER OF YOU WILL BE AVAILABLE AND YOU'LL ALREADY HAVE SOMEONE.
RIGHT. BUT...
...DON'T LOOK AT *ME* WITH THAT GLINT IN YOUR EYE, OKAY?
DON'T!
THERE'S NO WAY I WOULD EVER SEE YOU THAT—
AHEM. DON'T BE RUDE.
"I WOULD NEVER CONSIDER DATING YOU"...
...ISN'T TRUE.
I'M SORRY. YOU'RE CHARMING, OF COURSE...
...BUT YOU ARE ABSOLUTELY, TOTALLY *NOT MY TYPE!*
I'LL FORGIVE YOU TODAY, BUT I'LL PUNCH YOU A LOT IF YOU EVER SAY THAT AGAIN.

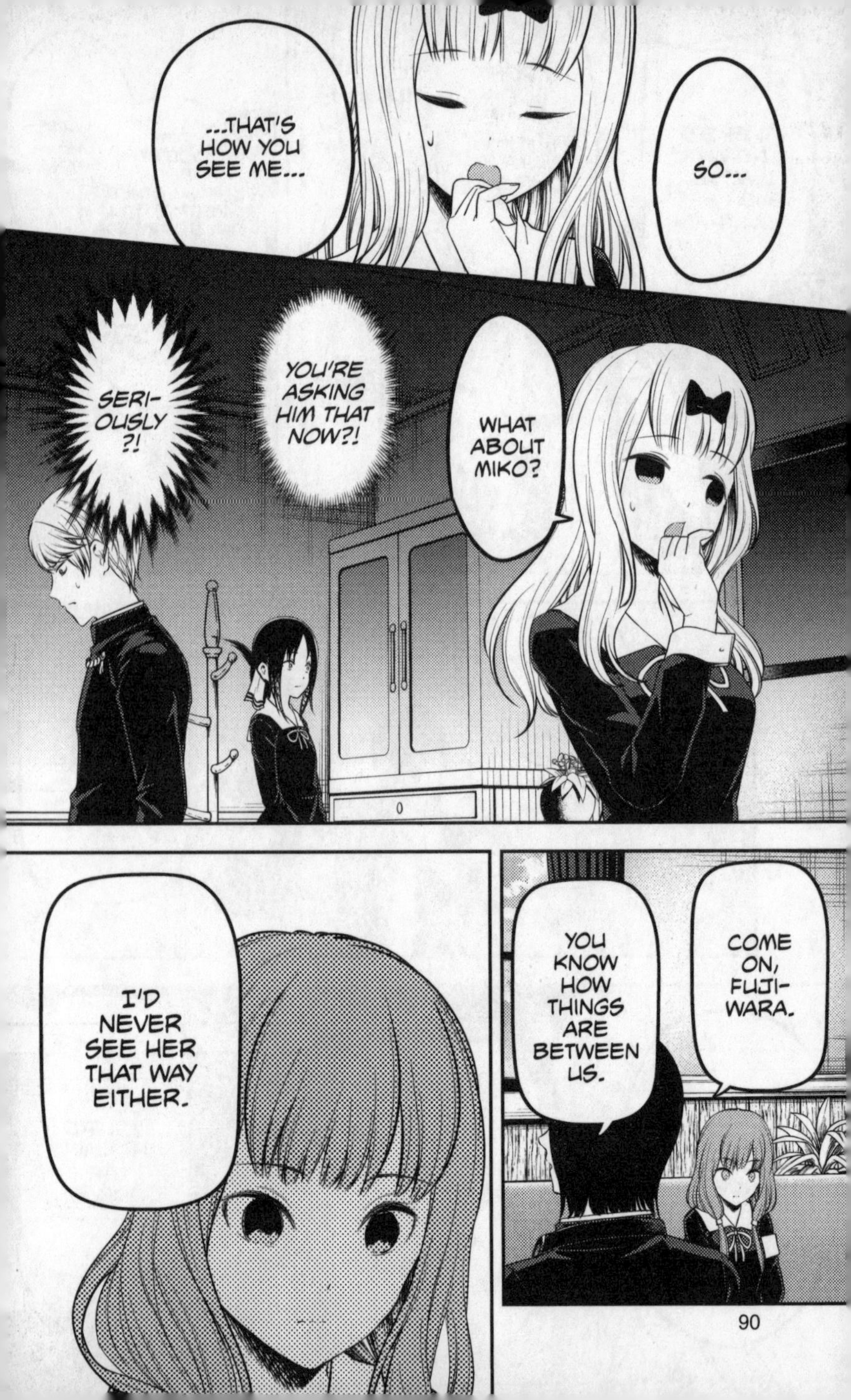
...THAT'S HOW YOU SEE ME...
SO...
WHAT ABOUT MIKO?
YOU'RE ASKING HIM THAT NOW?!
SERI-OUSLY?!
COME ON, FUJI-WARA.
YOU KNOW HOW THINGS ARE BETWEEN US.
I'D NEVER SEE HER THAT WAY EITHER.

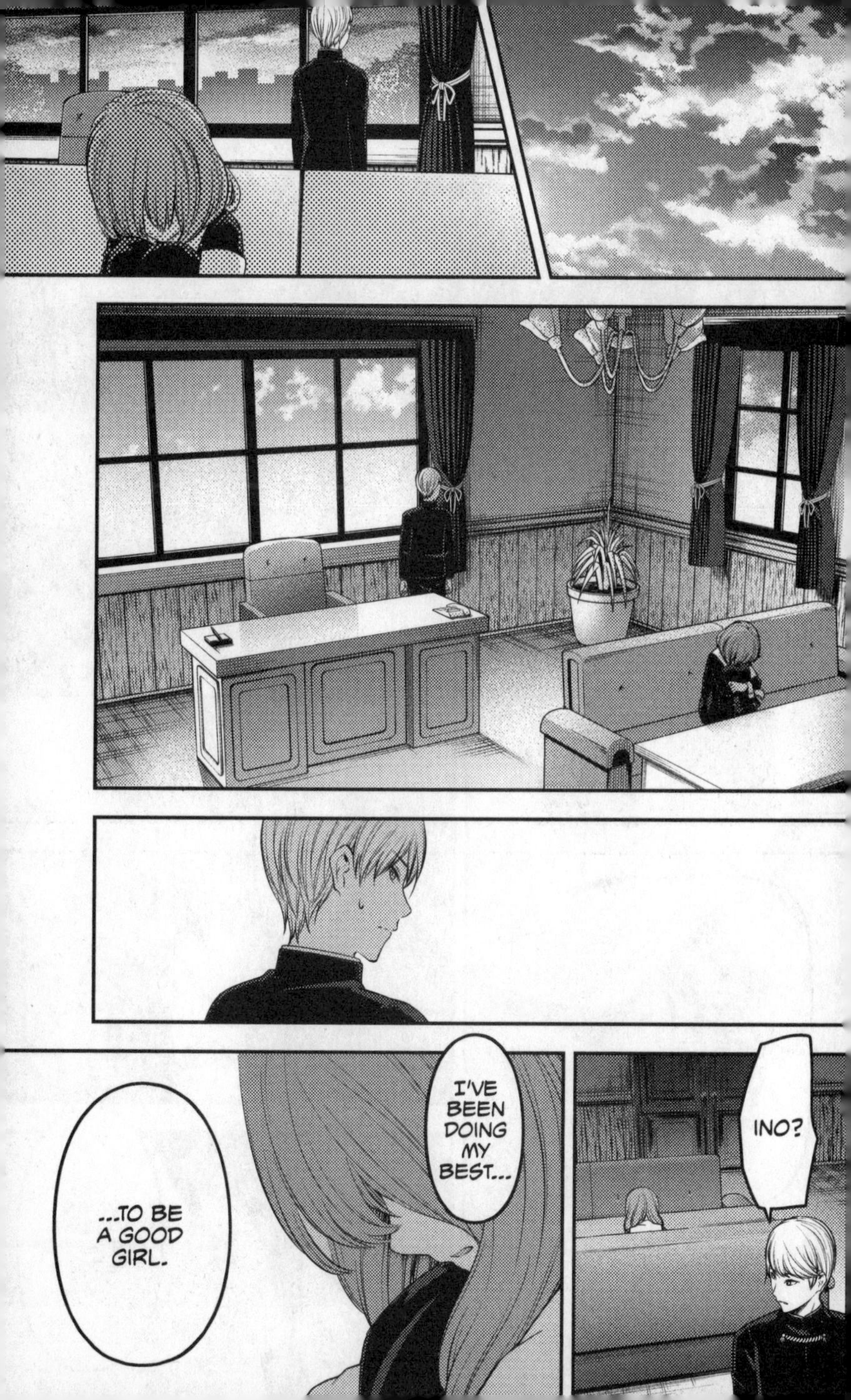
INO?
I'VE BEEN DOING MY BEST...
...TO BE A GOOD GIRL.

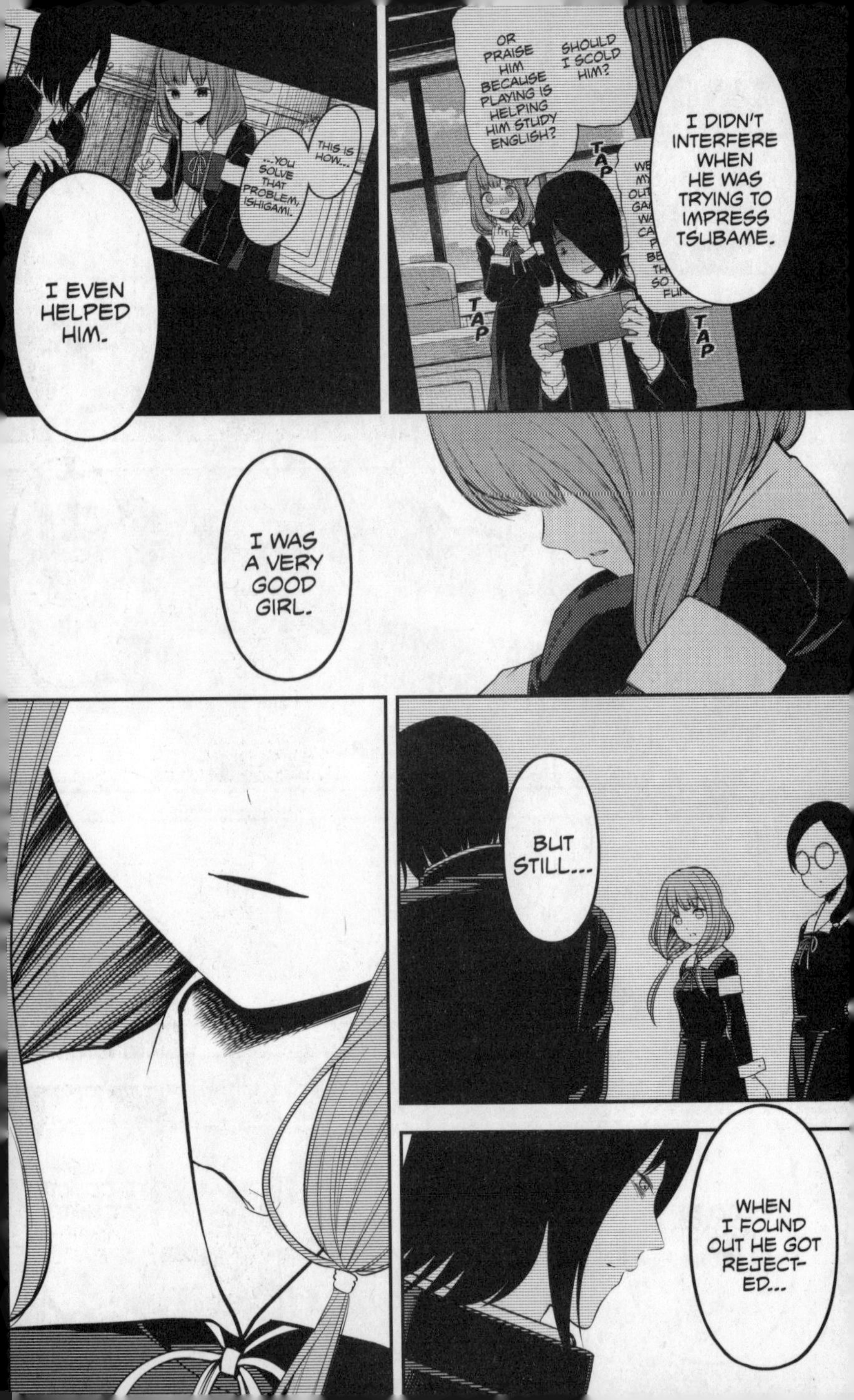
I DIDN'T INTERFERE WHEN HE WAS TRYING TO IMPRESS TSUBAME.
SHOULD I SCOLD HIM?
OR PRAISE HIM BECAUSE PLAYING IS HELPING HIM STUDY ENGLISH?
TAP
TAP
TAP
THIS IS HOW...
...YOU SOLVE THAT PROBLEM, ISHIGAMI.
I EVEN HELPED HIM.
I WAS A VERY GOOD GIRL.
BUT STILL...
WHEN I FOUND OUT HE GOT REJECT-ED...

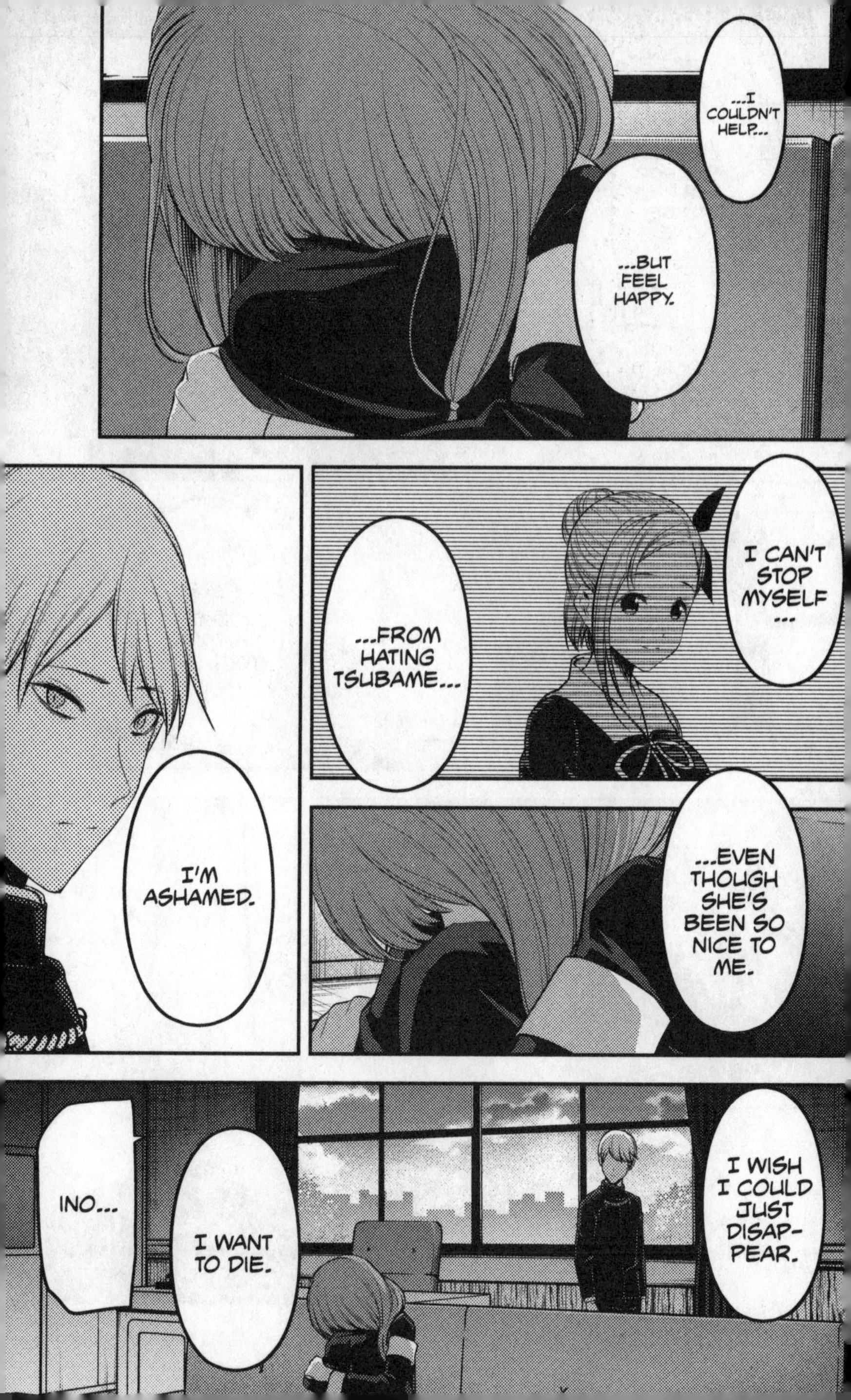
...I COULDN'T HELP...
...BUT FEEL HAPPY.
I CAN'T STOP MYSELF ...
...FROM HATING TSUBAME...
...EVEN THOUGH SHE'S BEEN SO NICE TO ME.
I'M ASHAMED.
I WISH I COULD JUST DISAP-PEAR.
I WANT TO DIE.
INO...

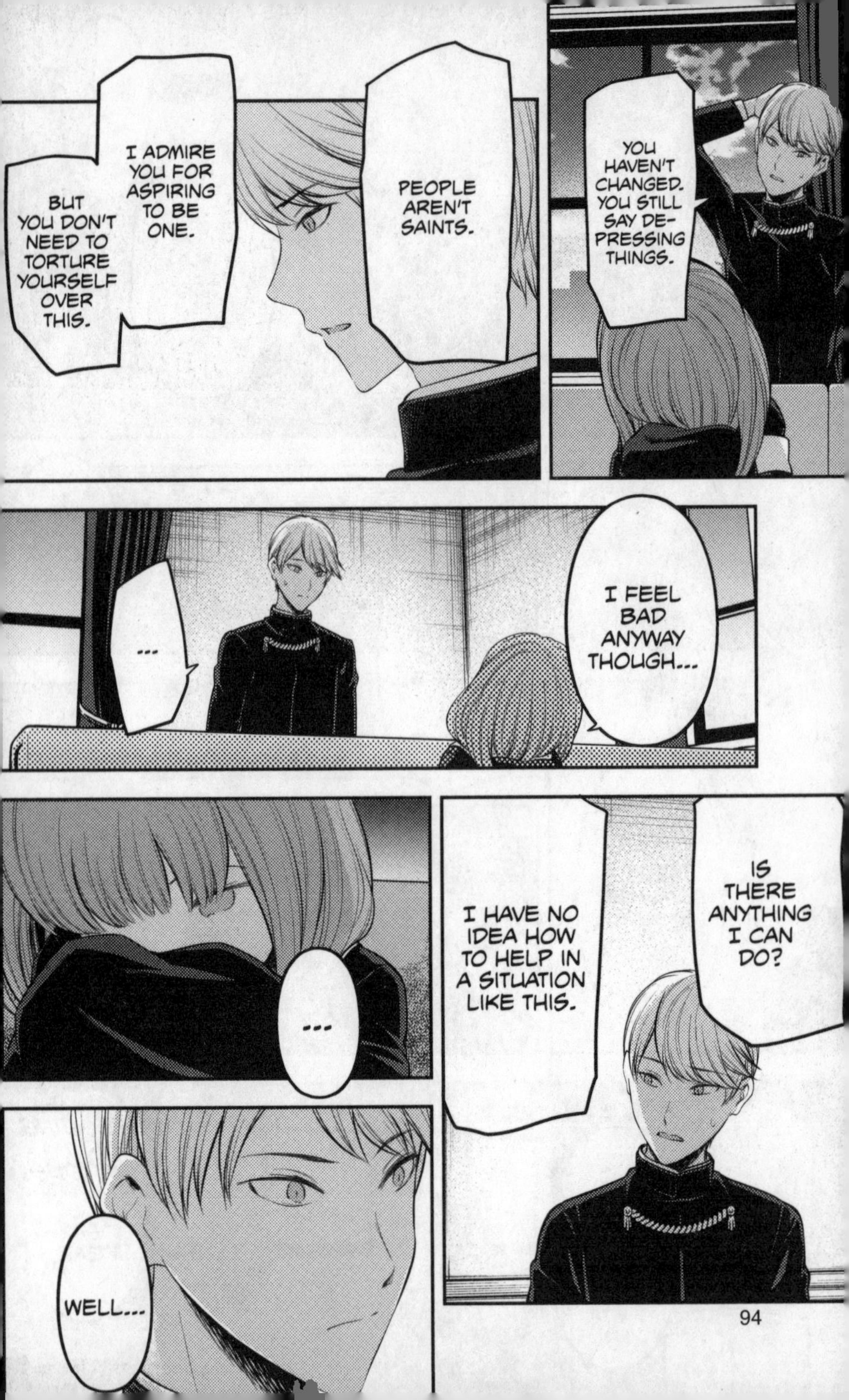
YOU HAVEN'T CHANGED. YOU STILL SAY DE-PRESSING THINGS.
PEOPLE AREN'T SAINTS.
I ADMIRE YOU FOR ASPIRING TO BE ONE.
BUT YOU DON'T NEED TO TORTURE YOURSELF OVER THIS.
I FEEL BAD ANYWAY THOUGH...
...
IS THERE ANYTHING I CAN DO?
I HAVE NO IDEA HOW TO HELP IN A SITUATION LIKE THIS.
...
WELL...

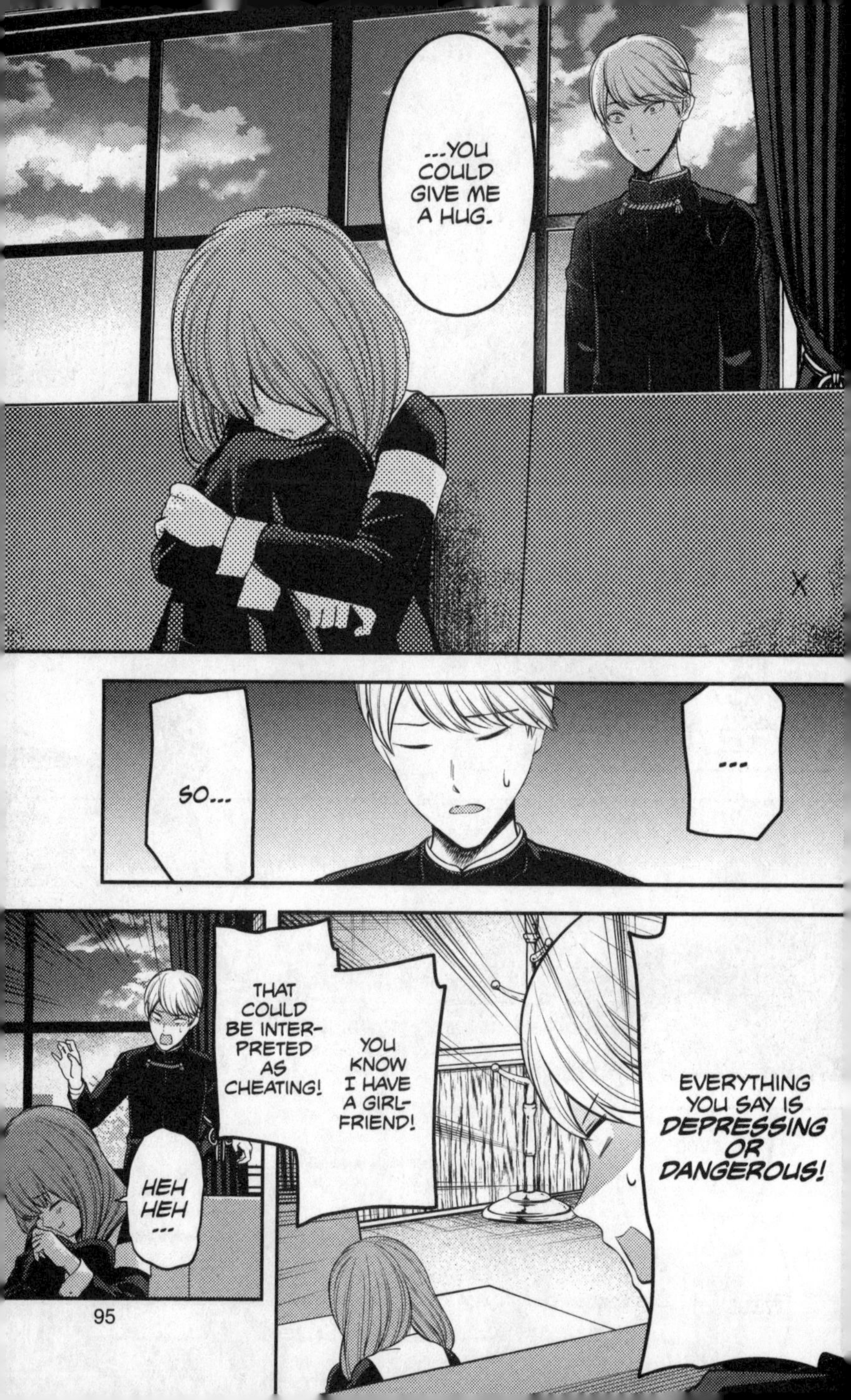
...YOU COULD GIVE ME A HUG.
...
SO...
EVERYTHING YOU SAY IS *DEPRESSING OR DANGEROUS!*
YOU KNOW I HAVE A GIRL-FRIEND!
THAT COULD BE INTER-PRETED AS CHEATING!
HEH HEH...

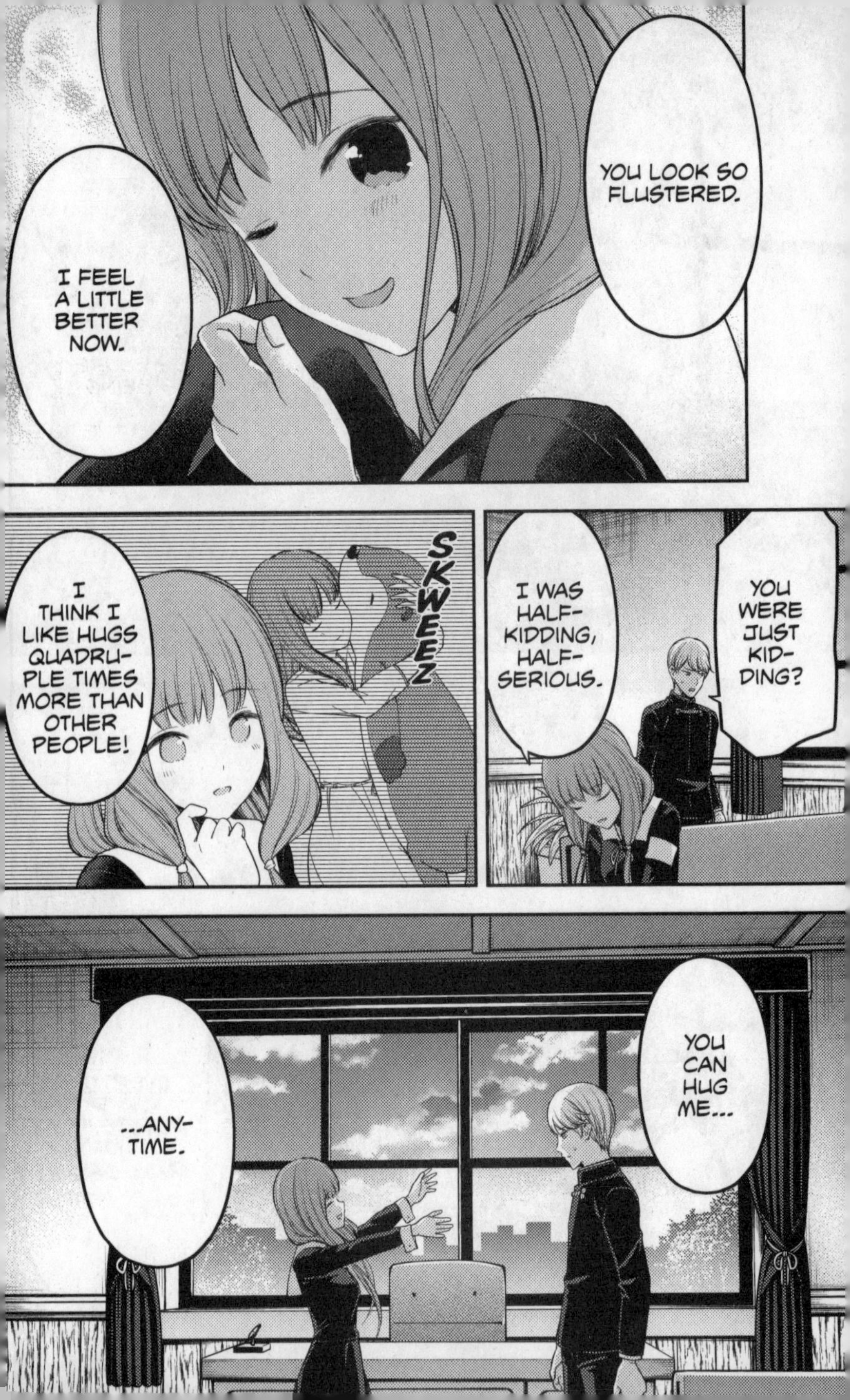
YOU LOOK SO FLUSTERED.
I FEEL A LITTLE BETTER NOW.
YOU WERE JUST KIDDING?
I WAS HALF-KIDDING, HALF-SERIOUS.
SKWEEZ
I THINK I LIKE HUGS QUADRUPLE TIMES MORE THAN OTHER PEOPLE!
YOU CAN HUG ME...
...ANYTIME.

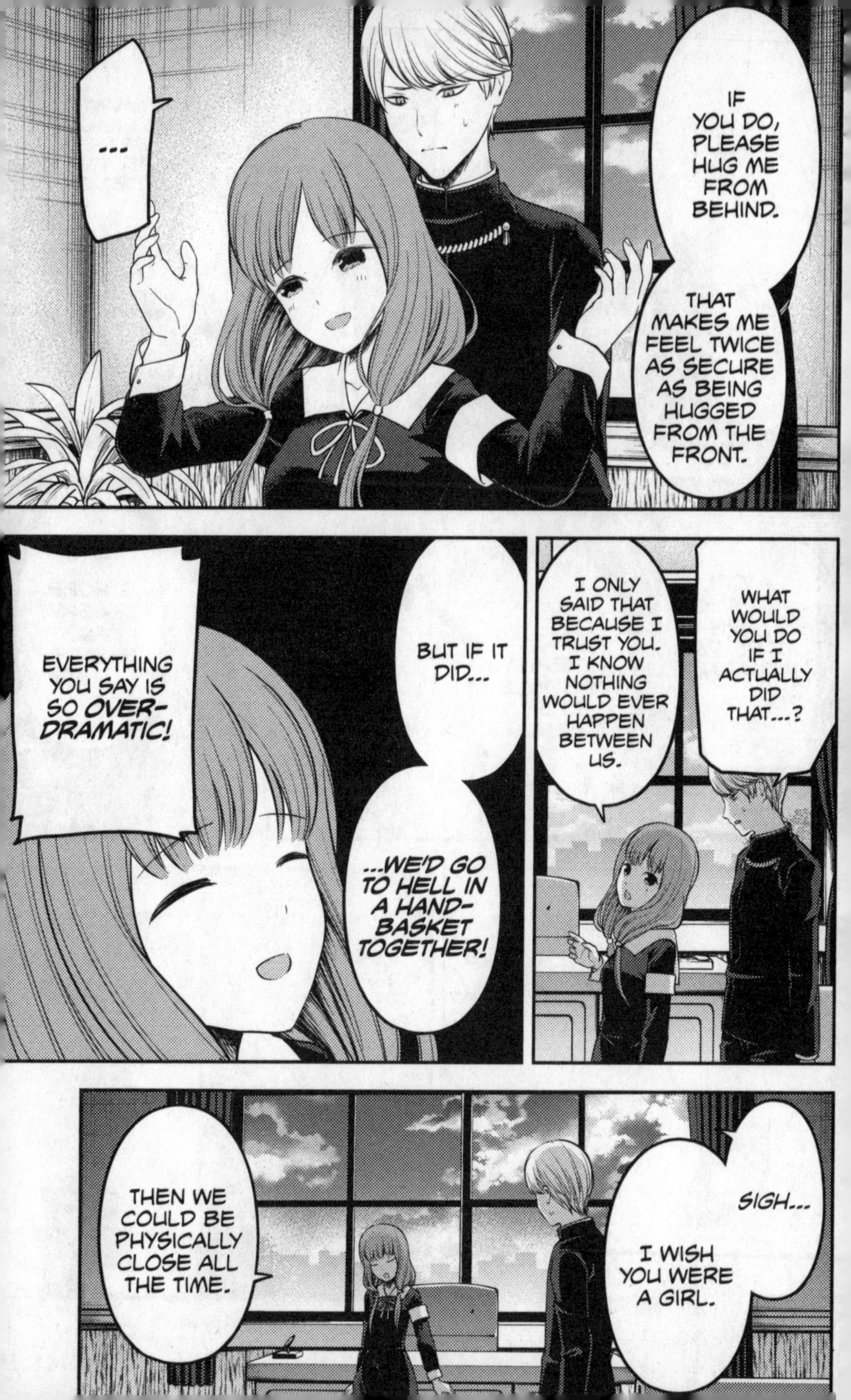
IF YOU DO, PLEASE HUG ME FROM BEHIND.
THAT MAKES ME FEEL TWICE AS SECURE AS BEING HUGGED FROM THE FRONT.
...
WHAT WOULD YOU DO IF I ACTUALLY DID THAT...?
I ONLY SAID THAT BECAUSE I TRUST YOU. I KNOW NOTHING WOULD EVER HAPPEN BETWEEN US.
BUT IF IT DID...
...WE'D GO TO HELL IN A HAND-BASKET TOGETHER!
EVERYTHING YOU SAY IS SO *OVER-DRAMATIC!*
SIGH...
I WISH YOU WERE A GIRL.
THEN WE COULD BE PHYSICALLY CLOSE ALL THE TIME.

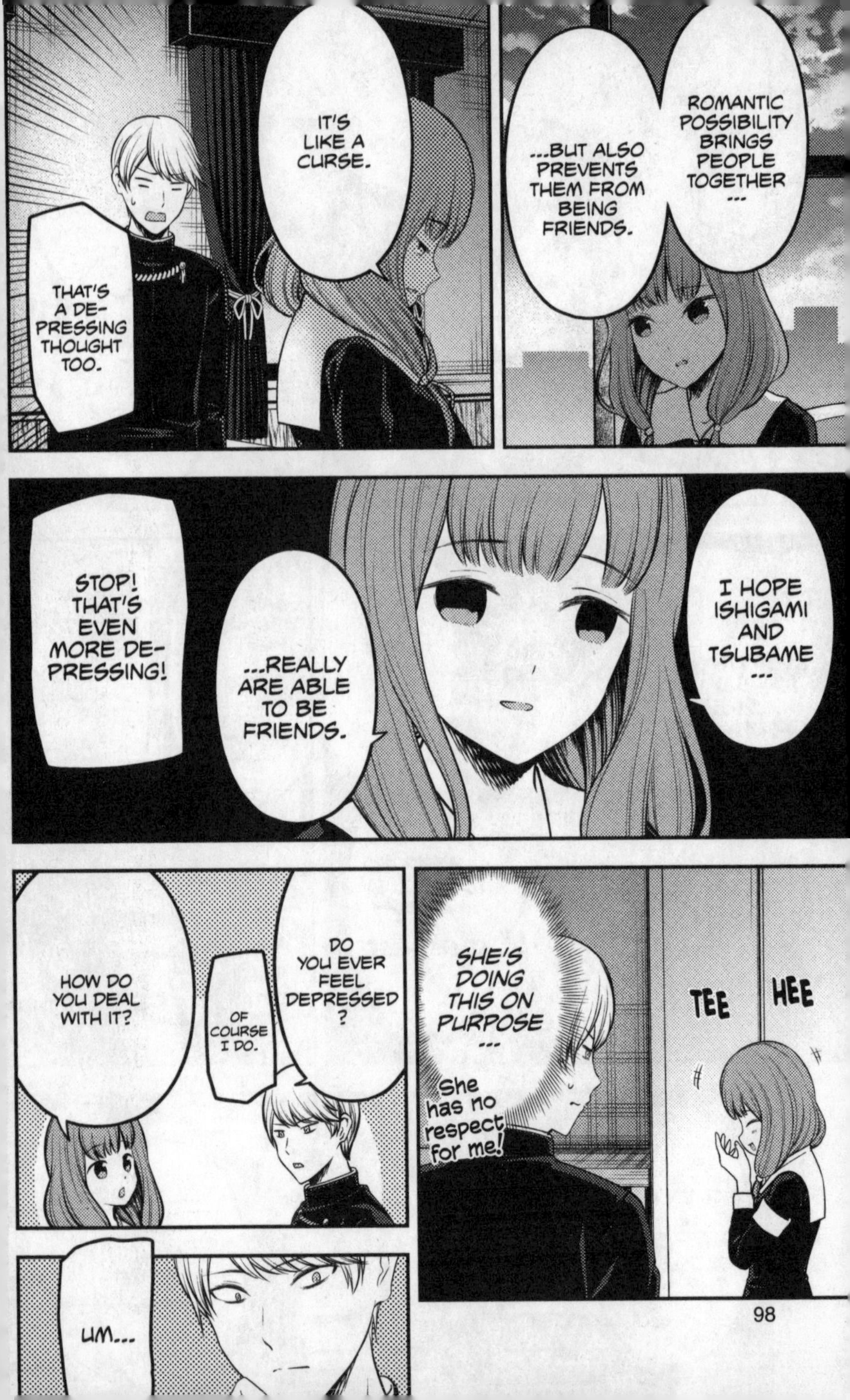
ROMANTIC POSSIBILITY BRINGS PEOPLE TOGETHER...
...BUT ALSO PREVENTS THEM FROM BEING FRIENDS.
IT'S LIKE A CURSE.
THAT'S A DE-PRESSING THOUGHT TOO.
I HOPE ISHIGAMI AND TSUBAME...
...REALLY ARE ABLE TO BE FRIENDS.
STOP! THAT'S EVEN MORE DE-PRESSING!
TEE HEE
SHE'S DOING THIS ON PURPOSE...
She has no respect for me!
DO YOU EVER FEEL DEPRESSED?
OF COURSE I DO.
HOW DO YOU DEAL WITH IT?
UM...

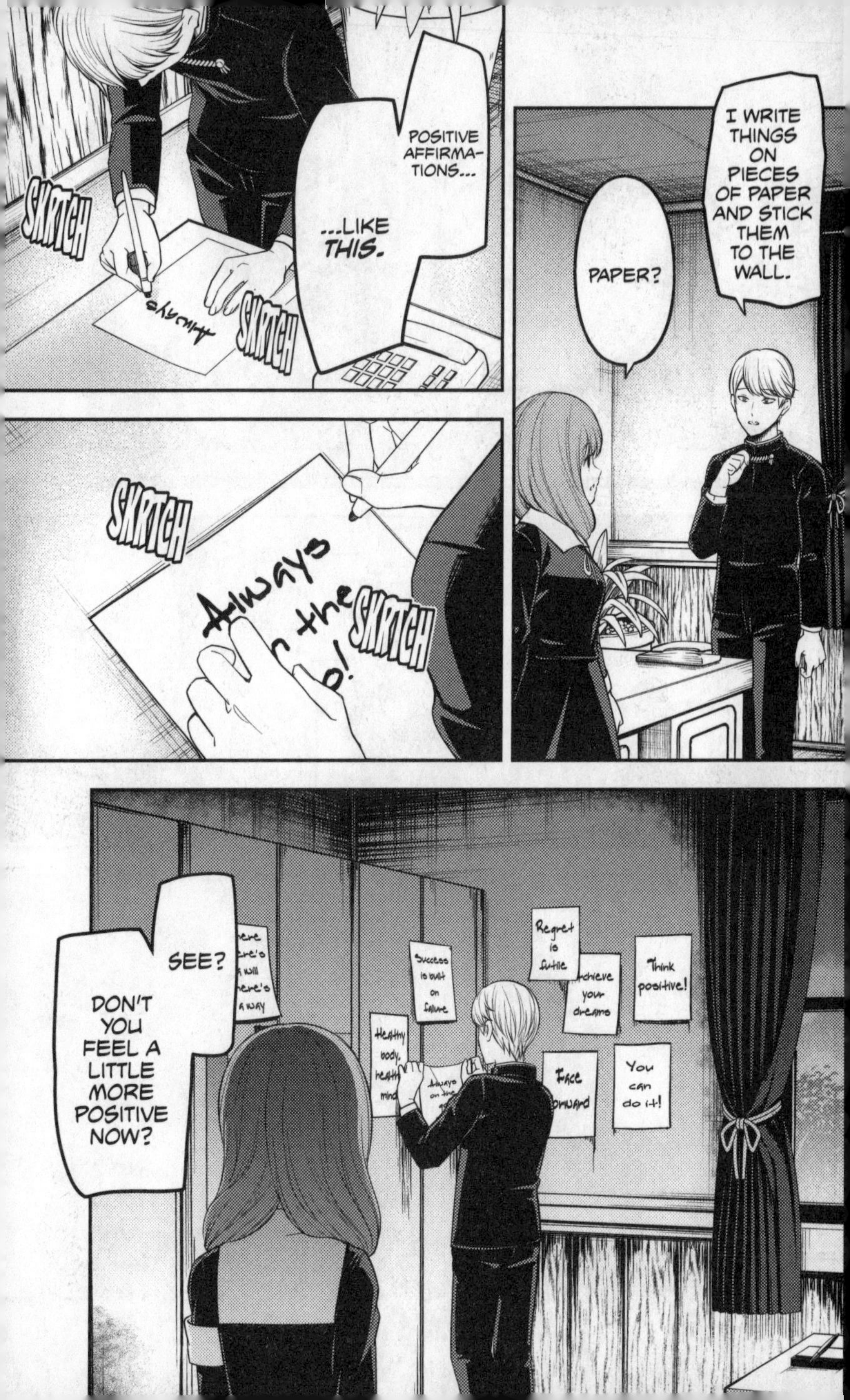
I WRITE THINGS ON PIECES OF PAPER AND STICK THEM TO THE WALL.
PAPER?
POSITIVE AFFIRMATIONS...
...LIKE THIS.
SKRTCH
SKRTCH
Always
SKRTCH
SKRTCH
Always on the go!
Regret is futile
Think positive!
Success is built on failure
You can do it!
SEE?
DON'T YOU FEEL A LITTLE MORE POSITIVE NOW?

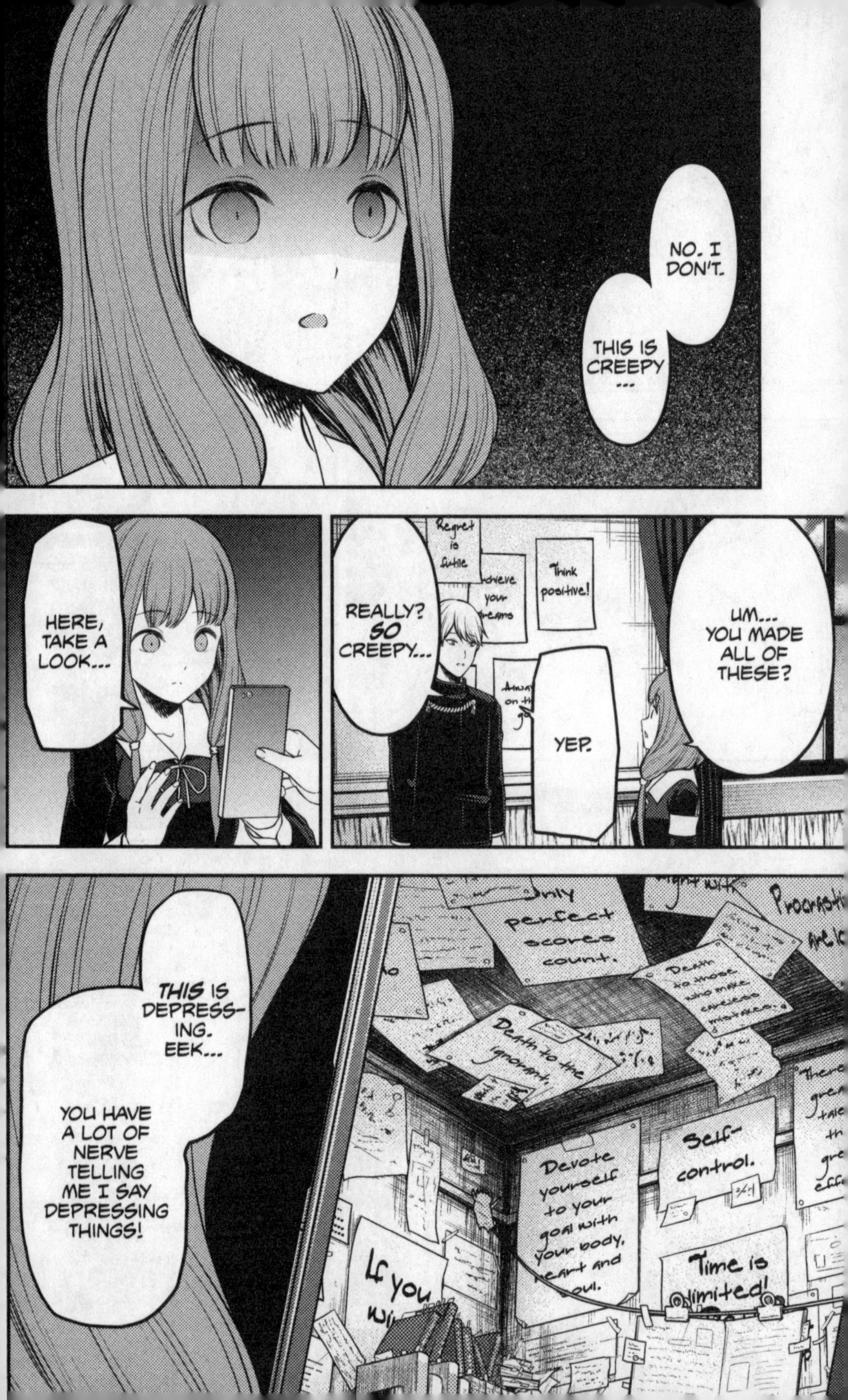
NO. I DON'T.
THIS IS CREEPY...
Regret is futile
Think positive!
UM... YOU MADE ALL OF THESE?
YEP.
REALLY? SO CREEPY...
HERE, TAKE A LOOK...
Death to those who make careless mistakes.
Death to the ignorant.
Self-control.
Time is limited!
THIS IS DEPRESSING. EEK...
YOU HAVE A LOT OF NERVE TELLING ME I SAY DEPRESSING THINGS!

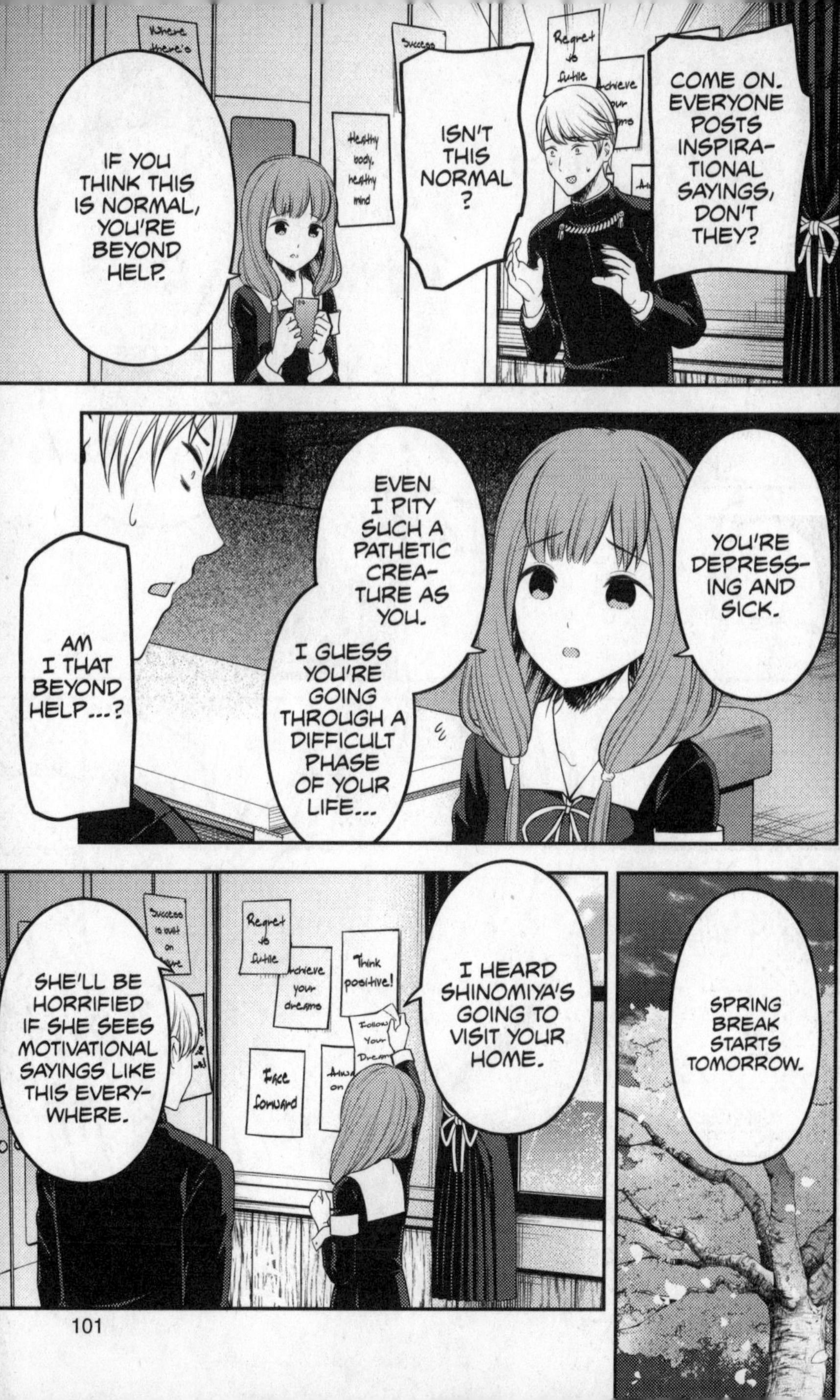
COME ON. EVERYONE POSTS INSPIRATIONAL SAYINGS, DON'T THEY?
ISN'T THIS NORMAL?
Healthy body, healthy mind
IF YOU THINK THIS IS NORMAL, YOU'RE BEYOND HELP.
YOU'RE DEPRESSING AND SICK.
EVEN I PITY SUCH A PATHETIC CREATURE AS YOU.
I GUESS YOU'RE GOING THROUGH A DIFFICULT PHASE OF YOUR LIFE...
AM I THAT BEYOND HELP...?
SPRING BREAK STARTS TOMORROW.
I HEARD SHINOMIYA'S GOING TO VISIT YOUR HOME.
Think positive!
Face forward
SHE'LL BE HORRIFIED IF SHE SEES MOTIVATIONAL SAYINGS LIKE THIS EVERYWHERE.

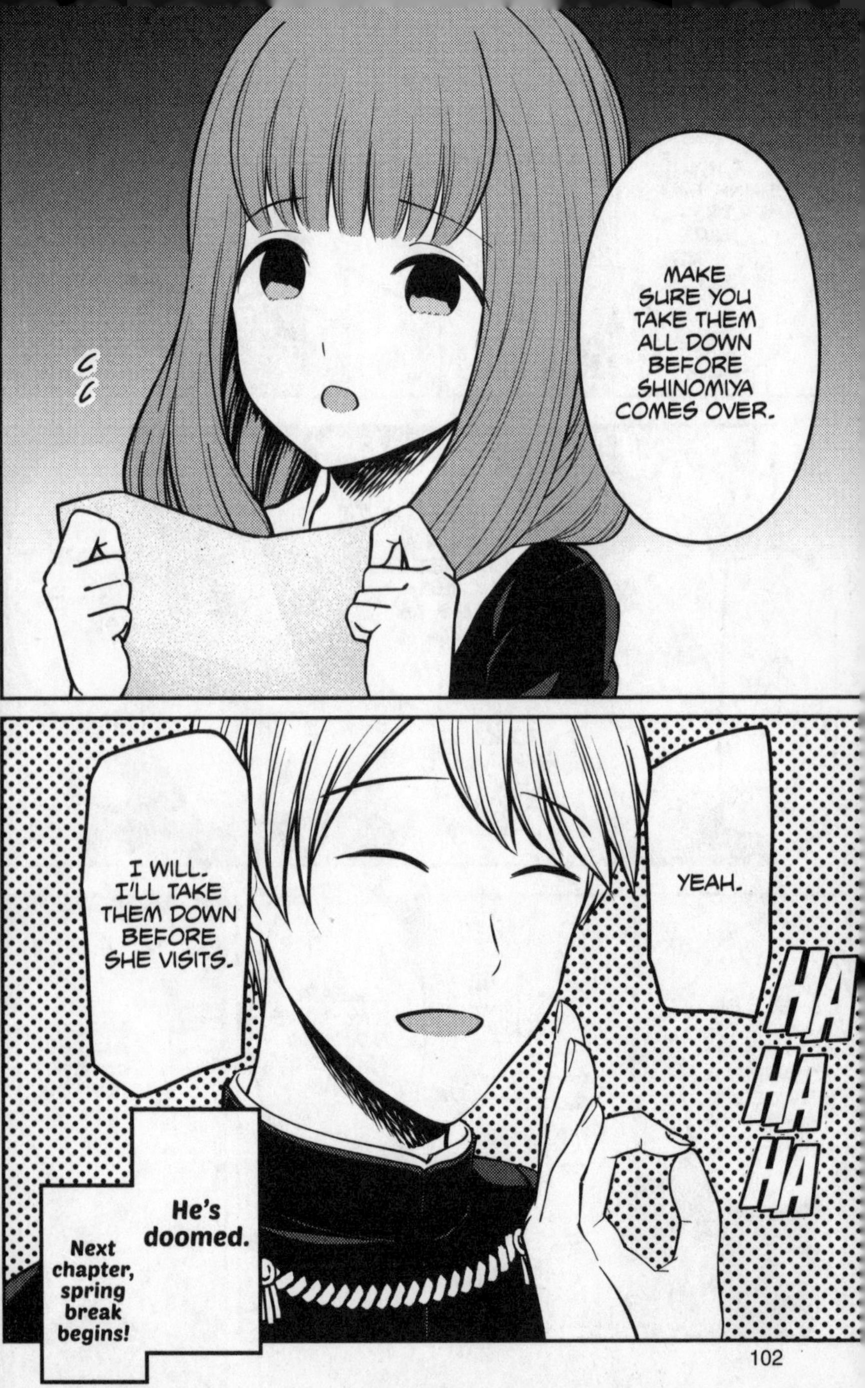

MAKE SURE YOU TAKE THEM ALL DOWN BEFORE SHINOMIYA COMES OVER.
YEAH.
HA HA HA HA
I WILL. I'LL TAKE THEM DOWN BEFORE SHE VISITS.
He's doomed.
Next chapter, spring break begins!

...a good girl
after all...

I'm not...

KAGUYA-SAMA
LOVE IS WAR

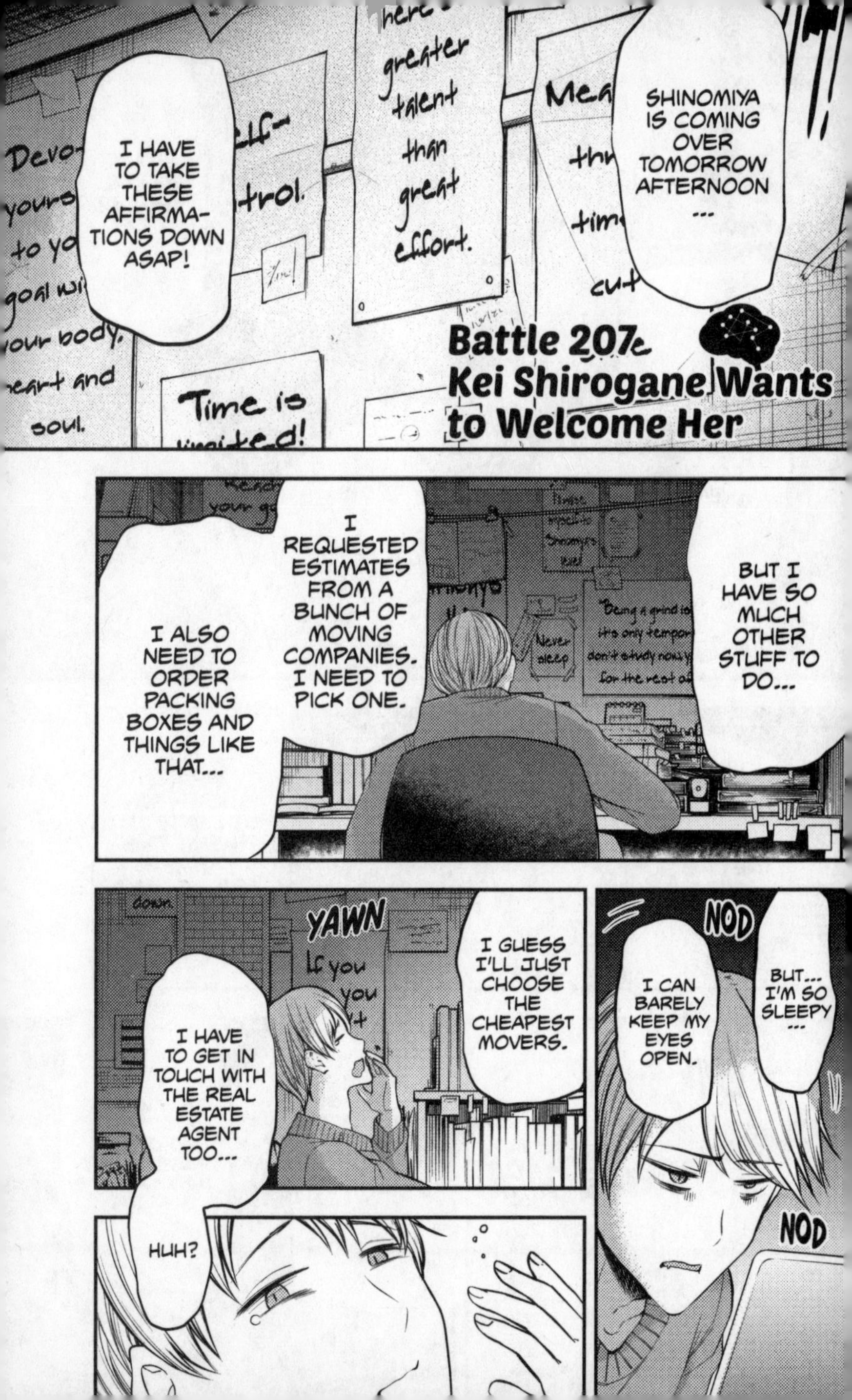
SHINOMIYA IS COMING OVER TOMORROW AFTERNOON ...
I HAVE TO TAKE THESE AFFIRMATIONS DOWN ASAP!
greater talent than great effort.
Time is limited!
Battle 207 Kei Shirogane Wants to Welcome Her
BUT I HAVE SO MUCH OTHER STUFF TO DO...
I REQUESTED ESTIMATES FROM A BUNCH OF MOVING COMPANIES. I NEED TO PICK ONE.
I ALSO NEED TO ORDER PACKING BOXES AND THINGS LIKE THAT...
NOD
BUT... I'M SO SLEEPY ...
I CAN BARELY KEEP MY EYES OPEN.
NOD
I GUESS I'LL JUST CHOOSE THE CHEAPEST MOVERS.
YAWN
I HAVE TO GET IN TOUCH WITH THE REAL ESTATE AGENT TOO...
HUH?

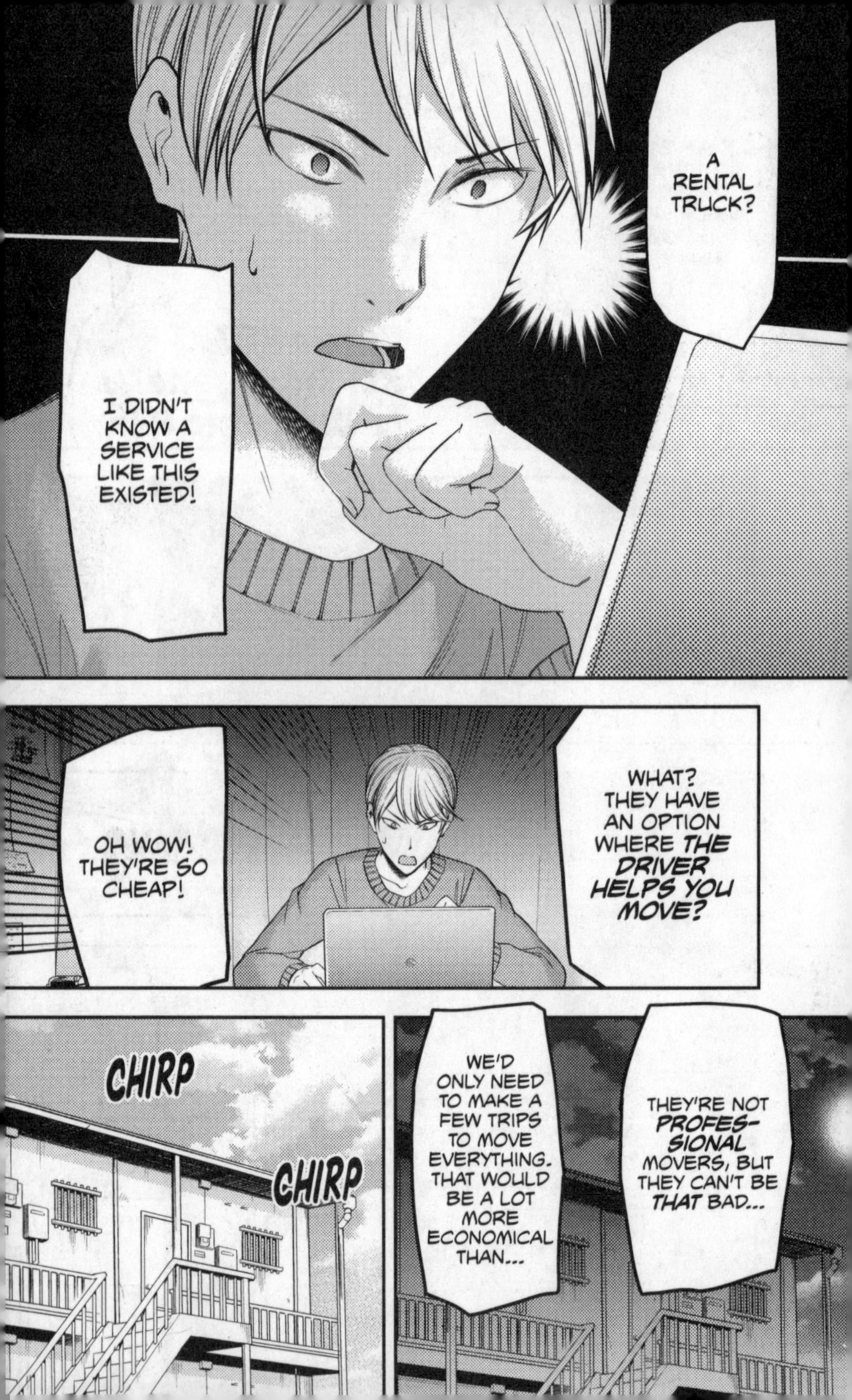
A RENTAL TRUCK?
I DIDN'T KNOW A SERVICE LIKE THIS EXISTED!
WHAT? THEY HAVE AN OPTION WHERE *THE DRIVER HELPS YOU MOVE?*
OH WOW! THEY'RE SO CHEAP!
THEY'RE NOT *PROFES-SIONAL* MOVERS, BUT THEY CAN'T BE *THAT* BAD...
WE'D ONLY NEED TO MAKE A FEW TRIPS TO MOVE EVERYTHING. THAT WOULD BE A LOT MORE ECONOMICAL THAN...
CHIRP
CHIRP

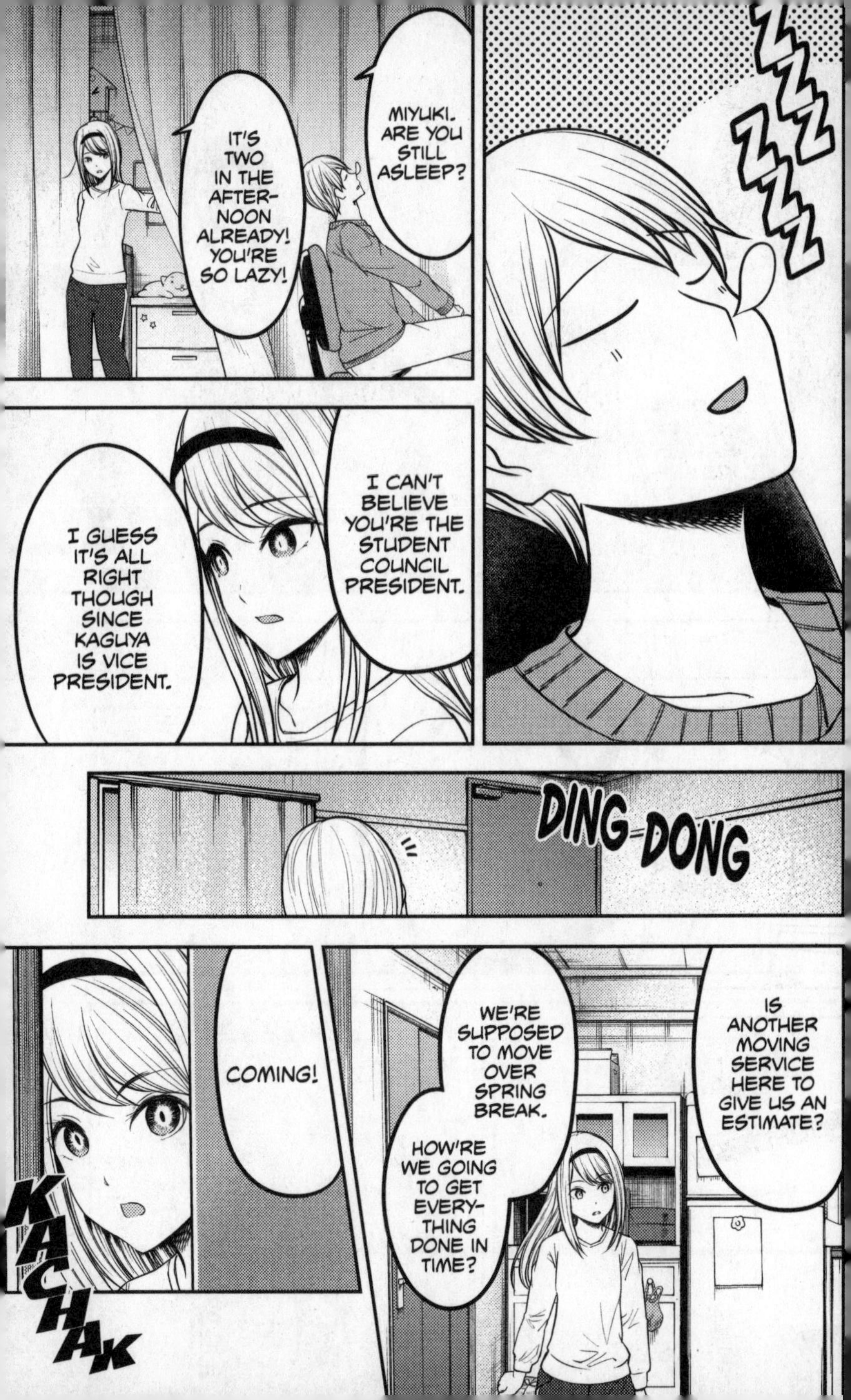
ZZZZZZ
MIYUKI. ARE YOU STILL ASLEEP?
IT'S TWO IN THE AFTERNOON ALREADY! YOU'RE SO LAZY!
I CAN'T BELIEVE YOU'RE THE STUDENT COUNCIL PRESIDENT.
I GUESS IT'S ALL RIGHT THOUGH SINCE KAGUYA IS VICE PRESIDENT.
DING-DONG
IS ANOTHER MOVING SERVICE HERE TO GIVE US AN ESTIMATE?
WE'RE SUPPOSED TO MOVE OVER SPRING BREAK.
HOW'RE WE GOING TO GET EVERYTHING DONE IN TIME?
COMING!
KACHAK

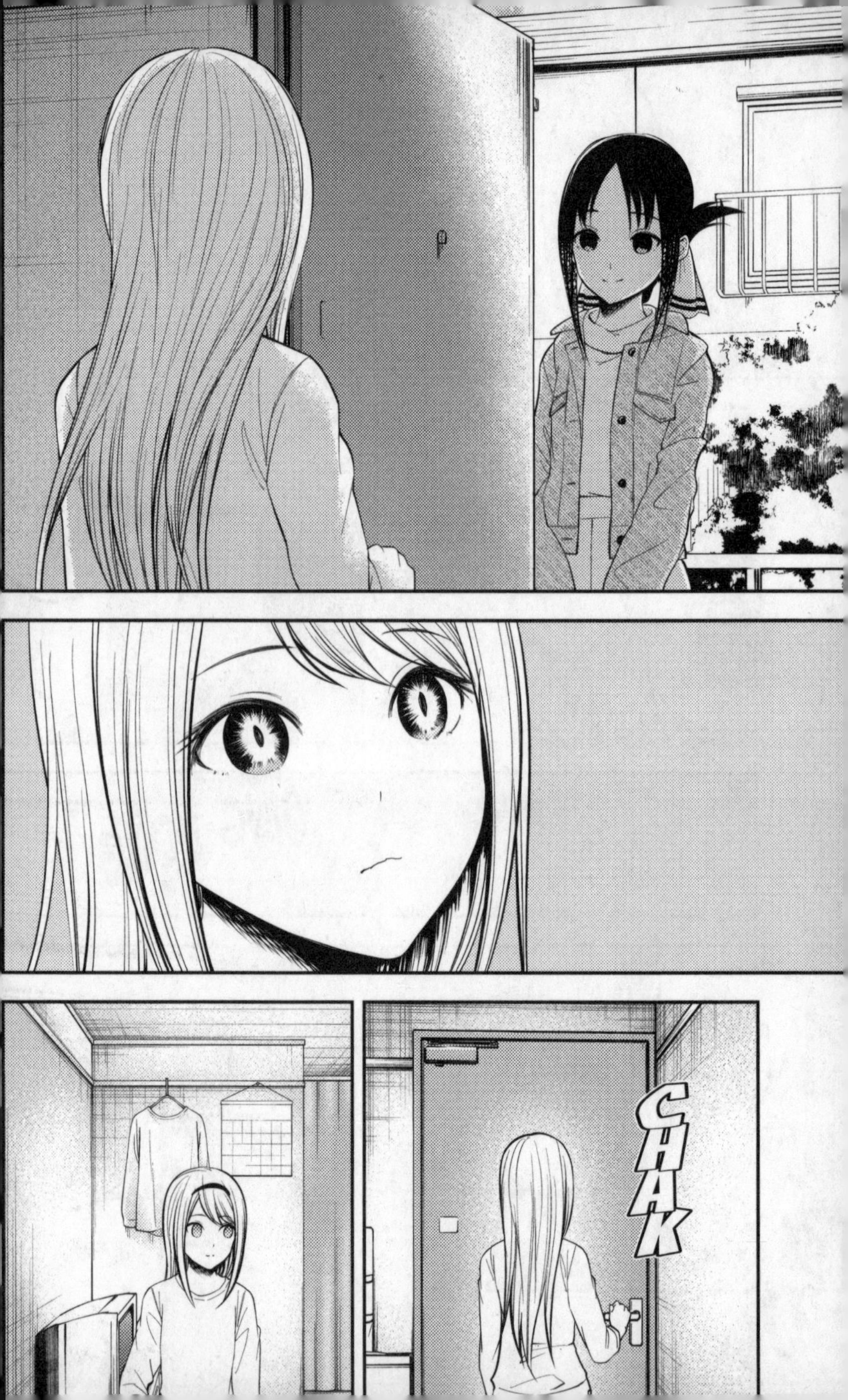
CHAK

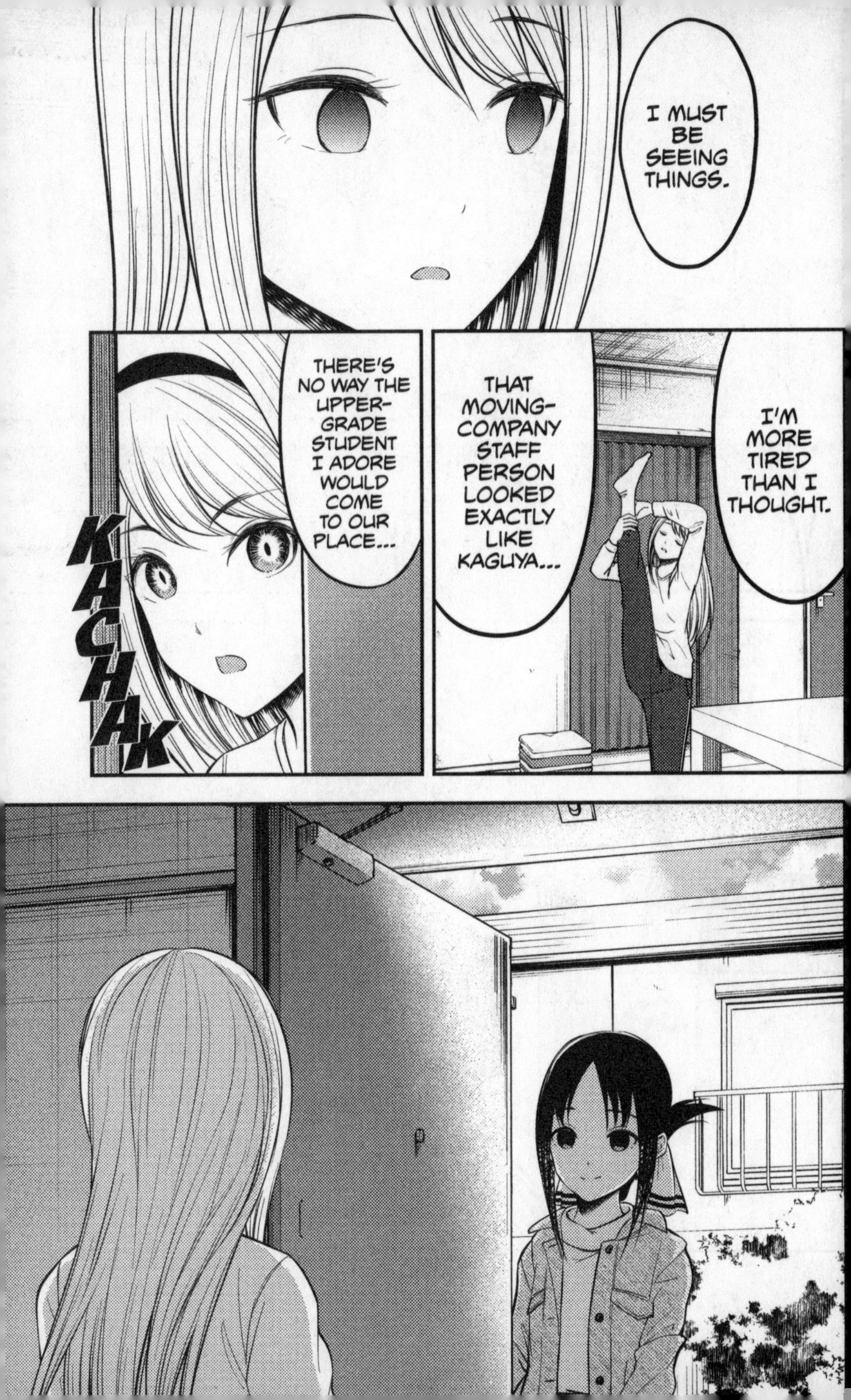
I MUST BE SEEING THINGS.
I'M MORE TIRED THAN I THOUGHT.
THAT MOVING-COMPANY STAFF PERSON LOOKED EXACTLY LIKE KAGUYA...
THERE'S NO WAY THE UPPER-GRADE STUDENT I ADORE WOULD COME TO OUR PLACE...
KACHAK

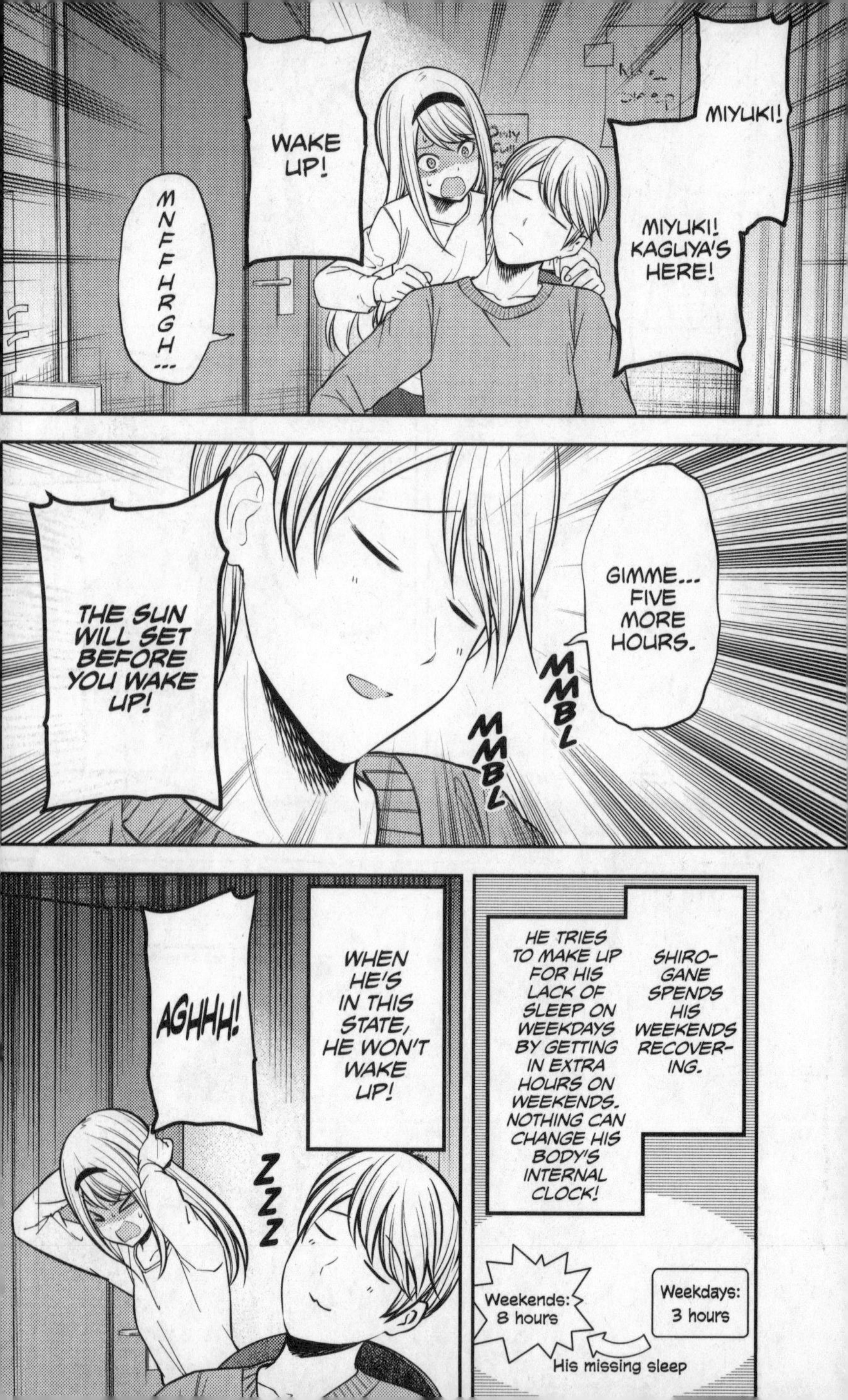
MIYUKI!
MIYUKI! KAGUYA'S HERE!
WAKE UP!
MNFFHRGH...
GIMME... FIVE MORE HOURS.
MMBL
MMBL
THE SUN WILL SET BEFORE YOU WAKE UP!
SHIROGANE SPENDS HIS WEEKENDS RECOVERING.
HE TRIES TO MAKE UP FOR HIS LACK OF SLEEP ON WEEKDAYS BY GETTING IN EXTRA HOURS ON WEEKENDS. NOTHING CAN CHANGE HIS BODY'S INTERNAL CLOCK!
Weekdays: 3 hours
His missing sleep
Weekends: 8 hours
WHEN HE'S IN THIS STATE, HE WON'T WAKE UP!
AGHHH!
ZZZ

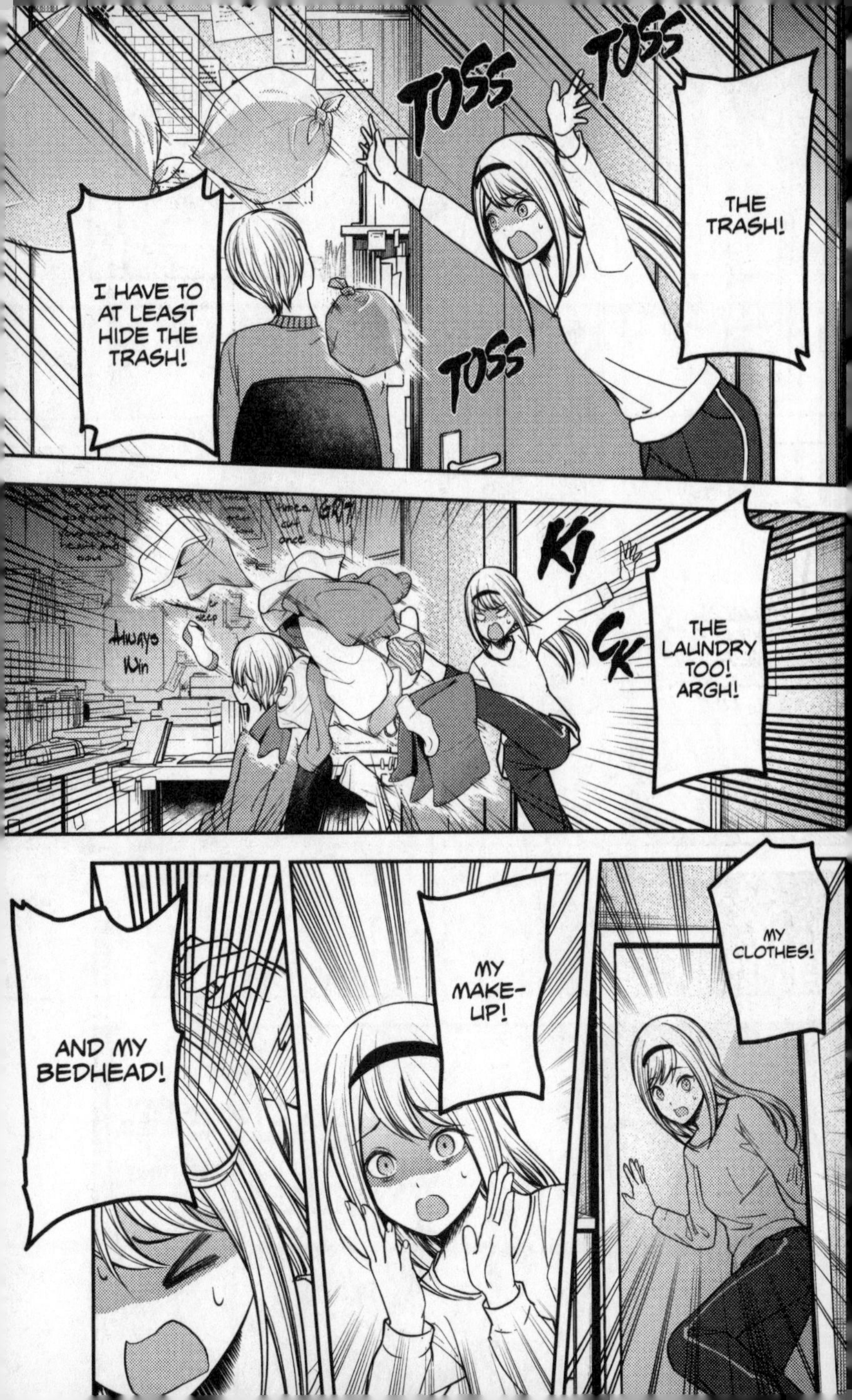
TOSS
TOSS
THE TRASH!
I HAVE TO AT LEAST HIDE THE TRASH!
TOSS
KICK
THE LAUNDRY TOO! ARGH!
MY CLOTHES!
MY MAKE-UP!
AND MY BEDHEAD!

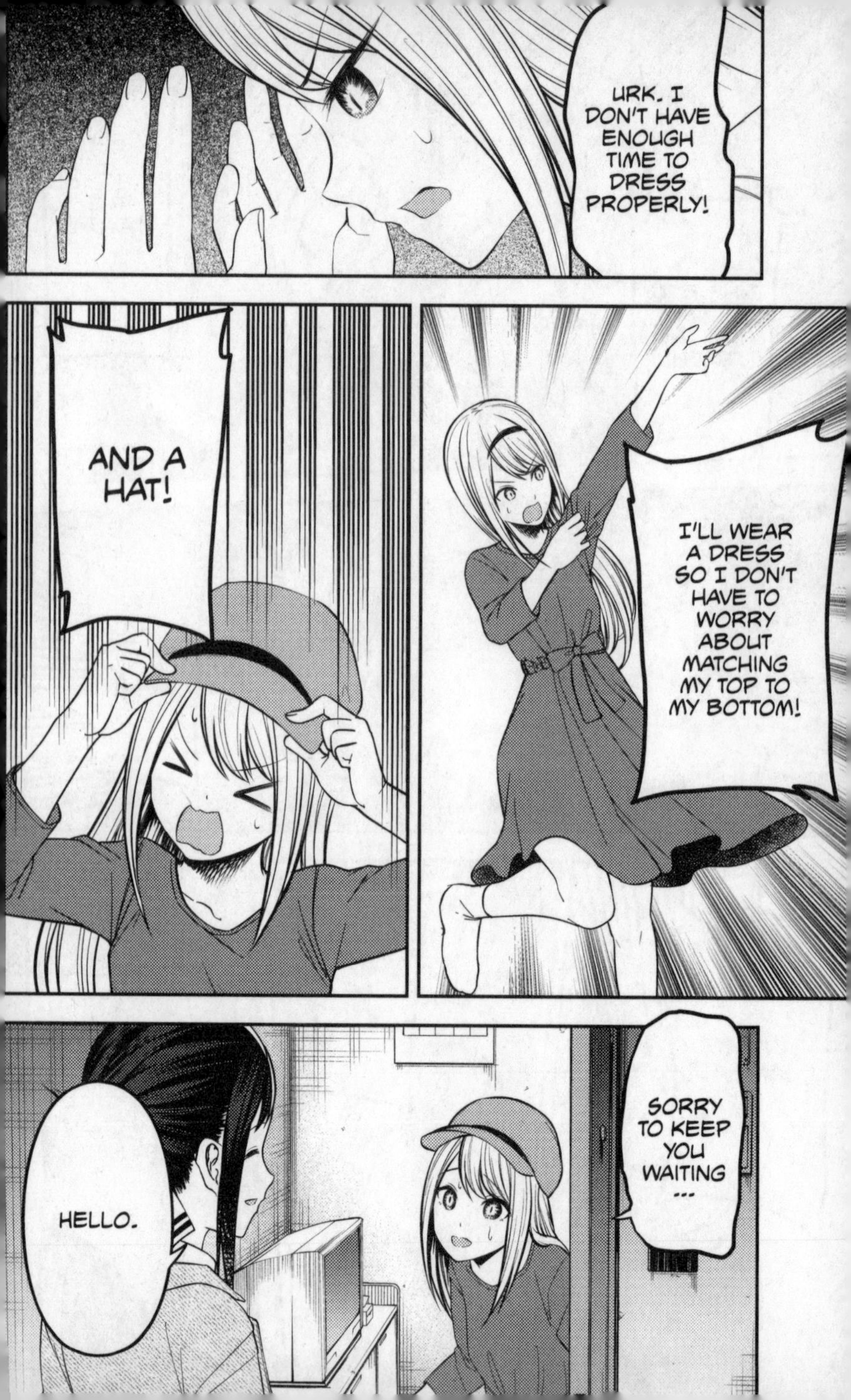
URK. I DON'T HAVE ENOUGH TIME TO DRESS PROPERLY!
I'LL WEAR A DRESS SO I DON'T HAVE TO WORRY ABOUT MATCHING MY TOP TO MY BOTTOM!
AND A HAT!
SORRY TO KEEP YOU WAITING...
HELLO.

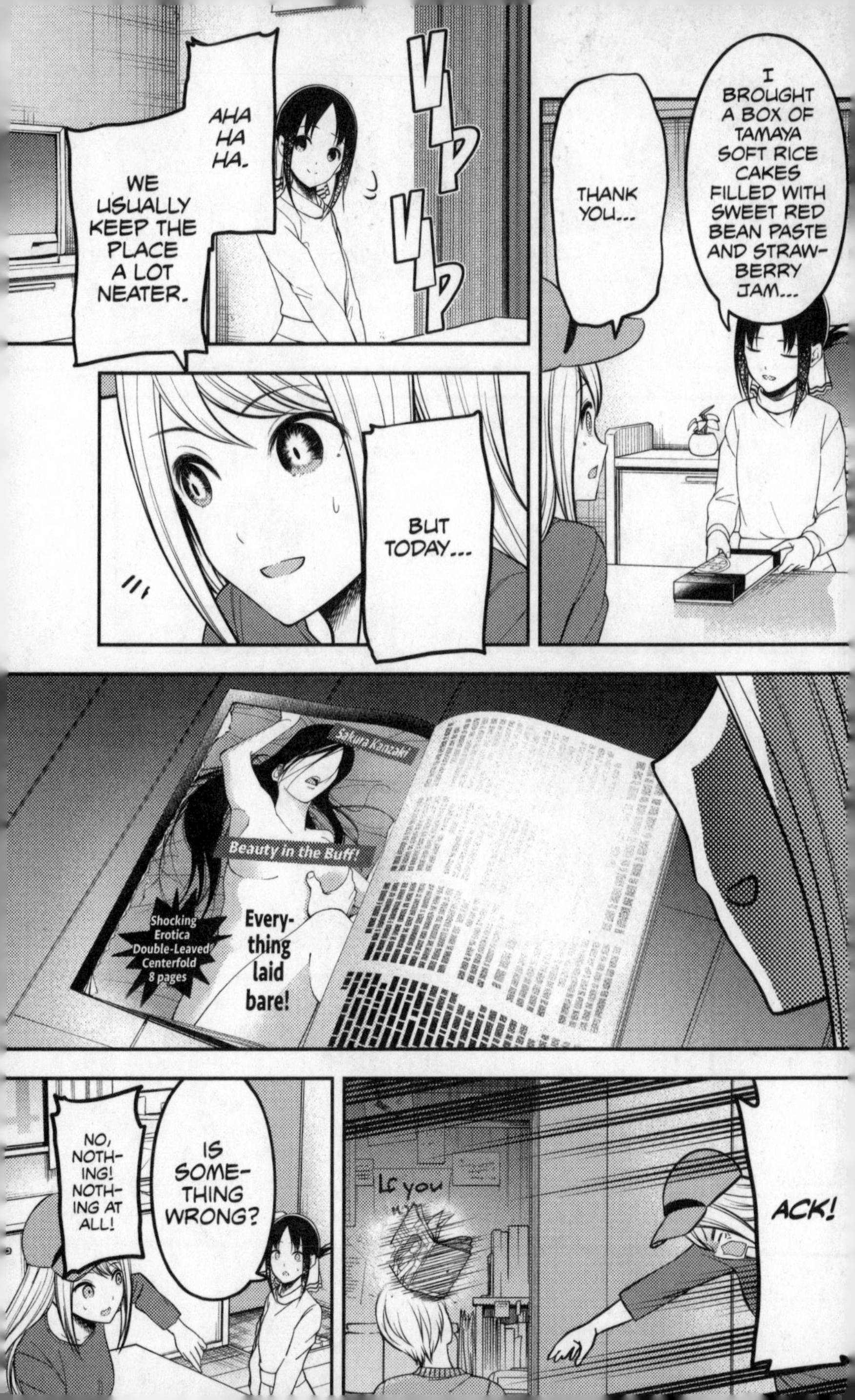
I BROUGHT A BOX OF TAMAYA SOFT RICE CAKES FILLED WITH SWEET RED BEAN PASTE AND STRAW-BERRY JAM...
THANK YOU...
VIP
VIP
AHA HA HA.
WE USUALLY KEEP THE PLACE A LOT NEATER.
BUT TODAY...
Sakura Kanzaki
Beauty in the Buff!
Shocking Erotica Double-Leaved Centerfold 8 pages
Every-thing laid bare!
ACK!
IS SOME-THING WRONG?
NO, NOTH-ING! NOTH-ING AT ALL!

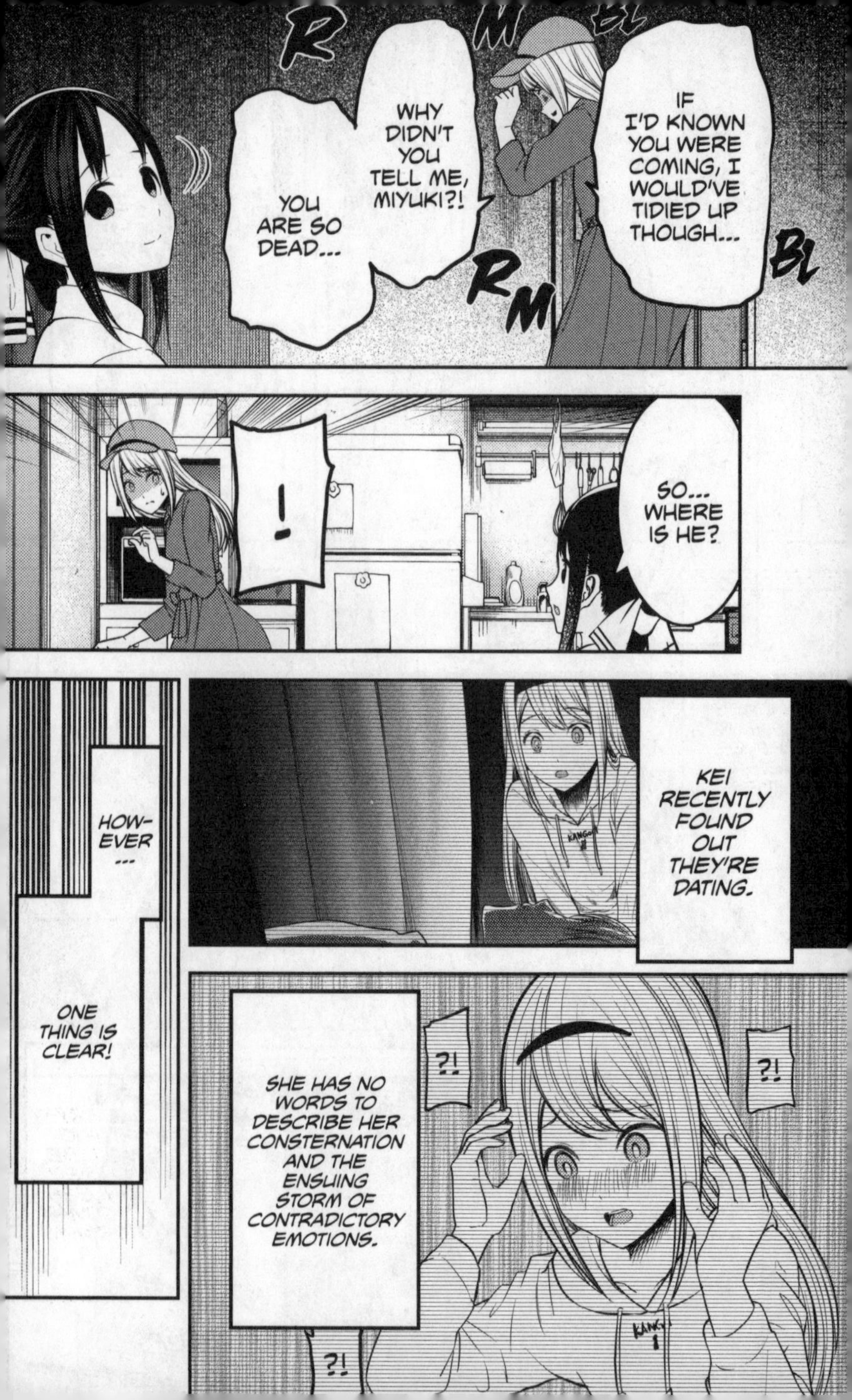
RMBL
IF I'D KNOWN YOU WERE COMING, I WOULD'VE TIDIED UP THOUGH...
WHY DIDN'T YOU TELL ME, MIYUKI?!
YOU ARE SO DEAD...
RMBL
SO... WHERE IS HE?
!
KEI RECENTLY FOUND OUT THEY'RE DATING.
HOW-EVER...
ONE THING IS CLEAR!
?!
?!
SHE HAS NO WORDS TO DESCRIBE HER CONSTERNATION AND THE ENSUING STORM OF CONTRADICTORY EMOTIONS.
?!

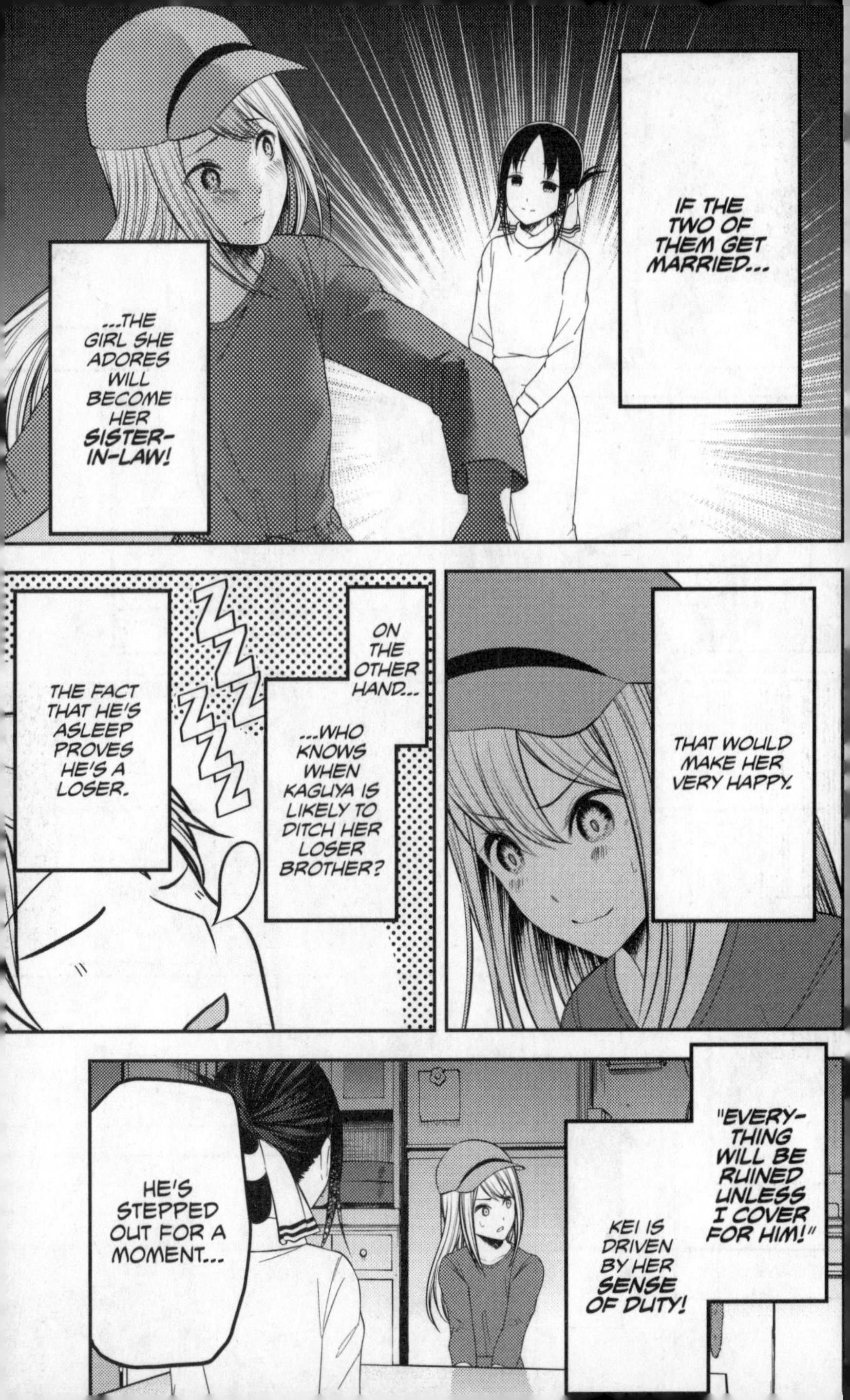
IF THE TWO OF THEM GET MARRIED...
...THE GIRL SHE ADORES WILL BECOME HER SISTER-IN-LAW!
THAT WOULD MAKE HER VERY HAPPY.
ON THE OTHER HAND...
...WHO KNOWS WHEN KAGUYA IS LIKELY TO DITCH HER LOSER BROTHER?
THE FACT THAT HE'S ASLEEP PROVES HE'S A LOSER.
"EVERY-THING WILL BE RUINED UNLESS I COVER FOR HIM!"
KEI IS DRIVEN BY HER SENSE OF DUTY!
HE'S STEPPED OUT FOR A MOMENT...

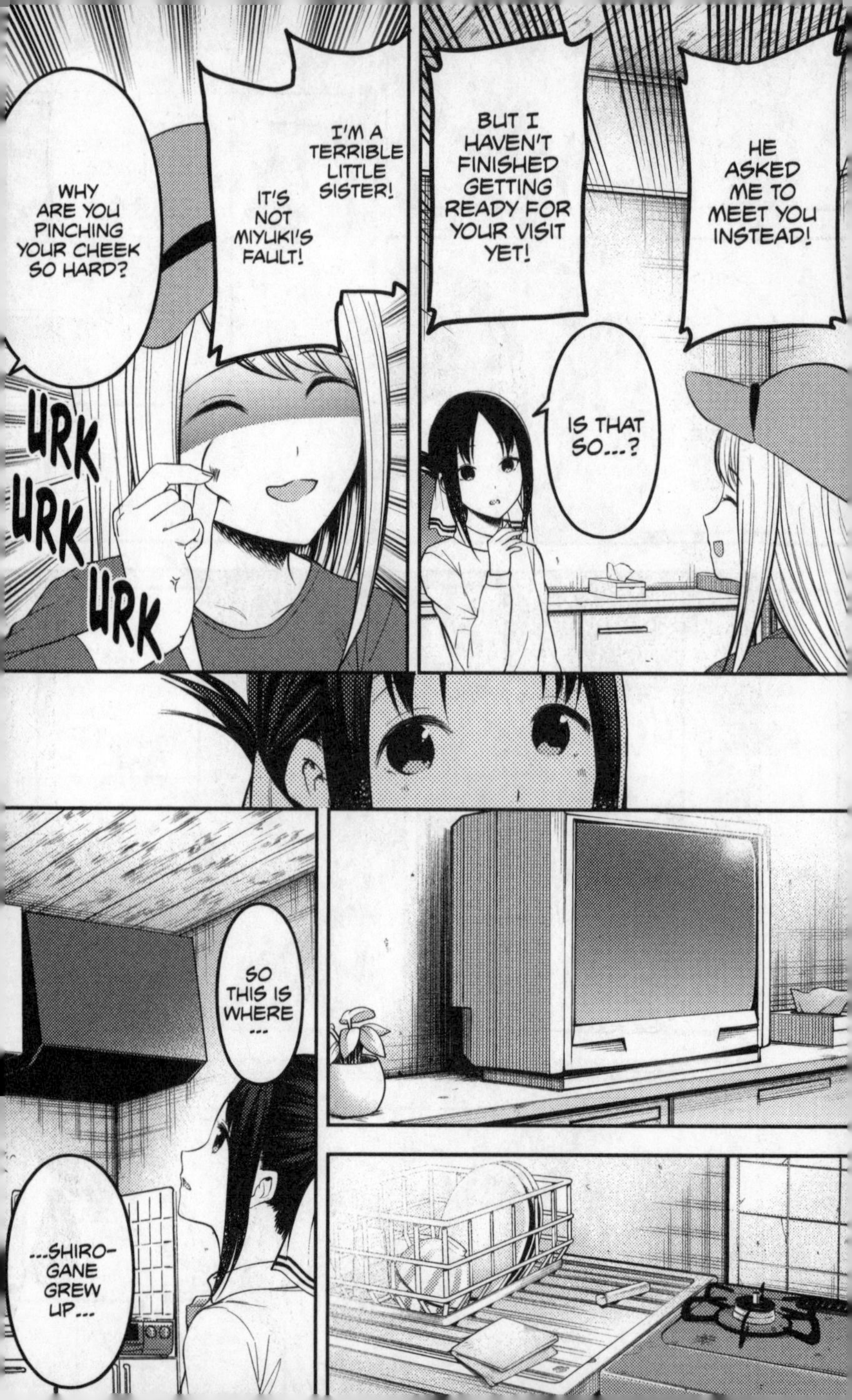
HE ASKED ME TO MEET YOU INSTEAD!
BUT I HAVEN'T FINISHED GETTING READY FOR YOUR VISIT YET!
IS THAT SO...?
I'M A TERRIBLE LITTLE SISTER!
IT'S NOT MIYUKI'S FAULT!
WHY ARE YOU PINCHING YOUR CHEEK SO HARD?
URK
URK
URK
SO THIS IS WHERE ...
...SHIRO-GANE GREW UP...

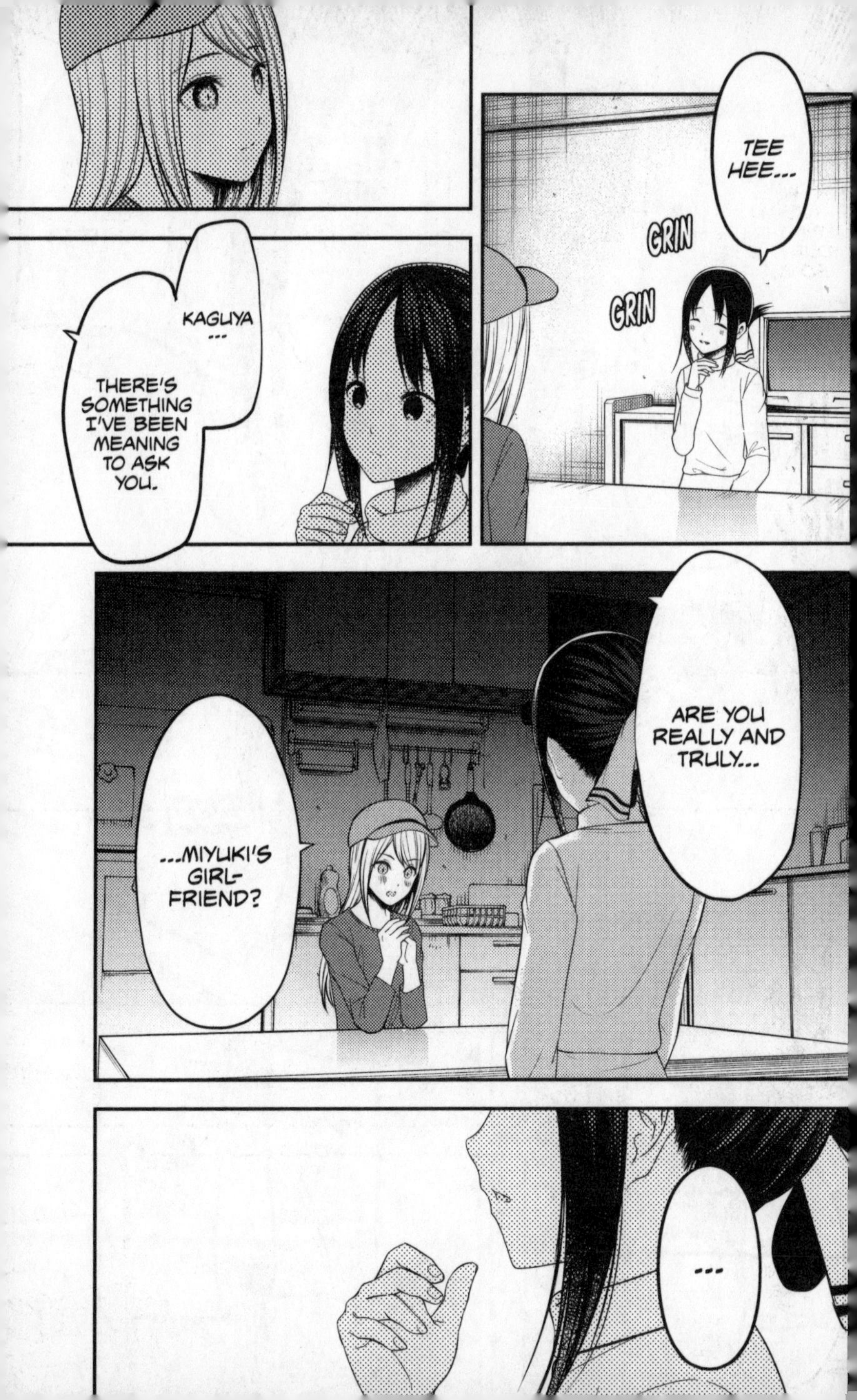
TEE HEE...
GRIN
GRIN
KAGUYA...
THERE'S SOMETHING I'VE BEEN MEANING TO ASK YOU.
ARE YOU REALLY AND TRULY...
...MIYUKI'S GIRL-FRIEND?
...

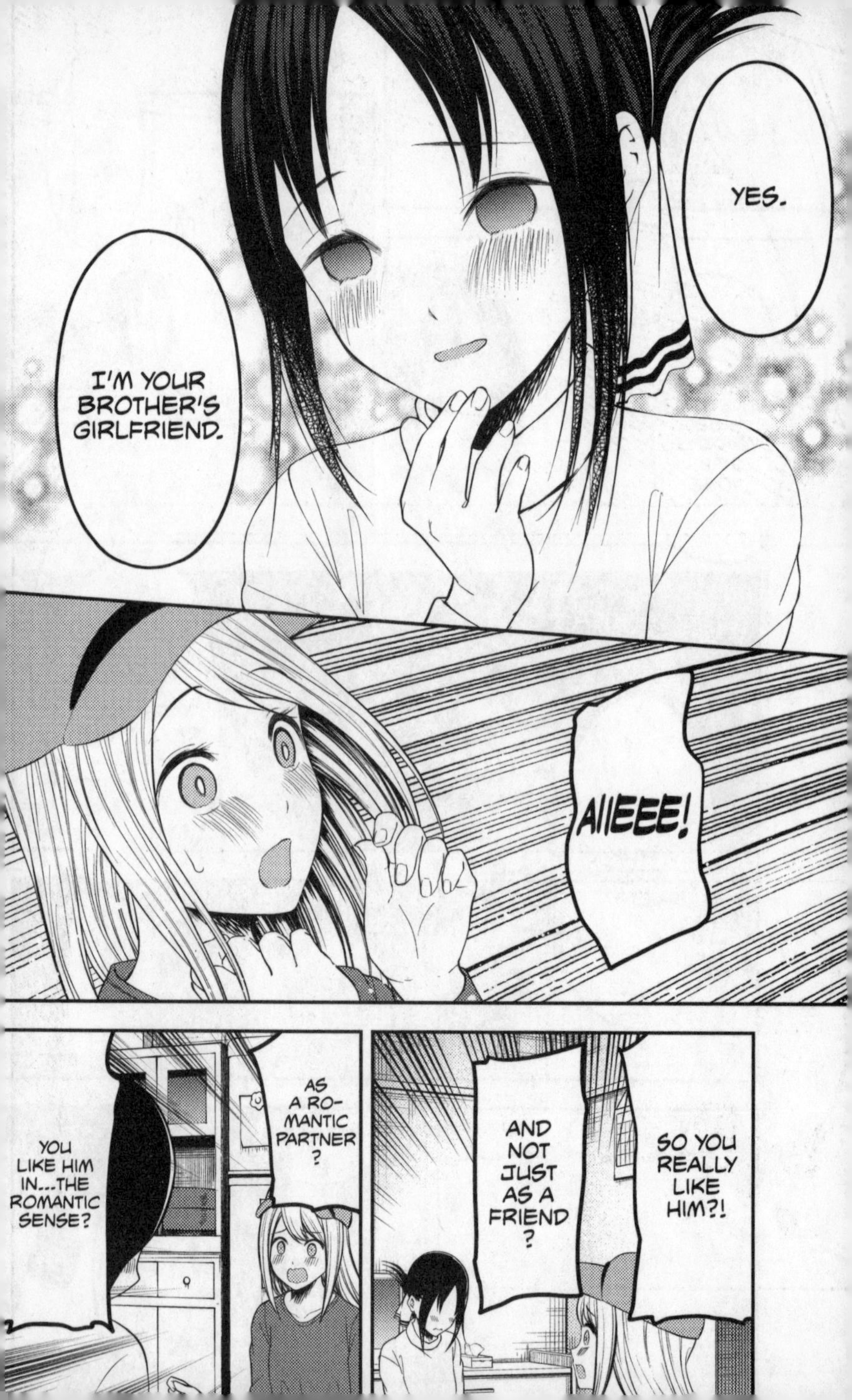
YES.
I'M YOUR BROTHER'S GIRLFRIEND.
AIIEEE!
SO YOU REALLY LIKE HIM?!
AND NOT JUST AS A FRIEND?
AS A RO-MANTIC PARTNER?
YOU LIKE HIM IN...THE ROMANTIC SENSE?

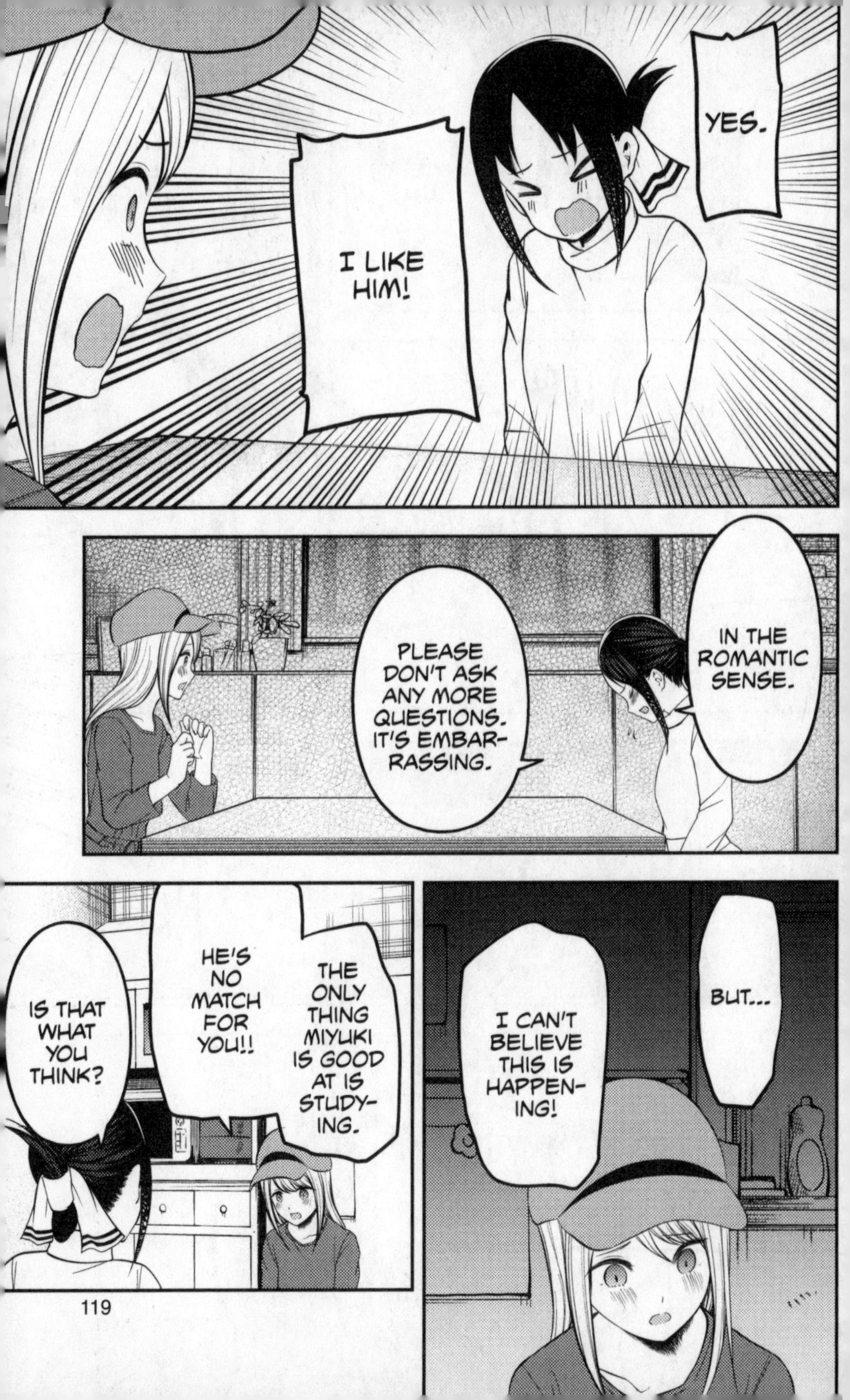
YES.
I LIKE HIM!
IN THE ROMANTIC SENSE.
PLEASE DON'T ASK ANY MORE QUESTIONS. IT'S EMBARRASSING.
BUT...
I CAN'T BELIEVE THIS IS HAPPENING!
THE ONLY THING MIYUKI IS GOOD AT IS STUDYING.
HE'S NO MATCH FOR YOU!!
IS THAT WHAT YOU THINK?

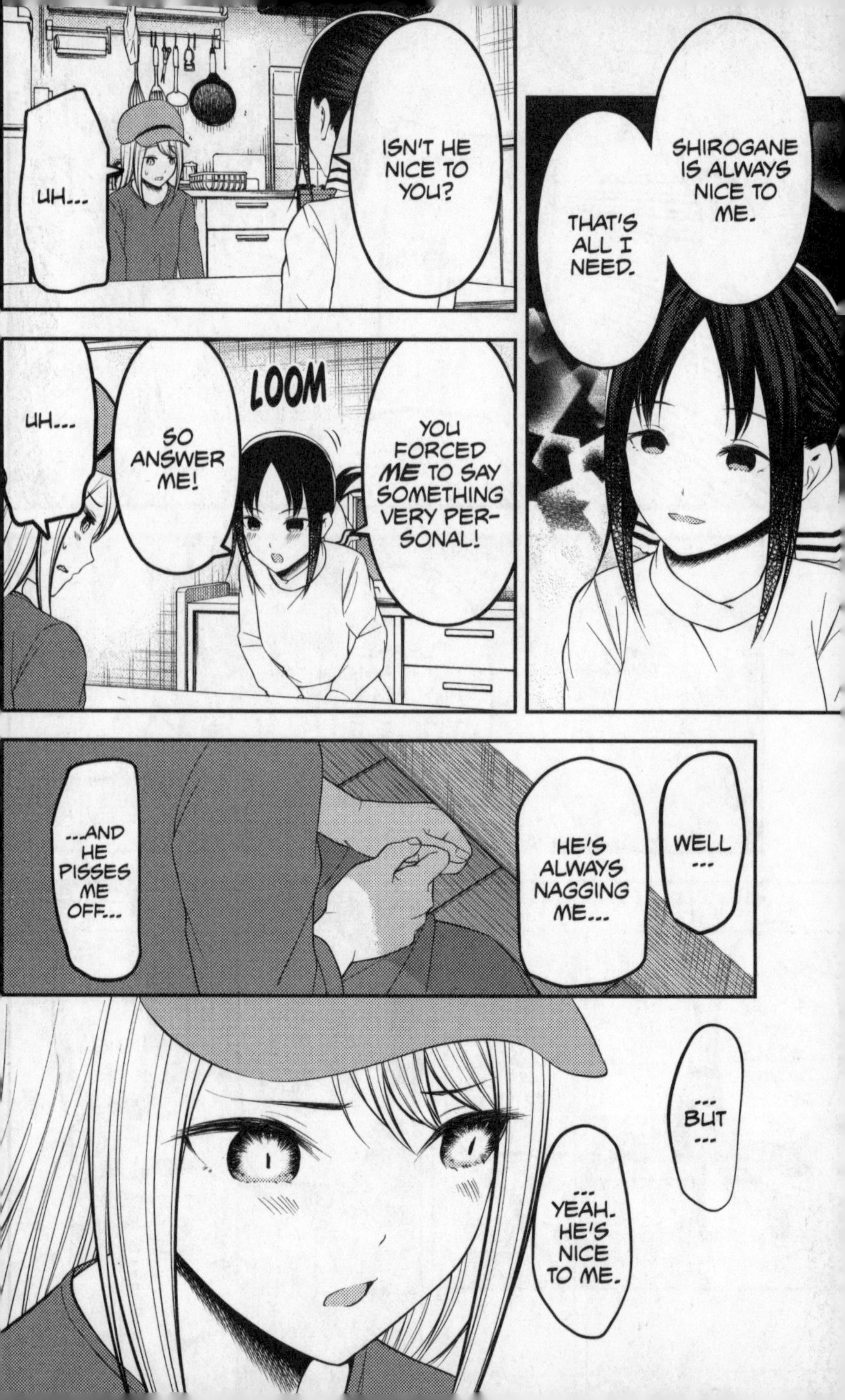
SHIROGANE IS ALWAYS NICE TO ME.
THAT'S ALL I NEED.
ISN'T HE NICE TO YOU?
UH...
YOU FORCED *ME* TO SAY SOMETHING VERY PER-SONAL!
LOOM
SO ANSWER ME!
UH...
WELL...
HE'S ALWAYS NAGGING ME...
...AND HE PISSES ME OFF...
...BUT...
...YEAH. HE'S NICE TO ME.

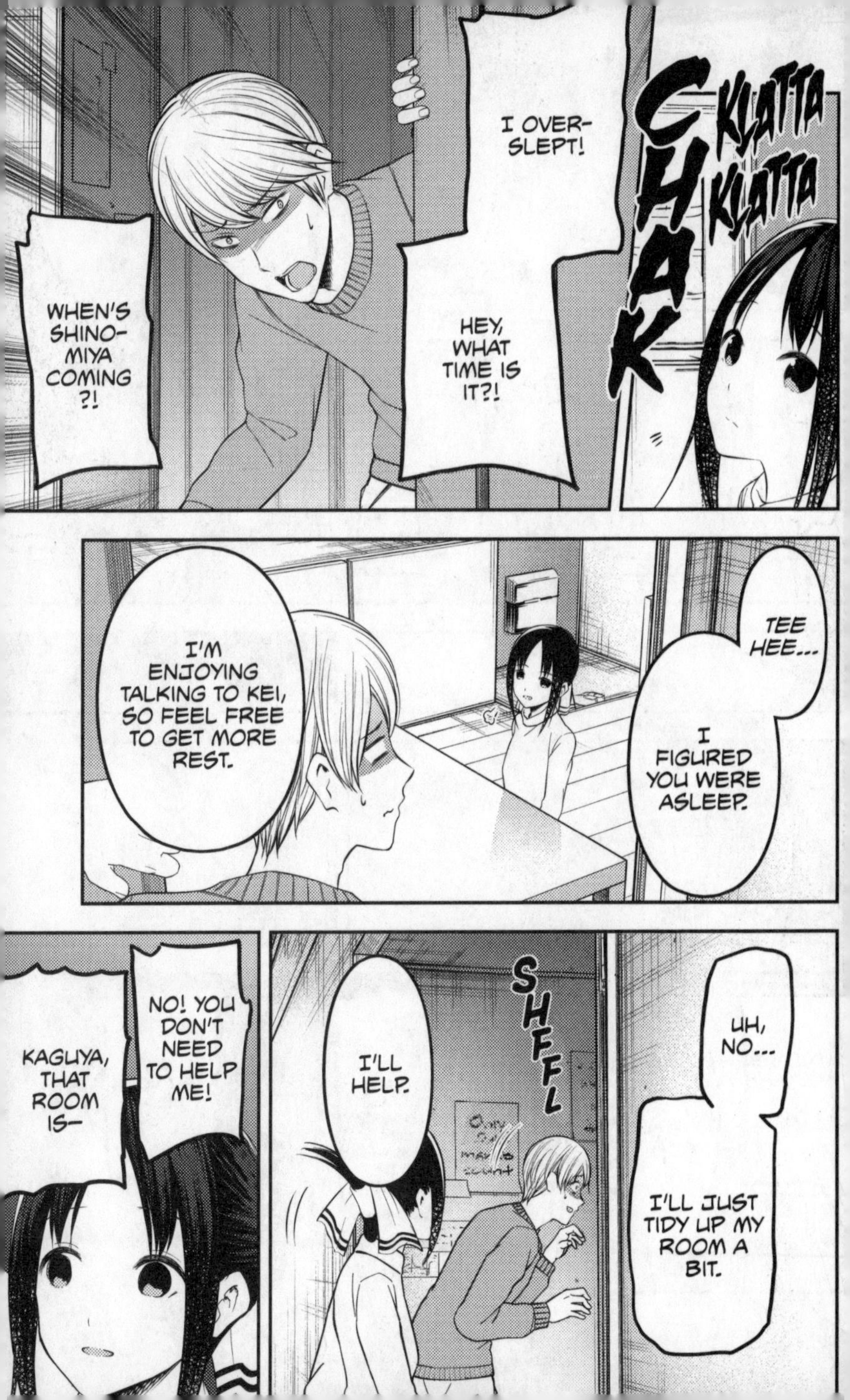
CHAK
KLATTA KLATTA
I OVER-SLEPT!
HEY, WHAT TIME IS IT?!
WHEN'S SHINO-MIYA COMING?!
TEE HEE...
I FIGURED YOU WERE ASLEEP.
I'M ENJOYING TALKING TO KEI, SO FEEL FREE TO GET MORE REST.
UH, NO...
I'LL JUST TIDY UP MY ROOM A BIT.
SHFFL
I'LL HELP.
NO! YOU DON'T NEED TO HELP ME!
KAGUYA, THAT ROOM IS—

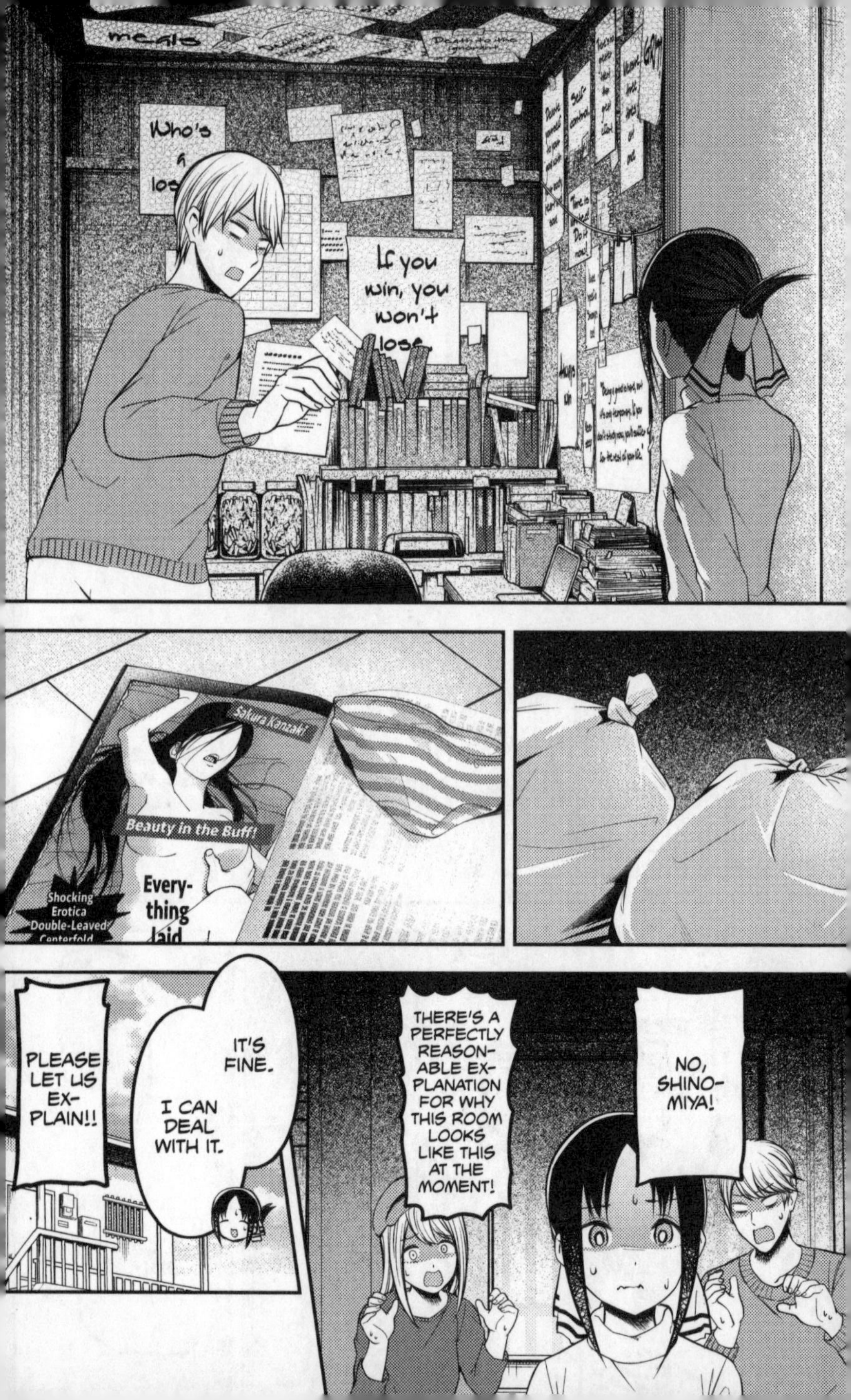
If you win, you won't lose.
Do it now!
Sakura Kanzaki
Beauty in the Buff!
Every-thing laid
Shocking Erotica Double-Leaved Centerfold
NO, SHINO-MIYA!
THERE'S A PERFECTLY REASON-ABLE EX-PLANATION FOR WHY THIS ROOM LOOKS LIKE THIS AT THE MOMENT!
IT'S FINE.
I CAN DEAL WITH IT.
PLEASE LET US EX-PLAIN!!

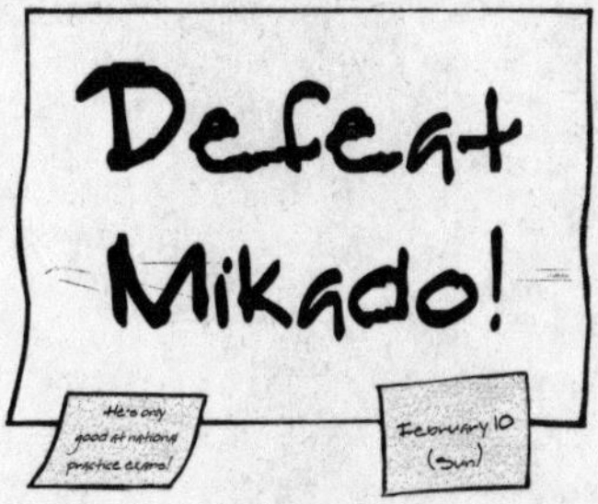
Defeat Mikado!
He's only good at national practice exams!
February 10 (Sun)

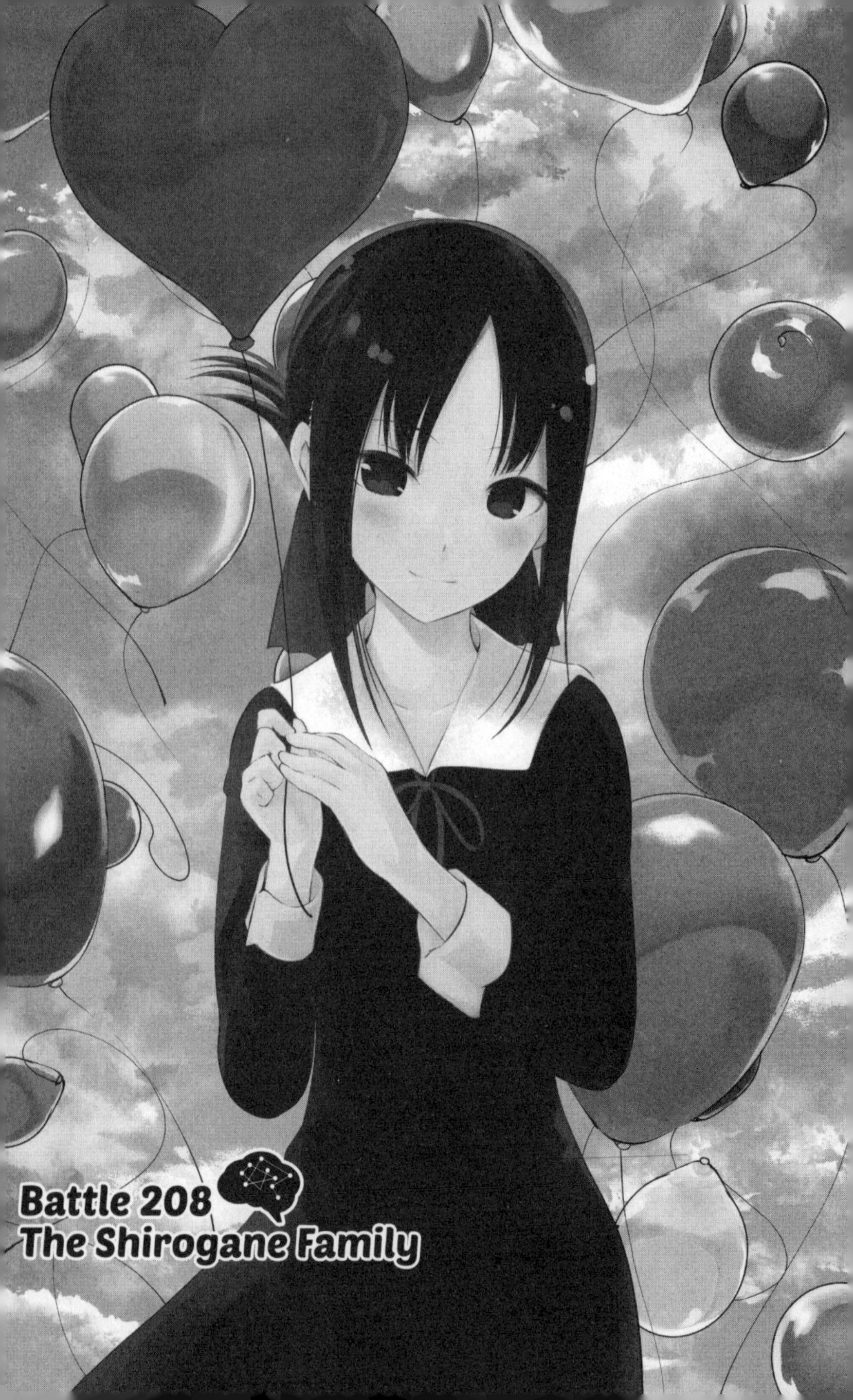
Battle 208
The Shirogane Family

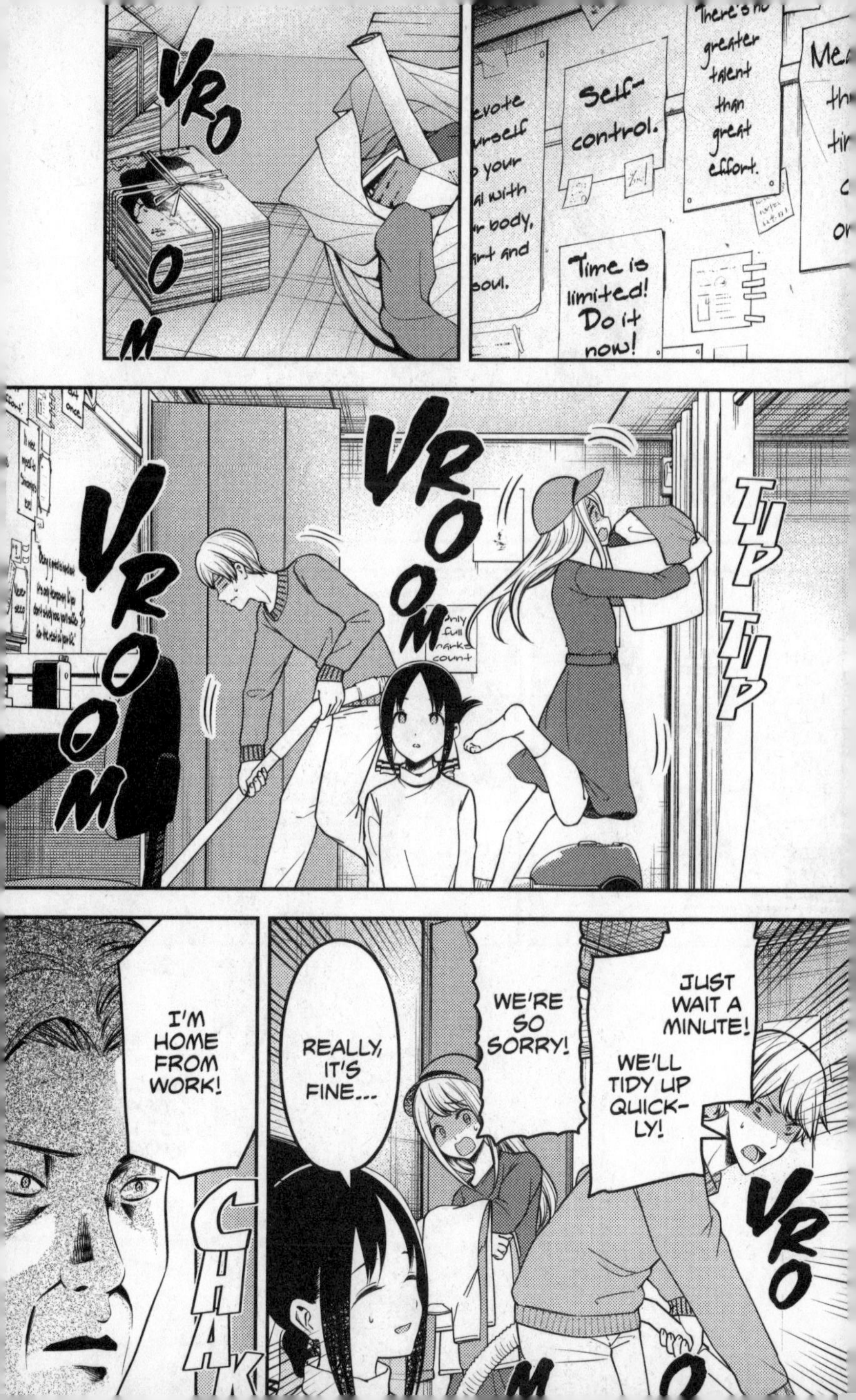
There's no greater talent than great effort.
Self-control.
Time is limited! Do it now!
VROOM
TUP TUP TUP
VROOM
VROOM
JUST WAIT A MINUTE!
WE'LL TIDY UP QUICKLY!
WE'RE SO SORRY!
REALLY, IT'S FINE...
VROOM
I'M HOME FROM WORK!
CHAK

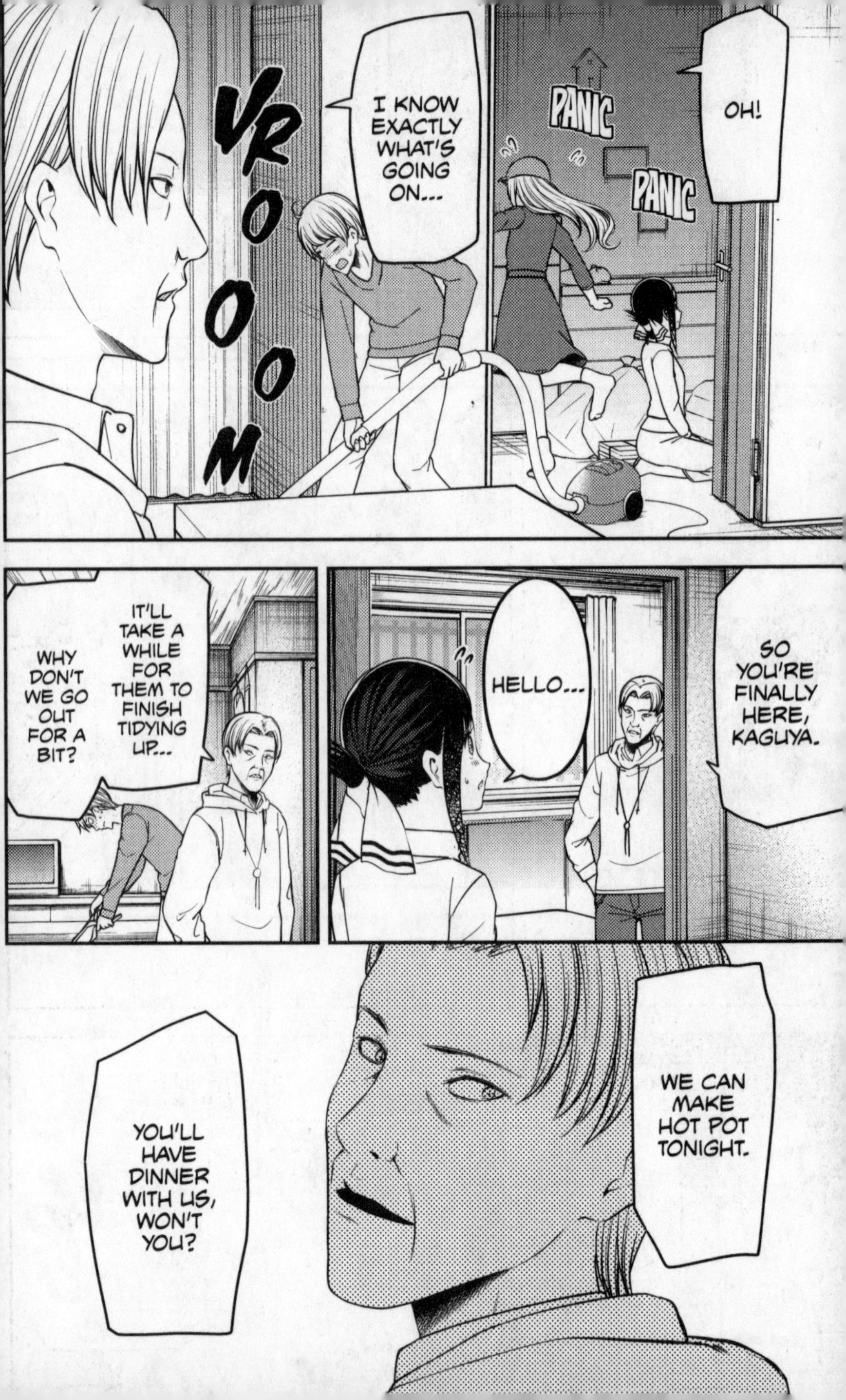
OH!
PANIC
PANIC
I KNOW EXACTLY WHAT'S GOING ON...
VROOOOM
SO YOU'RE FINALLY HERE, KAGUYA.
HELLO...
IT'LL TAKE A WHILE FOR THEM TO FINISH TIDYING UP...
WHY DON'T WE GO OUT FOR A BIT?
WE CAN MAKE HOT POT TONIGHT.
YOU'LL HAVE DINNER WITH US, WON'T YOU?

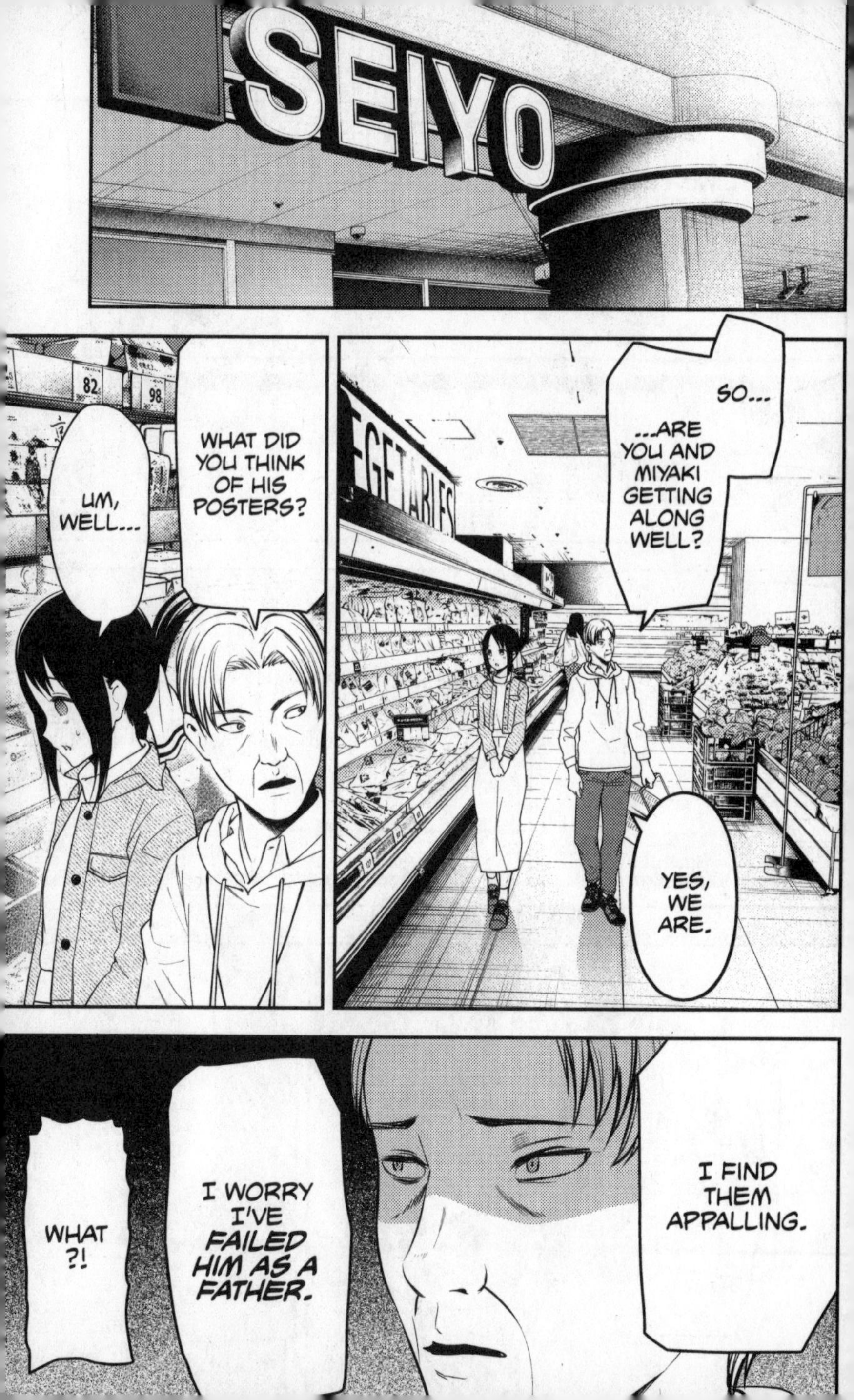
SEIYO
SO...
...ARE YOU AND MIYAKI GETTING ALONG WELL?
YES, WE ARE.
WHAT DID YOU THINK OF HIS POSTERS?
UM, WELL...
I FIND THEM APPALLING.
I WORRY I'VE *FAILED* HIM AS A FATHER.
WHAT?!

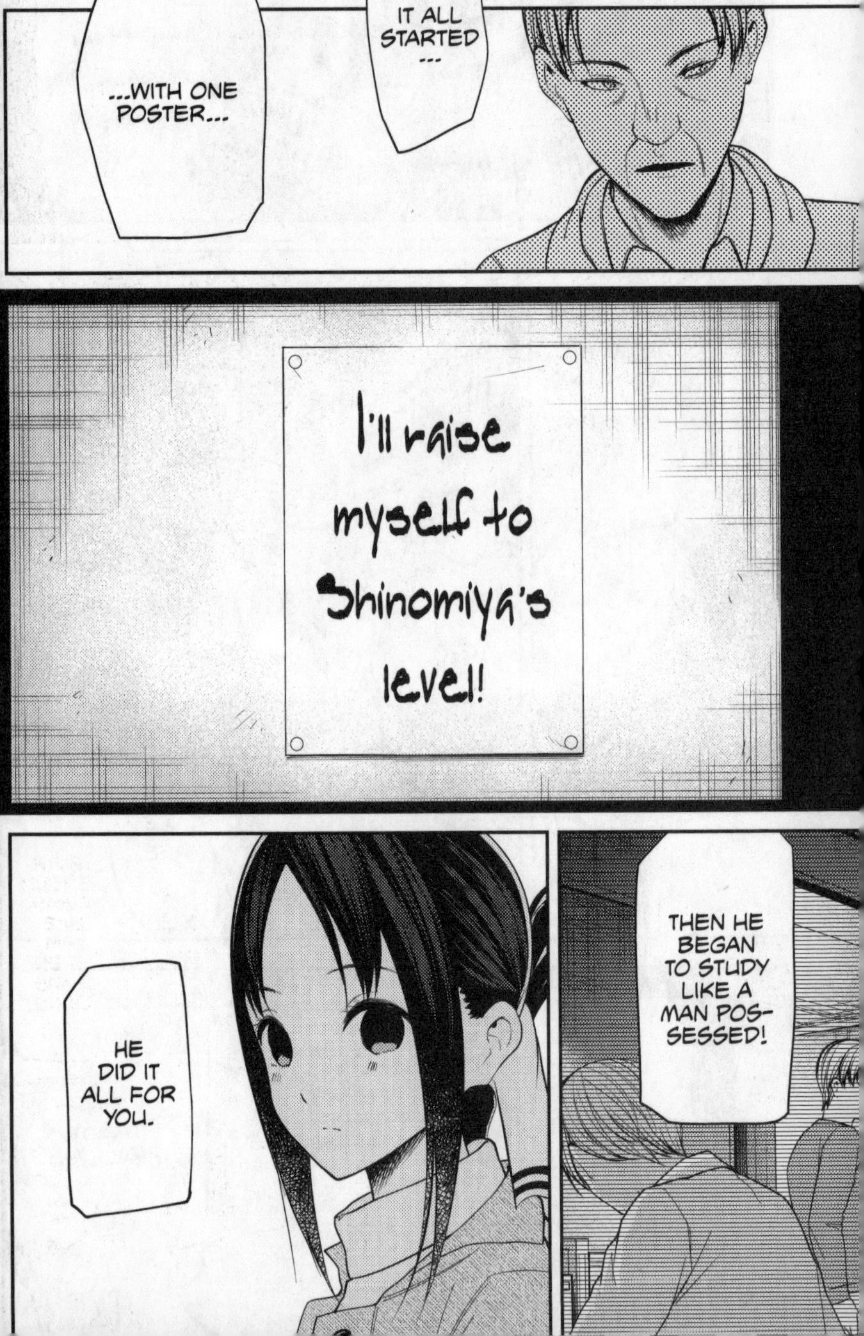
IT ALL STARTED ---
...WITH ONE POSTER...
I'll raise myself to Shinomiya's level!
THEN HE BEGAN TO STUDY LIKE A MAN POS-SESSED!
HE DID IT ALL FOR YOU.

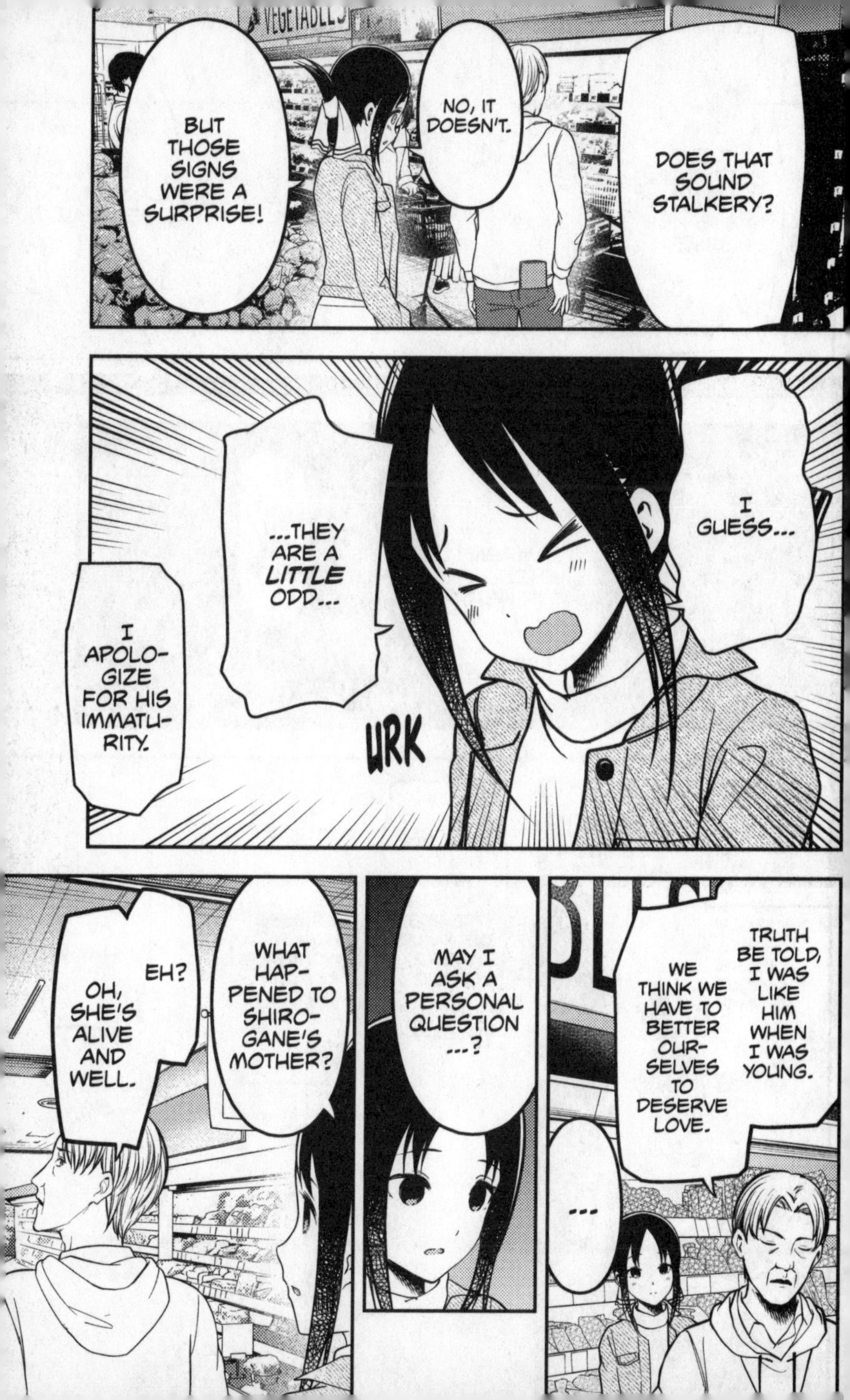
DOES THAT SOUND STALKERY?
NO, IT DOESN'T.
BUT THOSE SIGNS WERE A SURPRISE!
I GUESS...
...THEY ARE A *LITTLE* ODD...
URK
I APOLOGIZE FOR HIS IMMATURITY.
TRUTH BE TOLD, I WAS LIKE HIM WHEN I WAS YOUNG.
WE THINK WE HAVE TO BETTER OURSELVES TO DESERVE LOVE.
...
MAY I ASK A PERSONAL QUESTION...?
WHAT HAPPENED TO SHIROGANE'S MOTHER?
EH?
OH, SHE'S ALIVE AND WELL.

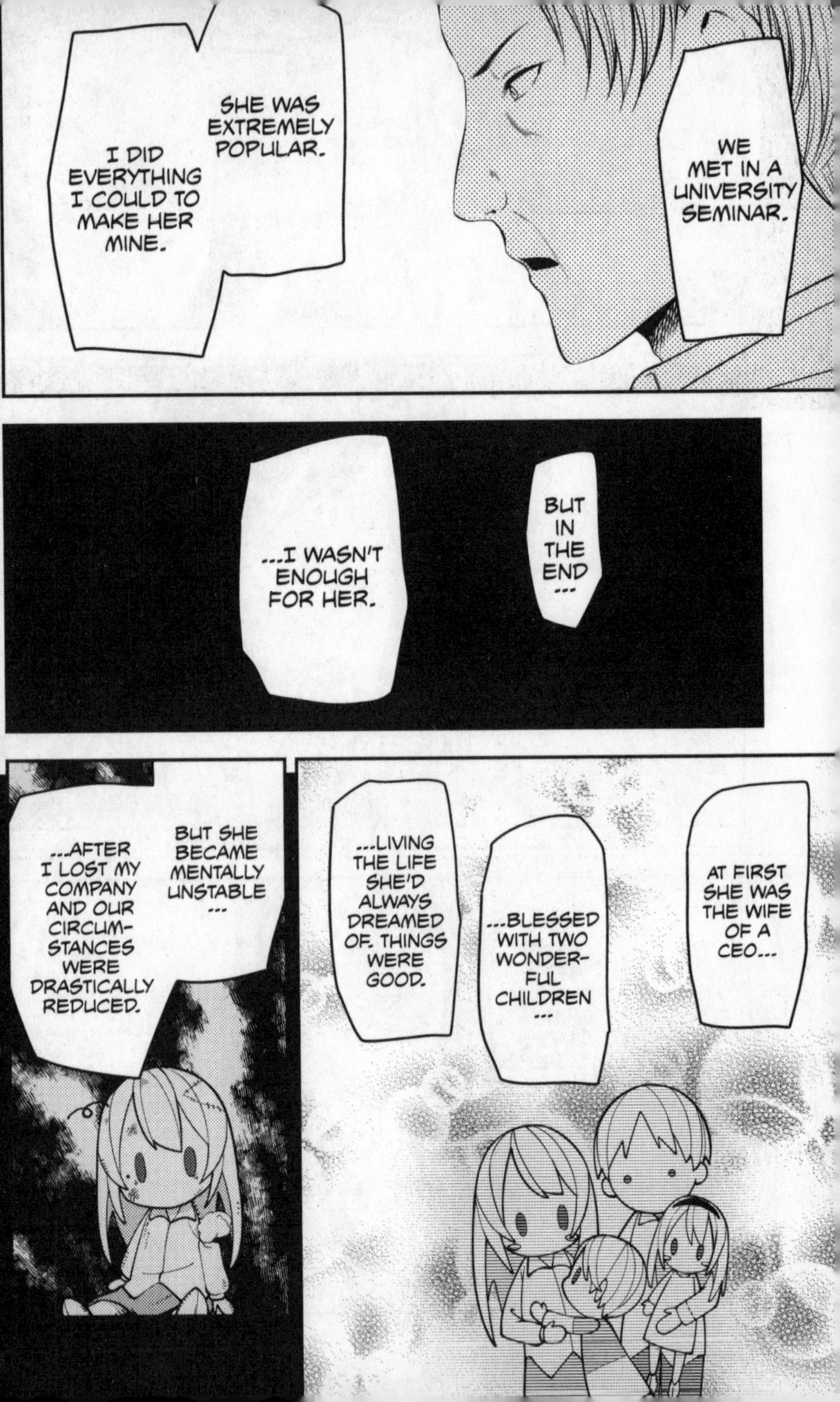
WE MET IN A UNIVERSITY SEMINAR.
SHE WAS EXTREMELY POPULAR.
I DID EVERYTHING I COULD TO MAKE HER MINE.
BUT IN THE END...
...I WASN'T ENOUGH FOR HER.
AT FIRST SHE WAS THE WIFE OF A CEO...
...BLESSED WITH TWO WONDERFUL CHILDREN...
...LIVING THE LIFE SHE'D ALWAYS DREAMED OF. THINGS WERE GOOD.
BUT SHE BECAME MENTALLY UNSTABLE...
...AFTER I LOST MY COMPANY AND OUR CIRCUMSTANCES WERE DRASTICALLY REDUCED.

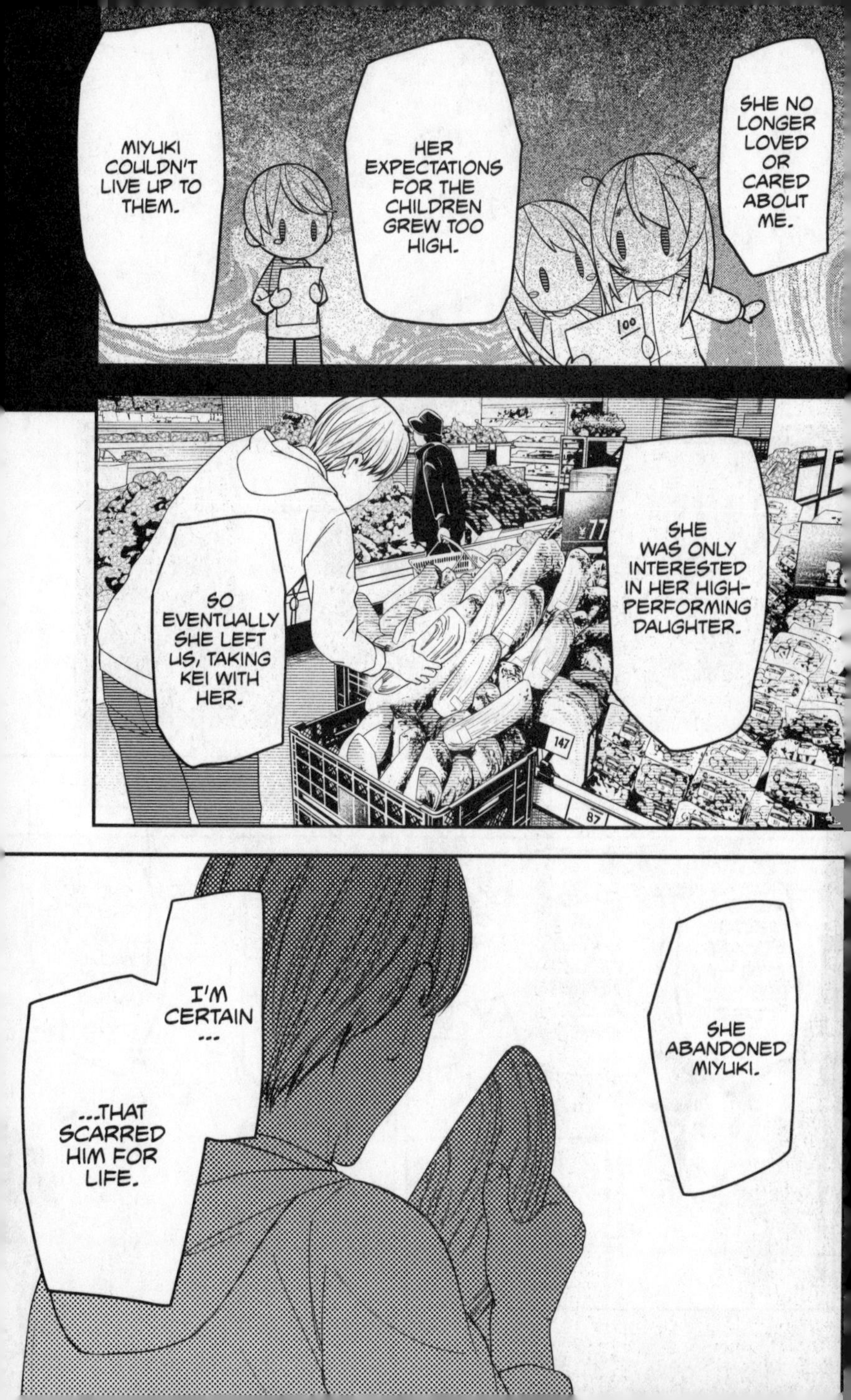
SHE NO LONGER LOVED OR CARED ABOUT ME.
HER EXPECTATIONS FOR THE CHILDREN GREW TOO HIGH.
MIYUKI COULDN'T LIVE UP TO THEM.
100
SHE WAS ONLY INTERESTED IN HER HIGH-PERFORMING DAUGHTER.
SO EVENTUALLY SHE LEFT US, TAKING KEI WITH HER.
147
87
SHE ABANDONED MIYUKI.
I'M CERTAIN...
...THAT SCARRED HIM FOR LIFE.

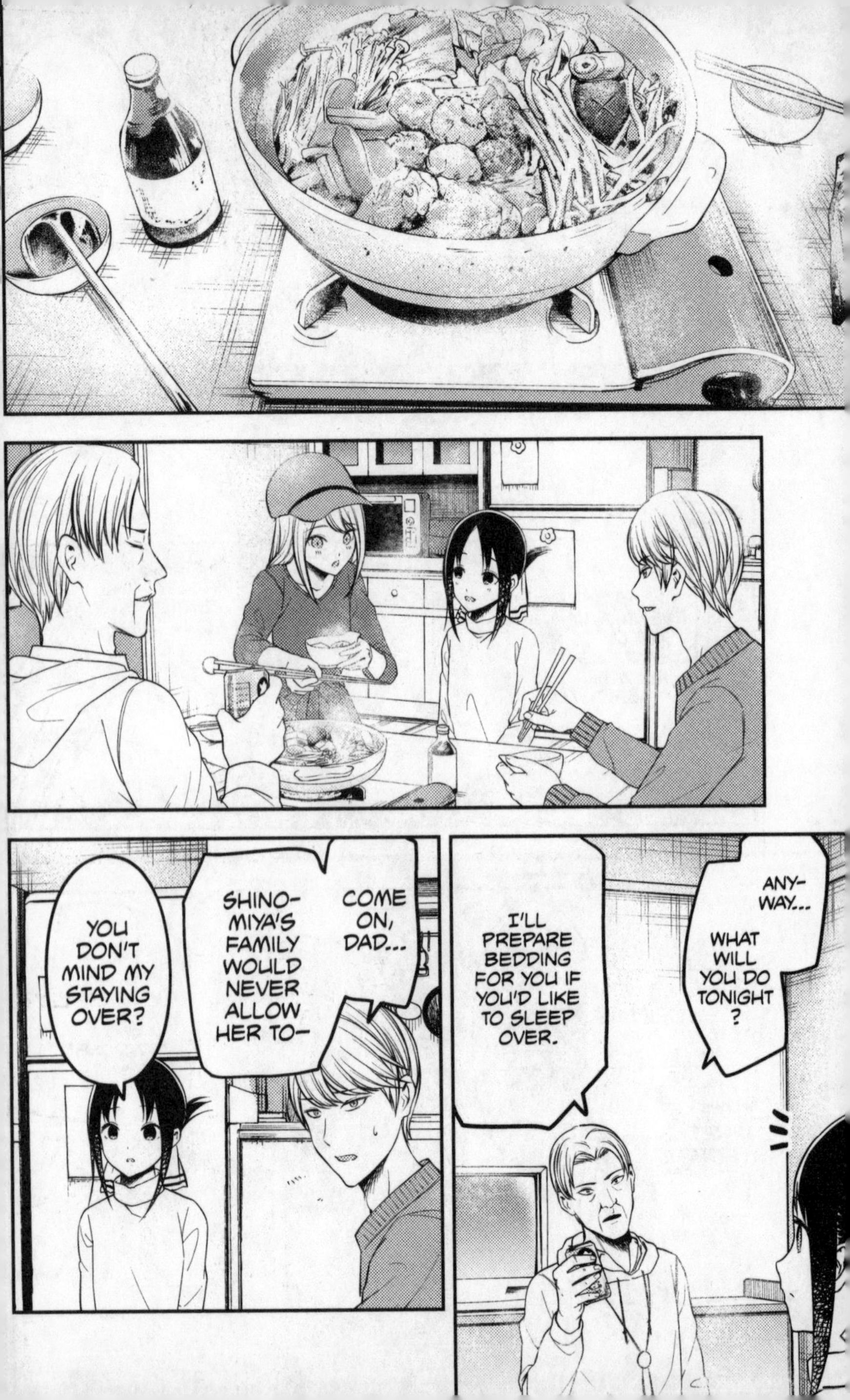
ANY-WAY... WHAT WILL YOU DO TONIGHT?
I'LL PREPARE BEDDING FOR YOU IF YOU'D LIKE TO SLEEP OVER.
COME ON, DAD... SHINO-MIYA'S FAMILY WOULD NEVER ALLOW HER TO—
YOU DON'T MIND MY STAYING OVER?

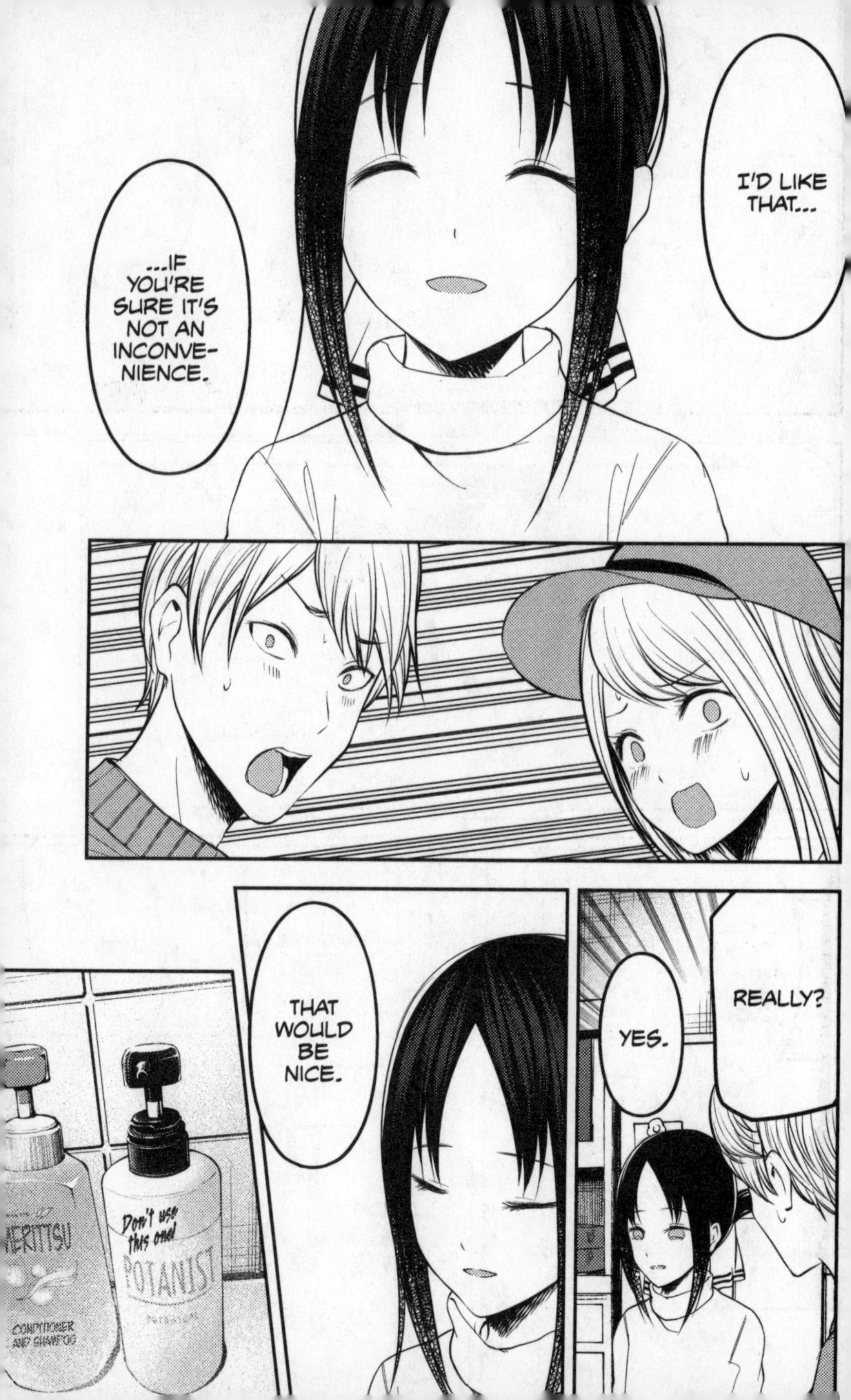
I'D LIKE THAT...
...IF YOU'RE SURE IT'S NOT AN INCONVENIENCE.
REALLY?
YES.
THAT WOULD BE NICE.
Don't use this one!
POTANIST
CONDITIONER AND SHAMPOO

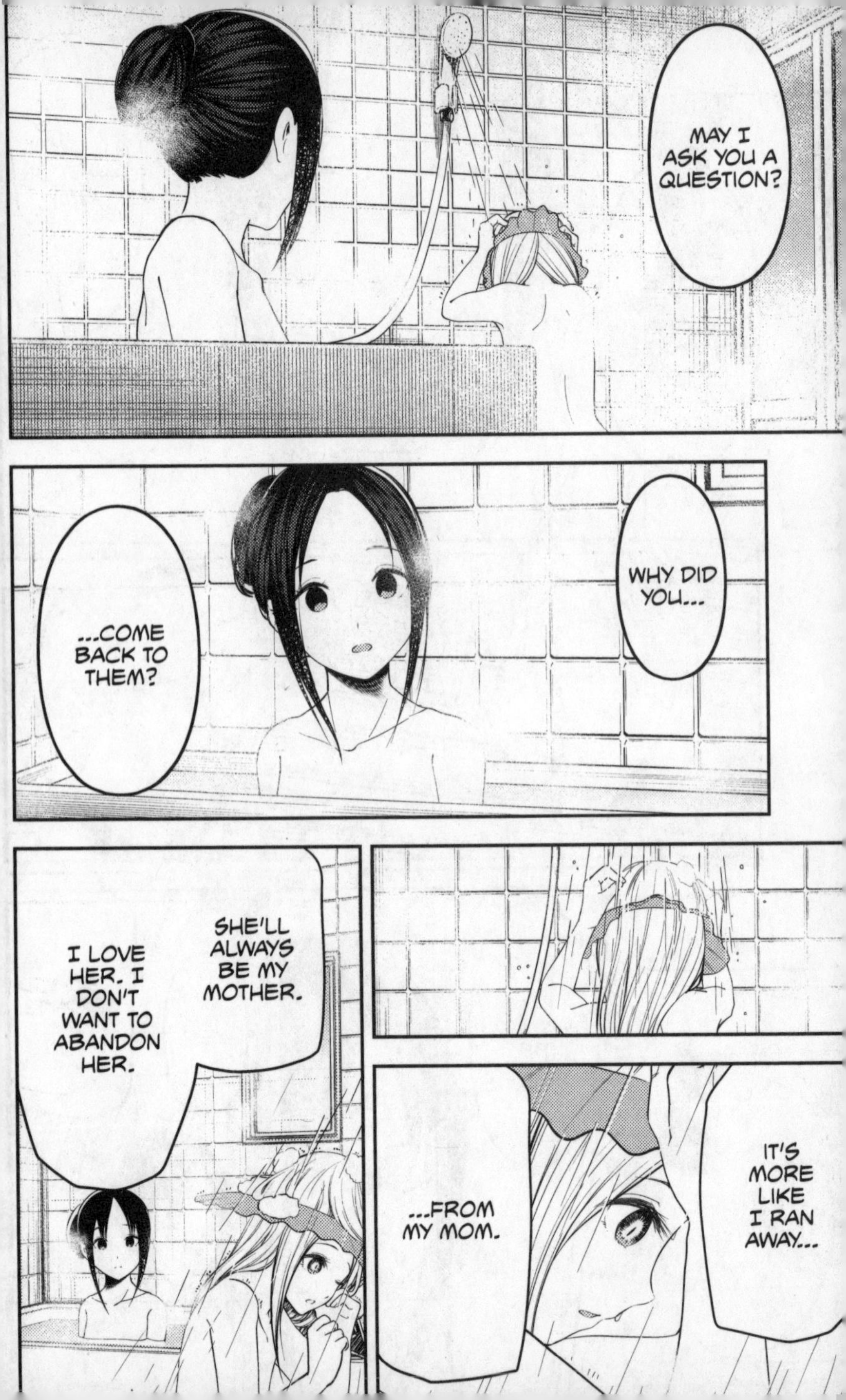
MAY I ASK YOU A QUESTION?
WHY DID YOU...
...COME BACK TO THEM?
IT'S MORE LIKE I RAN AWAY...
...FROM MY MOM.
SHE'LL ALWAYS BE MY MOTHER.
I LOVE HER. I DON'T WANT TO ABANDON HER.

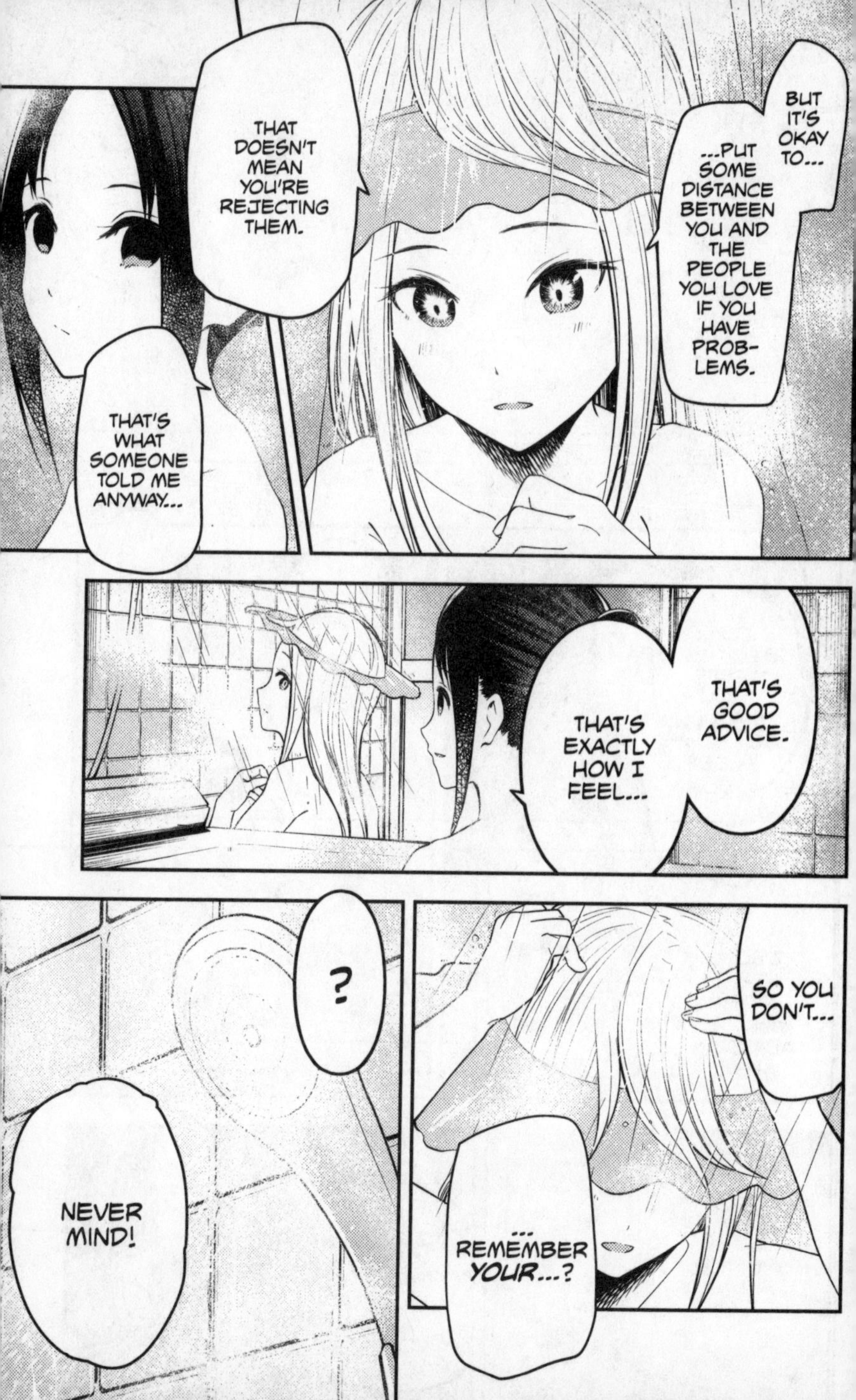
BUT IT'S OKAY TO...
...PUT SOME DISTANCE BETWEEN YOU AND THE PEOPLE YOU LOVE IF YOU HAVE PROB-LEMS.
THAT DOESN'T MEAN YOU'RE REJECTING THEM.
THAT'S WHAT SOMEONE TOLD ME ANYWAY...
THAT'S GOOD ADVICE.
THAT'S EXACTLY HOW I FEEL...
SO YOU DON'T...
...REMEMBER YOUR...?
?
NEVER MIND!

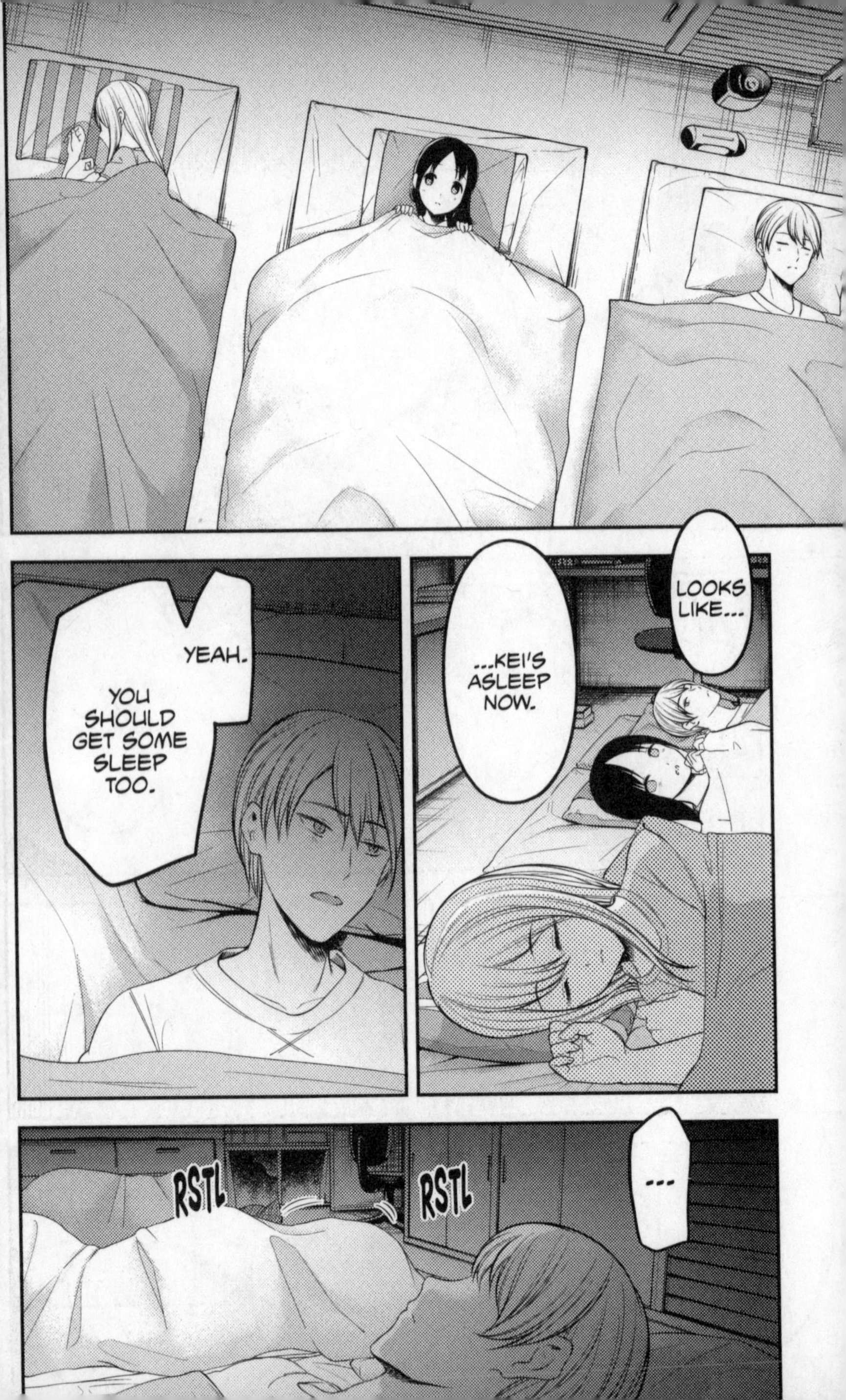
LOOKS LIKE...
...KEI'S ASLEEP NOW.
YEAH.
YOU SHOULD GET SOME SLEEP TOO.
...
RSTL
RSTL

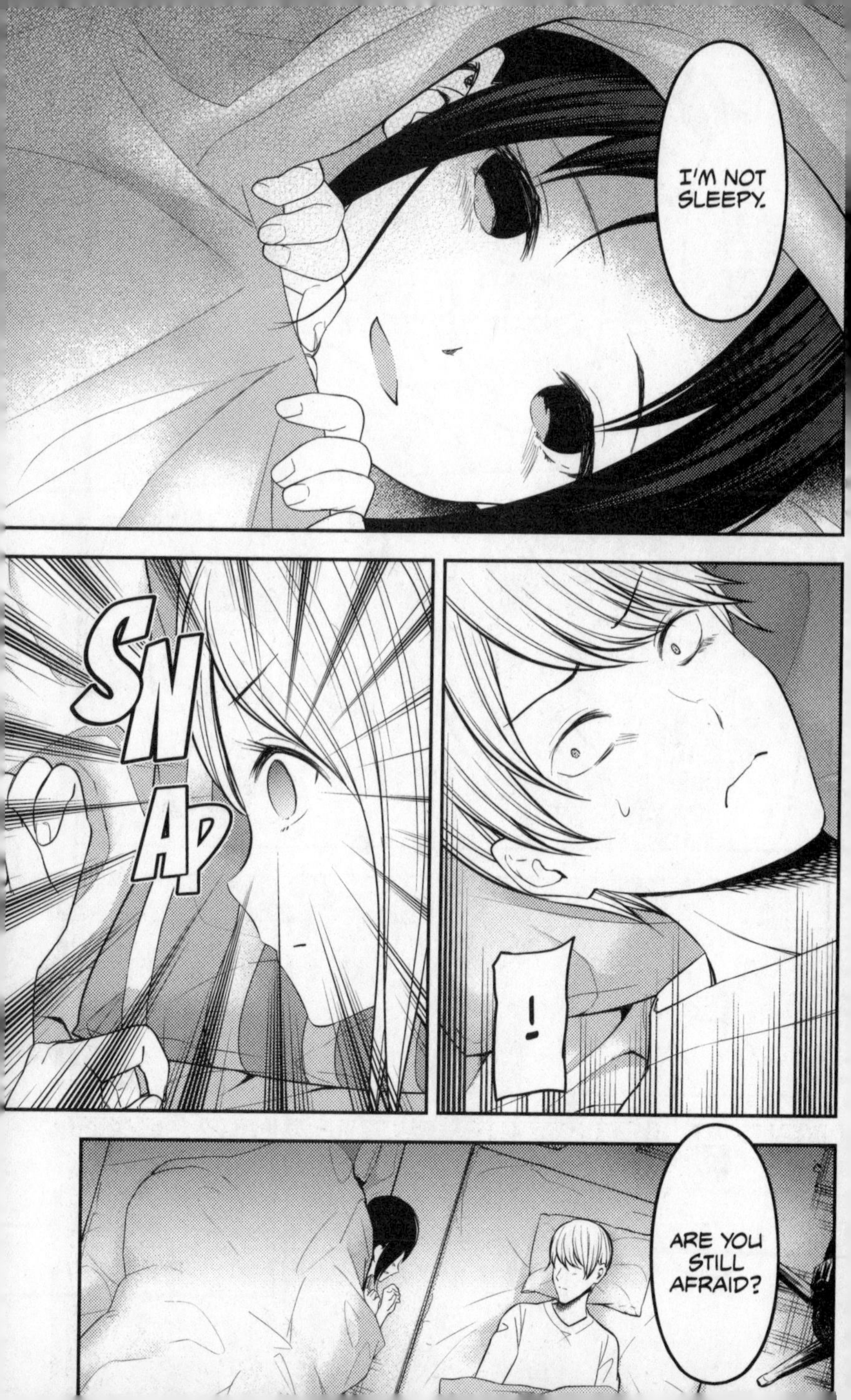
I'M NOT SLEEPY.
!
SNAP
ARE YOU STILL AFRAID?

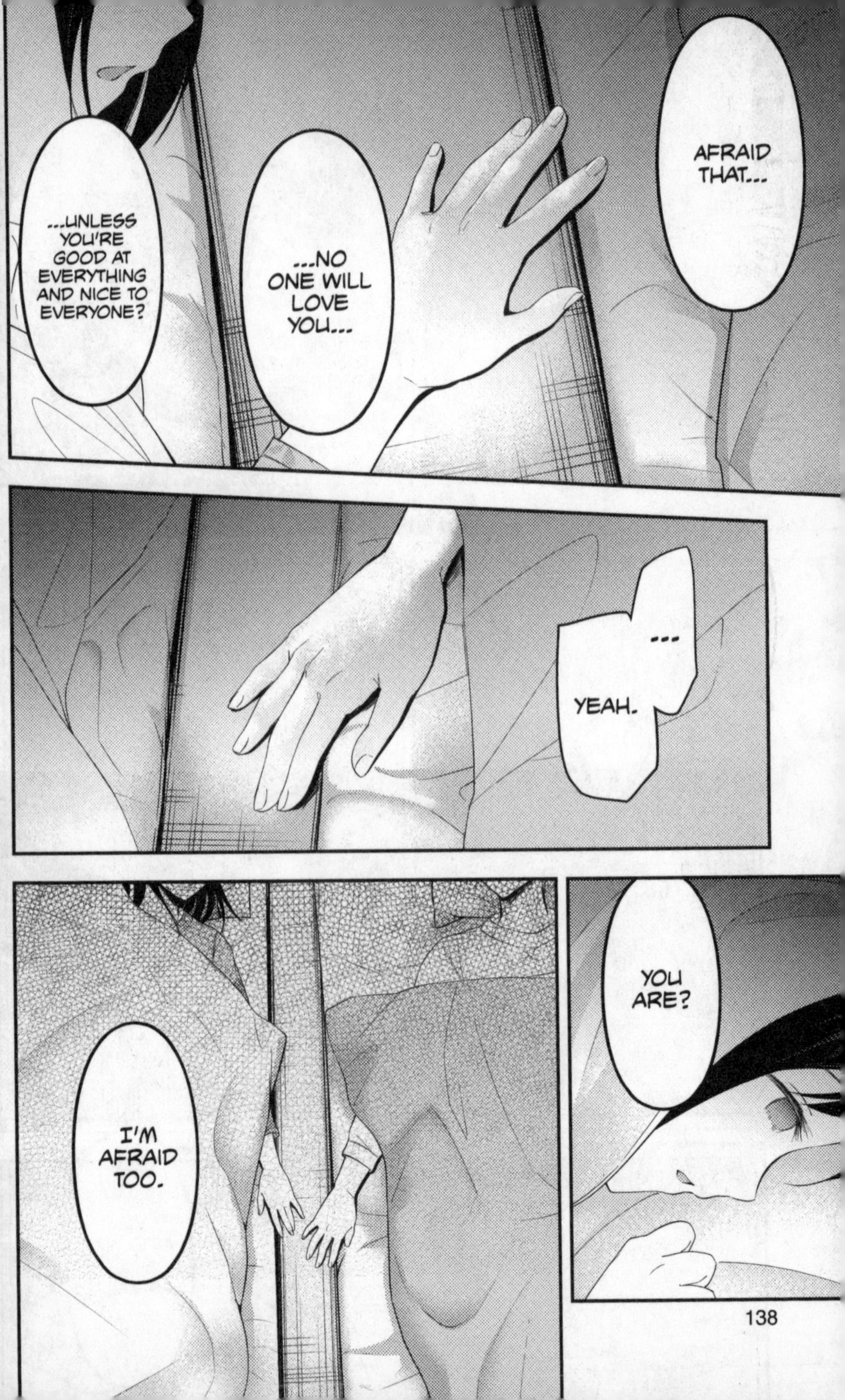
AFRAID THAT...
...NO ONE WILL LOVE YOU...
...UNLESS YOU'RE GOOD AT EVERYTHING AND NICE TO EVERYONE?
...
YEAH.
YOU ARE?
I'M AFRAID TOO.

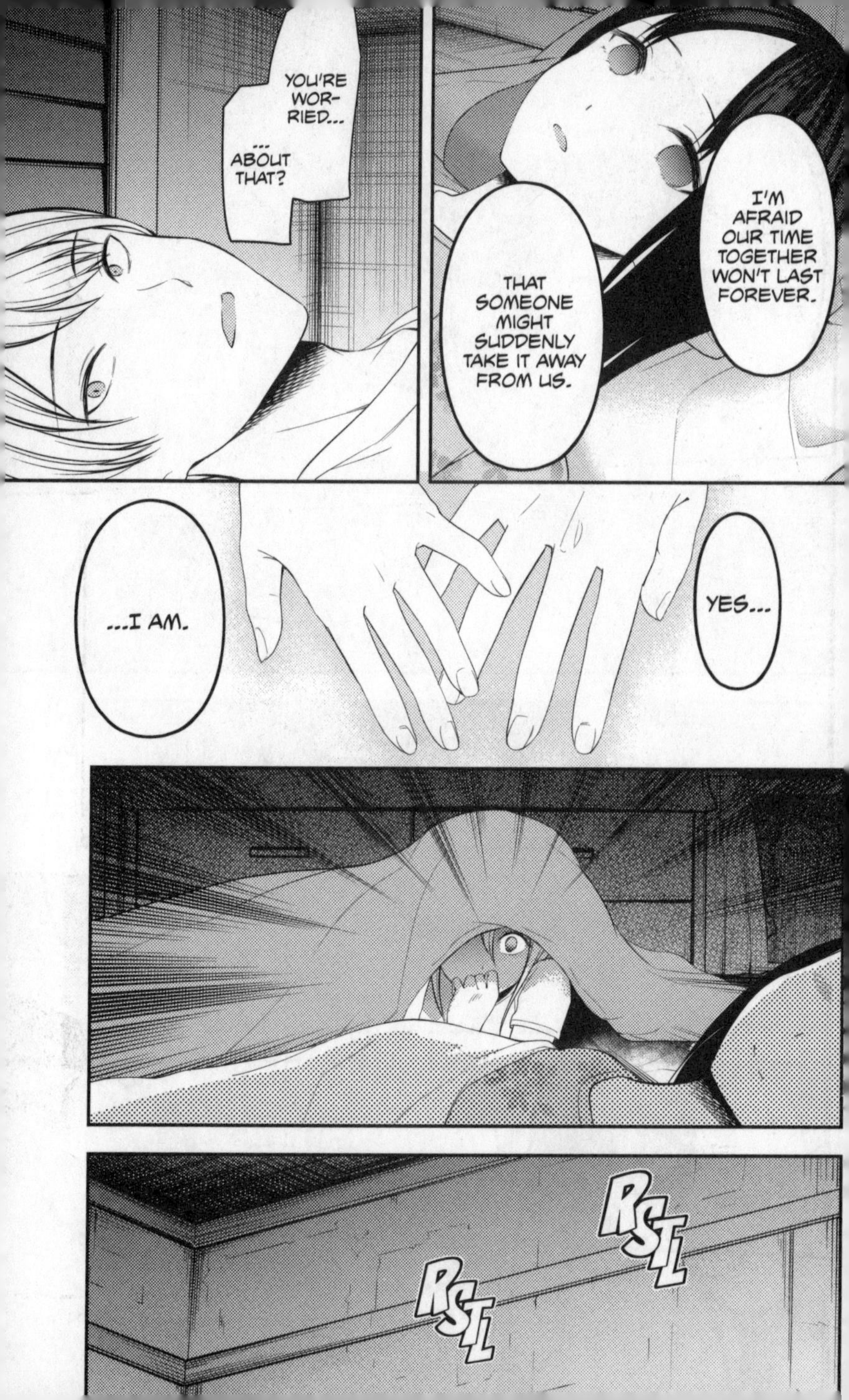
I'M AFRAID OUR TIME TOGETHER WON'T LAST FOREVER.
THAT SOMEONE MIGHT SUDDENLY TAKE IT AWAY FROM US.
YOU'RE WORRIED...
...ABOUT THAT?
YES...
...I AM.
RSTL
RSTL

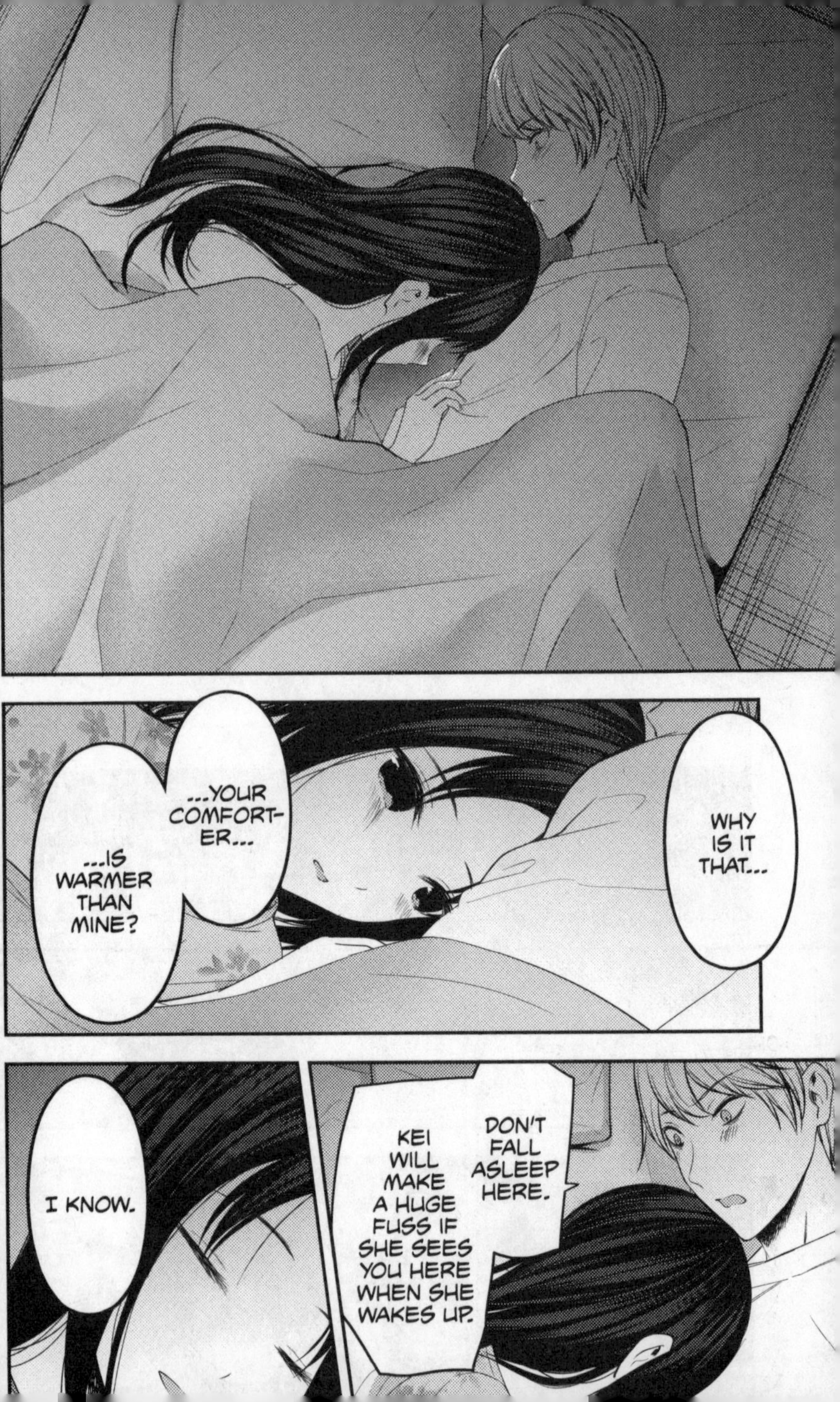
WHY IS IT THAT...
...YOUR COMFORTER...
...IS WARMER THAN MINE?
DON'T FALL ASLEEP HERE.
KEI WILL MAKE A HUGE FUSS IF SHE SEES YOU HERE WHEN SHE WAKES UP.
I KNOW.

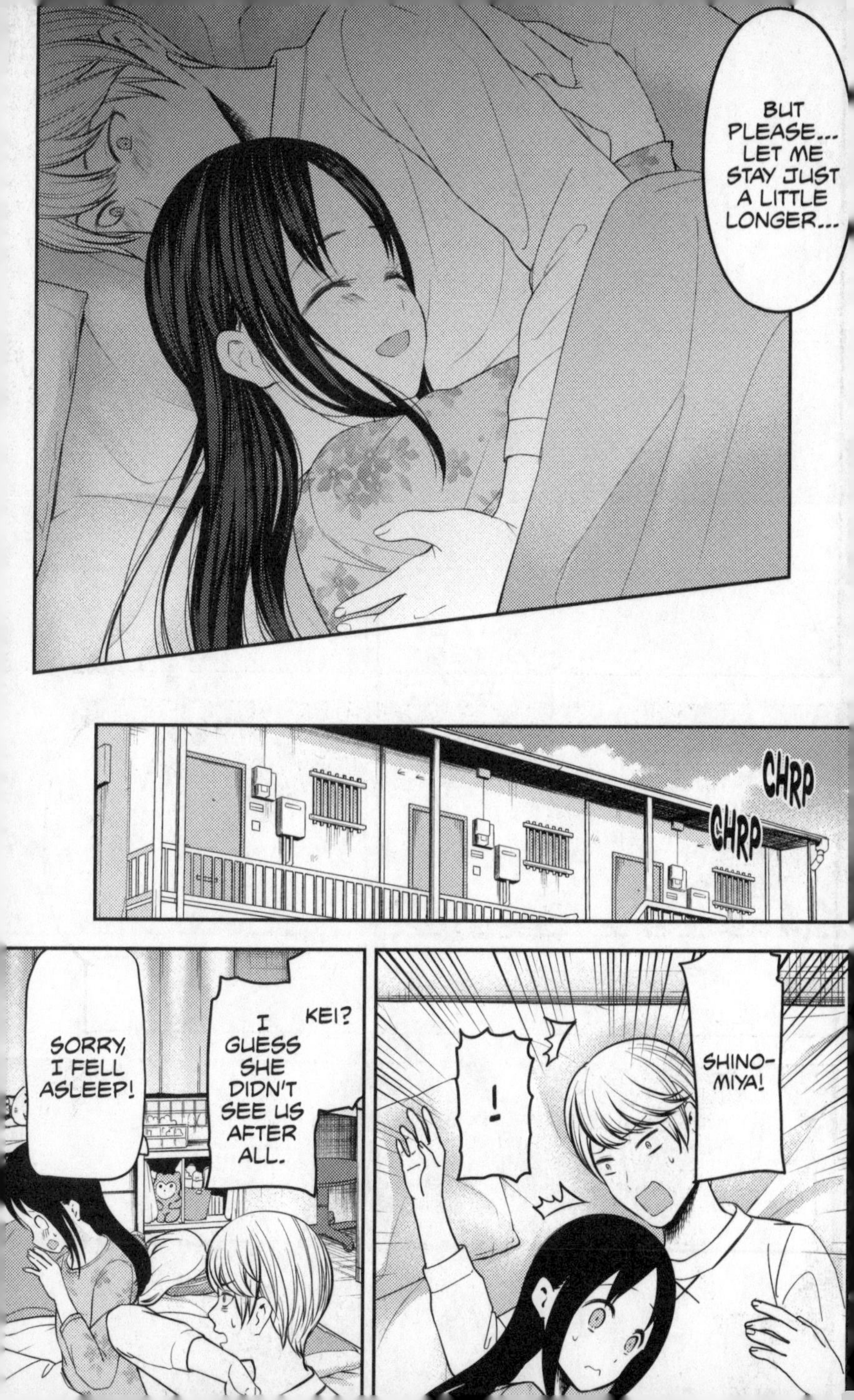
BUT PLEASE... LET ME STAY JUST A LITTLE LONGER...
CHRP
CHRP
SHINO-MIYA!
!
KEI?
I GUESS SHE DIDN'T SEE US AFTER ALL.
SORRY, I FELL ASLEEP!

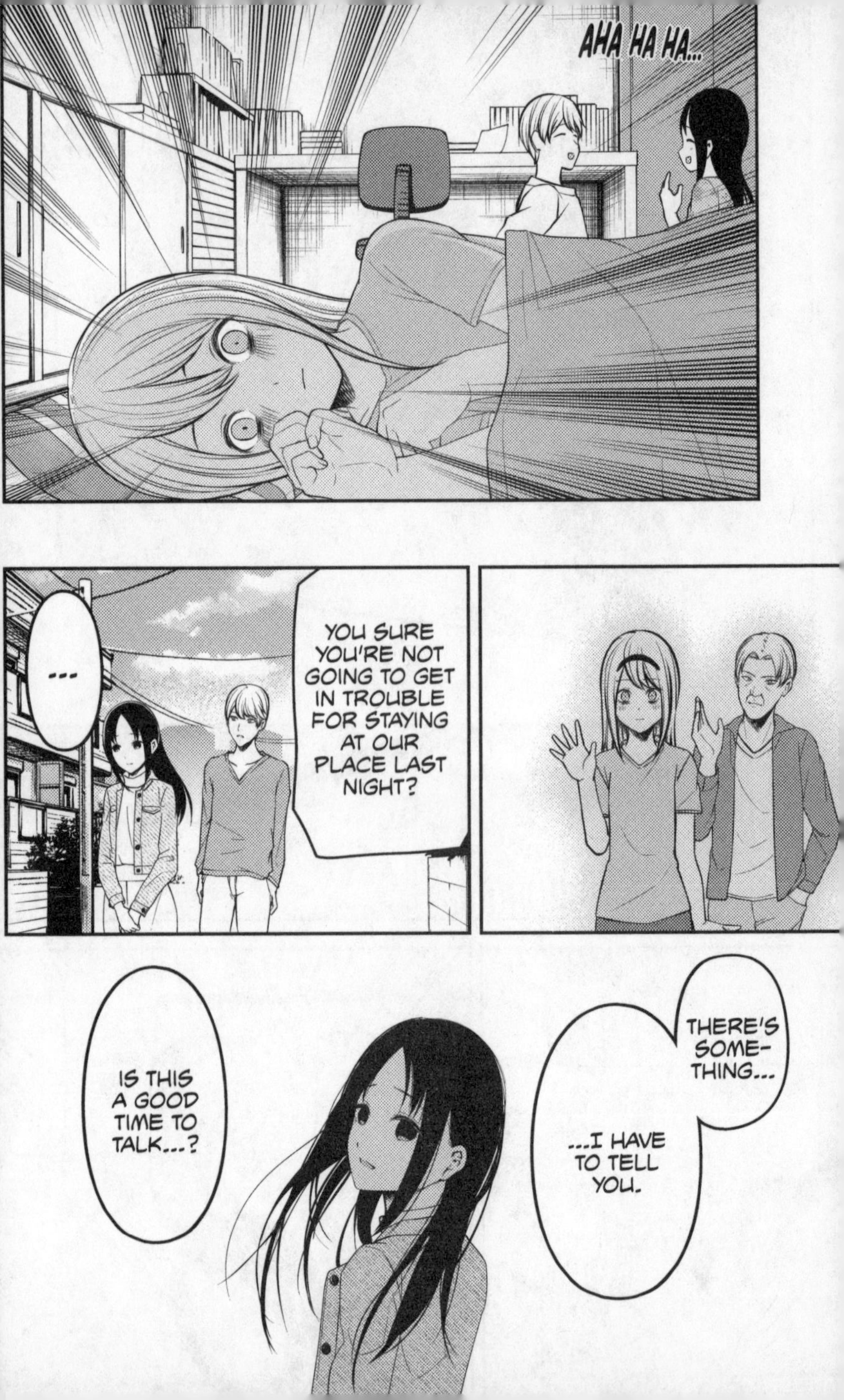
AHA HA HA...
YOU SURE YOU'RE NOT GOING TO GET IN TROUBLE FOR STAYING AT OUR PLACE LAST NIGHT?
...
THERE'S SOME-THING...
...I HAVE TO TELL YOU.
IS THIS A GOOD TIME TO TALK...?

Awake all night

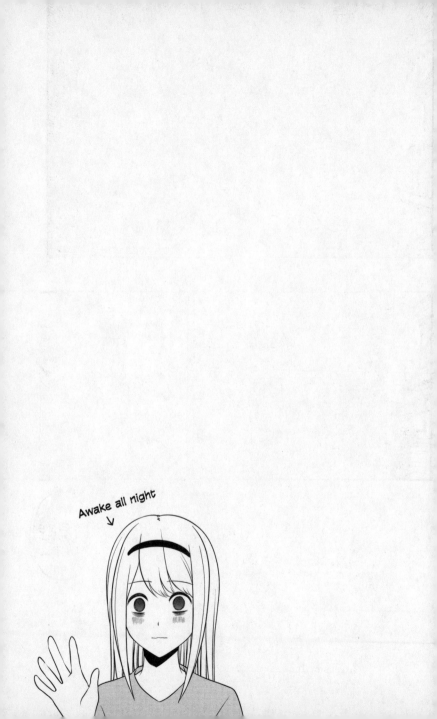

KAGUYA-SAMA
LOVE IS WAR

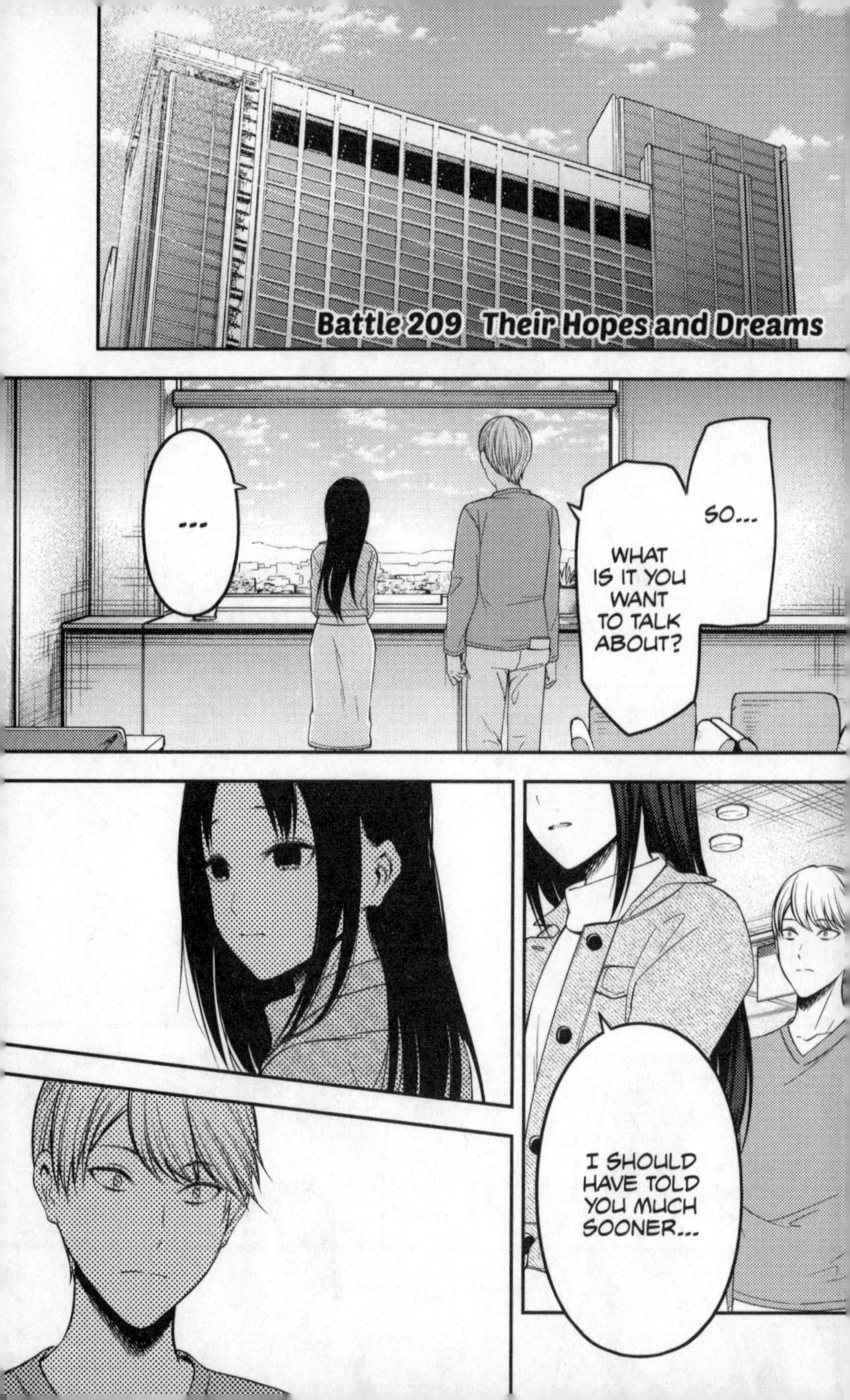
Battle 209 Their Hopes and Dreams
SO... WHAT IS IT YOU WANT TO TALK ABOUT?
...
I SHOULD HAVE TOLD YOU MUCH SOONER...

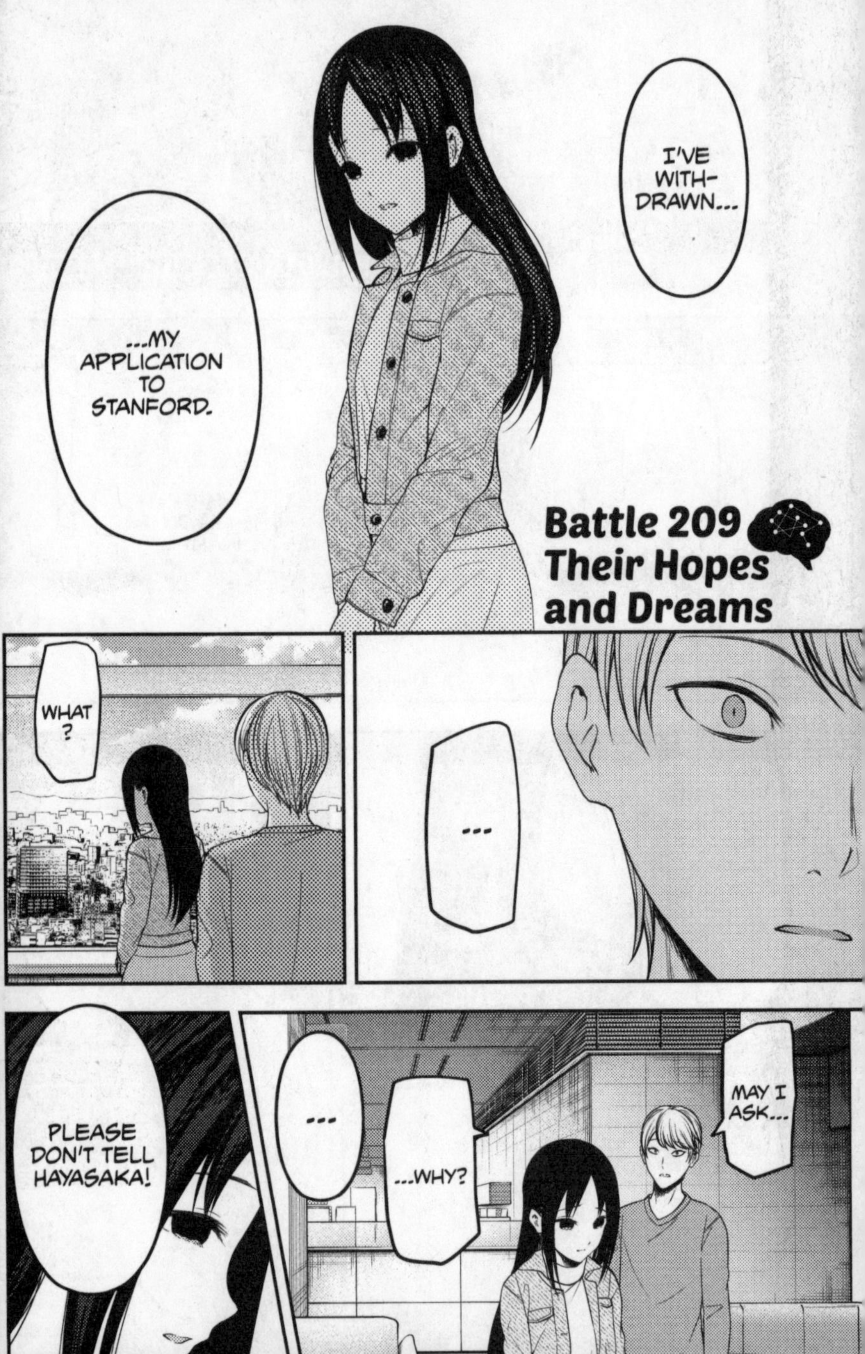
I'VE WITH-DRAWN...
...MY APPLICATION TO STANFORD.
Battle 209 Their Hopes and Dreams
...
WHAT?
MAY I ASK...
...WHY?
...
PLEASE DON'T TELL HAYASAKA!

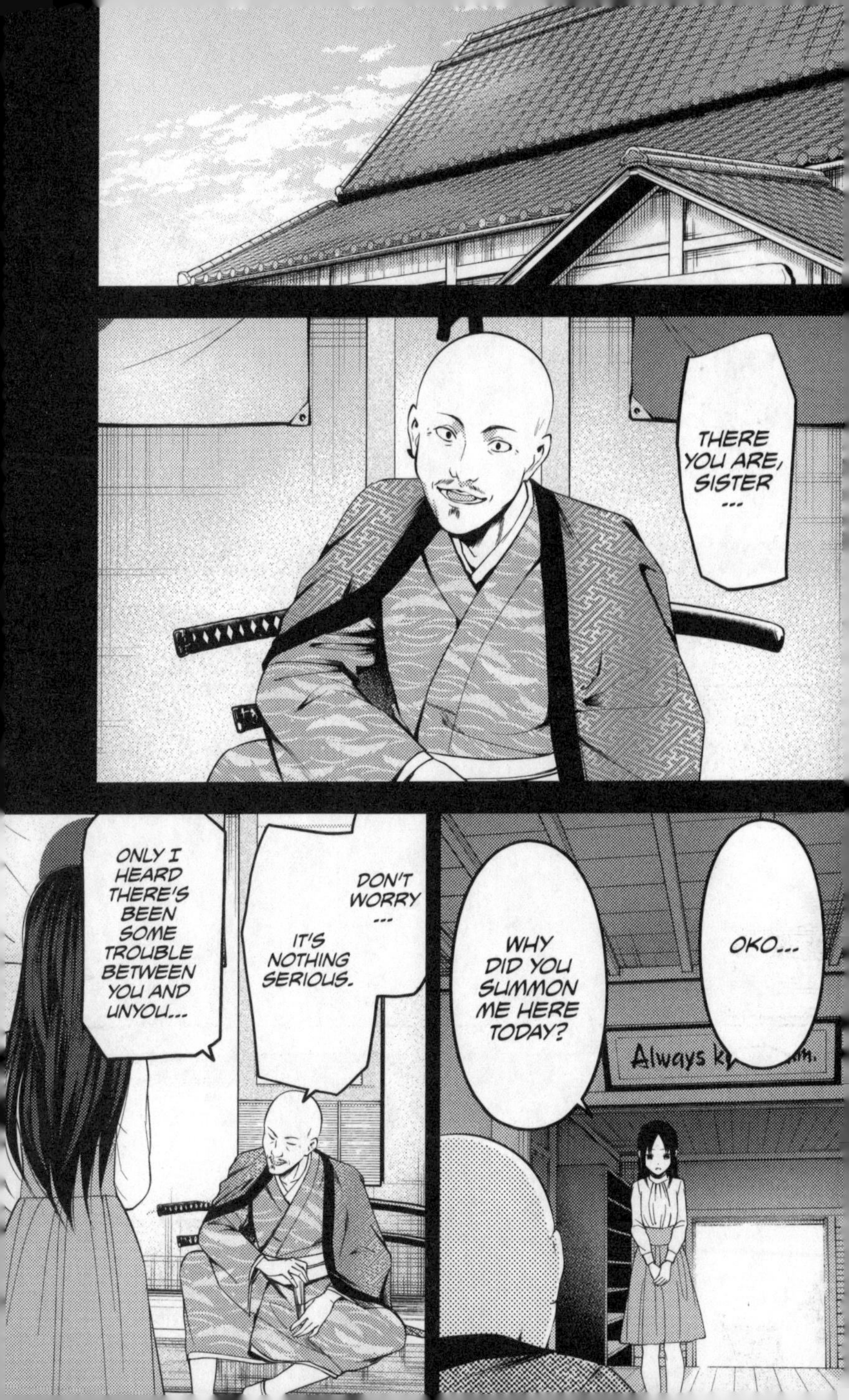
THERE YOU ARE, SISTER...
OKO...
WHY DID YOU SUMMON ME HERE TODAY?
DON'T WORRY...
IT'S NOTHING SERIOUS.
ONLY I HEARD THERE'S BEEN SOME TROUBLE BETWEEN YOU AND UNYOU...

I WAS WORRIED ABOUT MY SWEET LITTLE SISTER. I AM YOUR BIG BROTHER AFTER ALL.
YOU NEEDN'T CONCERN YOURSELF. IT DOESN'T AFFECT YOU.
YES, IT DOES.
THE HAYASAKA FAMILY ARE MY PAWNS.
IF YOU TWO QUARRELED OVER A HAYASAKA, I AM TO BLAME.
I'M THE ONE WHO LOANED AI HAYASAKA TO YOU OUT OF CONCERN FOR YOUR WELL-BEING.

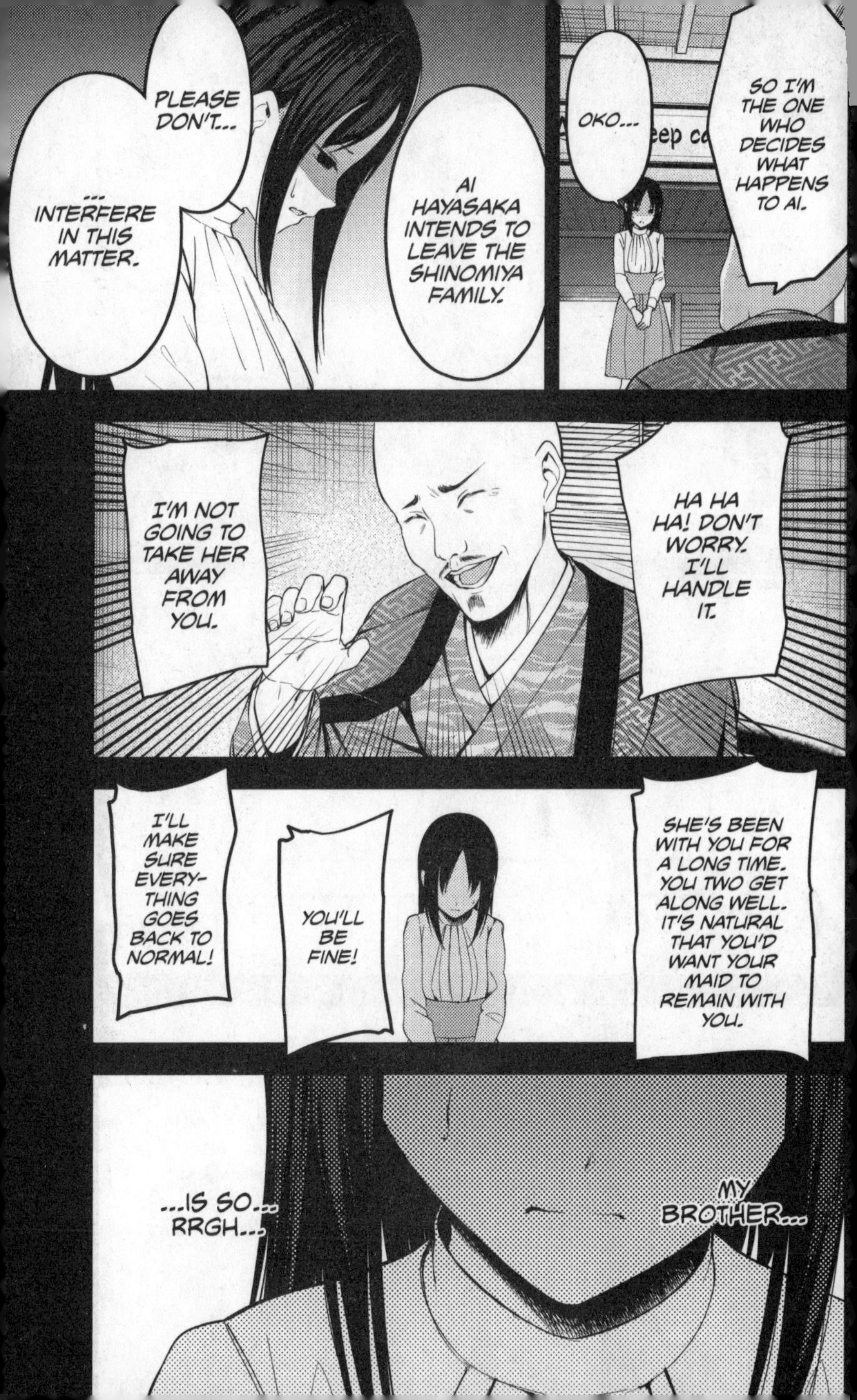
SO I'M THE ONE WHO DECIDES WHAT HAPPENS TO AI.
OKO...
AI HAYASAKA INTENDS TO LEAVE THE SHINOMIYA FAMILY.
PLEASE DON'T...
...INTERFERE IN THIS MATTER.
HA HA HA! DON'T WORRY. I'LL HANDLE IT.
I'M NOT GOING TO TAKE HER AWAY FROM YOU.
SHE'S BEEN WITH YOU FOR A LONG TIME. YOU TWO GET ALONG WELL. IT'S NATURAL THAT YOU'D WANT YOUR MAID TO REMAIN WITH YOU.
YOU'LL BE FINE!
I'LL MAKE SURE EVERY-THING GOES BACK TO NORMAL!
MY BROTHER...
...IS SO... RRGH...

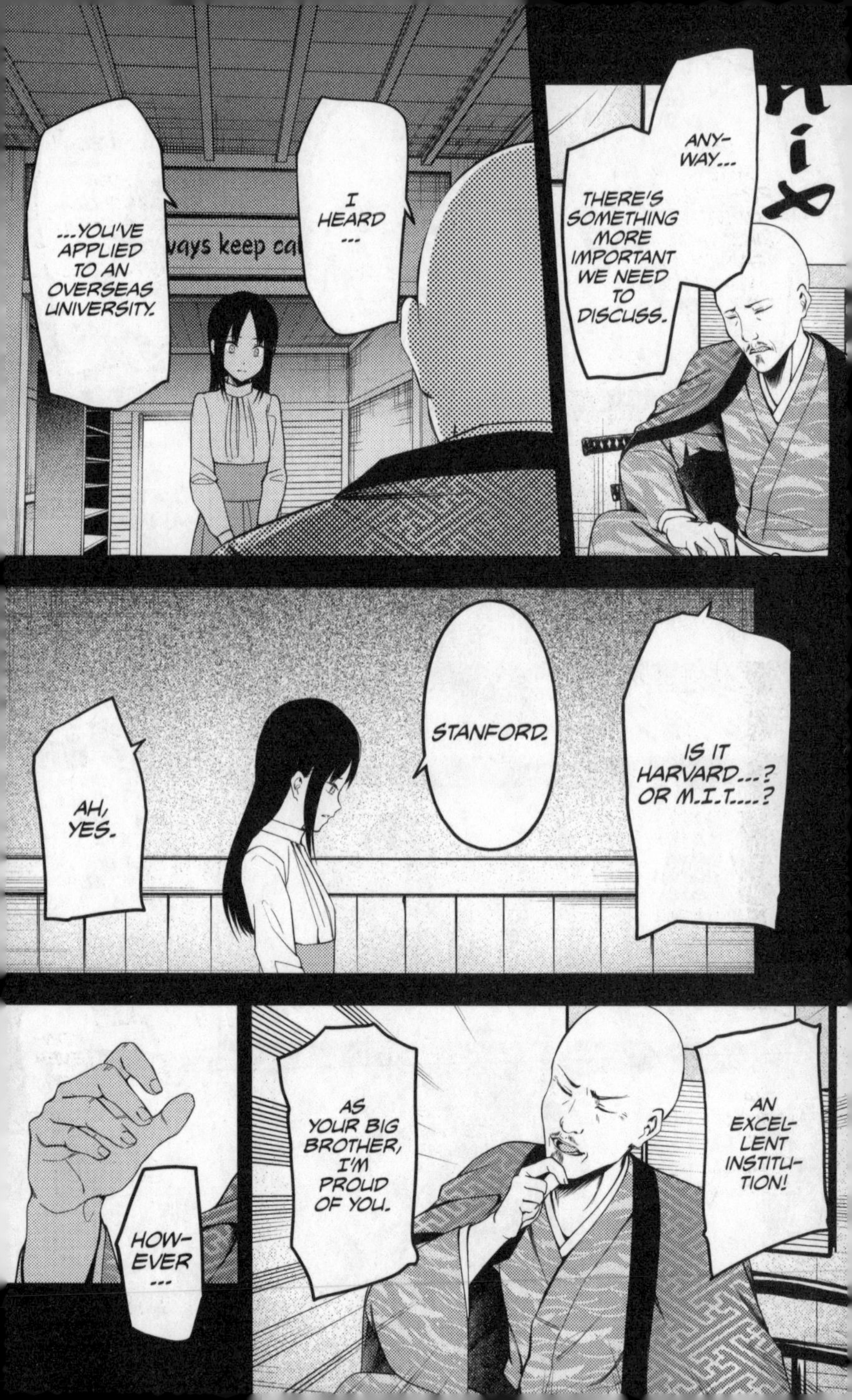
ANY-WAY...
THERE'S SOMETHING MORE IMPORTANT WE NEED TO DISCUSS.
I HEARD ---
...YOU'VE APPLIED TO AN OVERSEAS UNIVERSITY.
IS IT HARVARD...? OR M.I.T....?
STANFORD.
AH, YES.
AN EXCEL-LENT INSTITU-TION!
AS YOUR BIG BROTHER, I'M PROUD OF YOU.
HOW-EVER ---

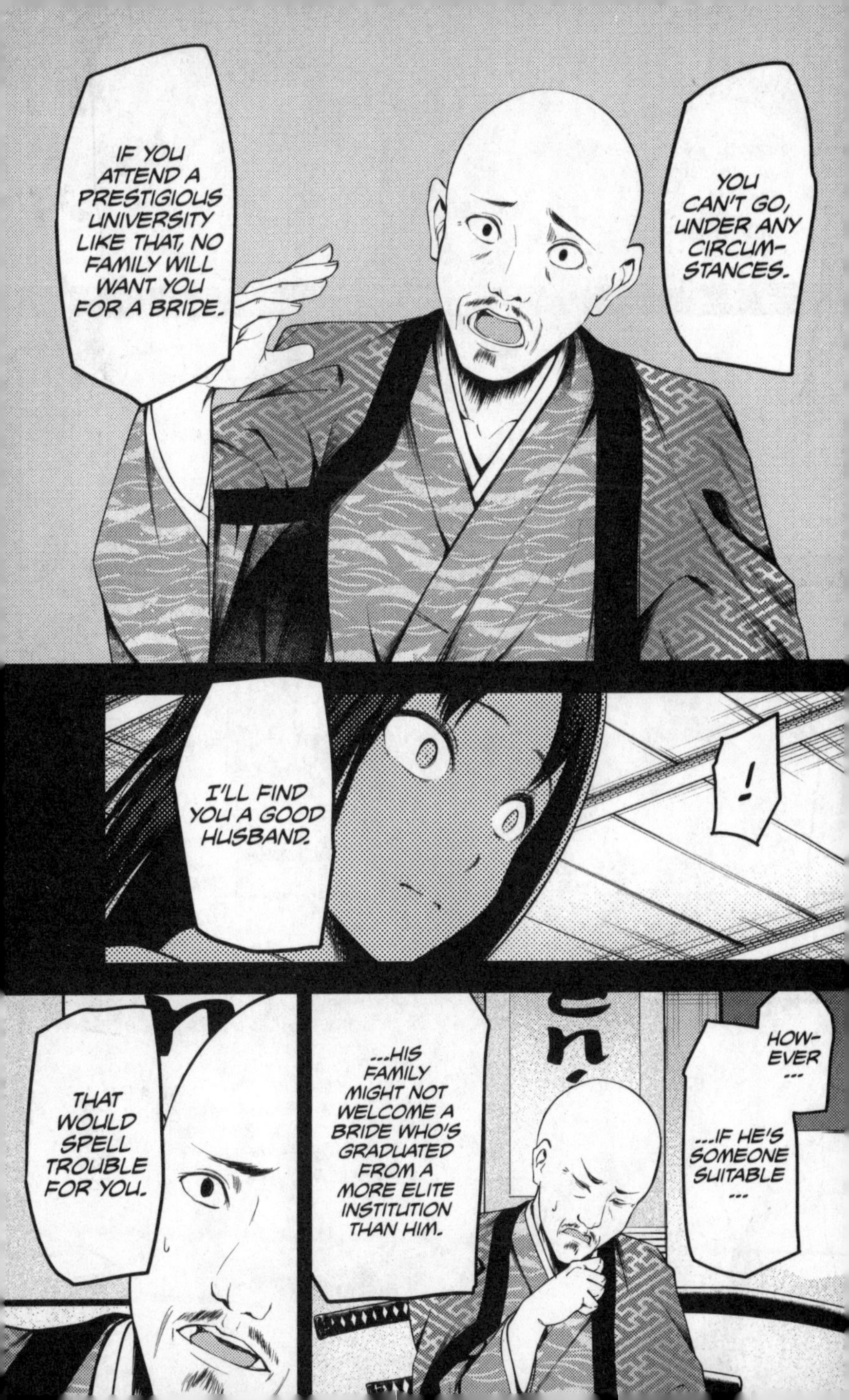

YOU CAN'T GO, UNDER ANY CIRCUM-STANCES.
IF YOU ATTEND A PRESTIGIOUS UNIVERSITY LIKE THAT, NO FAMILY WILL WANT YOU FOR A BRIDE.
!
I'LL FIND YOU A GOOD HUSBAND.
HOW-EVER...
...IF HE'S SOMEONE SUITABLE...
...HIS FAMILY MIGHT NOT WELCOME A BRIDE WHO'S GRADUATED FROM A MORE ELITE INSTITUTION THAN HIM.
THAT WOULD SPELL TROUBLE FOR YOU.

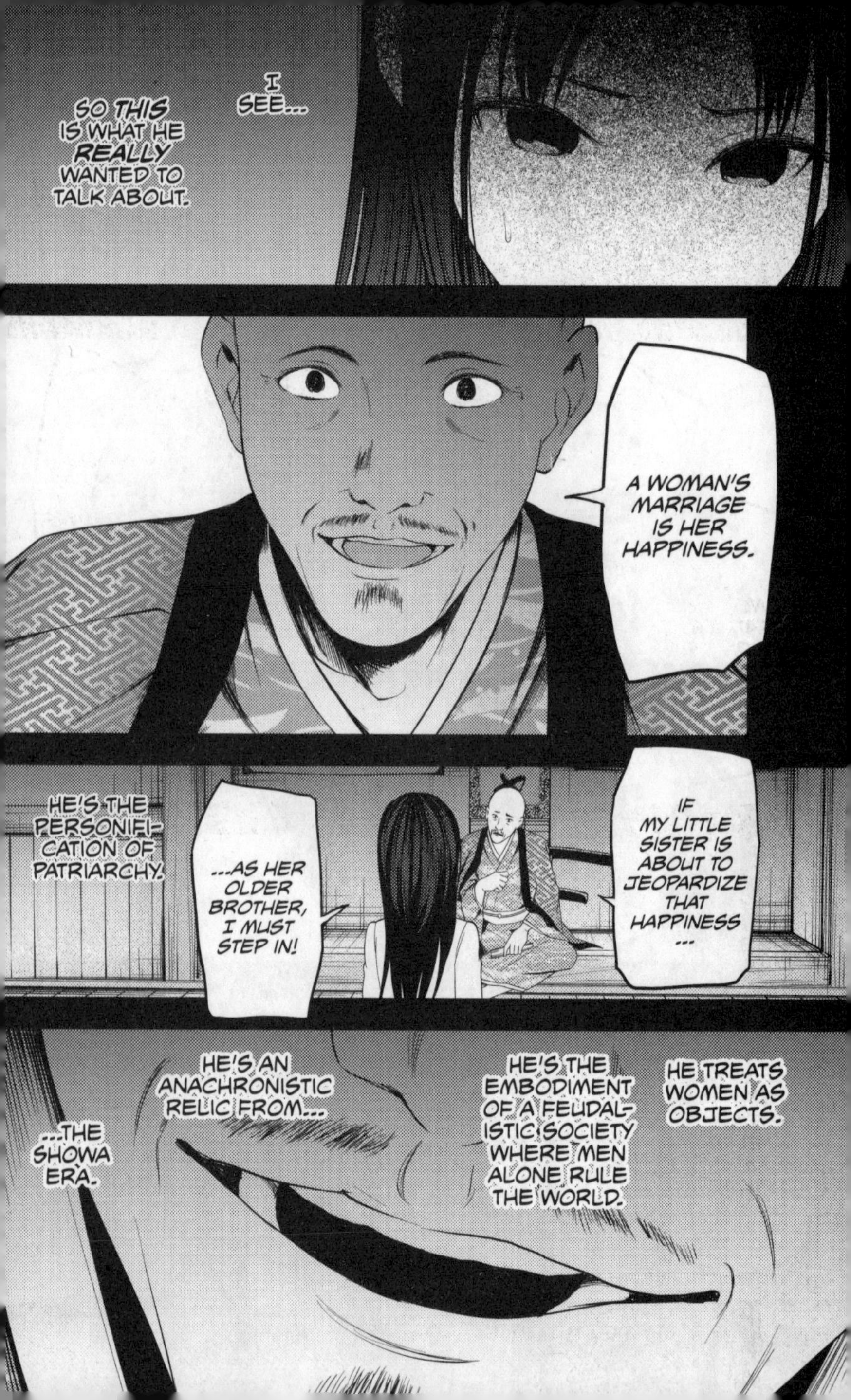
I SEE...
SO THIS IS WHAT HE REALLY WANTED TO TALK ABOUT.
A WOMAN'S MARRIAGE IS HER HAPPINESS.
IF MY LITTLE SISTER IS ABOUT TO JEOPARDIZE THAT HAPPINESS ...
...AS HER OLDER BROTHER, I MUST STEP IN!
HE'S THE PERSONIFI-CATION OF PATRIARCHY.
HE TREATS WOMEN AS OBJECTS.
HE'S THE EMBODIMENT OF A FEUDAL-ISTIC SOCIETY WHERE MEN ALONE RULE THE WORLD.
HE'S AN ANACHRONISTIC RELIC FROM...
...THE SHOWA ERA.

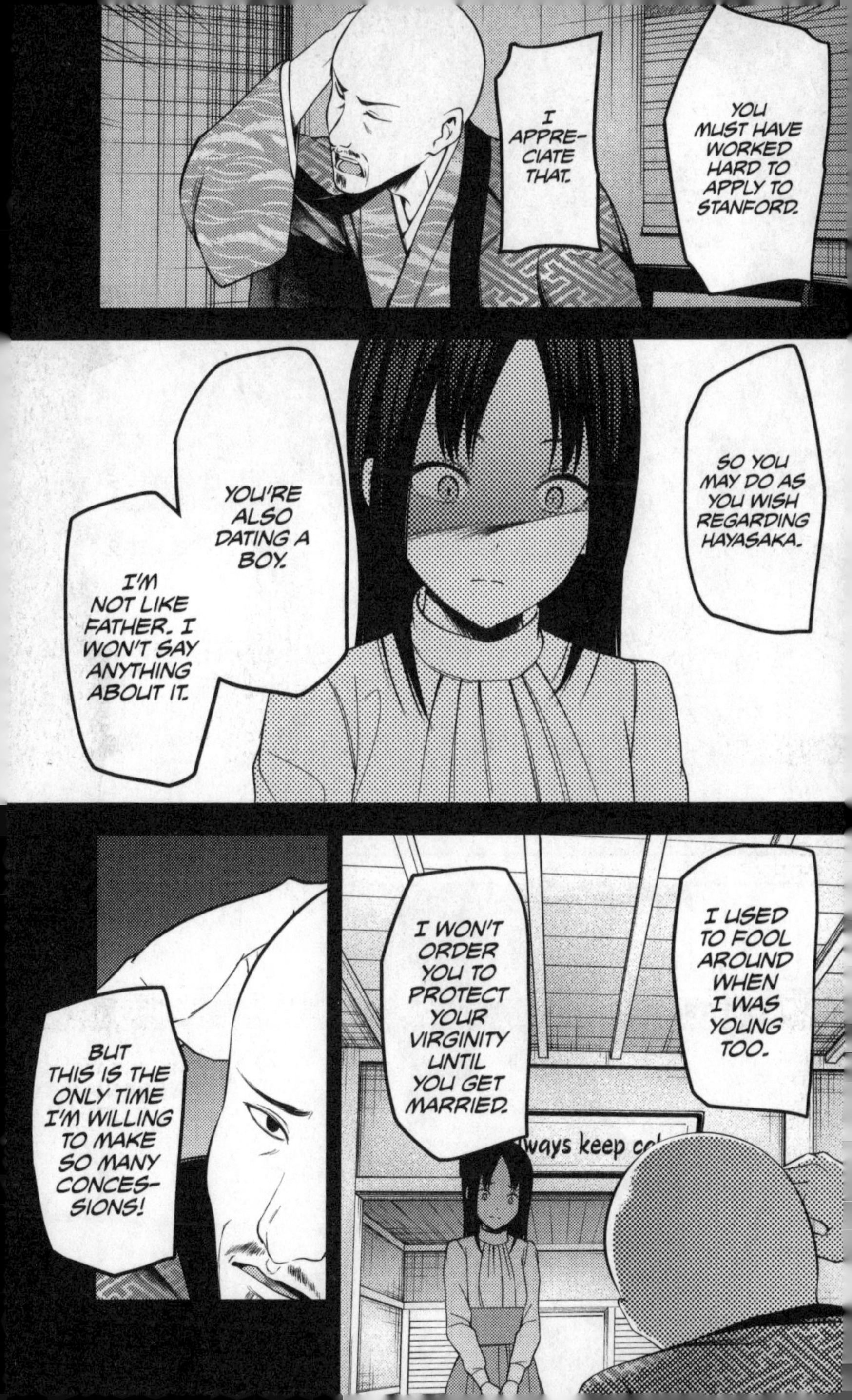
YOU MUST HAVE WORKED HARD TO APPLY TO STANFORD.
I APPRECIATE THAT.
SO YOU MAY DO AS YOU WISH REGARDING HAYASAKA.
YOU'RE ALSO DATING A BOY.
I'M NOT LIKE FATHER. I WON'T SAY ANYTHING ABOUT IT.
I USED TO FOOL AROUND WHEN I WAS YOUNG TOO.
I WON'T ORDER YOU TO PROTECT YOUR VIRGINITY UNTIL YOU GET MARRIED.
BUT THIS IS THE ONLY TIME I'M WILLING TO MAKE SO MANY CONCESSIONS!

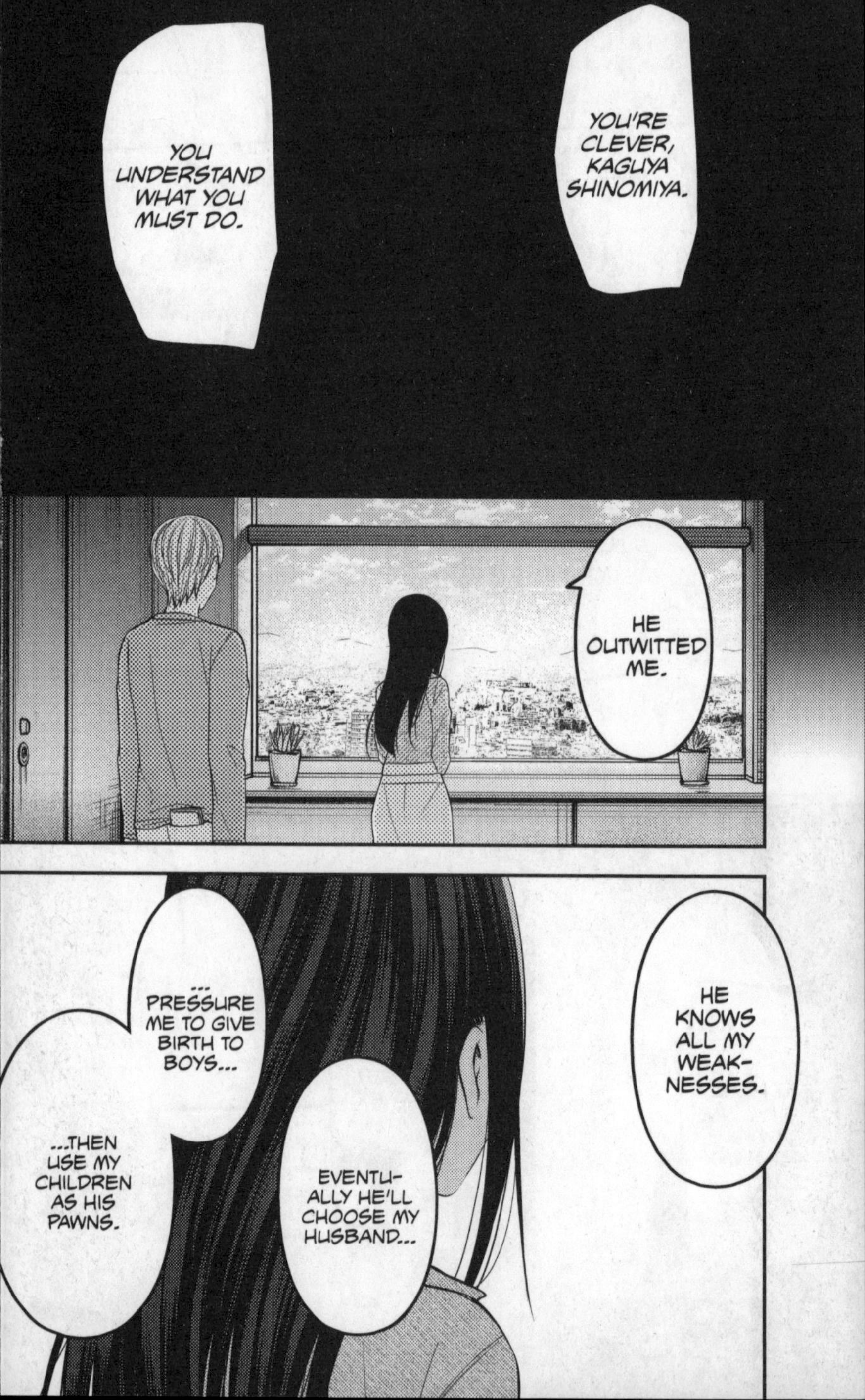
YOU'RE CLEVER, KAGUYA SHINOMIYA.
YOU UNDERSTAND WHAT YOU MUST DO.
HE OUTWITTED ME.
HE KNOWS ALL MY WEAK-NESSES.
EVENTU-ALLY HE'LL CHOOSE MY HUSBAND...
... PRESSURE ME TO GIVE BIRTH TO BOYS...
...THEN USE MY CHILDREN AS HIS PAWNS.

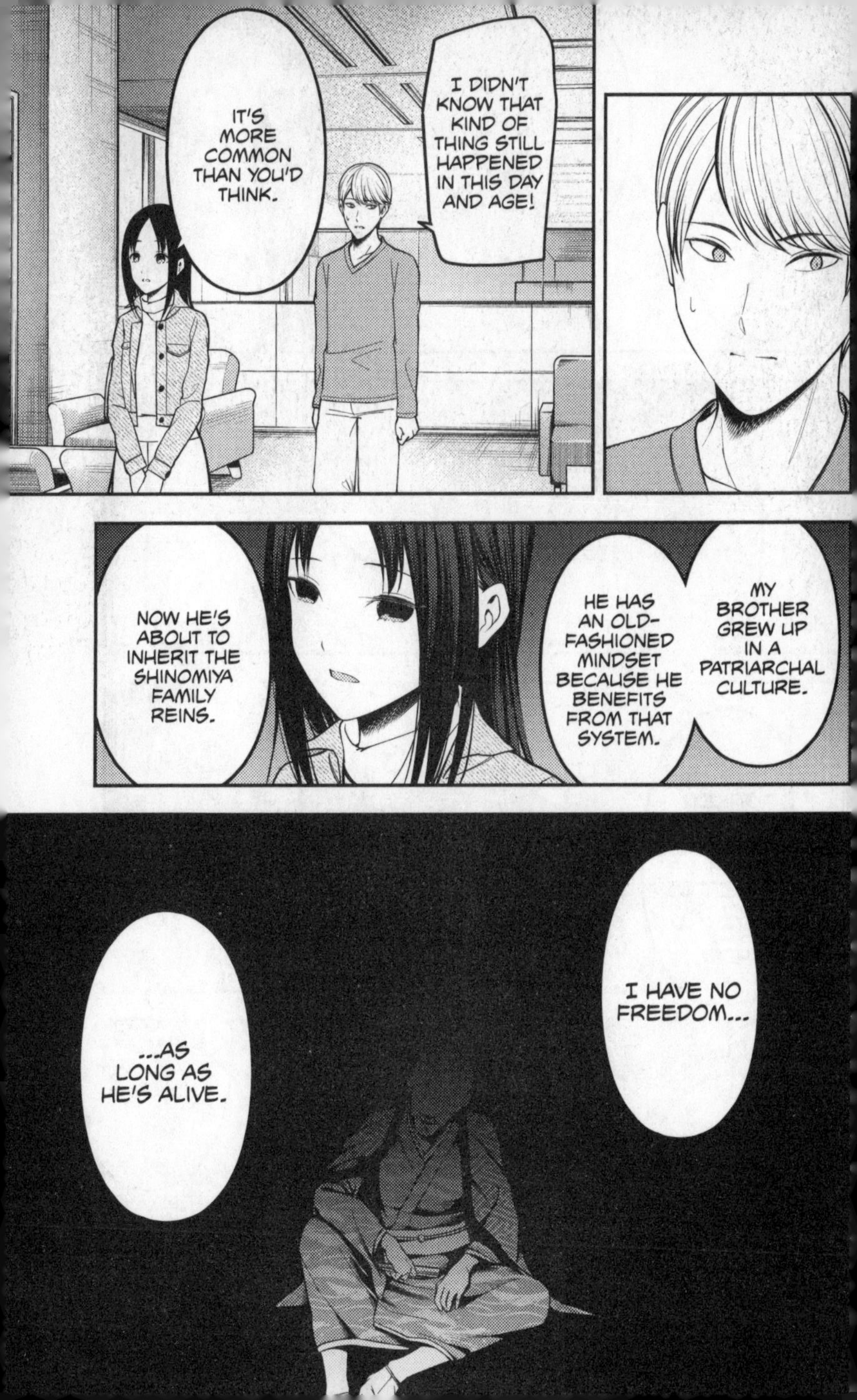
I DIDN'T KNOW THAT KIND OF THING STILL HAPPENED IN THIS DAY AND AGE!
IT'S MORE COMMON THAN YOU'D THINK.
MY BROTHER GREW UP IN A PATRIARCHAL CULTURE.
HE HAS AN OLD-FASHIONED MINDSET BECAUSE HE BENEFITS FROM THAT SYSTEM.
NOW HE'S ABOUT TO INHERIT THE SHINOMIYA FAMILY REINS.
I HAVE NO FREEDOM...
...AS LONG AS HE'S ALIVE.

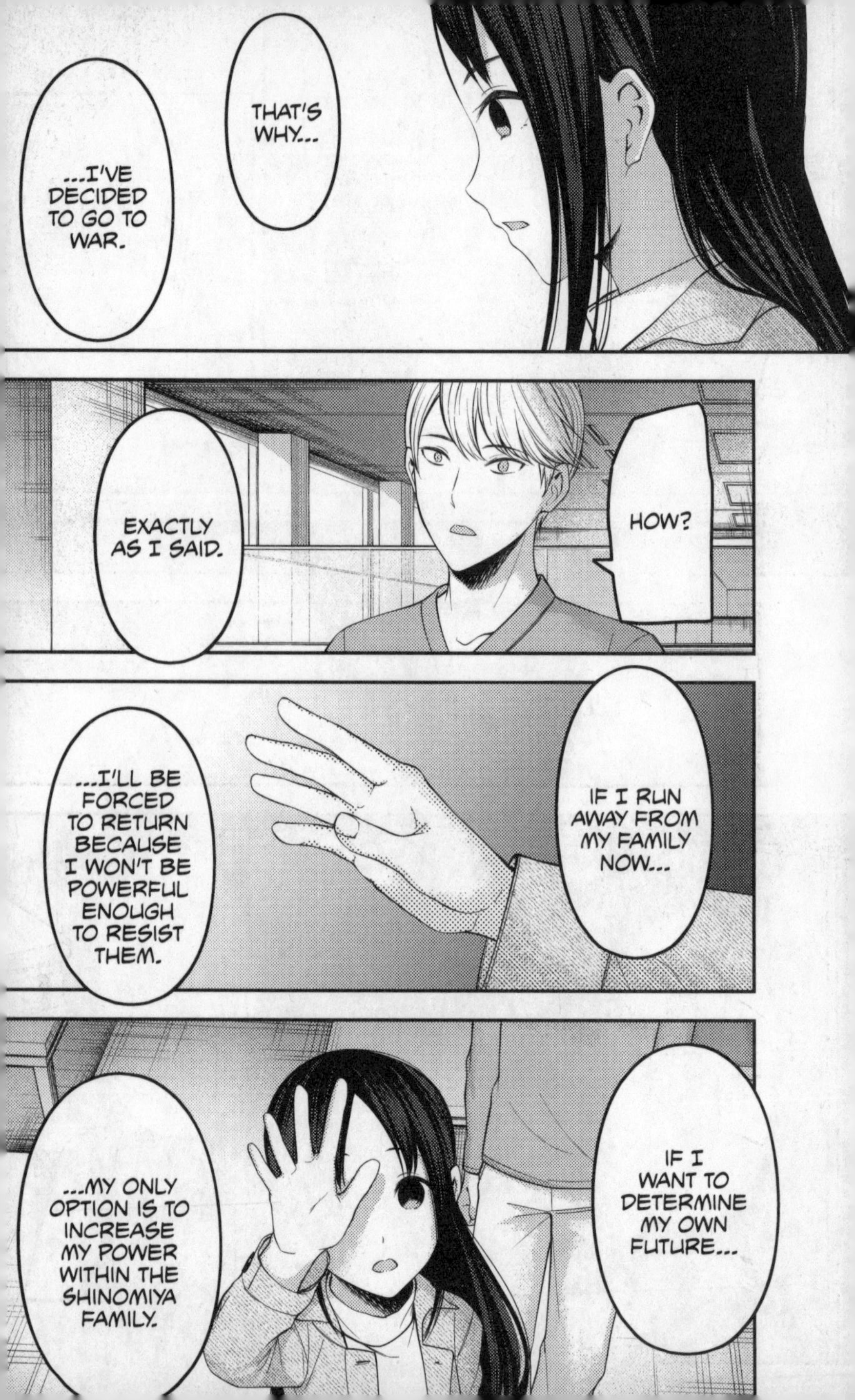
THAT'S WHY...
...I'VE DECIDED TO GO TO WAR.
HOW?
EXACTLY AS I SAID.
IF I RUN AWAY FROM MY FAMILY NOW...
...I'LL BE FORCED TO RETURN BECAUSE I WON'T BE POWERFUL ENOUGH TO RESIST THEM.
IF I WANT TO DETERMINE MY OWN FUTURE...
...MY ONLY OPTION IS TO INCREASE MY POWER WITHIN THE SHINOMIYA FAMILY.

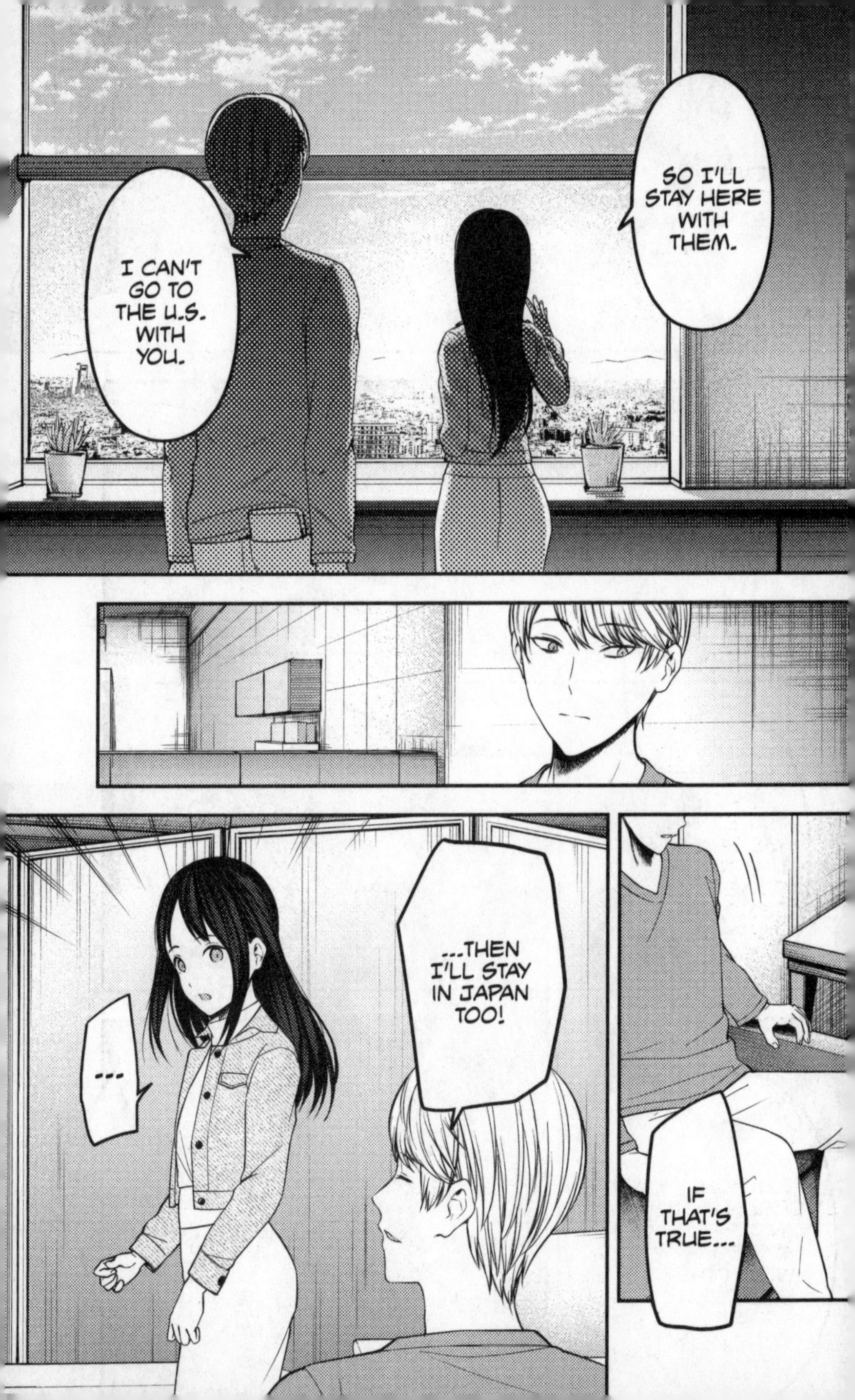
SO I'LL STAY HERE WITH THEM.
I CAN'T GO TO THE U.S. WITH YOU.
IF THAT'S TRUE...
...THEN I'LL STAY IN JAPAN TOO!
...

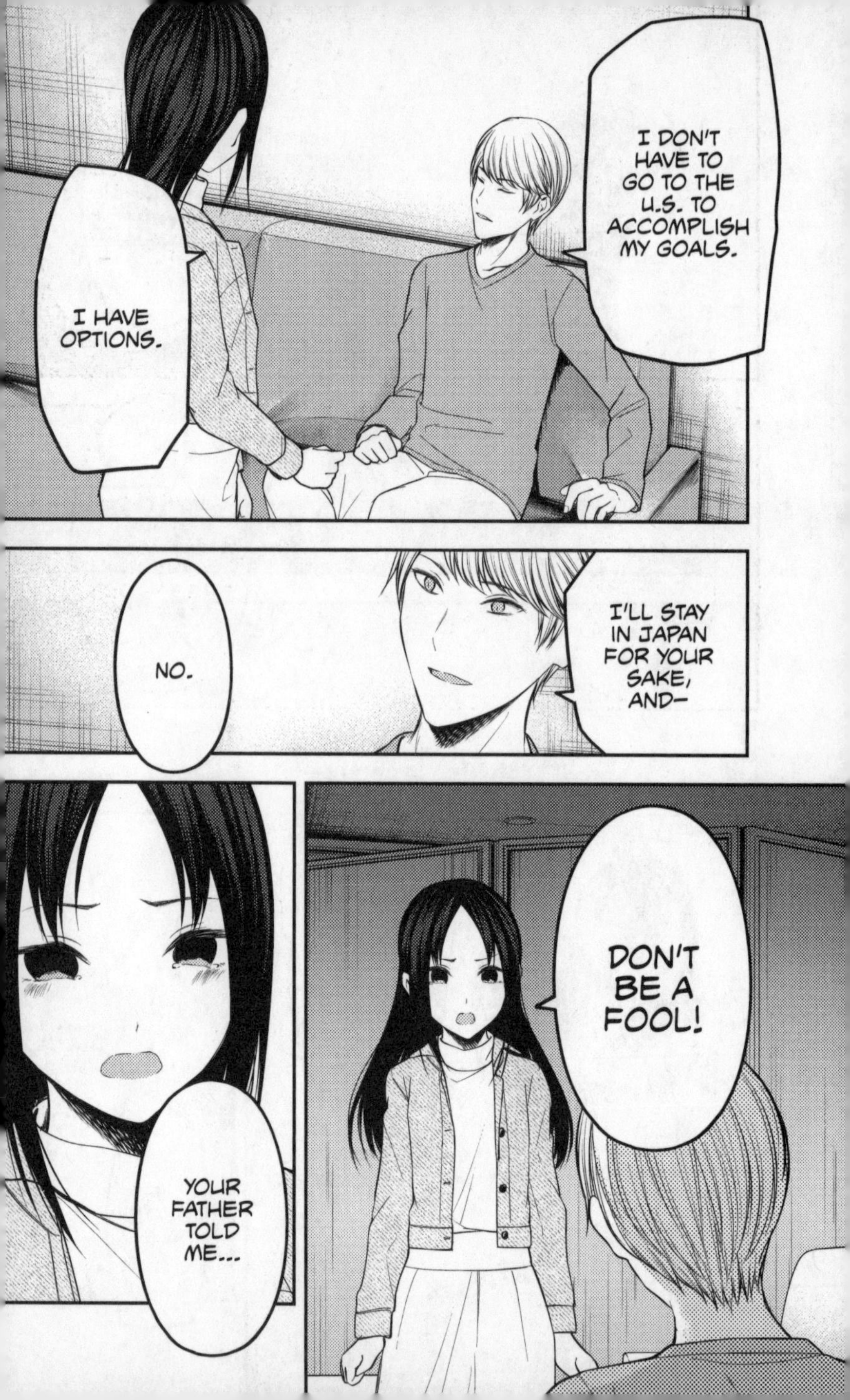
I DON'T HAVE TO GO TO THE U.S. TO ACCOMPLISH MY GOALS.
I HAVE OPTIONS.
I'LL STAY IN JAPAN FOR YOUR SAKE, AND—
NO.
DON'T BE A FOOL!
YOUR FATHER TOLD ME...

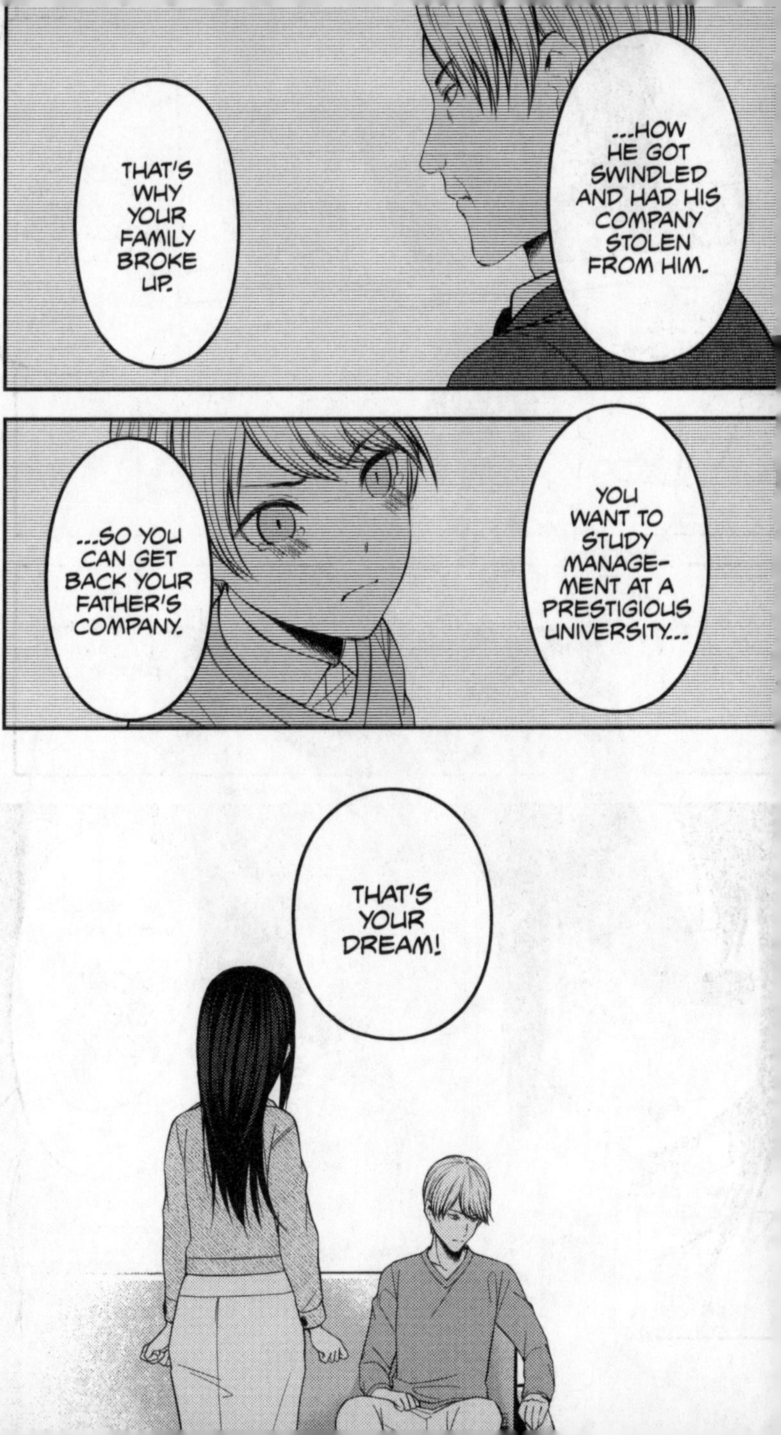
...HOW HE GOT SWINDLED AND HAD HIS COMPANY STOLEN FROM HIM.
THAT'S WHY YOUR FAMILY BROKE UP.
YOU WANT TO STUDY MANAGE-MENT AT A PRESTIGIOUS UNIVERSITY...
...SO YOU CAN GET BACK YOUR FATHER'S COMPANY.
THAT'S YOUR DREAM!

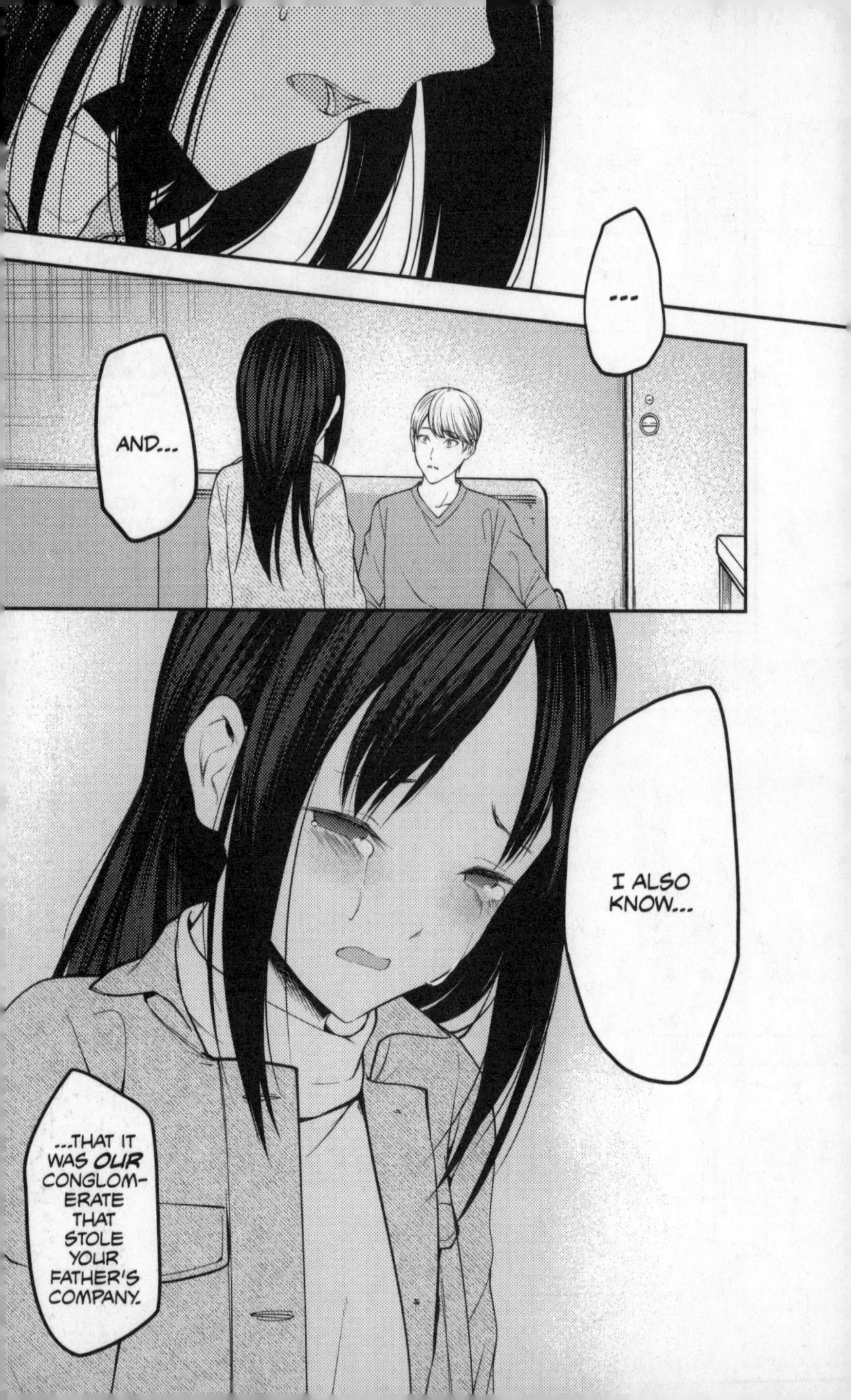
...
AND...
I ALSO KNOW...
...THAT IT WAS *OUR* CONGLOMERATE THAT STOLE YOUR FATHER'S COMPANY.

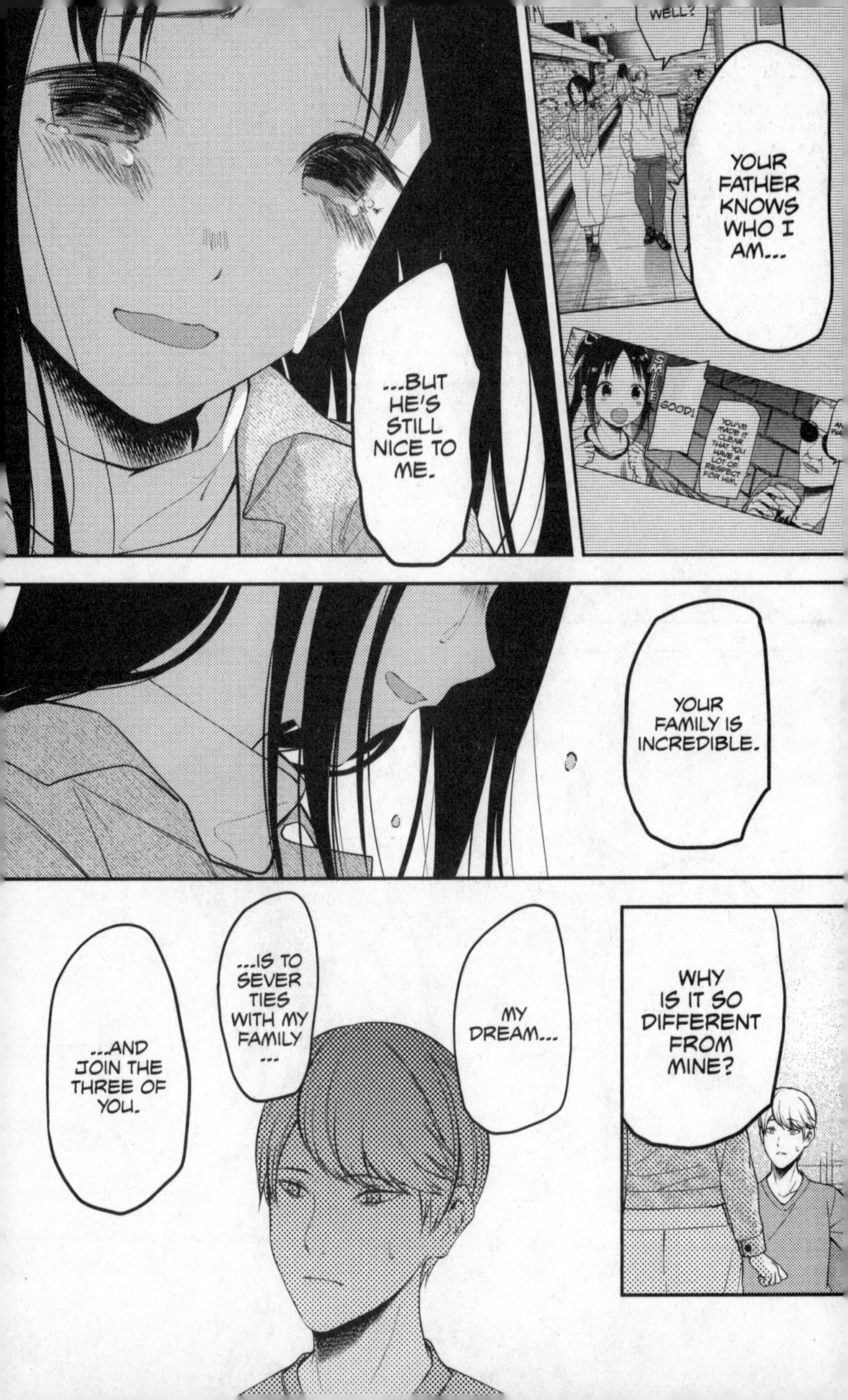
WELL?
YOUR FATHER KNOWS WHO I AM...
SMILE
GOOD!
YOU'VE MADE IT CLEAR THAT YOU HAVE A LOT OF RESPECT FOR HIM.
...BUT HE'S STILL NICE TO ME.
YOUR FAMILY IS INCREDIBLE.
WHY IS IT SO DIFFERENT FROM MINE?
MY DREAM...
...IS TO SEVER TIES WITH MY FAMILY...
...AND JOIN THE THREE OF YOU.

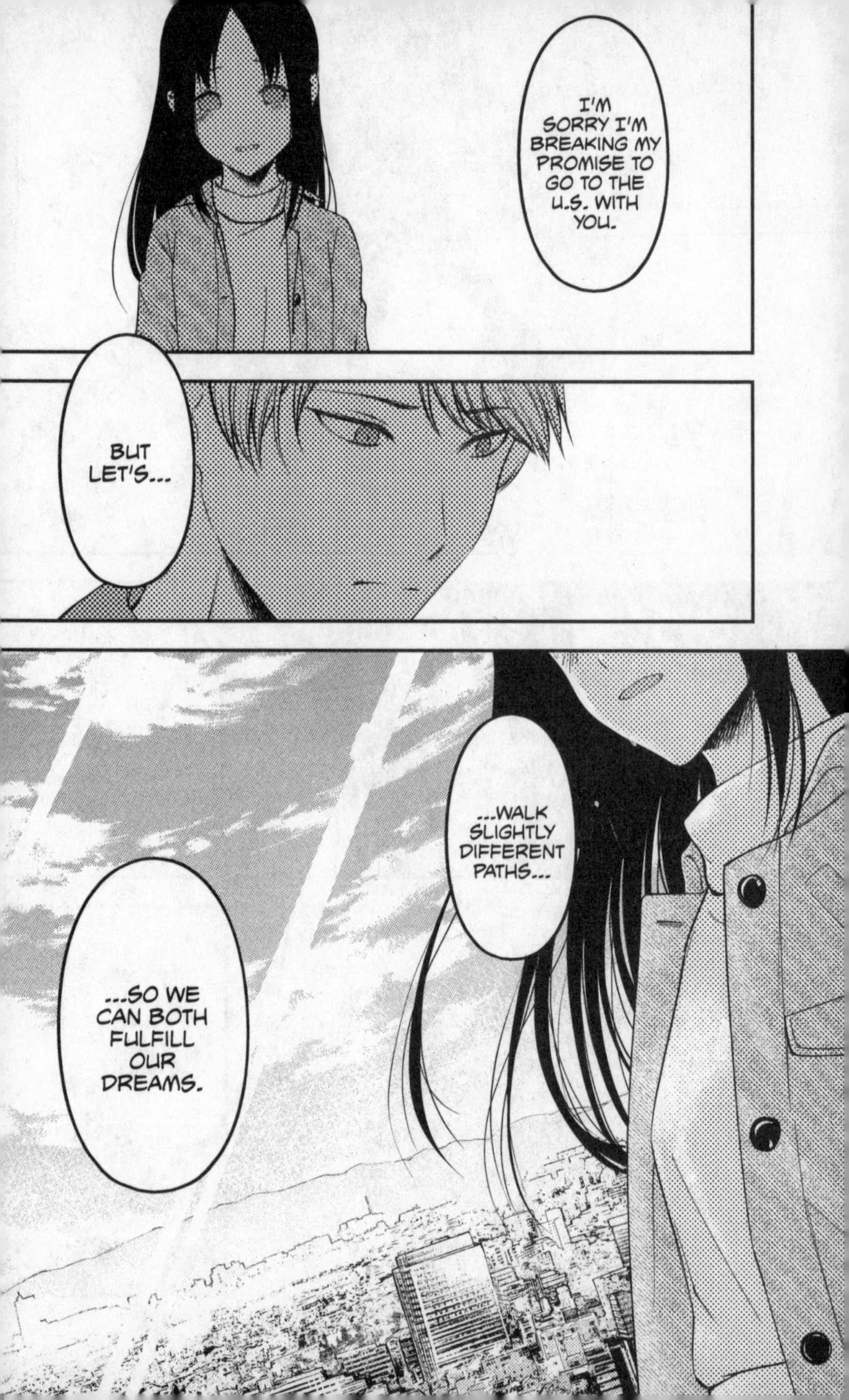
I'M SORRY I'M BREAKING MY PROMISE TO GO TO THE U.S. WITH YOU.
BUT LET'S...
...WALK SLIGHTLY DIFFERENT PATHS...
...SO WE CAN BOTH FULFILL OUR DREAMS.

Now you understand the Shinomiya family!
Old geezer
Ganan (father)
(first wife)
Nayotake (mistress)
(second wife)
Oko (first son)
(second son)
Unyou (third son)
Kaguya (first daughter)
Arrogant
Coward
Liar
Bad girl

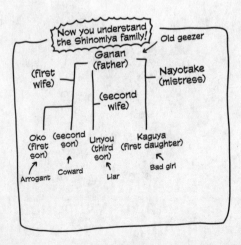

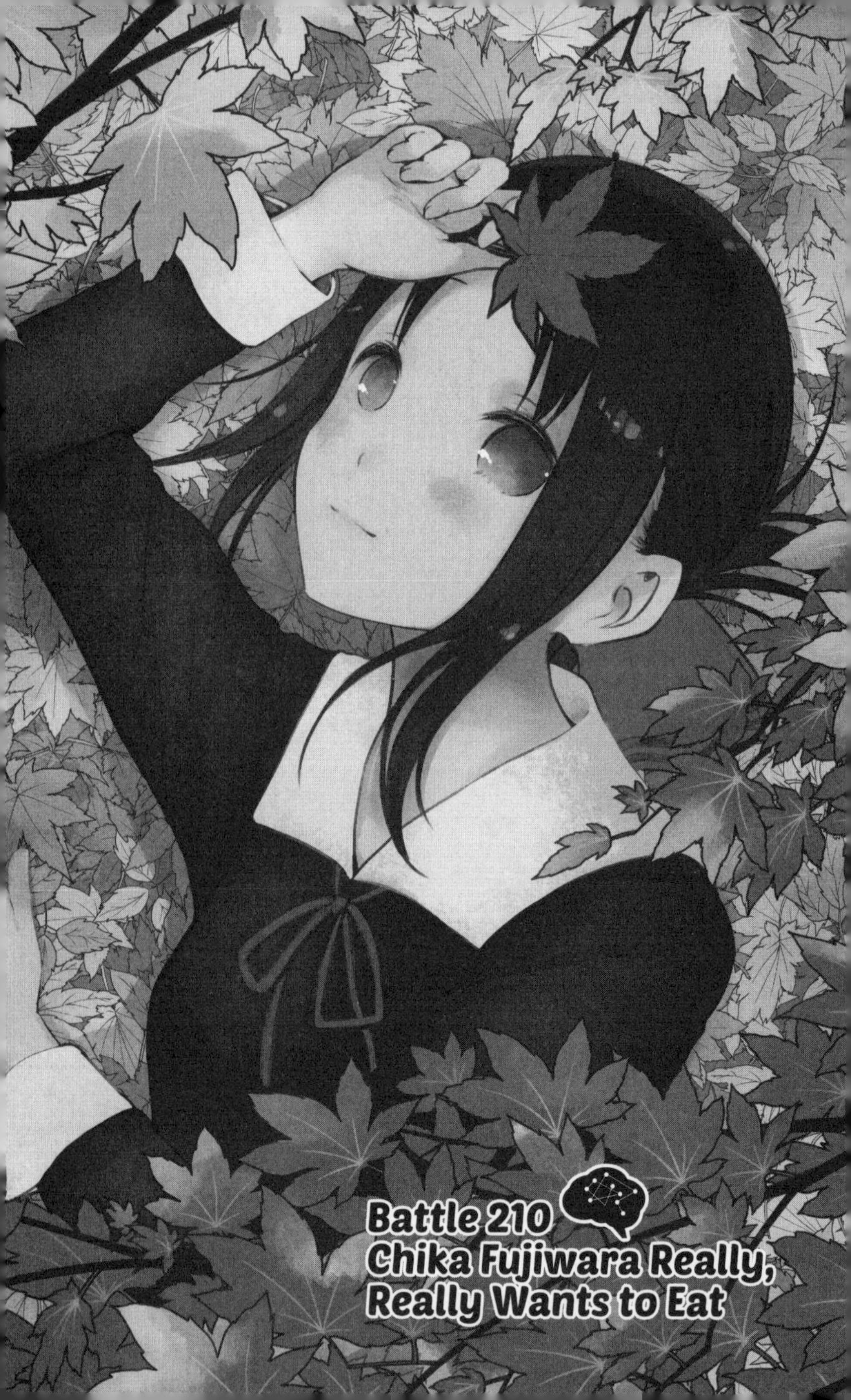
Battle 210
Chika Fujiwara Really, Really Wants to Eat

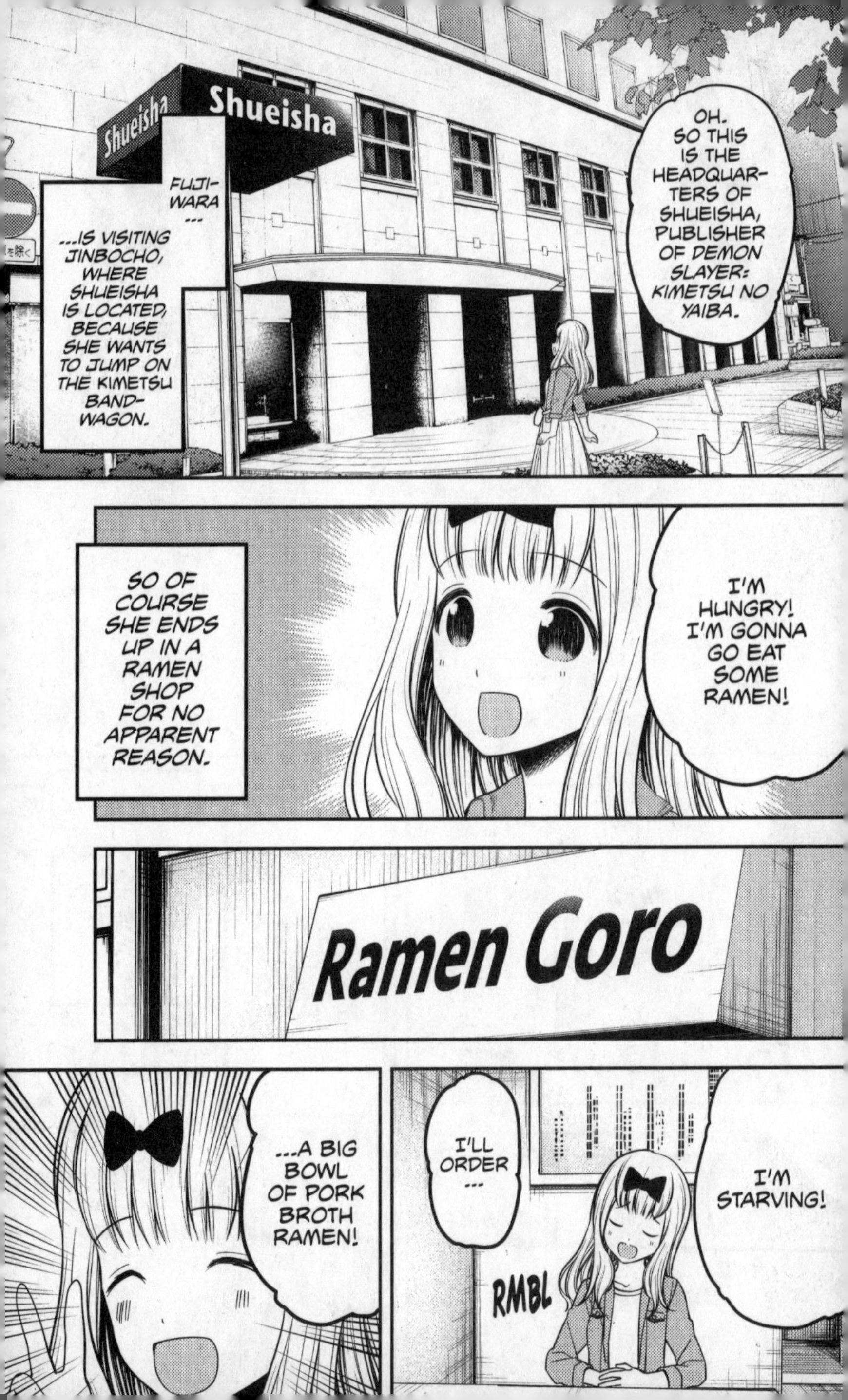
Shueisha
Shueisha
OH. SO THIS IS THE HEADQUARTERS OF SHUEISHA, PUBLISHER OF DEMON SLAYER: KIMETSU NO YAIBA.
FUJIWARA...
...IS VISITING JINBOCHO, WHERE SHUEISHA IS LOCATED, BECAUSE SHE WANTS TO JUMP ON THE KIMETSU BANDWAGON.
I'M HUNGRY! I'M GONNA GO EAT SOME RAMEN!
SO OF COURSE SHE ENDS UP IN A RAMEN SHOP FOR NO APPARENT REASON.
Ramen Goro
I'M STARVING!
RMBL
I'LL ORDER...
...A BIG BOWL OF PORK BROTH RAMEN!

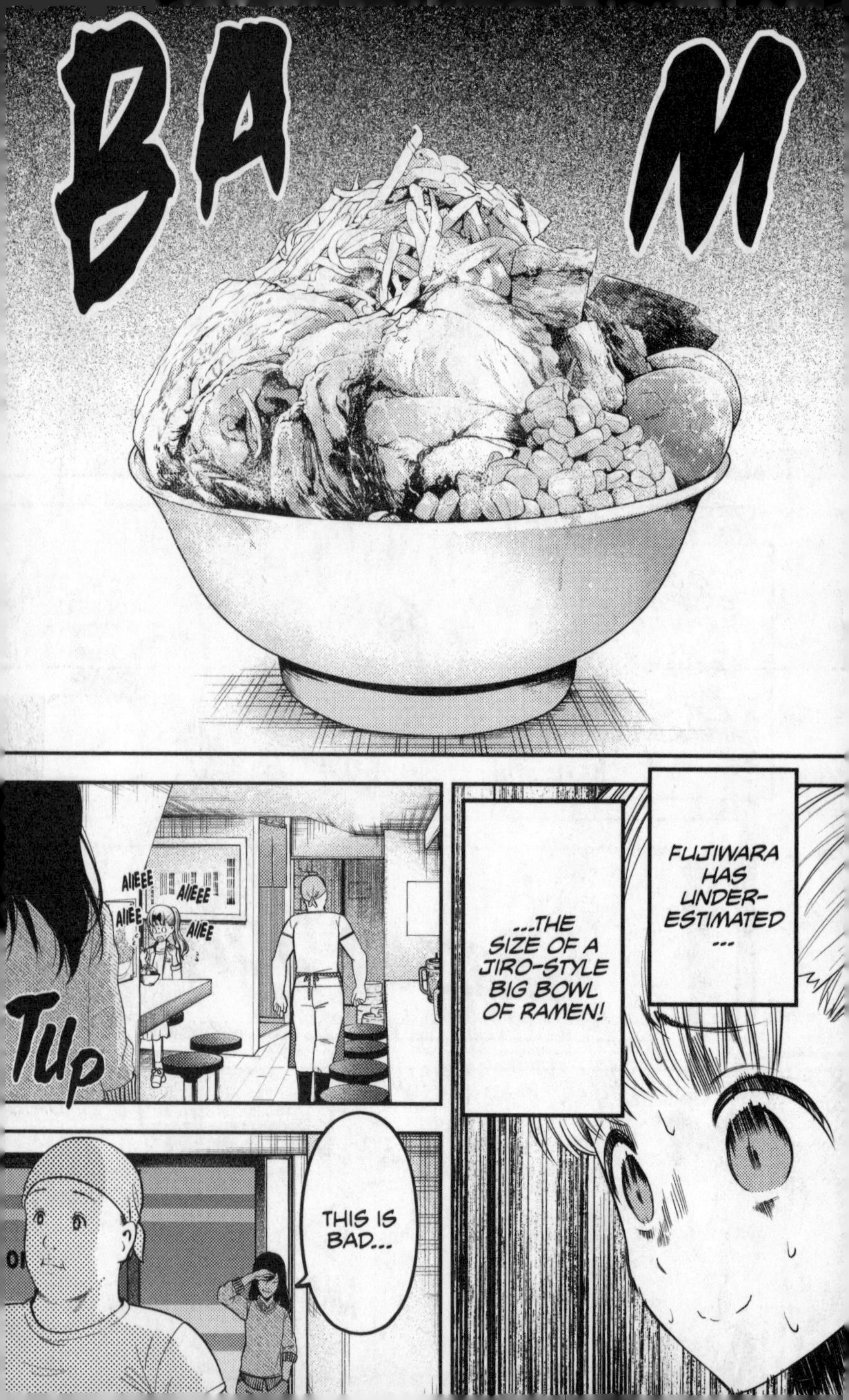
BAM
FUJIWARA HAS UNDER-ESTIMATED...
...THE SIZE OF A JIRO-STYLE BIG BOWL OF RAMEN!
AIIEEE
AIIEEE
AIIEE
AIIEE
TUP
THIS IS BAD...

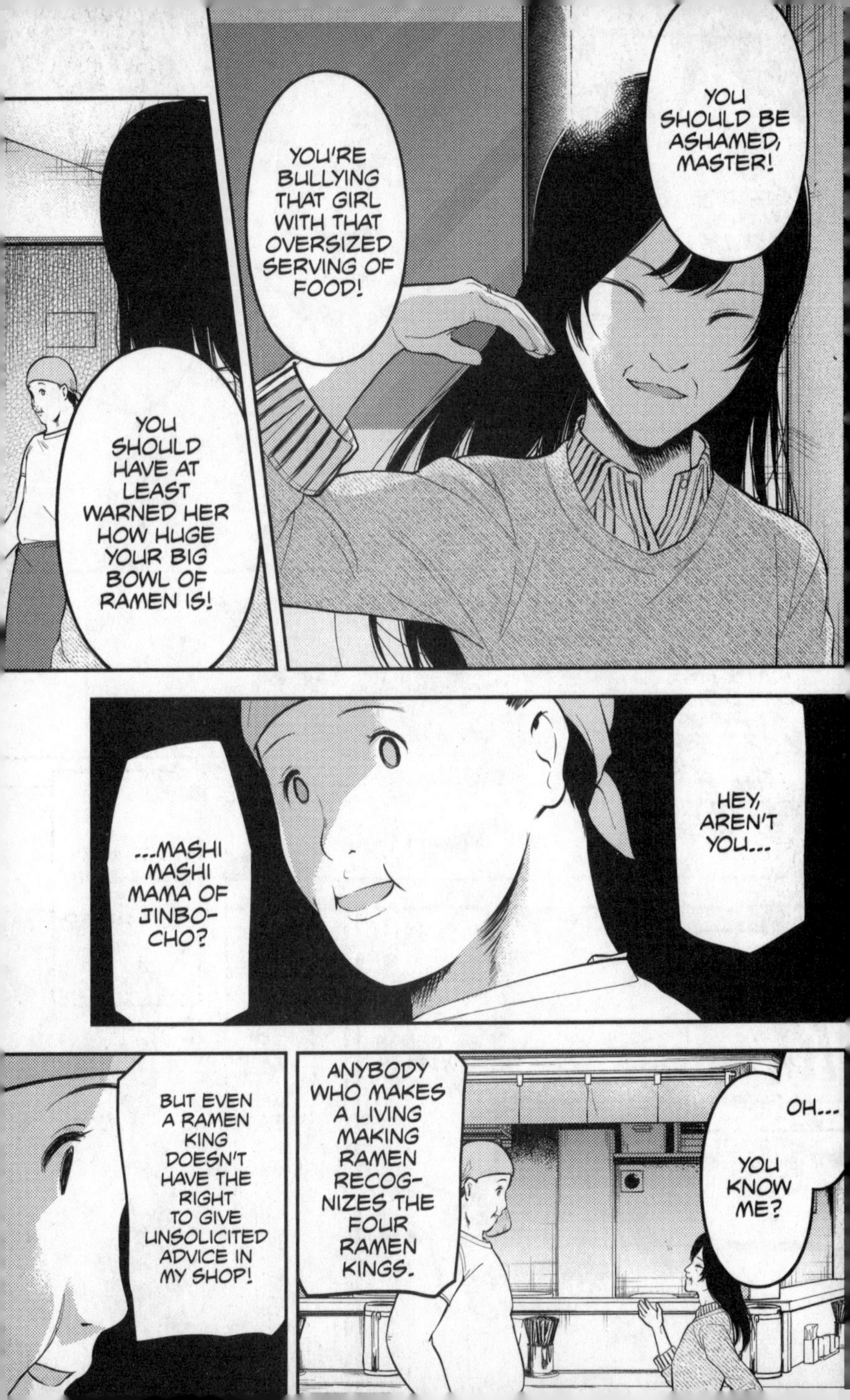
YOU SHOULD BE ASHAMED, MASTER!
YOU'RE BULLYING THAT GIRL WITH THAT OVERSIZED SERVING OF FOOD!
YOU SHOULD HAVE AT LEAST WARNED HER HOW HUGE YOUR BIG BOWL OF RAMEN IS!
HEY, AREN'T YOU...
...MASHI MASHI MAMA OF JINBOCHO?
OH... YOU KNOW ME?
ANYBODY WHO MAKES A LIVING MAKING RAMEN RECOGNIZES THE FOUR RAMEN KINGS.
BUT EVEN A RAMEN KING DOESN'T HAVE THE RIGHT TO GIVE UNSOLICITED ADVICE IN MY SHOP!

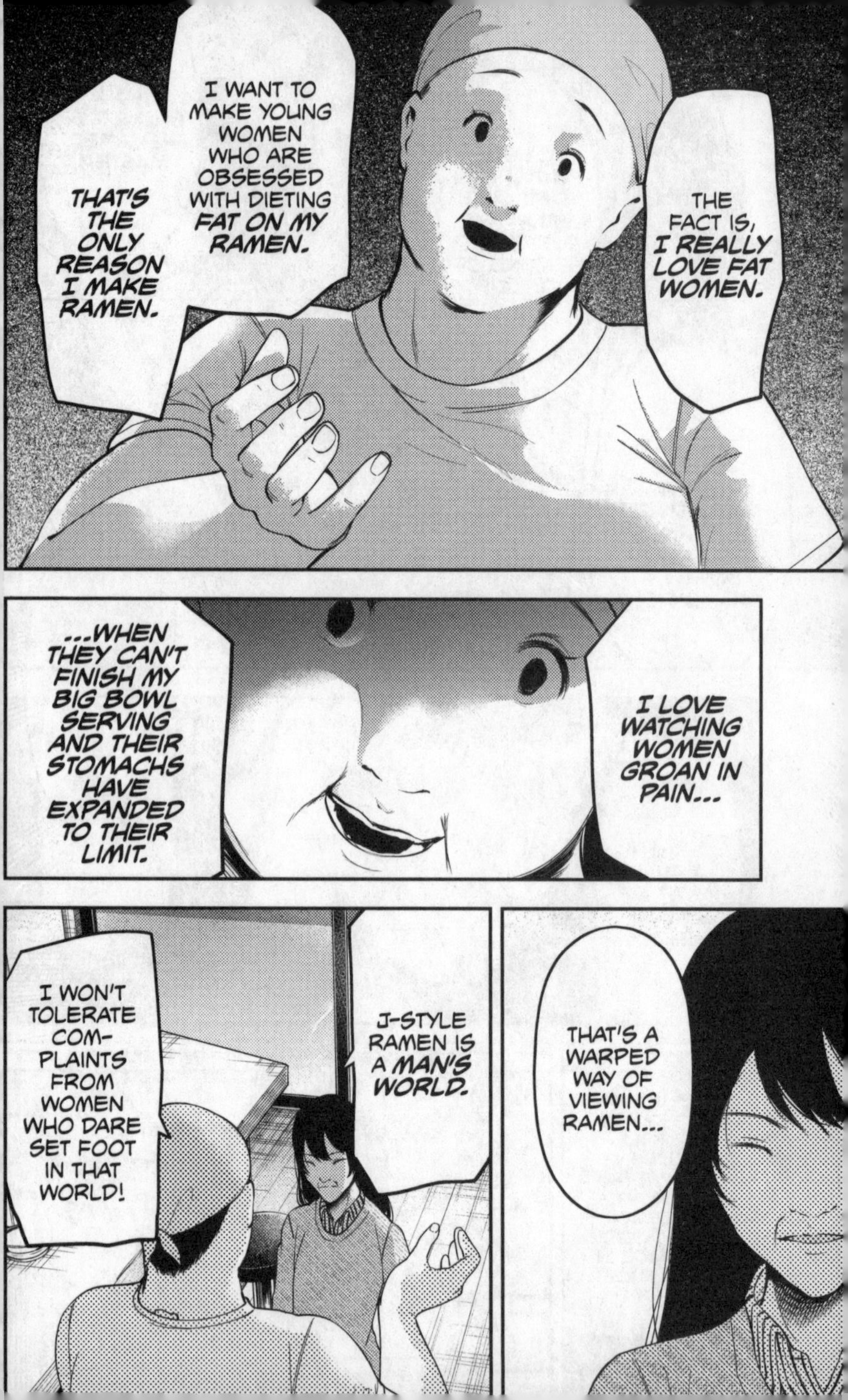
THE FACT IS, I REALLY LOVE FAT WOMEN.
I WANT TO MAKE YOUNG WOMEN WHO ARE OBSESSED WITH DIETING FAT ON MY RAMEN.
THAT'S THE ONLY REASON I MAKE RAMEN.
I LOVE WATCHING WOMEN GROAN IN PAIN...
...WHEN THEY CAN'T FINISH MY BIG BOWL SERVING AND THEIR STOMACHS HAVE EXPANDED TO THEIR LIMIT.
THAT'S A WARPED WAY OF VIEWING RAMEN...
J-STYLE RAMEN IS A MAN'S WORLD.
I WON'T TOLERATE COM-PLAINTS FROM WOMEN WHO DARE SET FOOT IN THAT WORLD!

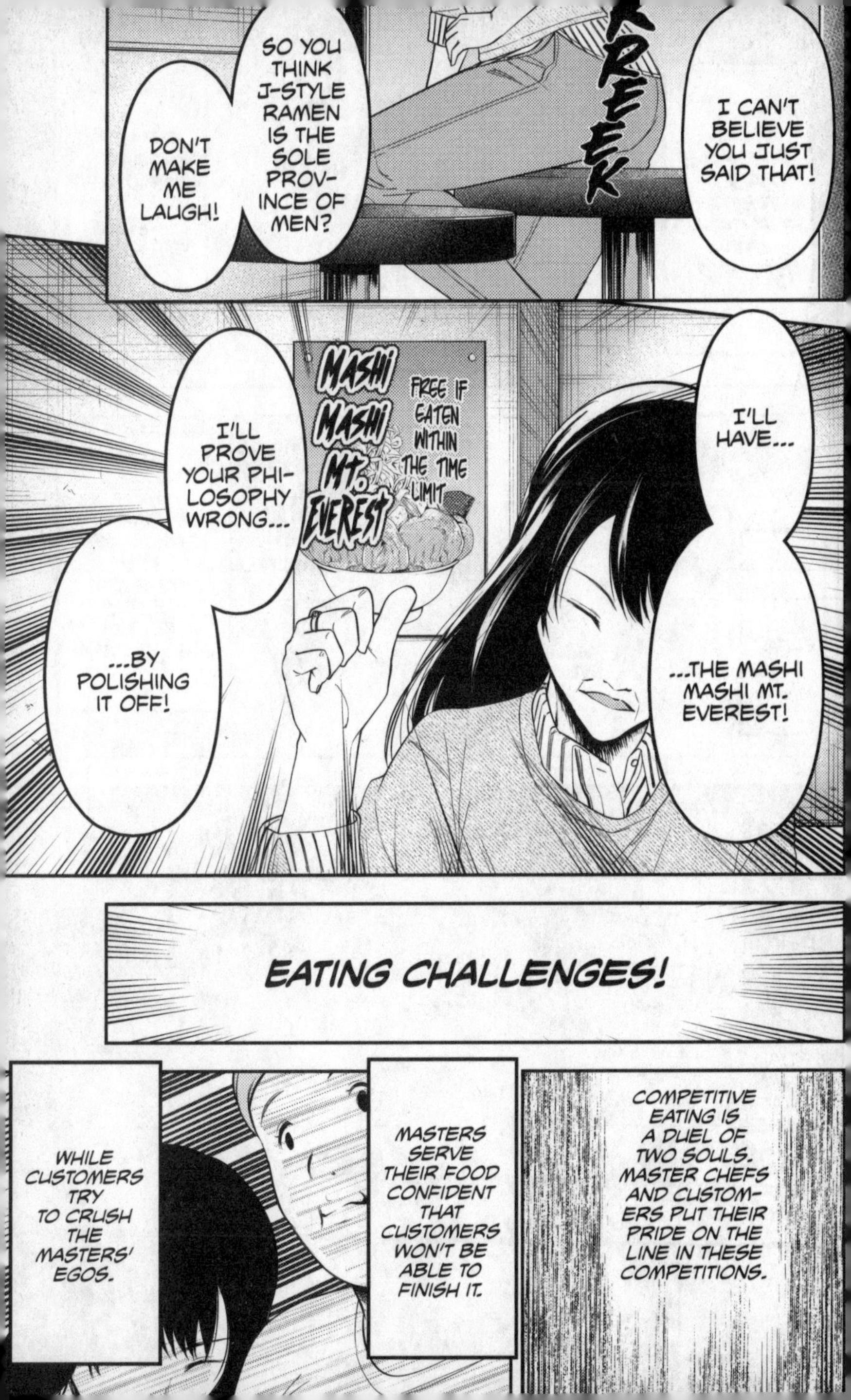
I CAN'T BELIEVE YOU JUST SAID THAT!
KREEK
SO YOU THINK J-STYLE RAMEN IS THE SOLE PROVINCE OF MEN?
DON'T MAKE ME LAUGH!
I'LL HAVE...
...THE MASHI MASHI MT. EVEREST!
MASHI MASHI MT. EVEREST
FREE IF EATEN WITHIN THE TIME LIMIT
I'LL PROVE YOUR PHILOSOPHY WRONG...
...BY POLISHING IT OFF!
EATING CHALLENGES!
COMPETITIVE EATING IS A DUEL OF TWO SOULS. MASTER CHEFS AND CUSTOMERS PUT THEIR PRIDE ON THE LINE IN THESE COMPETITIONS.
MASTERS SERVE THEIR FOOD CONFIDENT THAT CUSTOMERS WON'T BE ABLE TO FINISH IT.
WHILE CUSTOMERS TRY TO CRUSH THE MASTERS' EGOS.

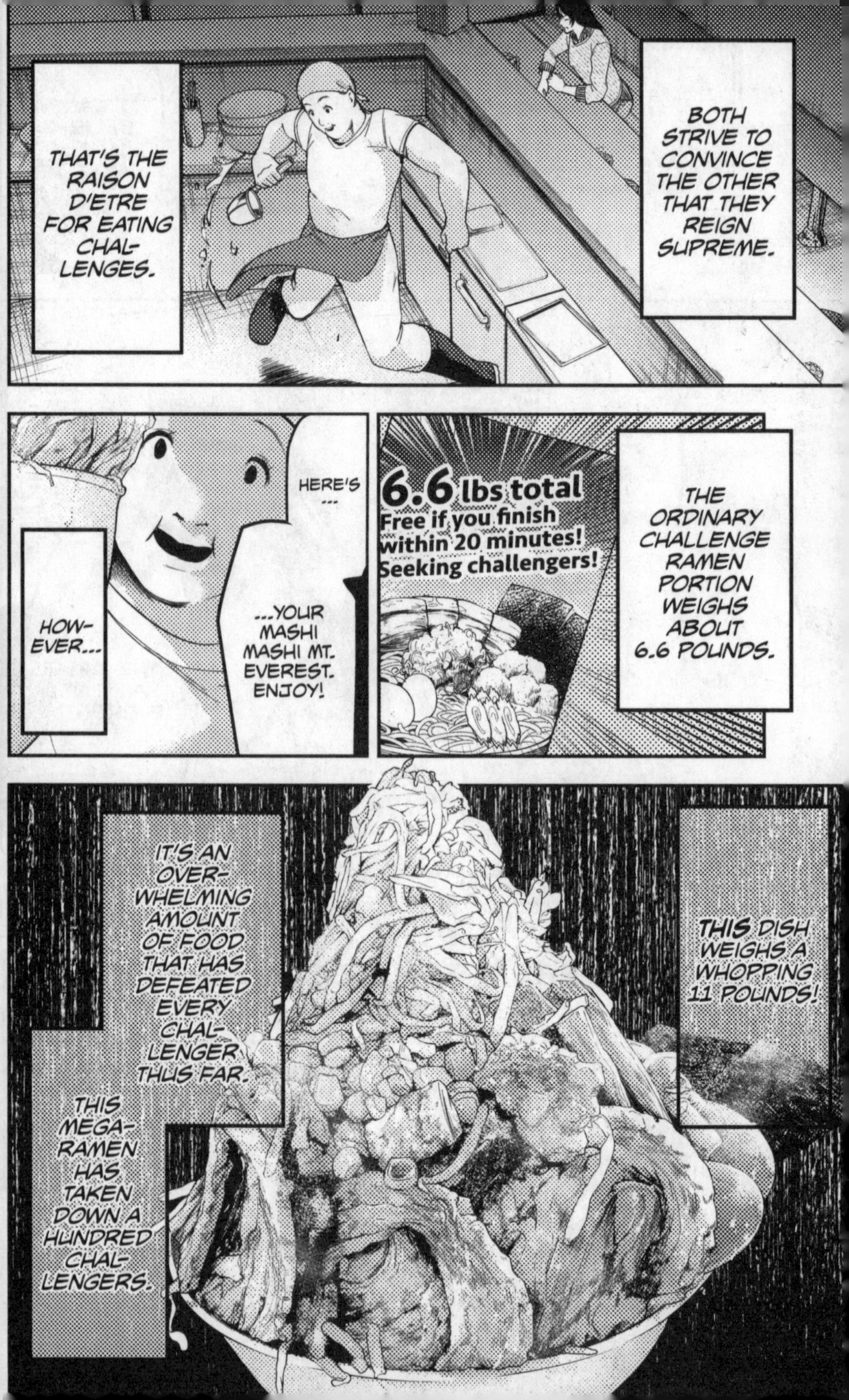
BOTH STRIVE TO CONVINCE THE OTHER THAT THEY REIGN SUPREME.
THAT'S THE RAISON D'ETRE FOR EATING CHAL-LENGES.
THE ORDINARY CHALLENGE RAMEN PORTION WEIGHS ABOUT 6.6 POUNDS.
6.6 lbs total
Free if you finish within 20 minutes! Seeking challengers!
HERE'S ---
---YOUR MASHI MASHI MT. EVEREST. ENJOY!
HOW-EVER...
THIS DISH WEIGHS A WHOPPING 11 POUNDS!
IT'S AN OVER-WHELMING AMOUNT OF FOOD THAT HAS DEFEATED EVERY CHAL-LENGER THUS FAR.
THIS MEGA-RAMEN HAS TAKEN DOWN A HUNDRED CHAL-LENGERS.

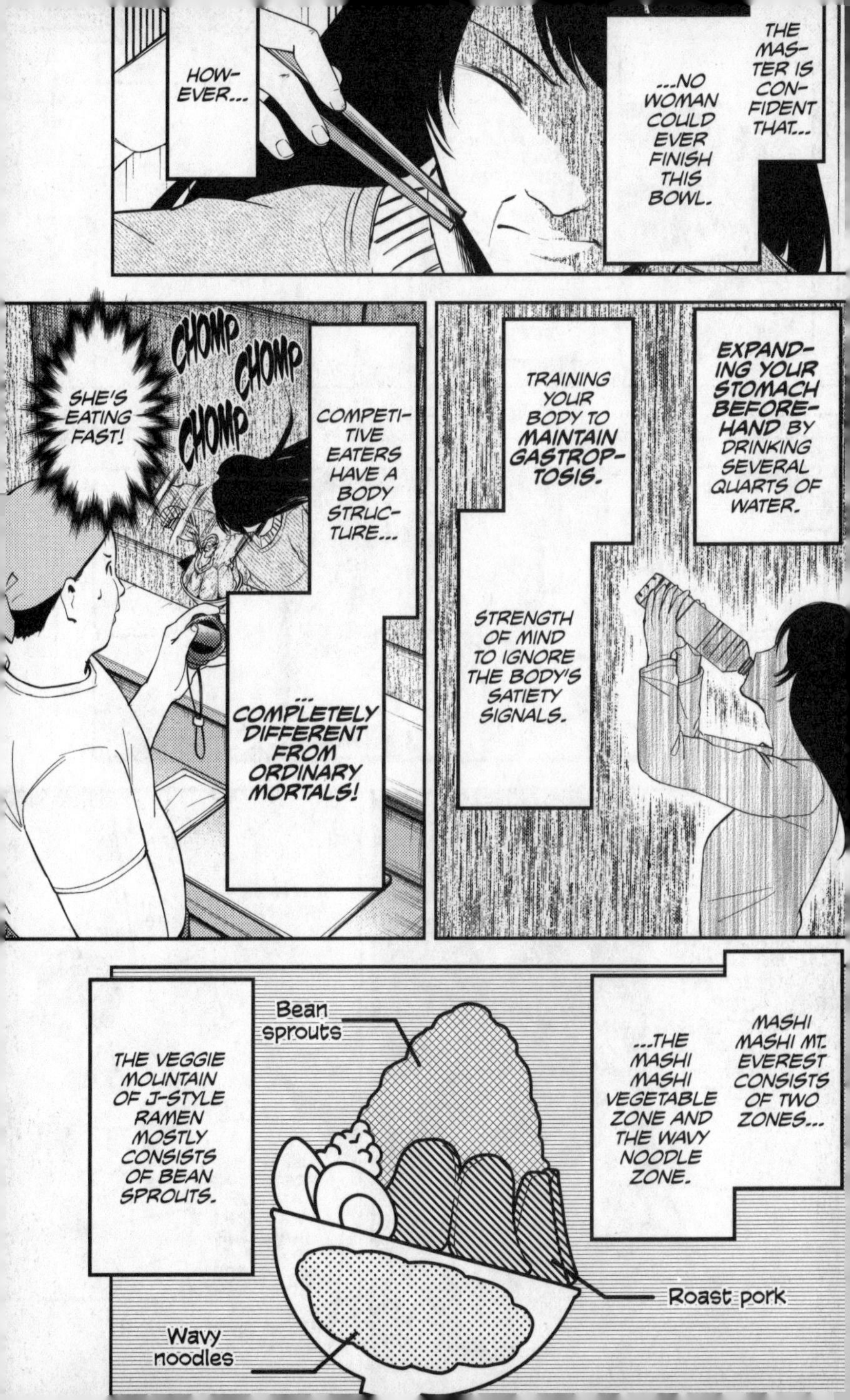
THE MASTER IS CONFIDENT THAT...
...NO WOMAN COULD EVER FINISH THIS BOWL.
HOWEVER...
EXPANDING YOUR STOMACH BEFOREHAND BY DRINKING SEVERAL QUARTS OF WATER.
TRAINING YOUR BODY TO MAINTAIN GASTROPTOSIS.
STRENGTH OF MIND TO IGNORE THE BODY'S SATIETY SIGNALS.
COMPETITIVE EATERS HAVE A BODY STRUCTURE...
...COMPLETELY DIFFERENT FROM ORDINARY MORTALS!
CHOMP
CHOMP
CHOMP
SHE'S EATING FAST!
MASHI MASHI MT. EVEREST CONSISTS OF TWO ZONES...
...THE MASHI MASHI VEGETABLE ZONE AND THE WAVY NOODLE ZONE.
THE VEGGIE MOUNTAIN OF J-STYLE RAMEN MOSTLY CONSISTS OF BEAN SPROUTS.
Bean sprouts
Roast pork
Wavy noodles

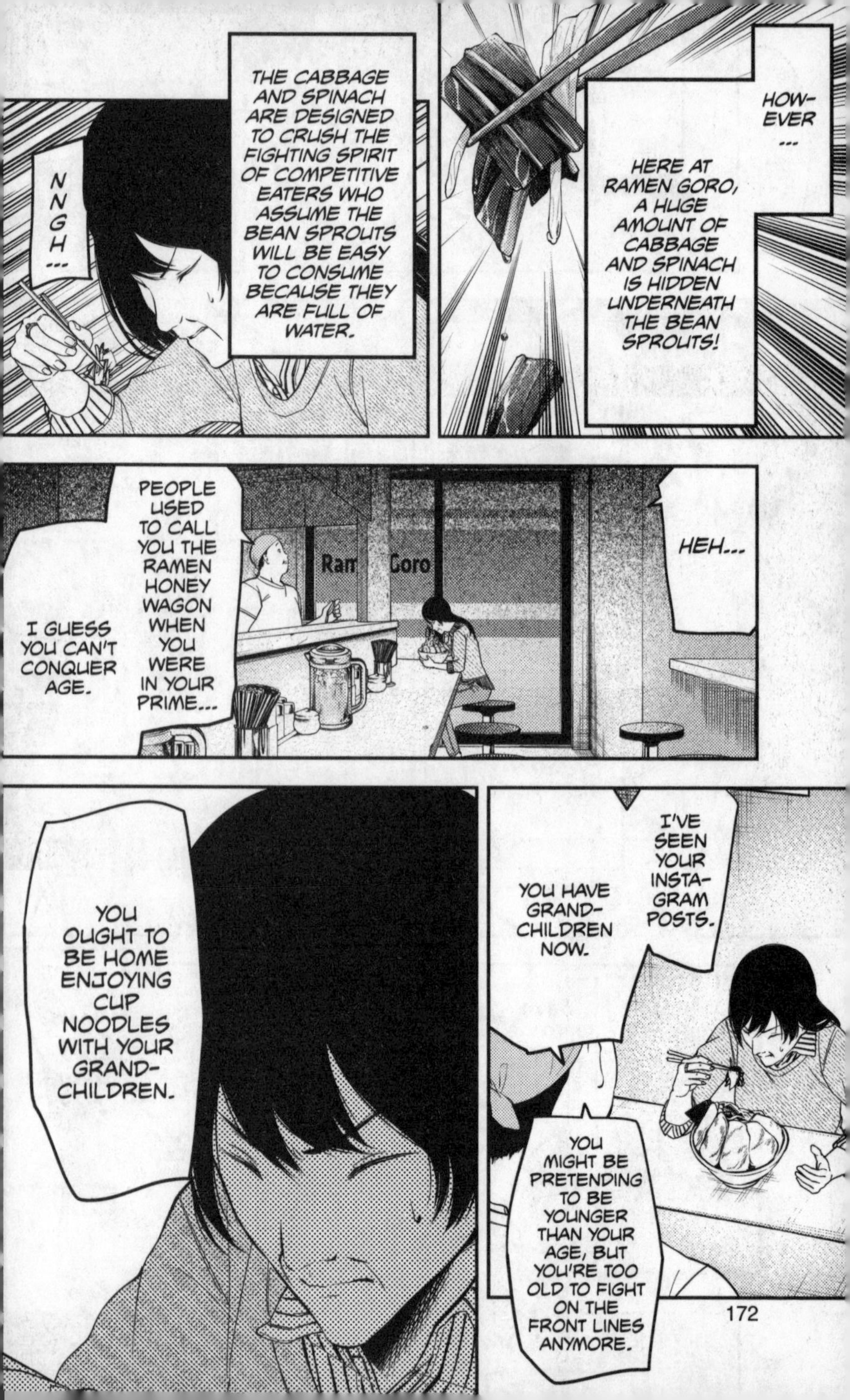
HOWEVER...
HERE AT RAMEN GORO, A HUGE AMOUNT OF CABBAGE AND SPINACH IS HIDDEN UNDERNEATH THE BEAN SPROUTS!
THE CABBAGE AND SPINACH ARE DESIGNED TO CRUSH THE FIGHTING SPIRIT OF COMPETITIVE EATERS WHO ASSUME THE BEAN SPROUTS WILL BE EASY TO CONSUME BECAUSE THEY ARE FULL OF WATER.
NNGH...
HEH...
Ram Goro
PEOPLE USED TO CALL YOU THE RAMEN HONEY WAGON WHEN YOU WERE IN YOUR PRIME...
I GUESS YOU CAN'T CONQUER AGE.
I'VE SEEN YOUR INSTAGRAM POSTS.
YOU HAVE GRANDCHILDREN NOW.
YOU MIGHT BE PRETENDING TO BE YOUNGER THAN YOUR AGE, BUT YOU'RE TOO OLD TO FIGHT ON THE FRONT LINES ANYMORE.
YOU OUGHT TO BE HOME ENJOYING CUP NOODLES WITH YOUR GRANDCHILDREN.

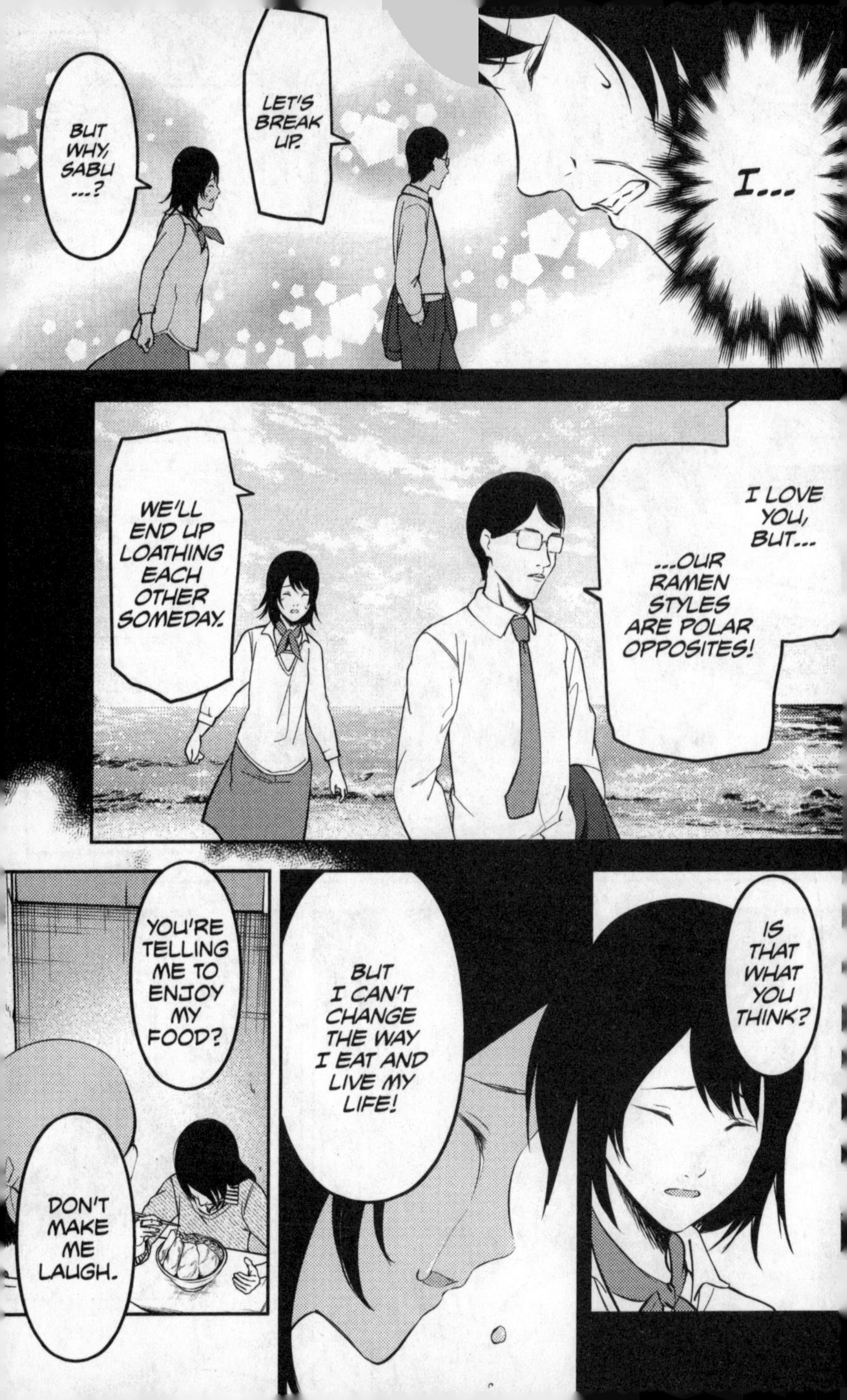
I...
LET'S BREAK UP.
BUT WHY, SABU...?
I LOVE YOU, BUT...
...OUR RAMEN STYLES ARE POLAR OPPOSITES!
WE'LL END UP LOATHING EACH OTHER SOMEDAY.
IS THAT WHAT YOU THINK?
BUT I CAN'T CHANGE THE WAY I EAT AND LIVE MY LIFE!
YOU'RE TELLING ME TO ENJOY MY FOOD?
DON'T MAKE ME LAUGH.

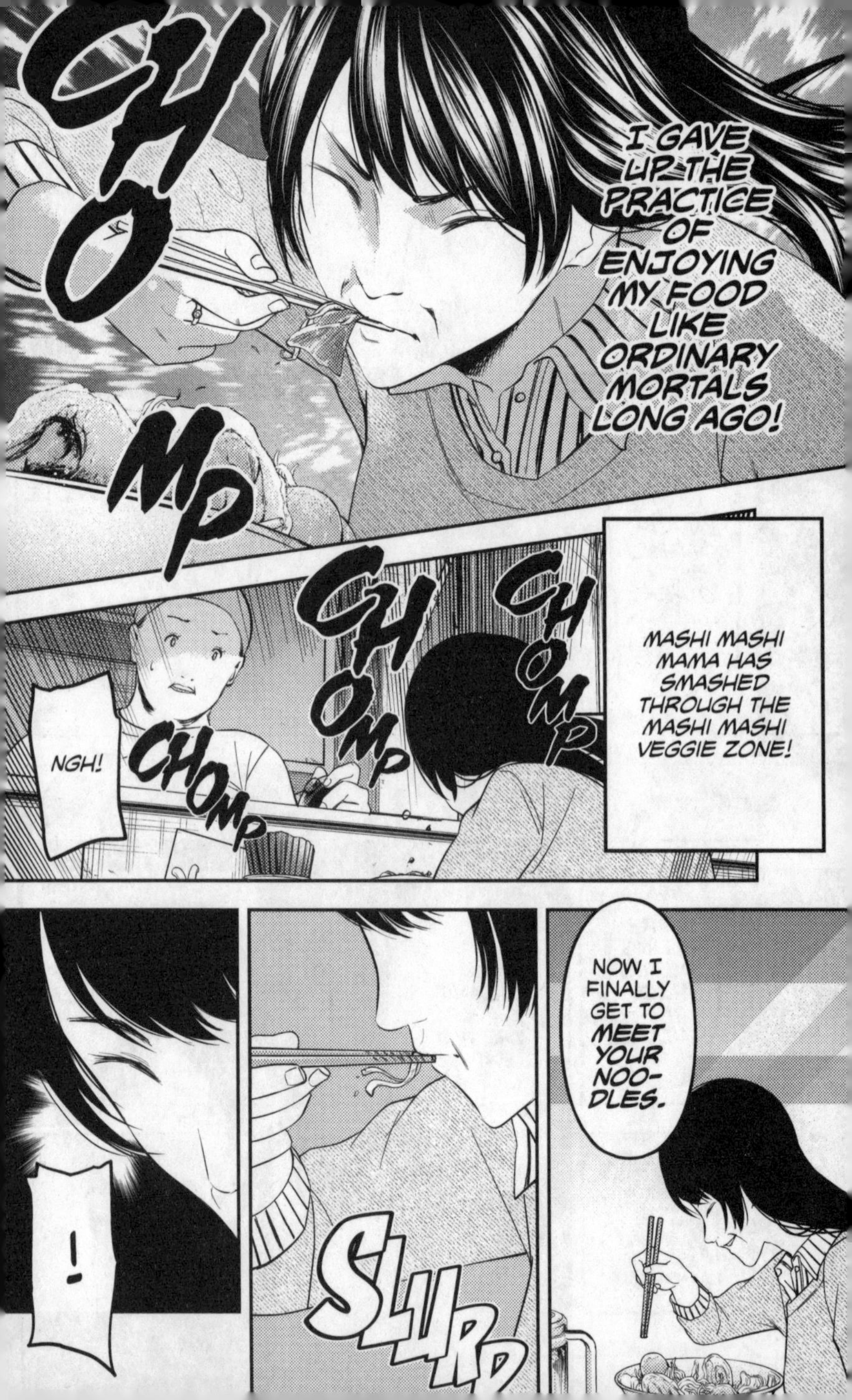
I GAVE UP THE PRACTICE OF ENJOYING MY FOOD LIKE ORDINARY MORTALS LONG AGO!
CHOMP
MASHI MASHI MAMA HAS SMASHED THROUGH THE MASHI MASHI VEGGIE ZONE!
CHOMP
CHOMP
CHOMP
NGH!
NOW I FINALLY GET TO MEET YOUR NOODLES.
SLURP
!

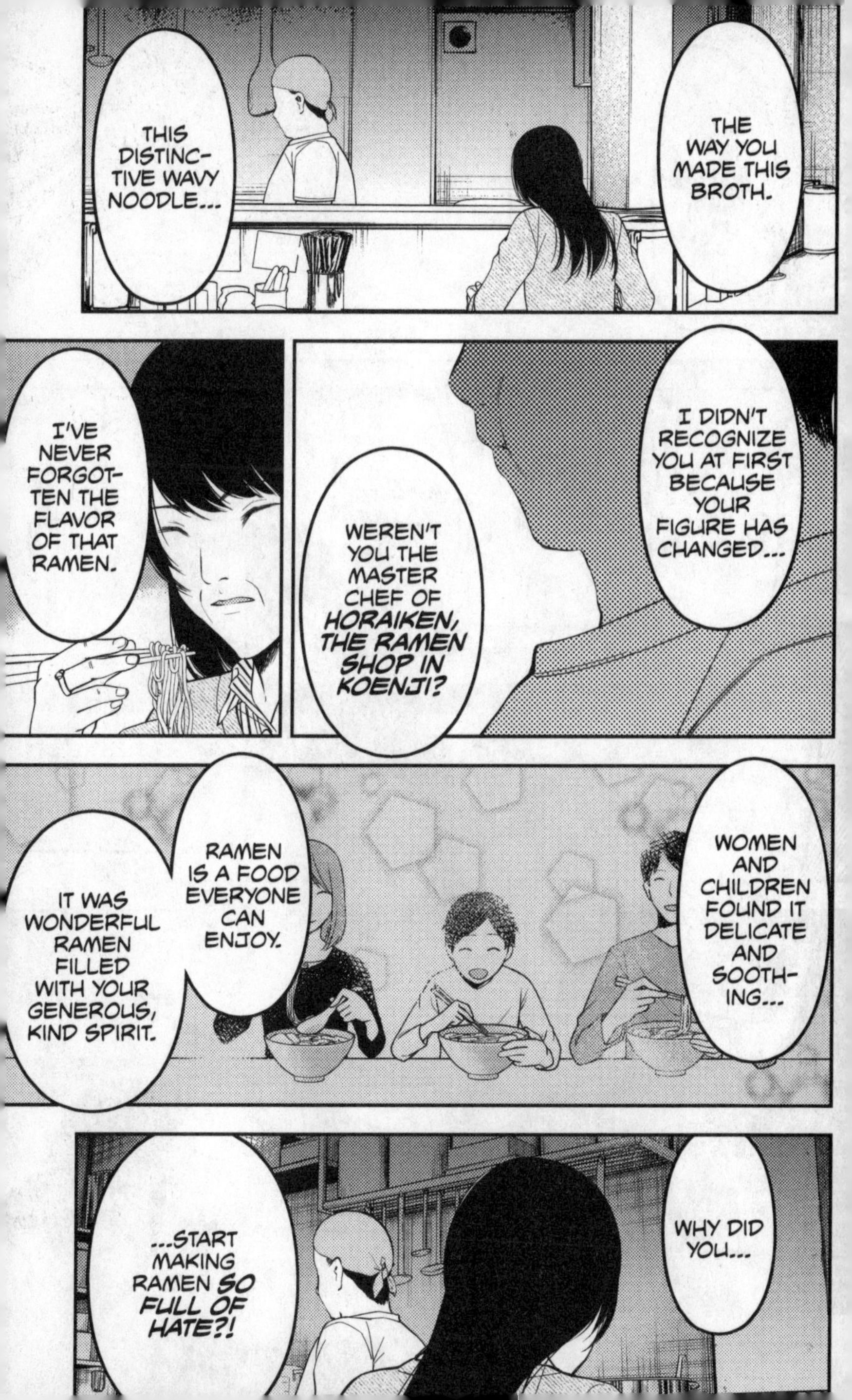
THE WAY YOU MADE THIS BROTH.
THIS DISTINCTIVE WAVY NOODLE...
I DIDN'T RECOGNIZE YOU AT FIRST BECAUSE YOUR FIGURE HAS CHANGED...
WEREN'T YOU THE MASTER CHEF OF *HORAIKEN, THE RAMEN SHOP IN KOENJI?*
I'VE NEVER FORGOTTEN THE FLAVOR OF THAT RAMEN.
WOMEN AND CHILDREN FOUND IT DELICATE AND SOOTHING...
RAMEN IS A FOOD EVERYONE CAN ENJOY.
IT WAS WONDERFUL RAMEN FILLED WITH YOUR GENEROUS, KIND SPIRIT.
WHY DID YOU...
...START MAKING RAMEN *SO FULL OF HATE?!*

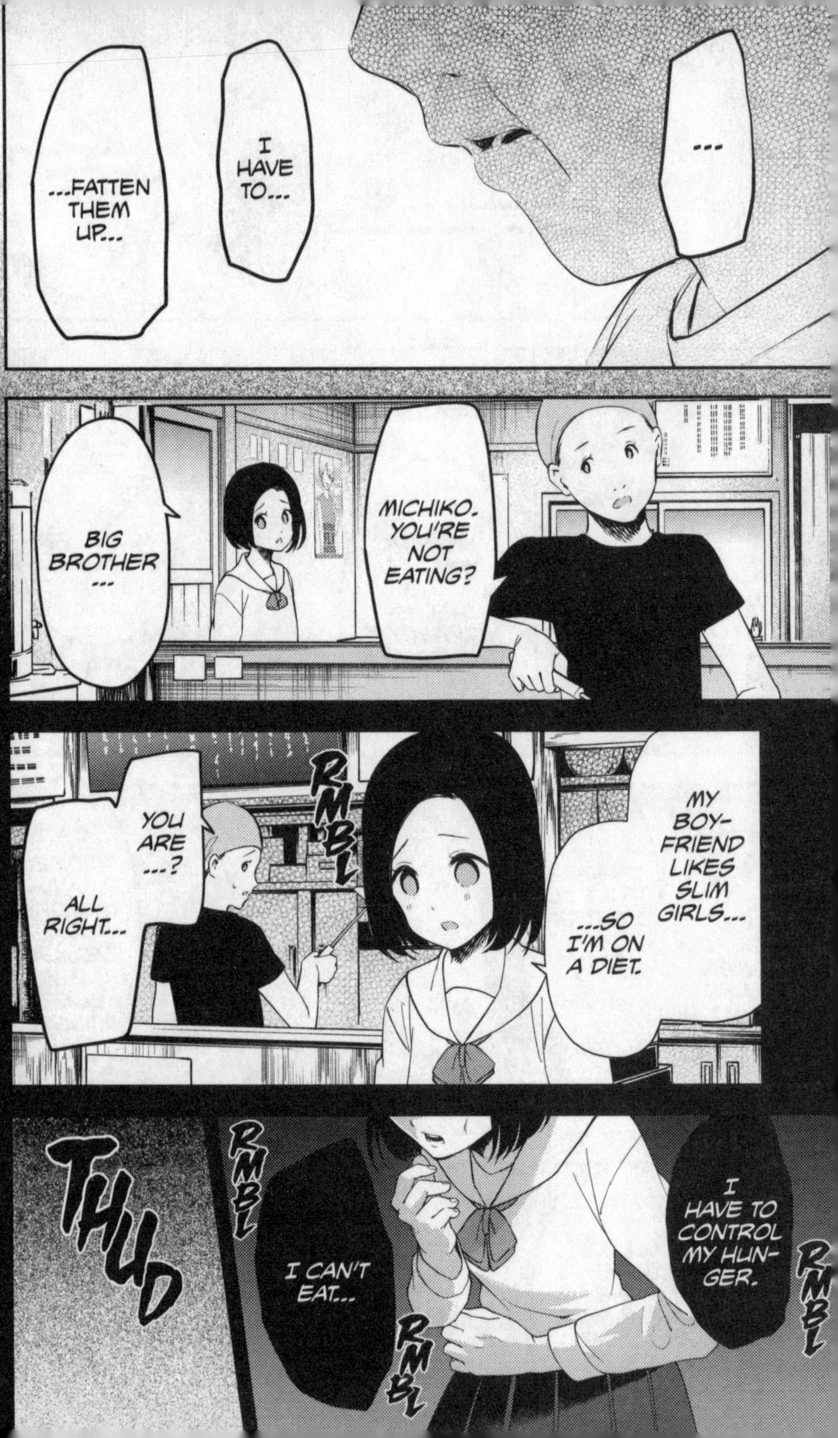
...
I HAVE TO...
...FATTEN THEM UP...
MICHIKO. YOU'RE NOT EATING?
BIG BROTHER ...
MY BOY-FRIEND LIKES SLIM GIRLS...
...SO I'M ON A DIET.
RMBL
YOU ARE ...?
ALL RIGHT...
RMBL
I HAVE TO CONTROL MY HUN-GER.
RMBL
I CAN'T EAT...
RMBL
THUD

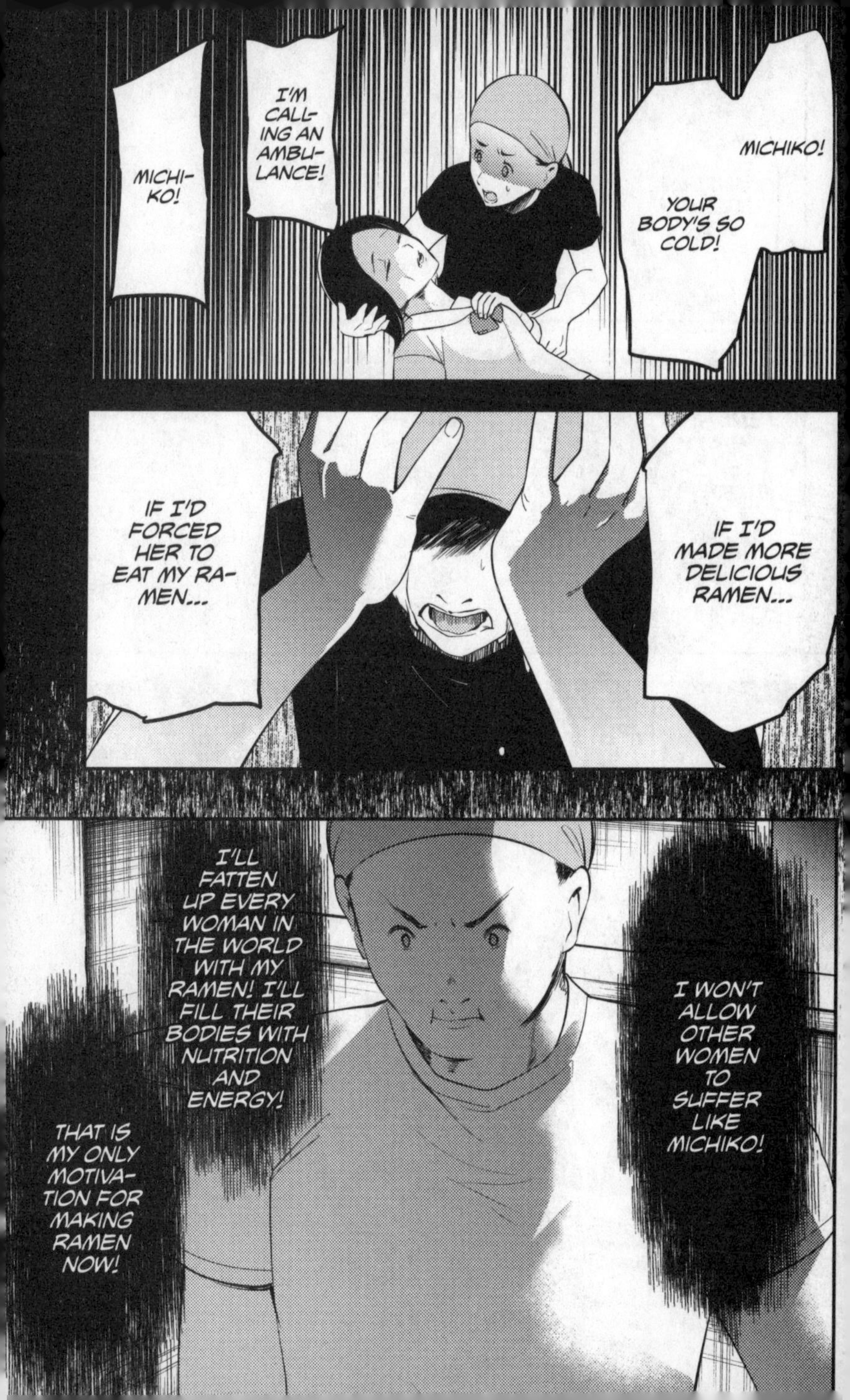
MICHIKO!
YOUR BODY'S SO COLD!
I'M CALLING AN AMBULANCE!
MICHIKO!
IF I'D MADE MORE DELICIOUS RAMEN...
IF I'D FORCED HER TO EAT MY RAMEN...
I WON'T ALLOW OTHER WOMEN TO SUFFER LIKE MICHIKO!
I'LL FATTEN UP EVERY WOMAN IN THE WORLD WITH MY RAMEN! I'LL FILL THEIR BODIES WITH NUTRITION AND ENERGY!
THAT IS MY ONLY MOTIVATION FOR MAKING RAMEN NOW!

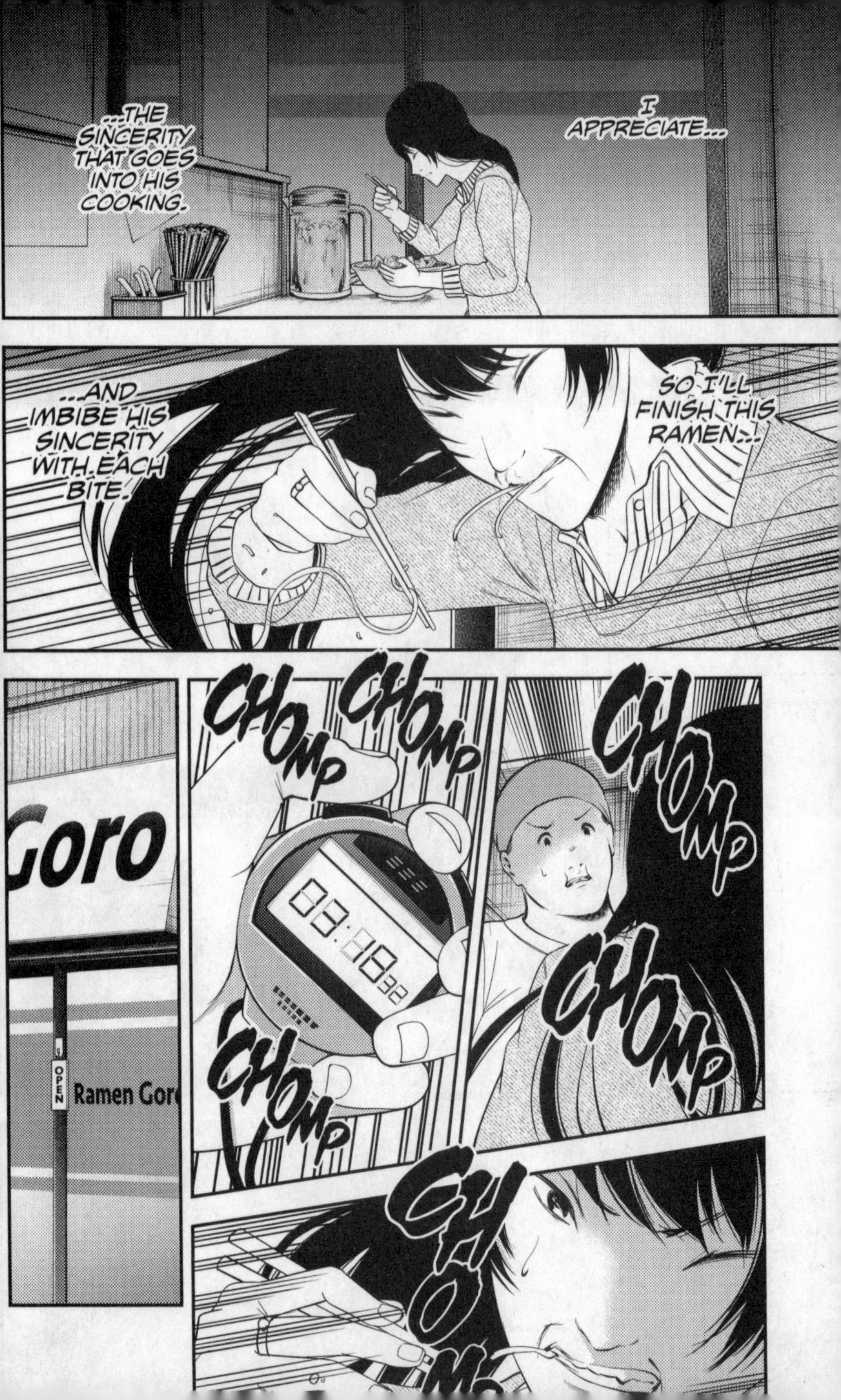
I APPRECIATE...
...THE SINCERITY THAT GOES INTO HIS COOKING.
SO I'LL FINISH THIS RAMEN...
...AND IMBIBE HIS SINCERITY WITH EACH BITE.
Goro
OPEN
Ramen Gor
CHOMP
CHOMP
CHOMP
CHOMP
CHOMP
CHOMP

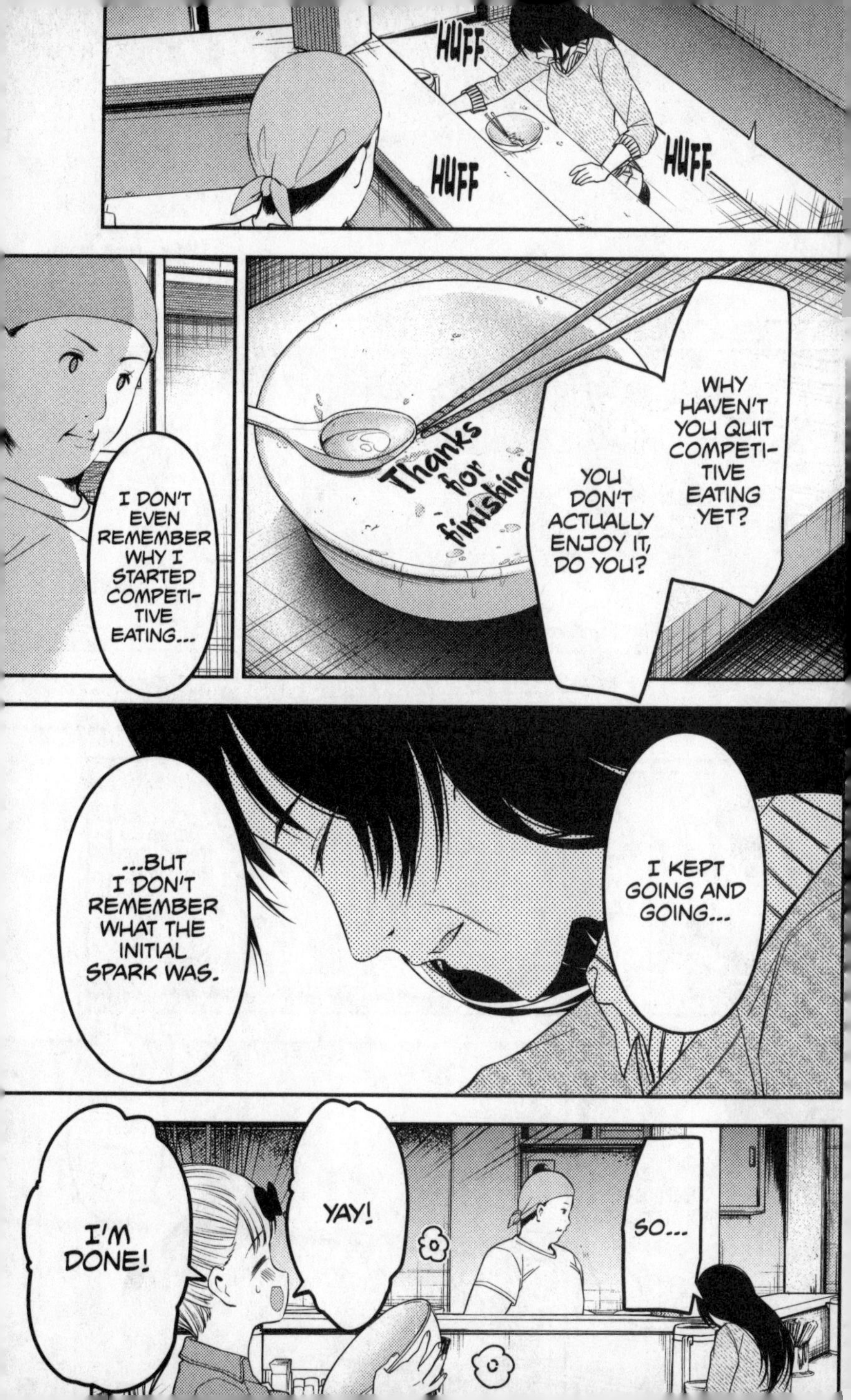
HUFF
HUFF
HUFF
WHY HAVEN'T YOU QUIT COMPETITIVE EATING YET?
YOU DON'T ACTUALLY ENJOY IT, DO YOU?
Thanks for finishing
I DON'T EVEN REMEMBER WHY I STARTED COMPETITIVE EATING...
I KEPT GOING AND GOING...
...BUT I DON'T REMEMBER WHAT THE INITIAL SPARK WAS.
SO...
YAY!
I'M DONE!

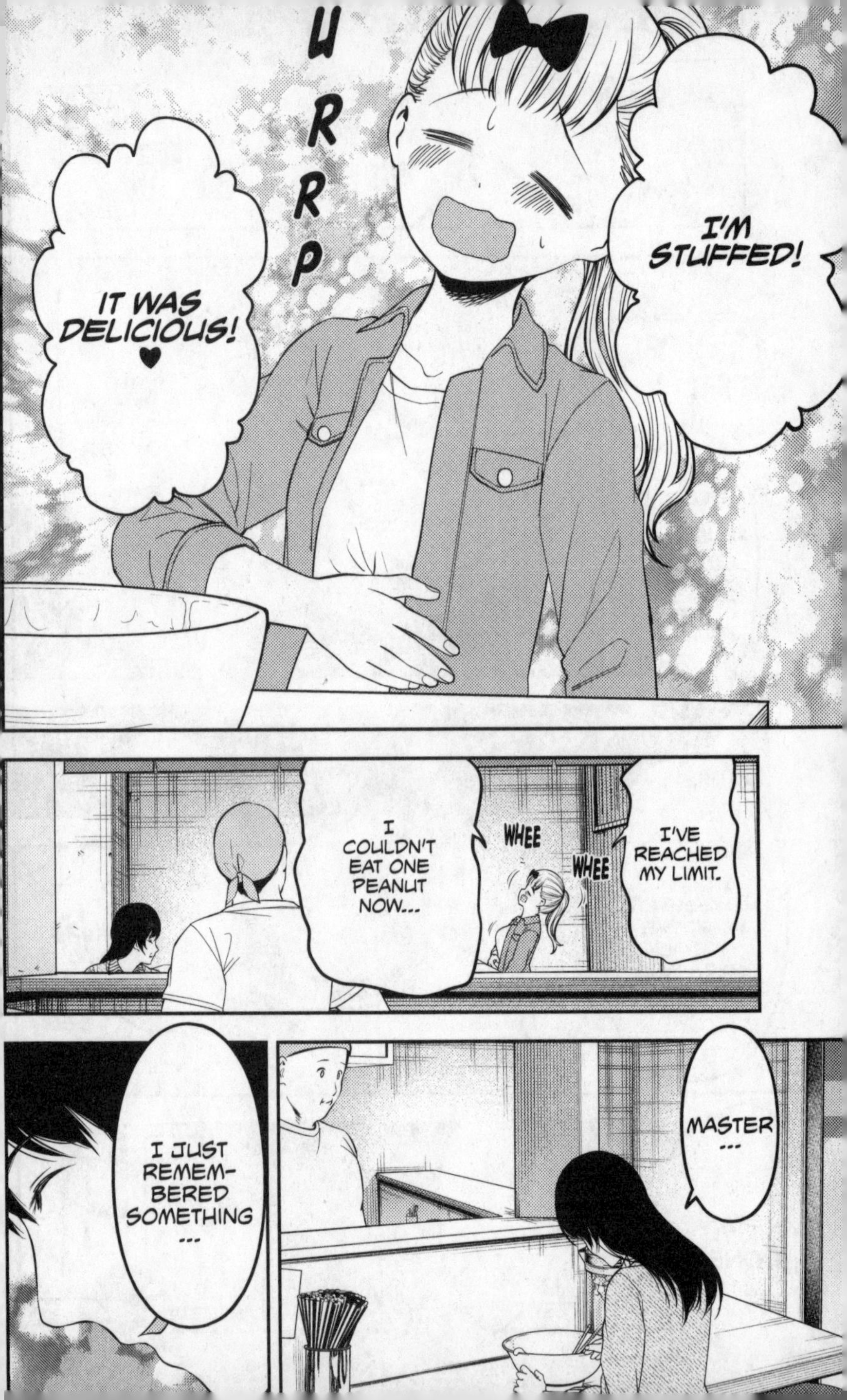
URRP
I'M STUFFED!
IT WAS DELICIOUS! ♥
I'VE REACHED MY LIMIT.
WHEE
WHEE
I COULDN'T EAT ONE PEANUT NOW...
MASTER...
I JUST REMEMBERED SOMETHING...

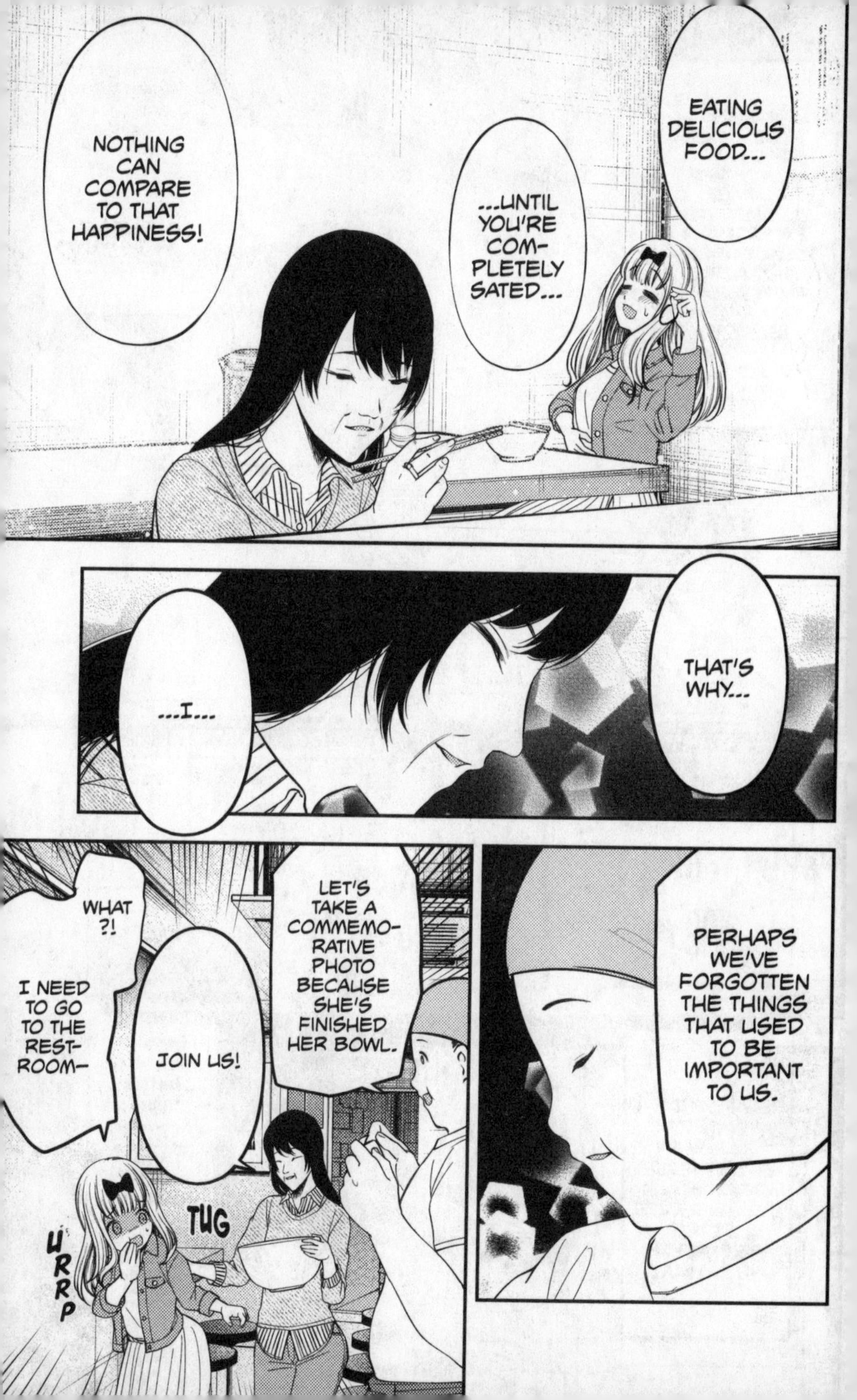
EATING DELICIOUS FOOD...
...UNTIL YOU'RE COM-PLETELY SATED...
NOTHING CAN COMPARE TO THAT HAPPINESS!
THAT'S WHY...
...I...
PERHAPS WE'VE FORGOTTEN THE THINGS THAT USED TO BE IMPORTANT TO US.
LET'S TAKE A COMMEMO-RATIVE PHOTO BECAUSE SHE'S FINISHED HER BOWL.
JOIN US!
WHAT?!
I NEED TO GO TO THE REST-ROOM—
TUG
URRP

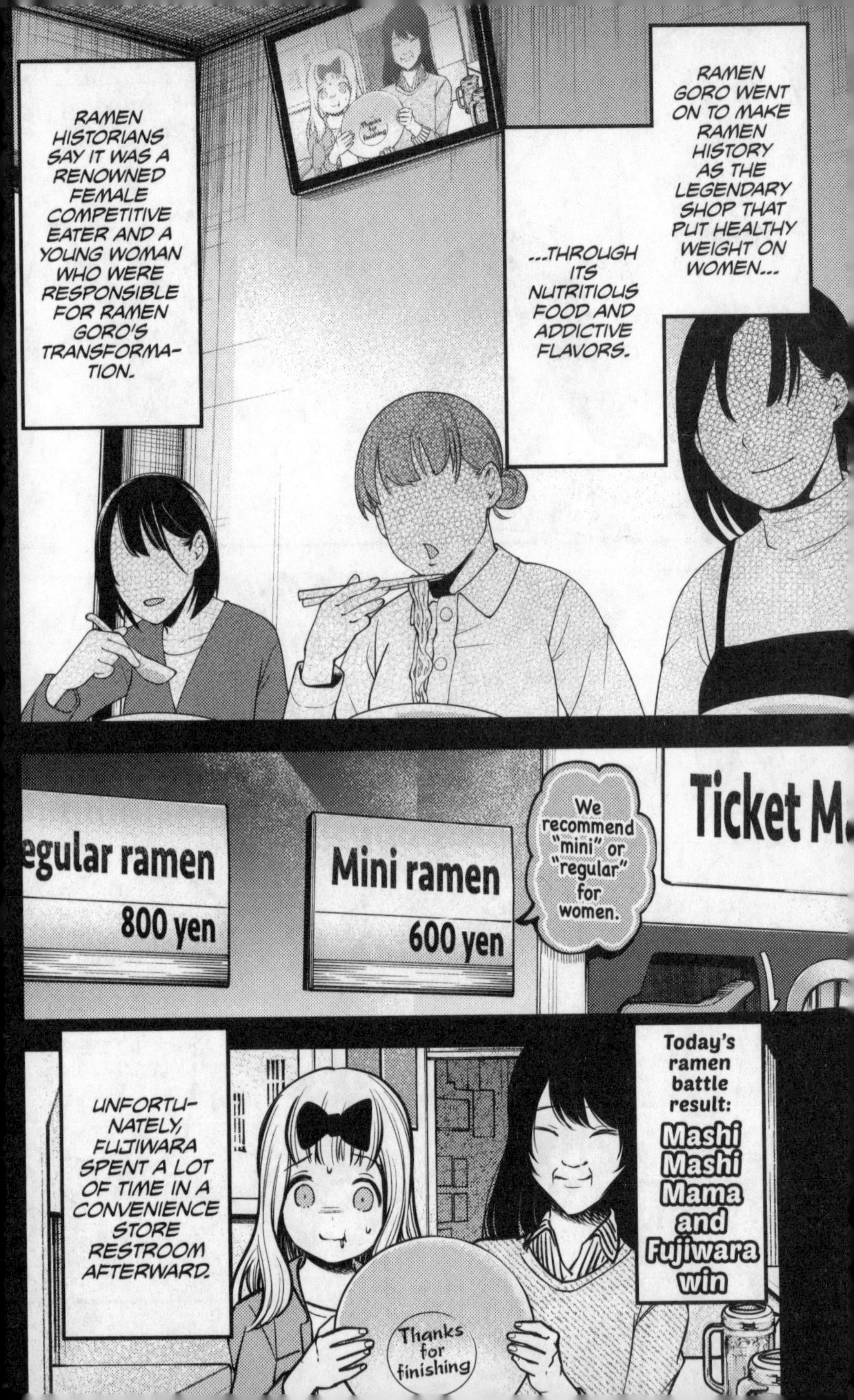
RAMEN GORO WENT ON TO MAKE RAMEN HISTORY AS THE LEGENDARY SHOP THAT PUT HEALTHY WEIGHT ON WOMEN...
...THROUGH ITS NUTRITIOUS FOOD AND ADDICTIVE FLAVORS.
RAMEN HISTORIANS SAY IT WAS A RENOWNED FEMALE COMPETITIVE EATER AND A YOUNG WOMAN WHO WERE RESPONSIBLE FOR RAMEN GORO'S TRANSFORMATION.
Ticket M
We recommend "mini" or "regular" for women.
Mini ramen
600 yen
egular ramen
800 yen
Today's ramen battle result: Mashi Mashi Mama and Fujiwara win
UNFORTUNATELY, FUJIWARA SPENT A LOT OF TIME IN A CONVENIENCE STORE RESTROOM AFTERWARD.
Thanks for finishing

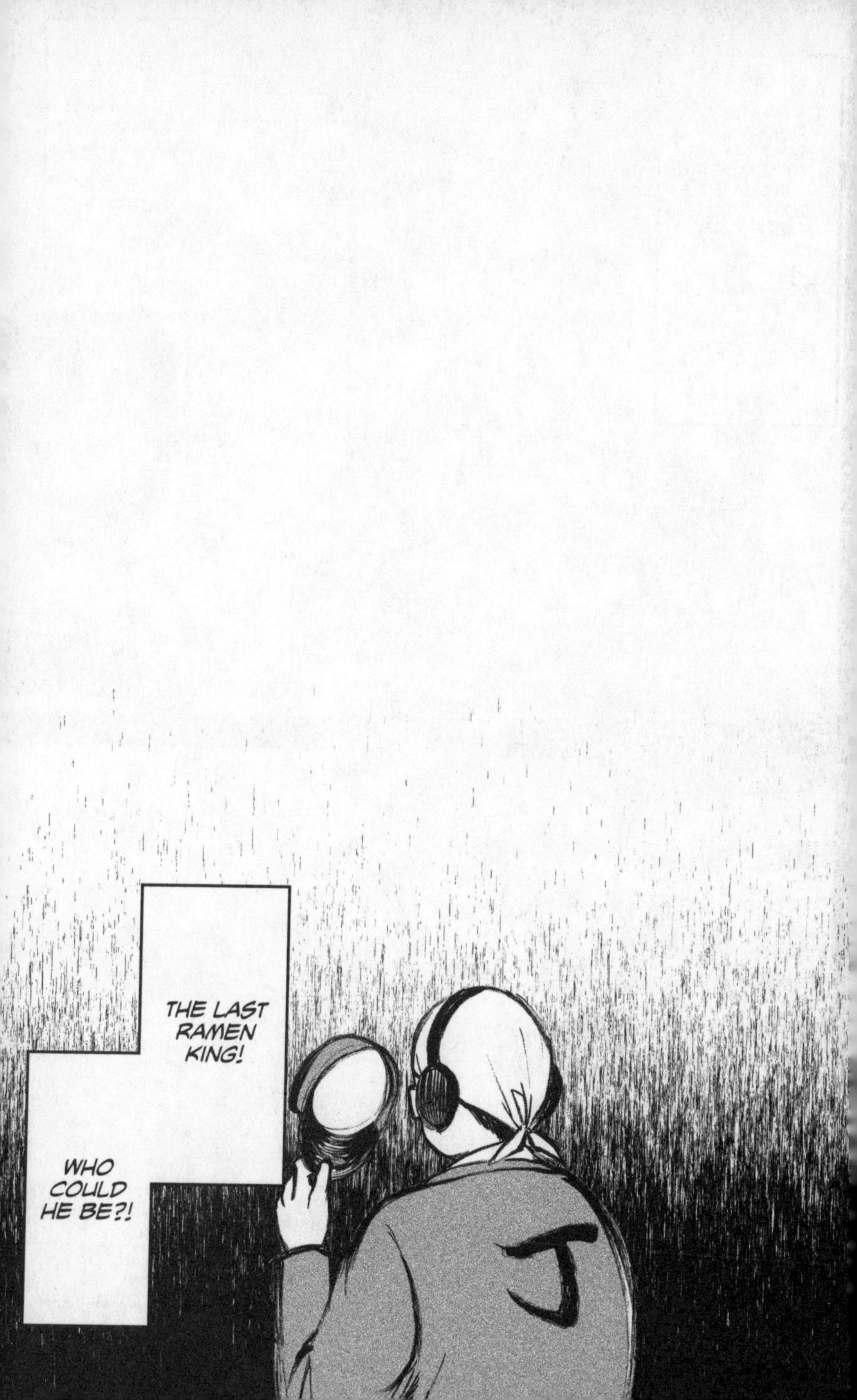
THE LAST RAMEN KING!
WHO COULD HE BE?!

KAGUYA-SAMA
LOVE IS WAR

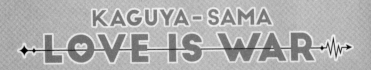

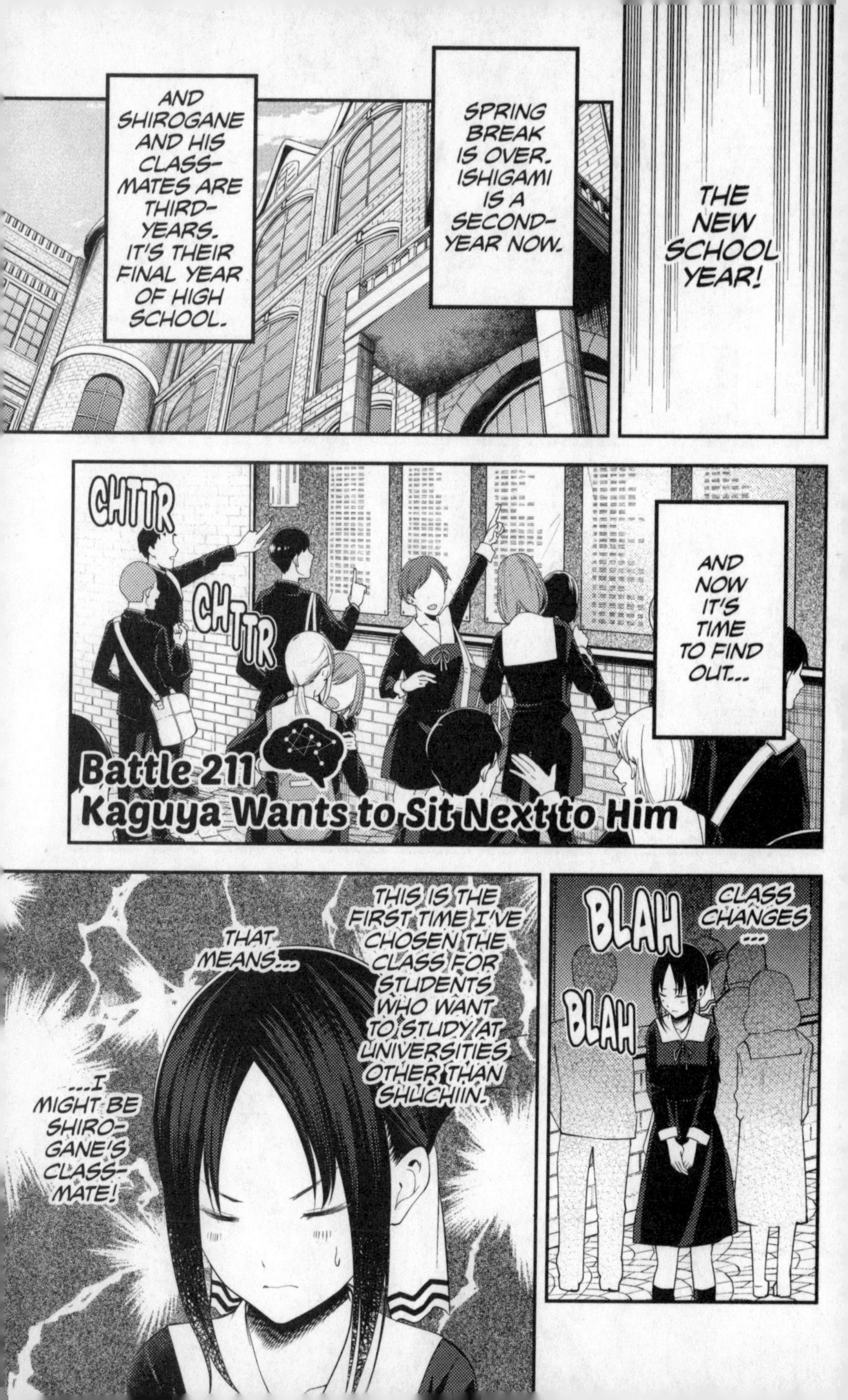
THE NEW SCHOOL YEAR!
SPRING BREAK IS OVER. ISHIGAMI IS A SECOND-YEAR NOW.
AND SHIROGANE AND HIS CLASSMATES ARE THIRD-YEARS. IT'S THEIR FINAL YEAR OF HIGH SCHOOL.
AND NOW IT'S TIME TO FIND OUT...
CHTTR
CHTTR
Battle 211
Kaguya Wants to Sit Next to Him
CLASS CHANGES...
BLAH
BLAH
THIS IS THE FIRST TIME I'VE CHOSEN THE CLASS FOR STUDENTS WHO WANT TO STUDY AT UNIVERSITIES OTHER THAN SHUCHIIN.
THAT MEANS...
...I MIGHT BE SHIROGANE'S CLASSMATE!

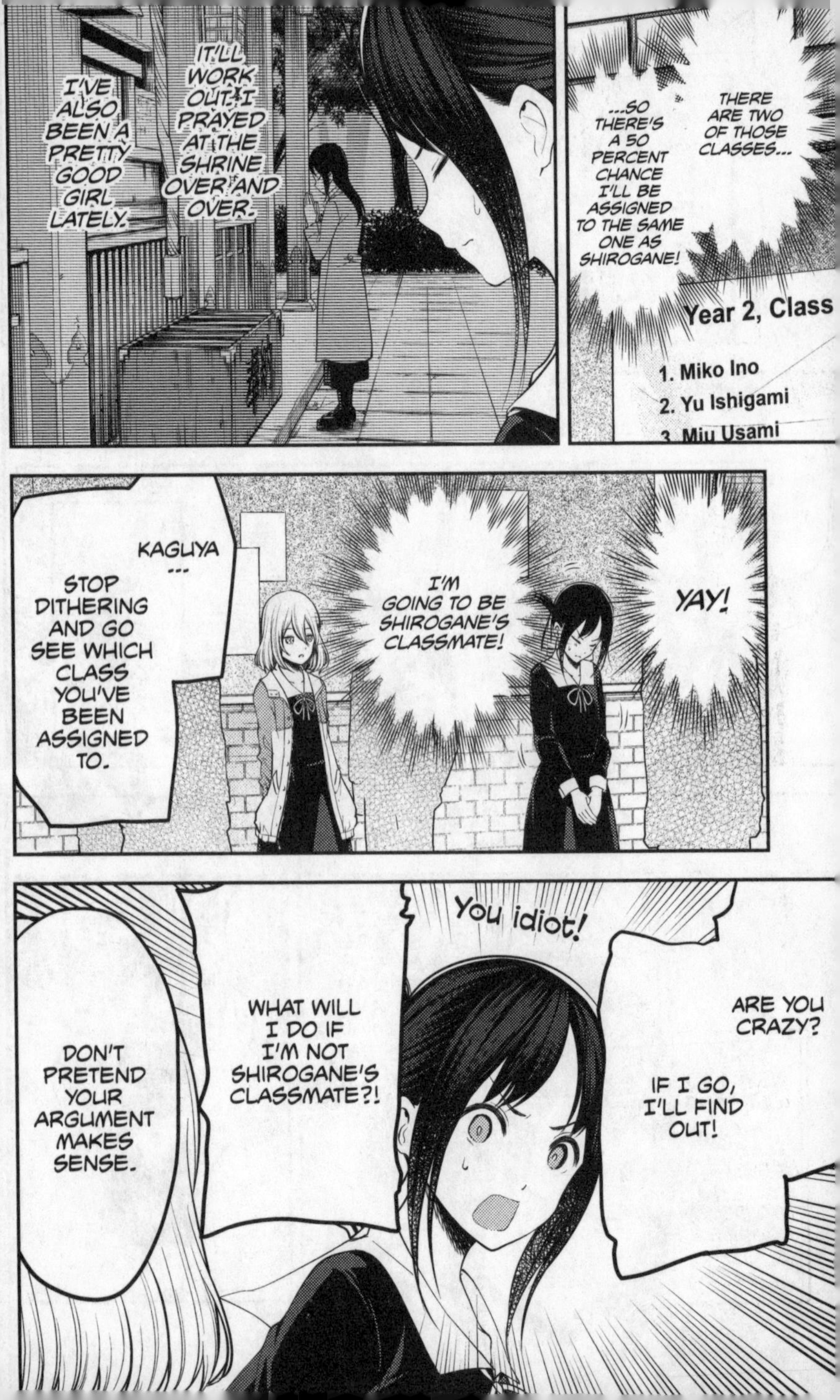
THERE ARE TWO OF THOSE CLASSES...
...SO THERE'S A 50 PERCENT CHANCE I'LL BE ASSIGNED TO THE SAME ONE AS SHIROGANE!
Year 2, Class
1. Miko Ino
2. Yu Ishigami
3. Miu Usami
IT'LL WORK OUT. I PRAYED AT THE SHRINE OVER AND OVER.
I'VE ALSO BEEN A PRETTY GOOD GIRL LATELY.
YAY!
I'M GOING TO BE SHIROGANE'S CLASSMATE!
KAGUYA...
STOP DITHERING AND GO SEE WHICH CLASS YOU'VE BEEN ASSIGNED TO.
ARE YOU CRAZY?
IF I GO, I'LL FIND OUT!
You idiot!
WHAT WILL I DO IF I'M NOT SHIROGANE'S CLASSMATE?!
DON'T PRETEND YOUR ARGUMENT MAKES SENSE.

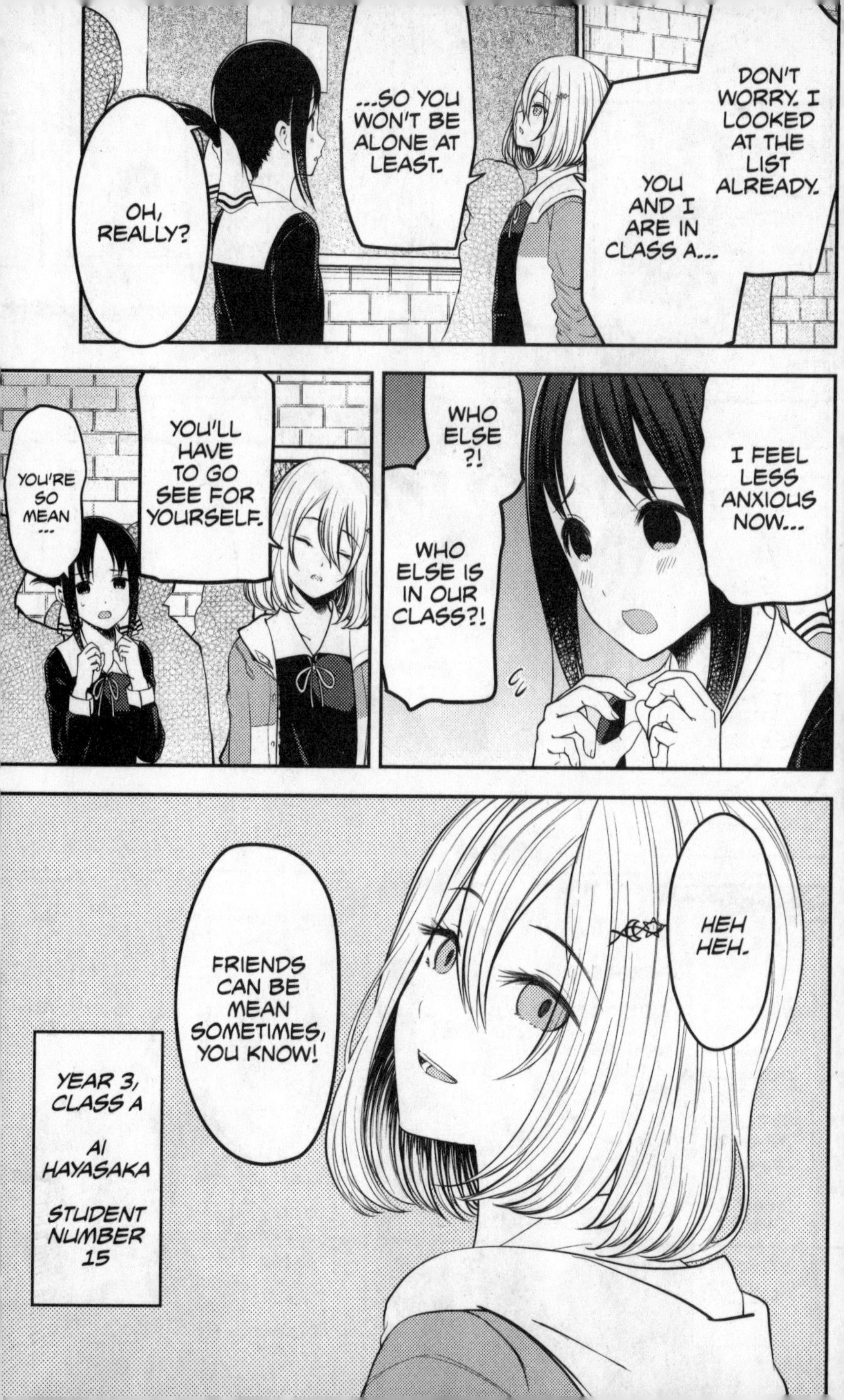
DON'T WORRY. I LOOKED AT THE LIST ALREADY.
YOU AND I ARE IN CLASS A...
...SO YOU WON'T BE ALONE AT LEAST.
OH, REALLY?
I FEEL LESS ANXIOUS NOW...
WHO ELSE ?!
WHO ELSE IS IN OUR CLASS?!
YOU'LL HAVE TO GO SEE FOR YOURSELF.
YOU'RE SO MEAN ...
HEH HEH.
FRIENDS CAN BE MEAN SOMETIMES, YOU KNOW!
YEAR 3, CLASS A
AI HAYASAKA
STUDENT NUMBER 15

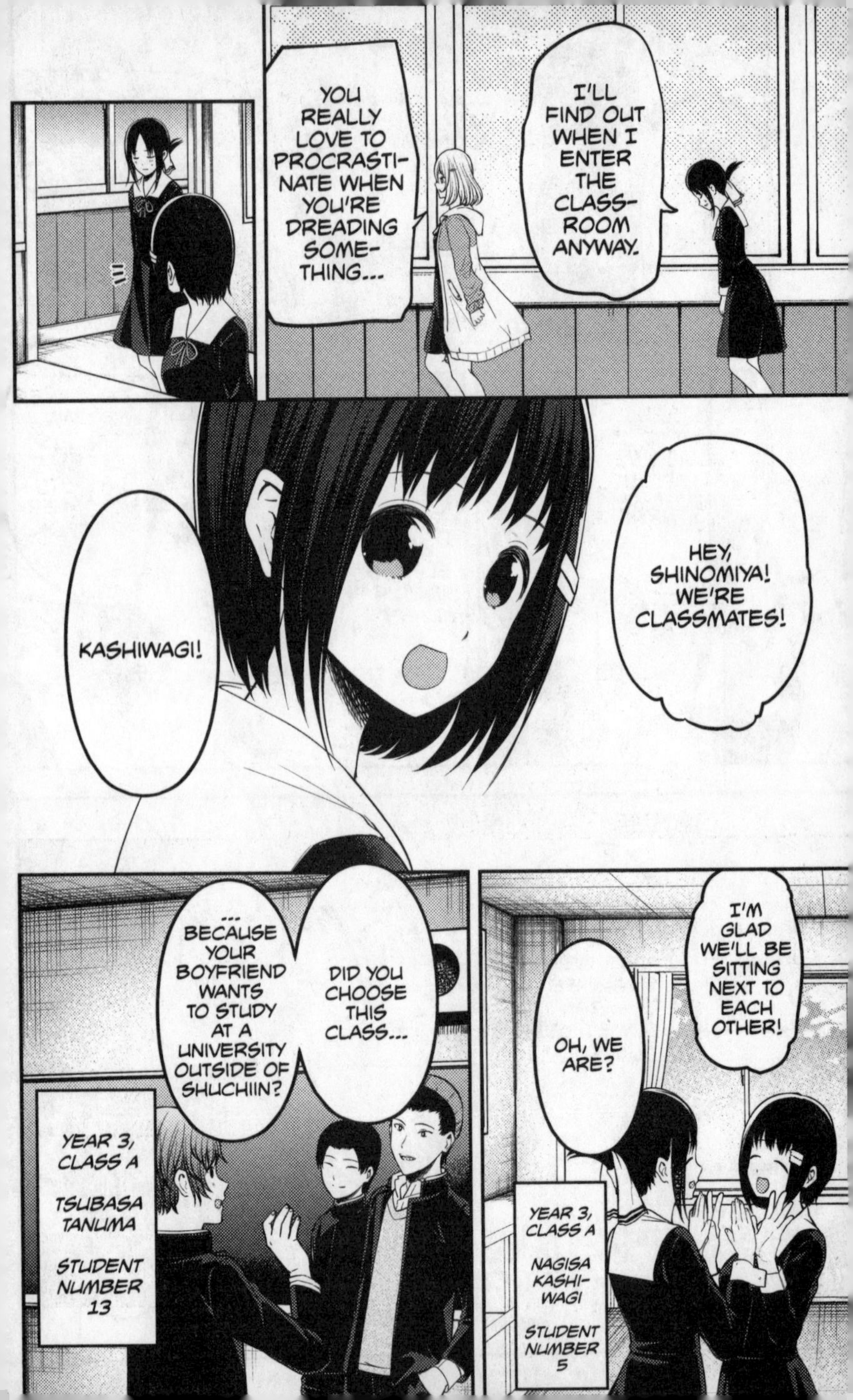
I'LL FIND OUT WHEN I ENTER THE CLASSROOM ANYWAY.
YOU REALLY LOVE TO PROCRASTINATE WHEN YOU'RE DREADING SOMETHING...
HEY, SHINOMIYA! WE'RE CLASSMATES!
KASHIWAGI!
I'M GLAD WE'LL BE SITTING NEXT TO EACH OTHER!
OH, WE ARE?
YEAR 3, CLASS A
NAGISA KASHIWAGI
STUDENT NUMBER 5
DID YOU CHOOSE THIS CLASS...
...BECAUSE YOUR BOYFRIEND WANTS TO STUDY AT A UNIVERSITY OUTSIDE OF SHUCHIIN?
YEAR 3, CLASS A
TSUBASA TANUMA
STUDENT NUMBER 13

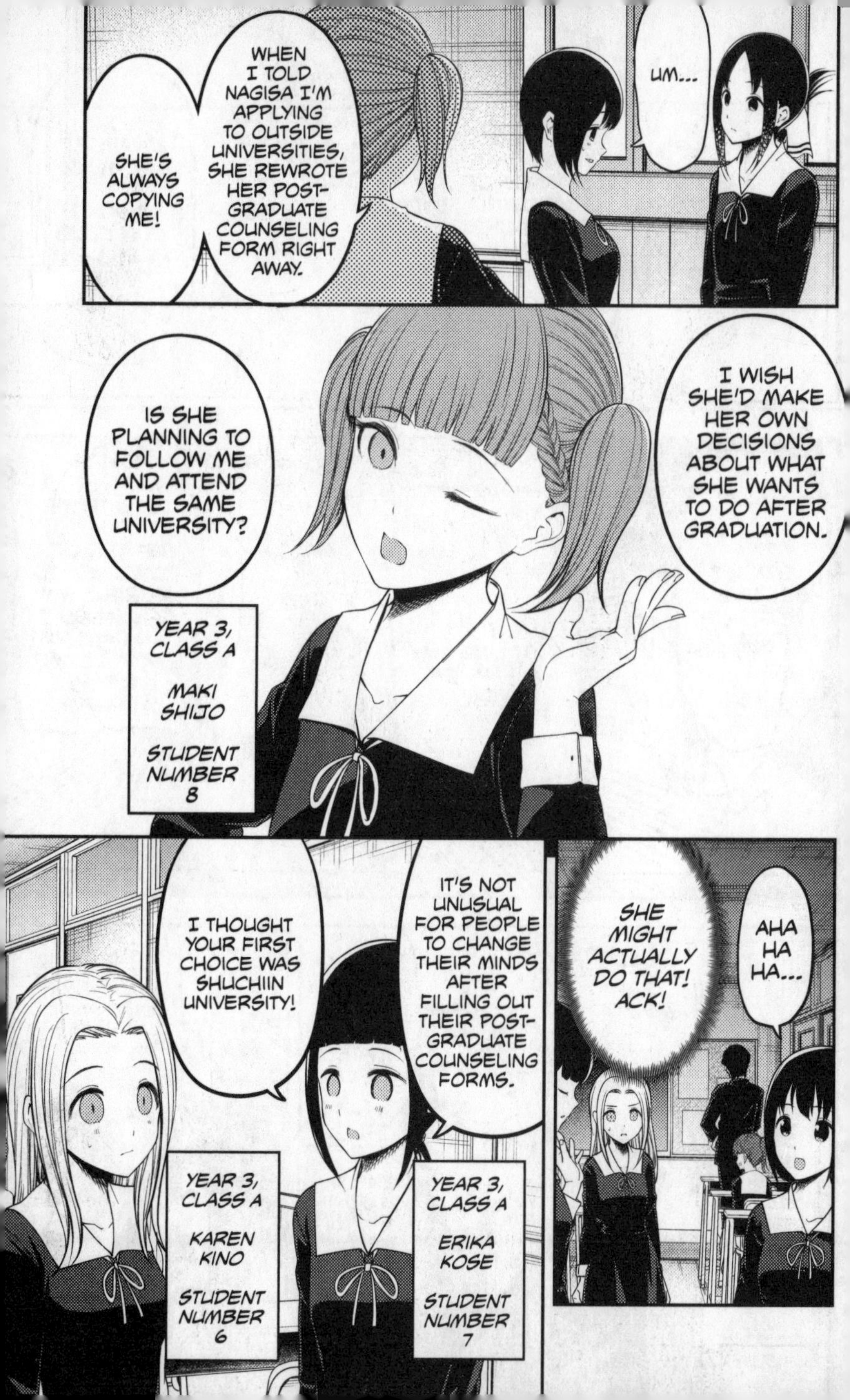
UM...
WHEN I TOLD NAGISA I'M APPLYING TO OUTSIDE UNIVERSITIES, SHE REWROTE HER POST-GRADUATE COUNSELING FORM RIGHT AWAY.
SHE'S ALWAYS COPYING ME!
I WISH SHE'D MAKE HER OWN DECISIONS ABOUT WHAT SHE WANTS TO DO AFTER GRADUATION.
IS SHE PLANNING TO FOLLOW ME AND ATTEND THE SAME UNIVERSITY?
YEAR 3, CLASS A MAKI SHIJO STUDENT NUMBER 8
AHA HA HA...
SHE MIGHT ACTUALLY DO THAT! ACK!
IT'S NOT UNUSUAL FOR PEOPLE TO CHANGE THEIR MINDS AFTER FILLING OUT THEIR POST-GRADUATE COUNSELING FORMS.
YEAR 3, CLASS A ERIKA KOSE STUDENT NUMBER 7
I THOUGHT YOUR FIRST CHOICE WAS SHUCHIIN UNIVERSITY!
YEAR 3, CLASS A KAREN KINO STUDENT NUMBER 6

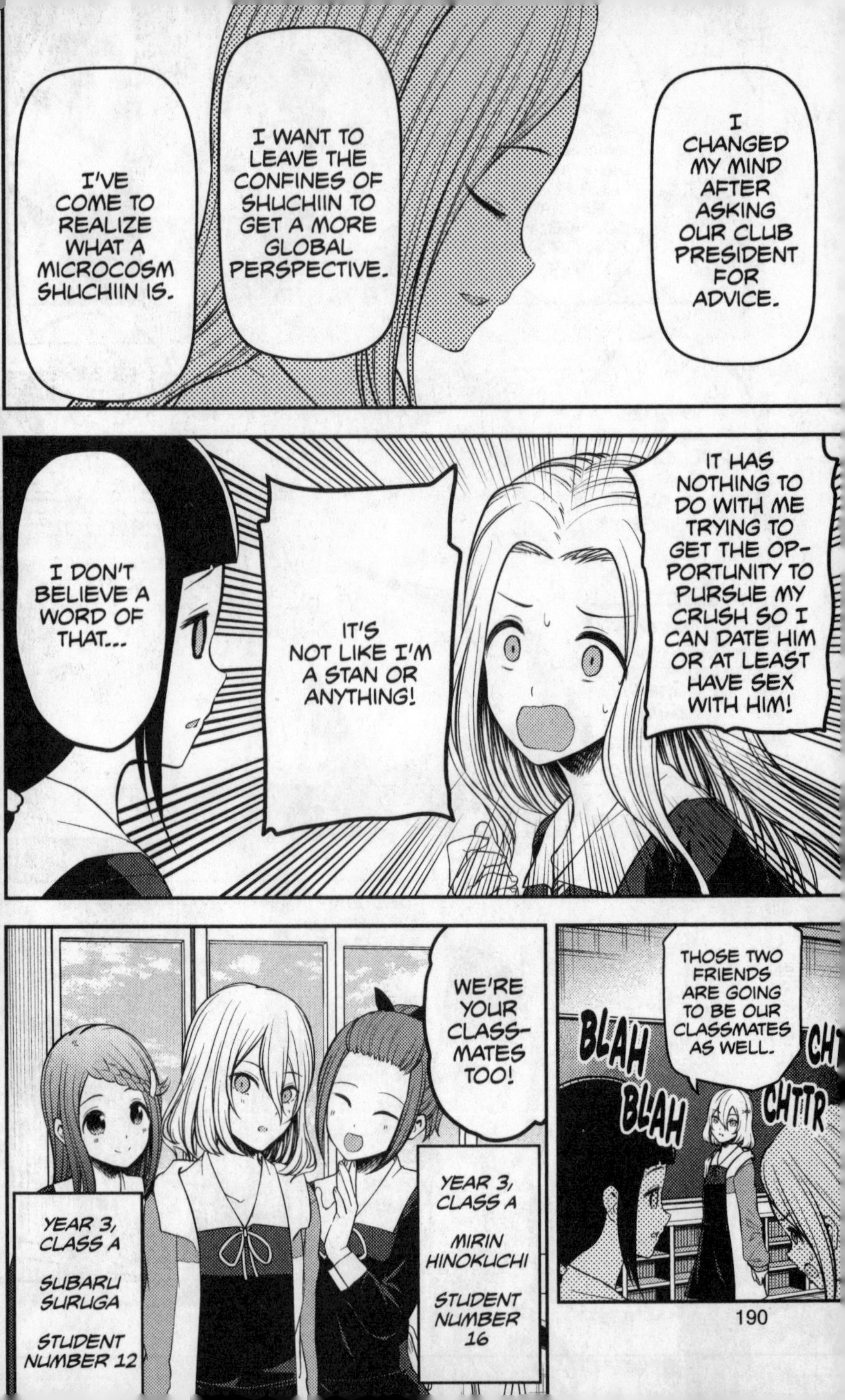
I CHANGED MY MIND AFTER ASKING OUR CLUB PRESIDENT FOR ADVICE.
I WANT TO LEAVE THE CONFINES OF SHUCHIIN TO GET A MORE GLOBAL PERSPECTIVE.
I'VE COME TO REALIZE WHAT A MICROCOSM SHUCHIIN IS.
IT HAS NOTHING TO DO WITH ME TRYING TO GET THE OP-PORTUNITY TO PURSUE MY CRUSH SO I CAN DATE HIM OR AT LEAST HAVE SEX WITH HIM!
IT'S NOT LIKE I'M A STAN OR ANYTHING!
I DON'T BELIEVE A WORD OF THAT...
THOSE TWO FRIENDS ARE GOING TO BE OUR CLASSMATES AS WELL.
CHT
CHTTR
BLAH
BLAH
WE'RE YOUR CLASS-MATES TOO!
YEAR 3, CLASS A
MIRIN HINOKUCHI
STUDENT NUMBER 16
YEAR 3, CLASS A
SUBARU SURUGA
STUDENT NUMBER 12

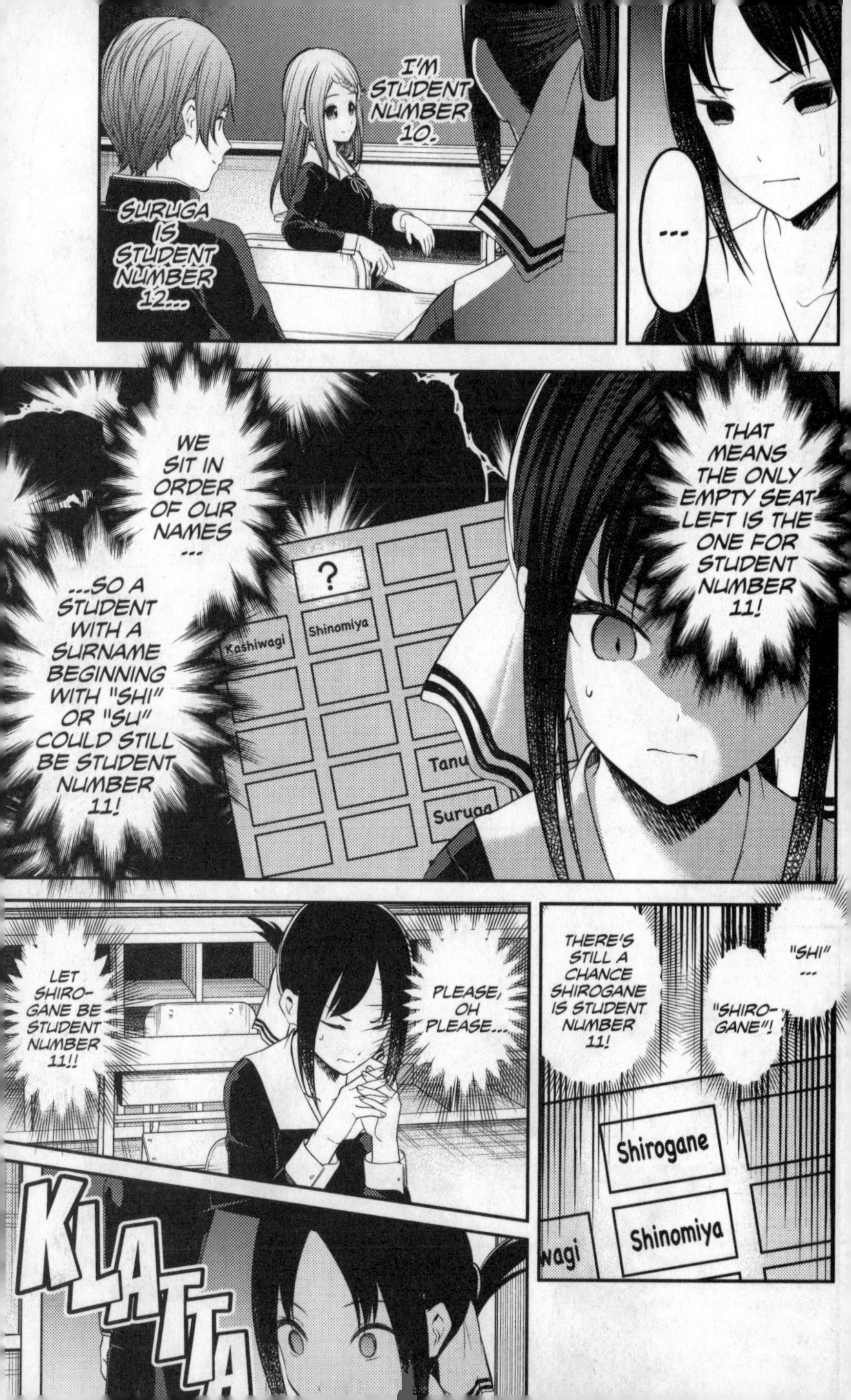
...
I'M STUDENT NUMBER 10.
SURUGA IS STUDENT NUMBER 12...
THAT MEANS THE ONLY EMPTY SEAT LEFT IS THE ONE FOR STUDENT NUMBER 11!
WE SIT IN ORDER OF OUR NAMES...
...SO A STUDENT WITH A SURNAME BEGINNING WITH "SHI" OR "SU" COULD STILL BE STUDENT NUMBER 11!
?
Shinomiya
Kashiwagi
Tanu
Suruga
"SHI"...
"SHIRO-GANE"!
THERE'S STILL A CHANCE SHIROGANE IS STUDENT NUMBER 11!
Shirogane
Shinomiya
wagi
PLEASE, OH PLEASE...
LET SHIRO-GANE BE STUDENT NUMBER 11!!
KLATTA

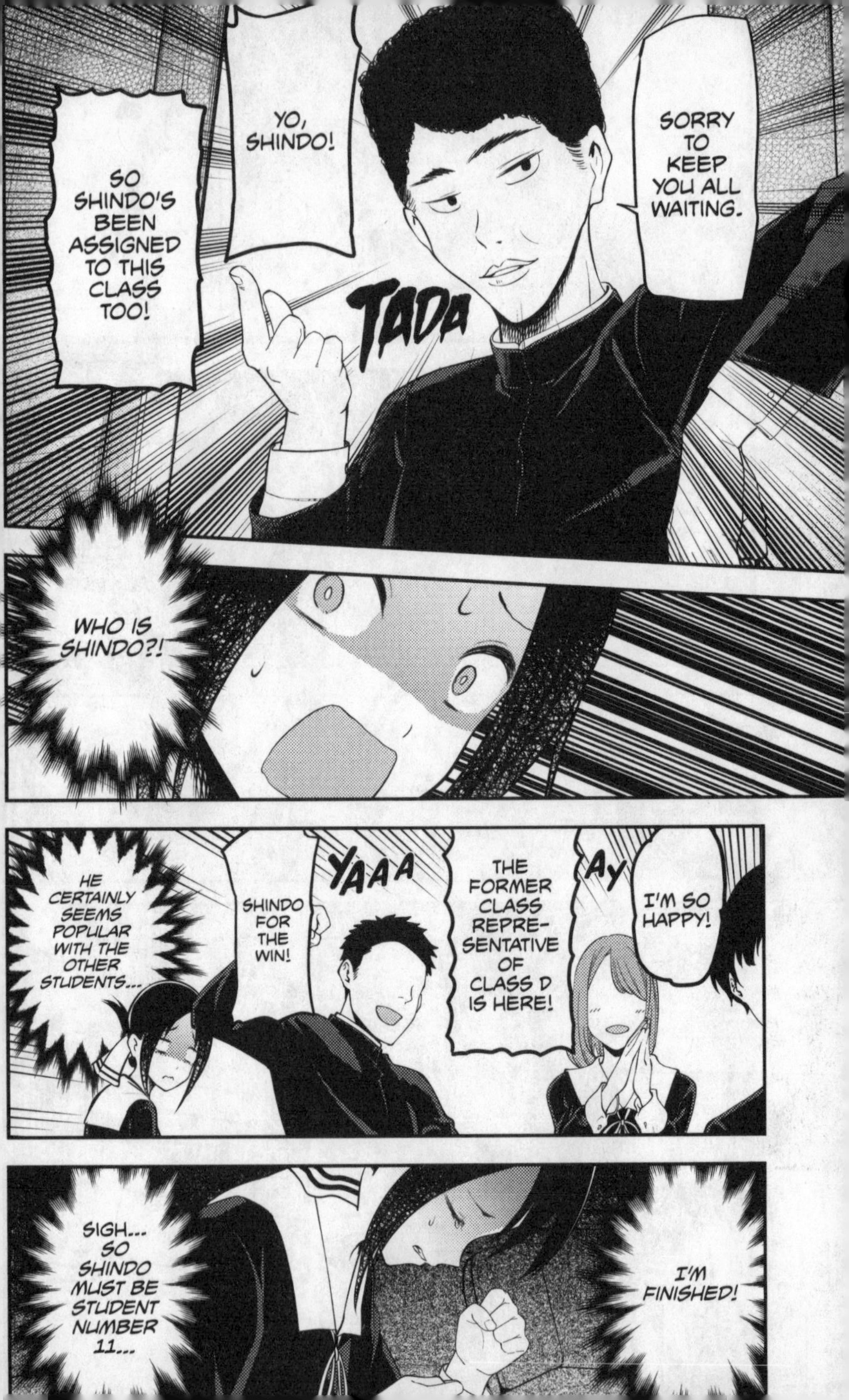
SORRY TO KEEP YOU ALL WAITING.
YO, SHINDO!
TADA
SO SHINDO'S BEEN ASSIGNED TO THIS CLASS TOO!
WHO IS SHINDO?!
I'M SO HAPPY!
Ay
THE FORMER CLASS REPRE-SENTATIVE OF CLASS D IS HERE!
YAAA
SHINDO FOR THE WIN!
HE CERTAINLY SEEMS POPULAR WITH THE OTHER STUDENTS...
I'M FINISHED!
SIGH... SO SHINDO MUST BE STUDENT NUMBER 11...

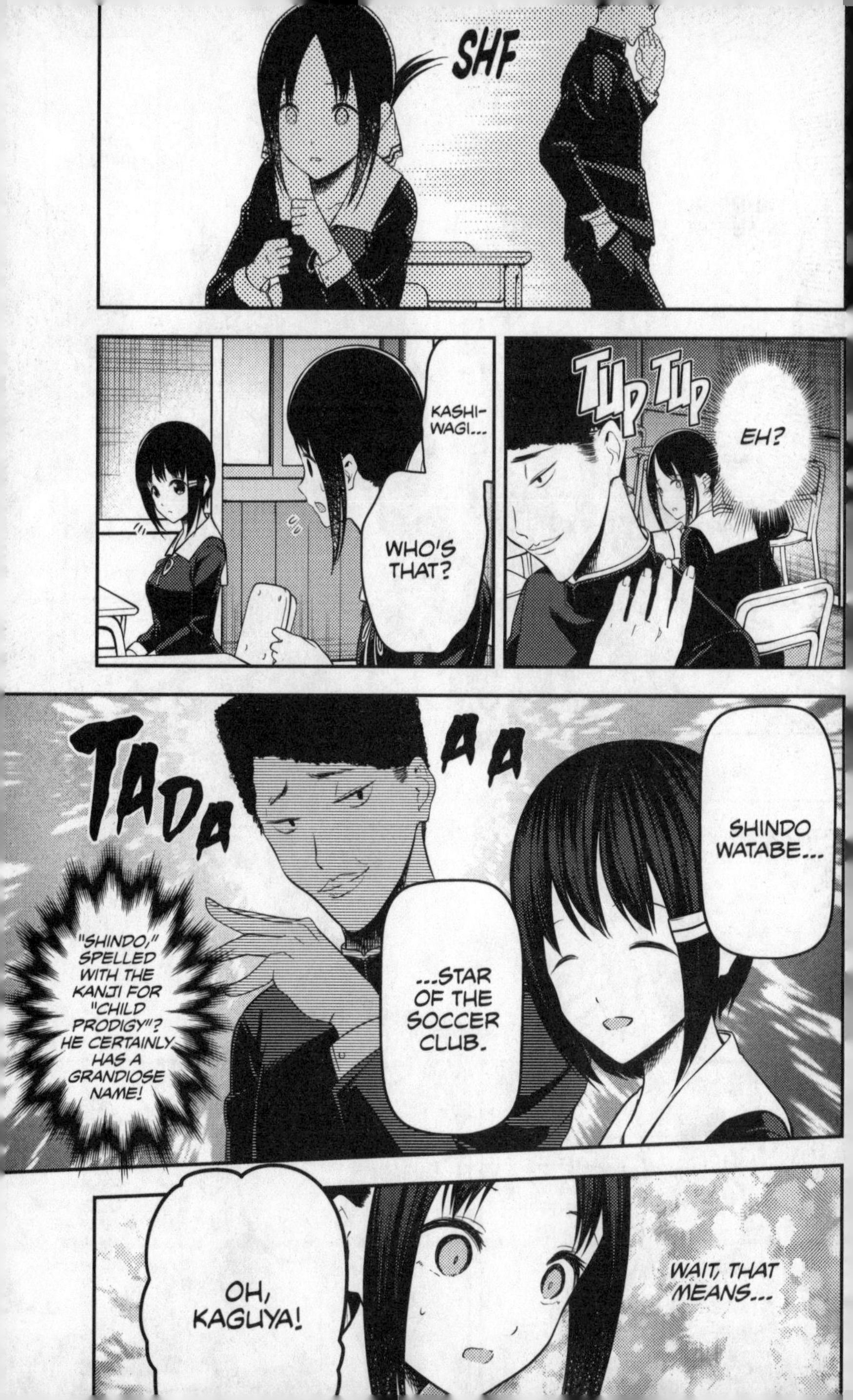
SHF
TUP TUP
EH?
KASHI-WAGI...
WHO'S THAT?
SHINDO WATABE...
...STAR OF THE SOCCER CLUB.
TADAA
"SHINDO," SPELLED WITH THE KANJI FOR "CHILD PRODIGY"? HE CERTAINLY HAS A GRANDIOSE NAME!
WAIT, THAT MEANS...
OH, KAGUYA!

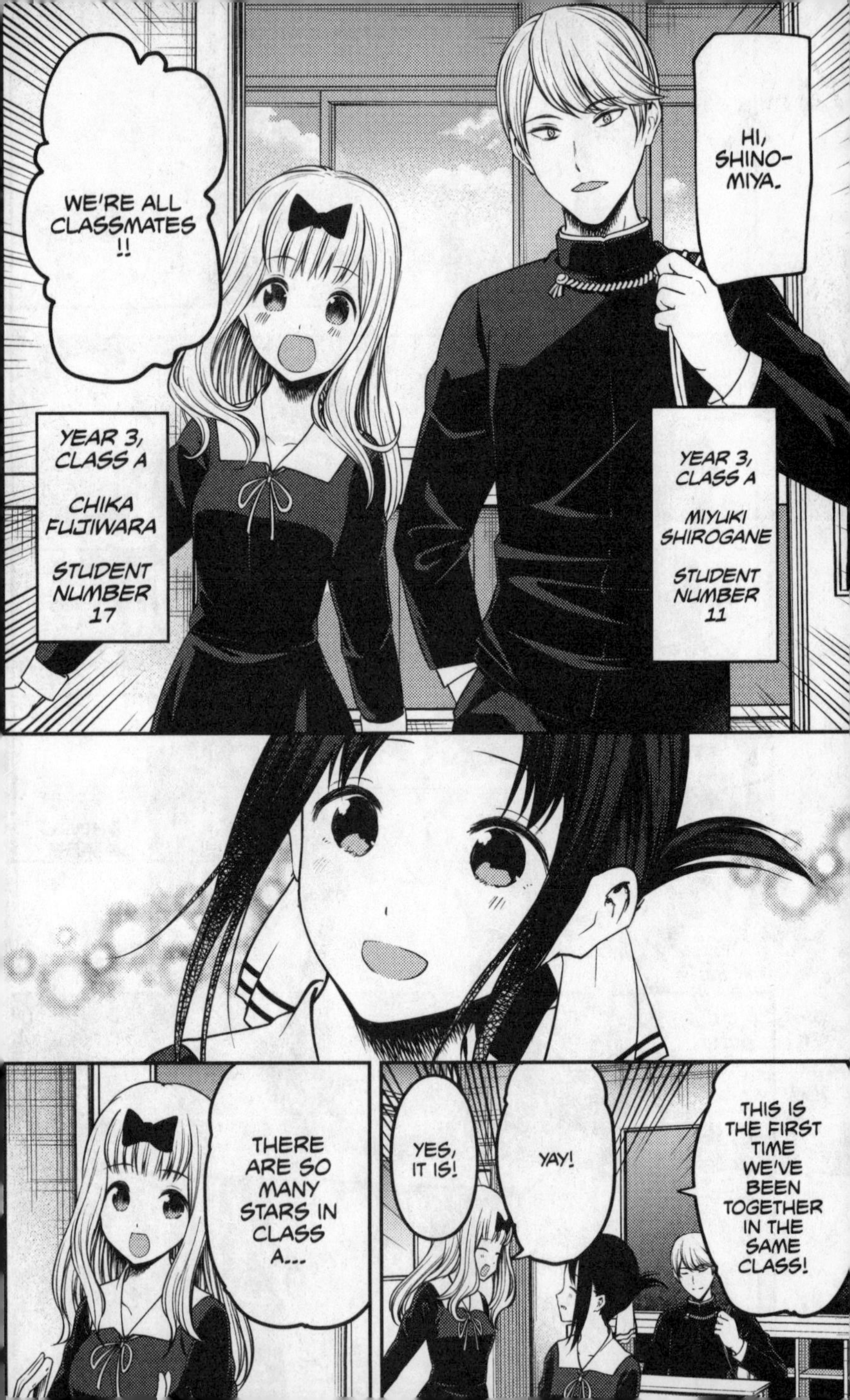
HI, SHINO-MIYA.
YEAR 3, CLASS A MIYUKI SHIROGANE STUDENT NUMBER 11
WE'RE ALL CLASSMATES !!
YEAR 3, CLASS A CHIKA FUJIWARA STUDENT NUMBER 17
THIS IS THE FIRST TIME WE'VE BEEN TOGETHER IN THE SAME CLASS!
YAY!
YES, IT IS!
THERE ARE SO MANY STARS IN CLASS A...

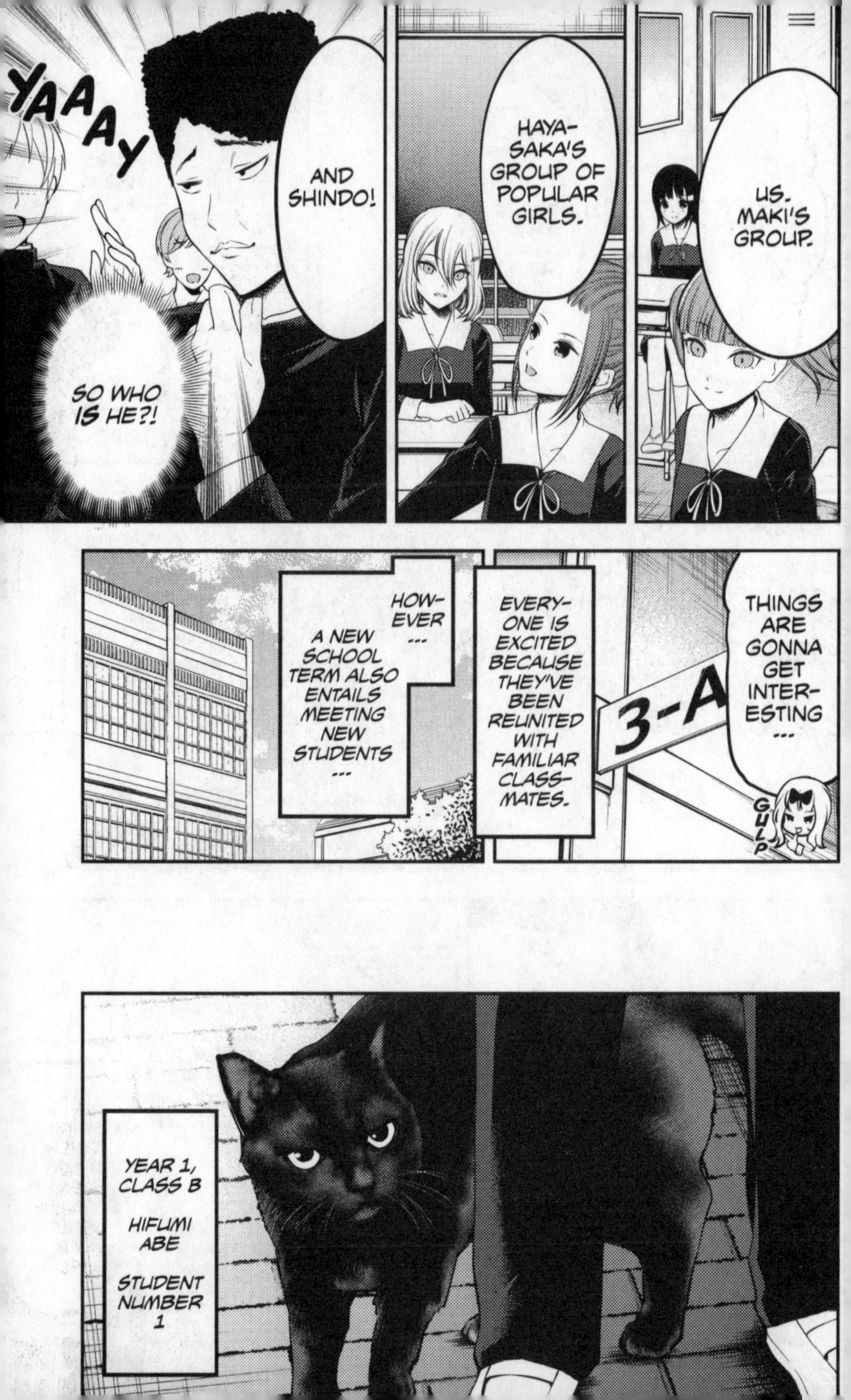
US. MAKI'S GROUP.
HAYA-SAKA'S GROUP OF POPULAR GIRLS.
AND SHINDO!
YAAAAY
SO WHO IS HE?!
THINGS ARE GONNA GET INTER-ESTING ...
3-A
GULP
EVERY-ONE IS EXCITED BECAUSE THEY'VE BEEN REUNITED WITH FAMILIAR CLASS-MATES.
HOW-EVER ... A NEW SCHOOL TERM ALSO ENTAILS MEETING NEW STUDENTS ...
YEAR 1, CLASS B
HIFUMI ABE
STUDENT NUMBER 1

THERE ARE RUMORS...
...THAT YOU ASSIGNED ALL YOUR FAVORITE STUDENTS TO CLASS A.
HEH HEH...
EDUCATORS ASSIGN STUDENTS TO CLASSES BASED ON WHAT THEY THINK IS IN THEIR BEST INTERESTS.
I CAME TO THE CONCLUSION THAT THESE WOULD BE THE BEST ASSIGNMENTS.
SHINOMIYA WILL NEED A LOT OF SUPPORT THIS YEAR.
THAT'S WHY...
...I ASSIGNED STUDENTS TO CLASS A WHO COULD HELP HER. AS MANY AS I COULD.
A TEACHER'S DUTY IS TO CREATE A SUPPORTIVE LEARNING ENVIRONMENT.
ISN'T THAT RIGHT, OBAYASHI?
NOT EVERY TEACHER IS A SAINT LIKE YOU.
AND YOU ASSIGNED *ME* TO THE PROBLEM CLASS!

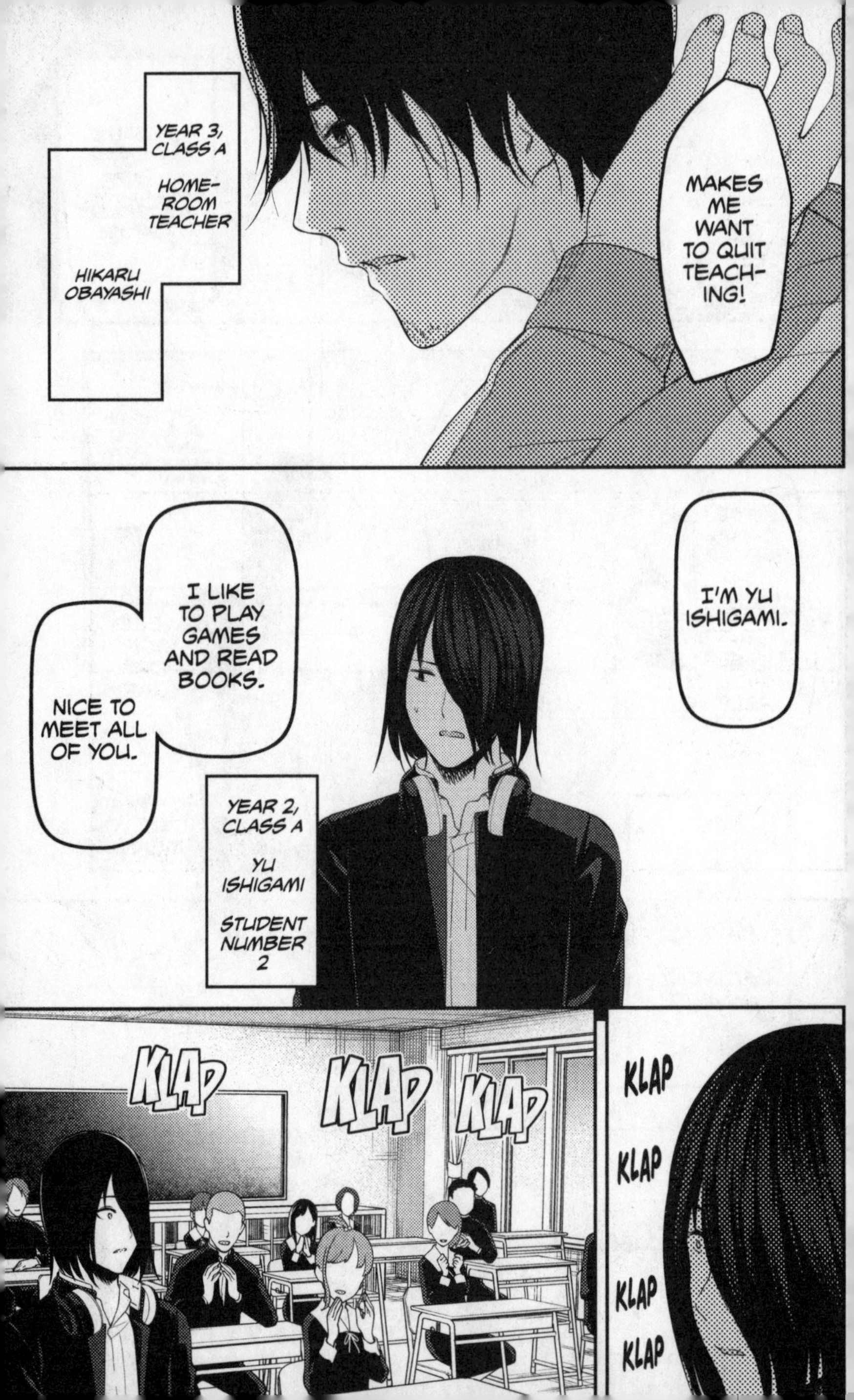
MAKES ME WANT TO QUIT TEACHING!
YEAR 3, CLASS A
HOMEROOM TEACHER
HIKARU OBAYASHI
I'M YU ISHIGAMI.
I LIKE TO PLAY GAMES AND READ BOOKS.
NICE TO MEET ALL OF YOU.
YEAR 2, CLASS A
YU ISHIGAMI
STUDENT NUMBER 2
KLAP
KLAP
KLAP
KLAP
KLAP
KLAP
KLAP

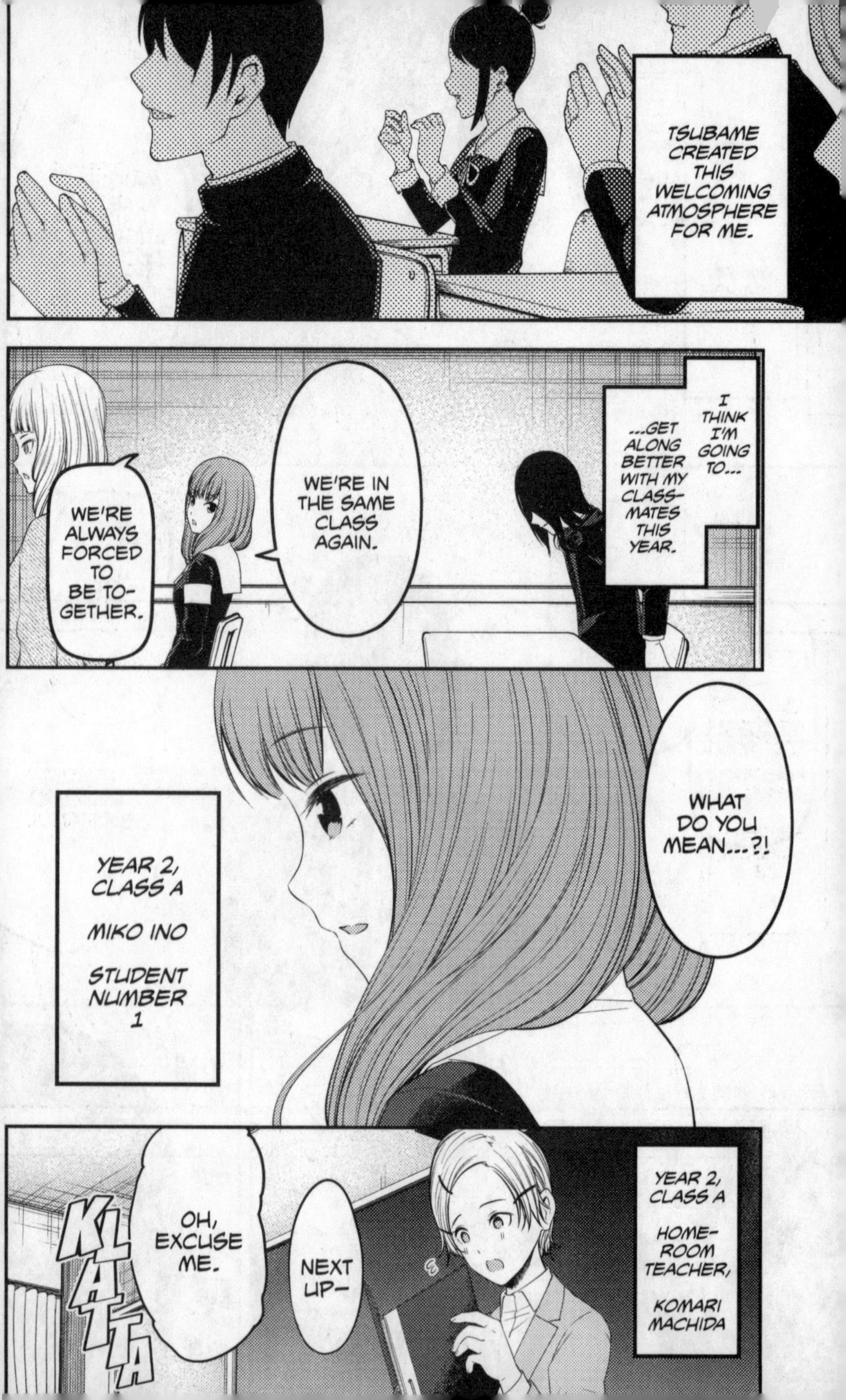
TSUBAME CREATED THIS WELCOMING ATMOSPHERE FOR ME.
I THINK I'M GOING TO...
...GET ALONG BETTER WITH MY CLASS-MATES THIS YEAR.
WE'RE IN THE SAME CLASS AGAIN.
WE'RE ALWAYS FORCED TO BE TO-GETHER.
WHAT DO YOU MEAN...?!
YEAR 2, CLASS A
MIKO INO
STUDENT NUMBER 1
YEAR 2, CLASS A HOME-ROOM TEACHER, KOMARI MACHIDA
NEXT UP—
OH, EXCUSE ME.
KLATTA

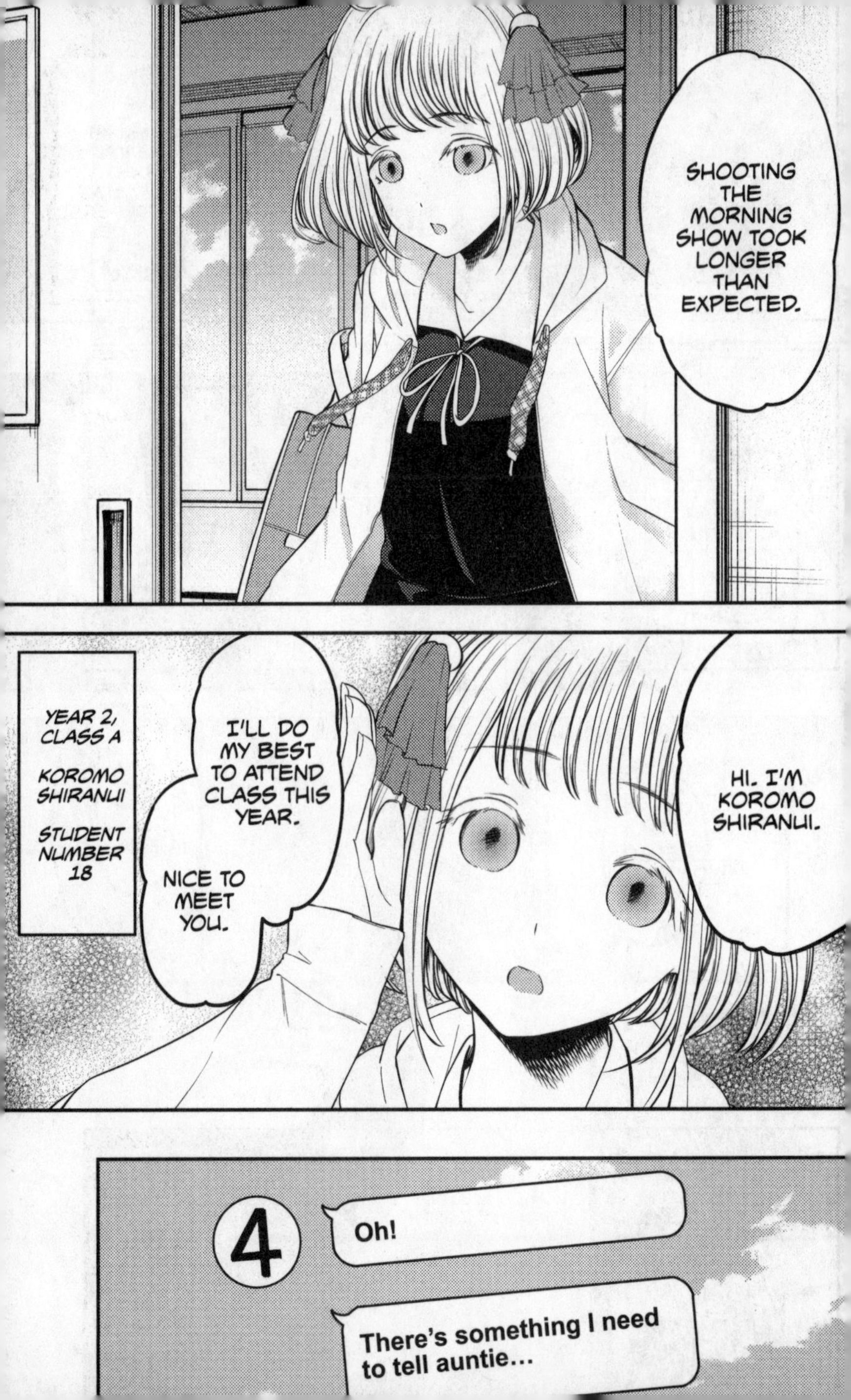
SHOOTING THE MORNING SHOW TOOK LONGER THAN EXPECTED.
HI. I'M KOROMO SHIRANUI.
I'LL DO MY BEST TO ATTEND CLASS THIS YEAR.
NICE TO MEET YOU.
YEAR 2, CLASS A
KOROMO SHIRANUI
STUDENT NUMBER 18
4
Oh!
There's something I need to tell auntie…

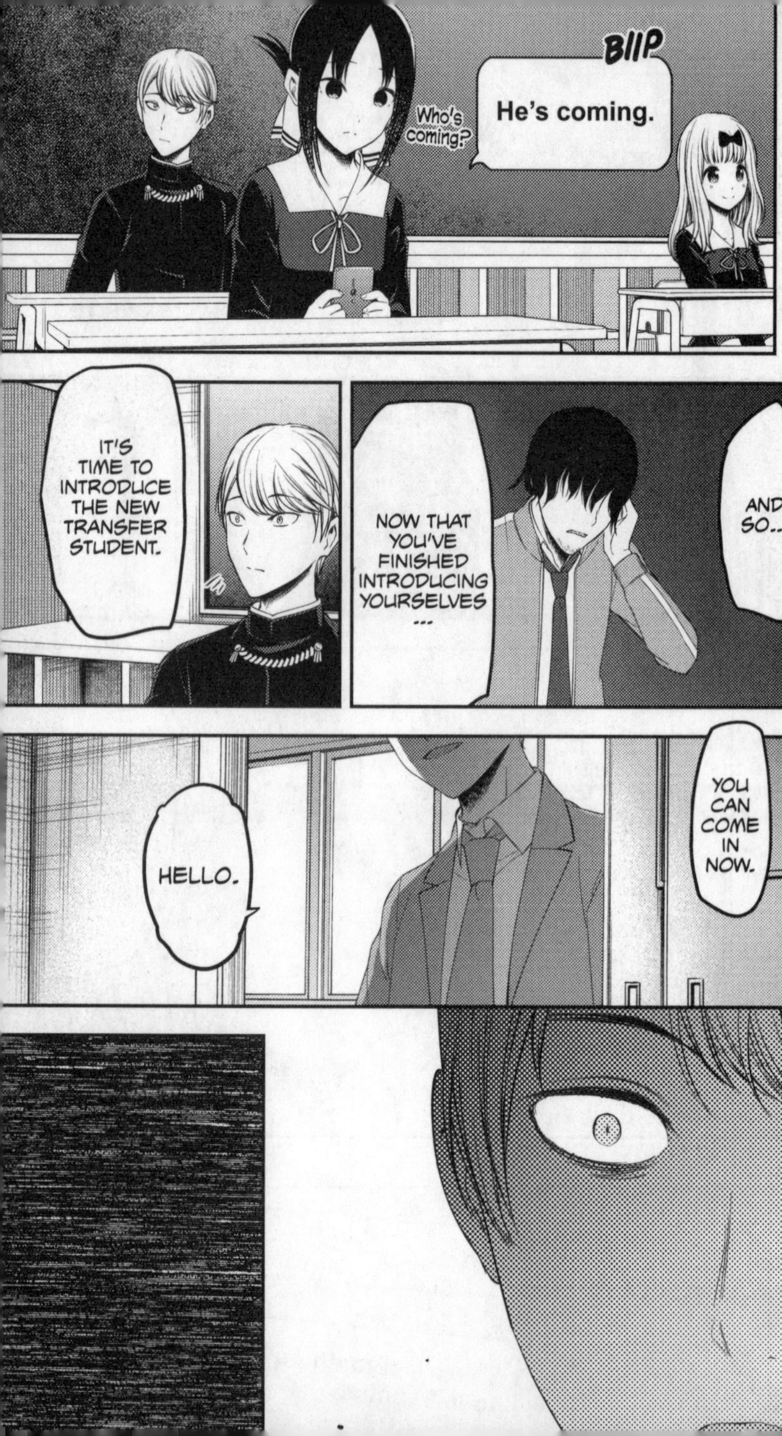
BIIP
He's coming.
Who's coming?
AND SO...
NOW THAT YOU'VE FINISHED INTRODUCING YOURSELVES...
IT'S TIME TO INTRODUCE THE NEW TRANSFER STUDENT.
YOU CAN COME IN NOW.
HELLO.

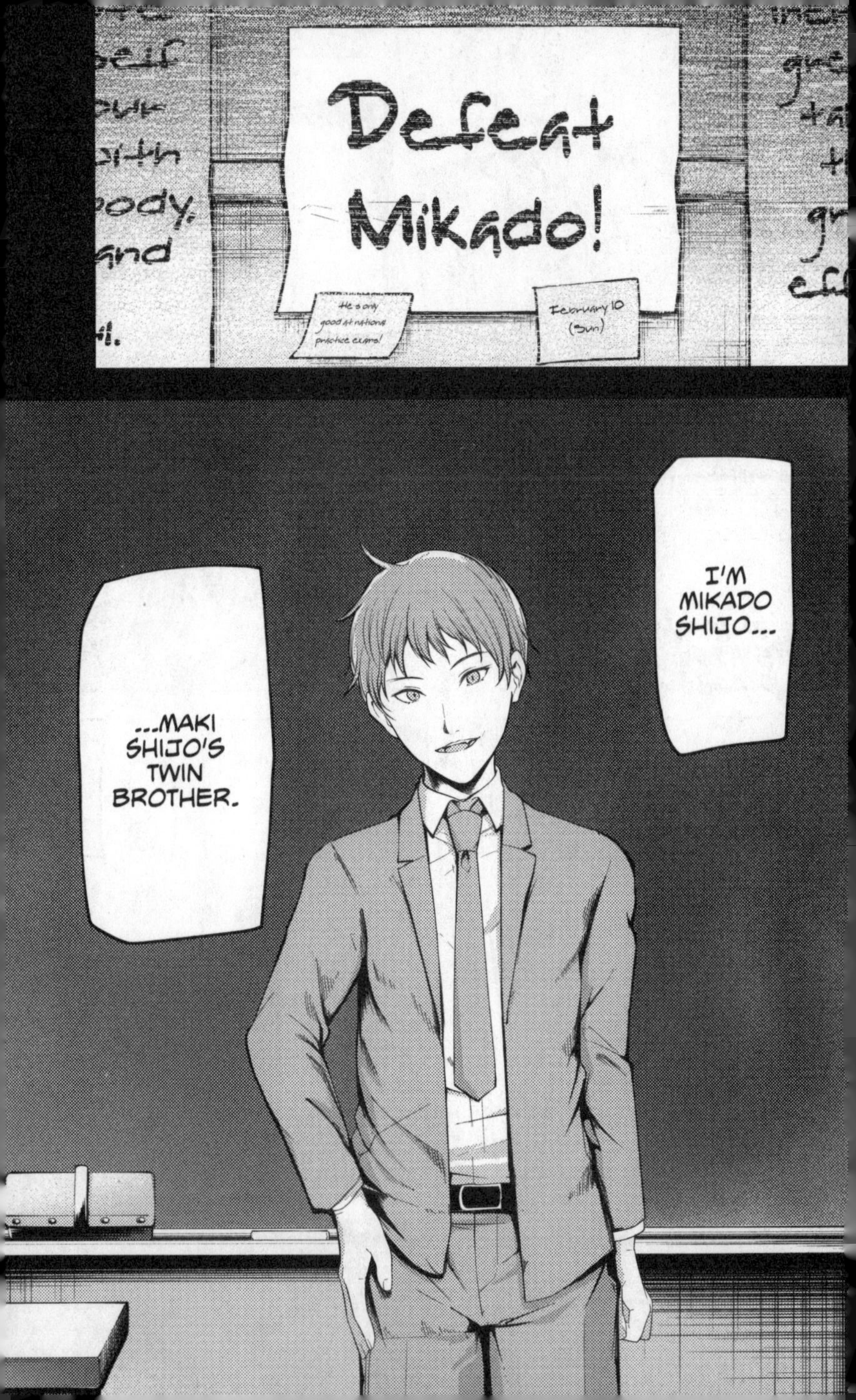
Defeat Mikado!
He's only good at national practice exams!
February 10 (Sun)
I'M MIKADO SHIJO...
...MAKI SHIJO'S TWIN BROTHER.

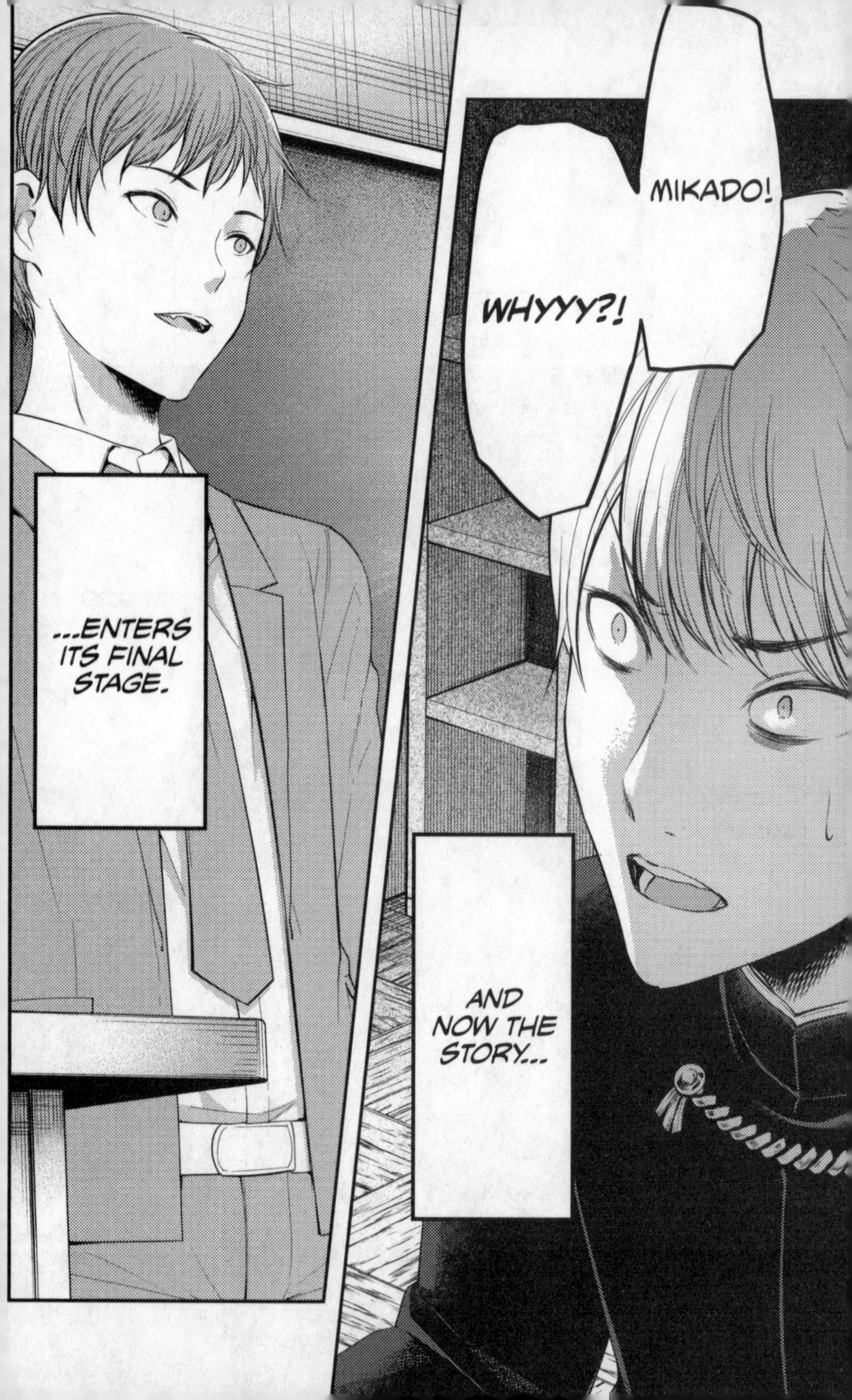
MIKADO!
WHYYY?!
AND NOW THE STORY...
...ENTERS ITS FINAL STAGE.

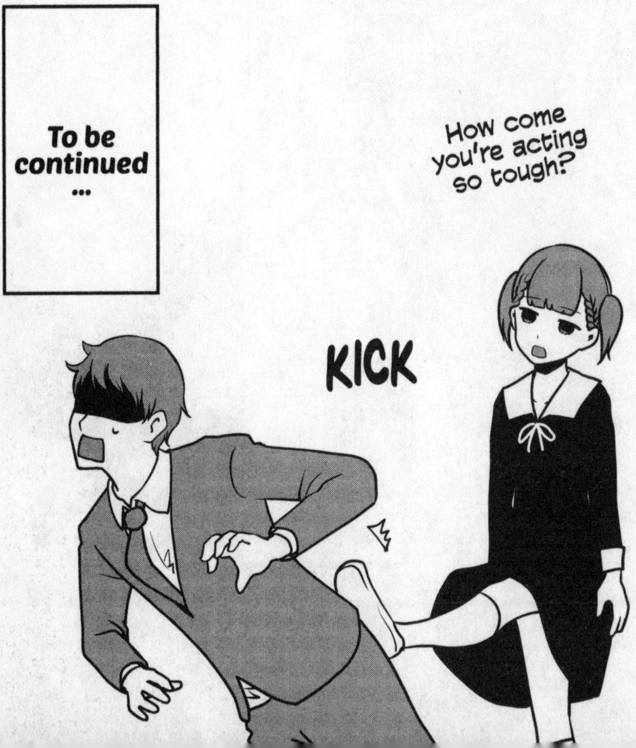
How come you're acting so tough?
KICK
To be continued ...

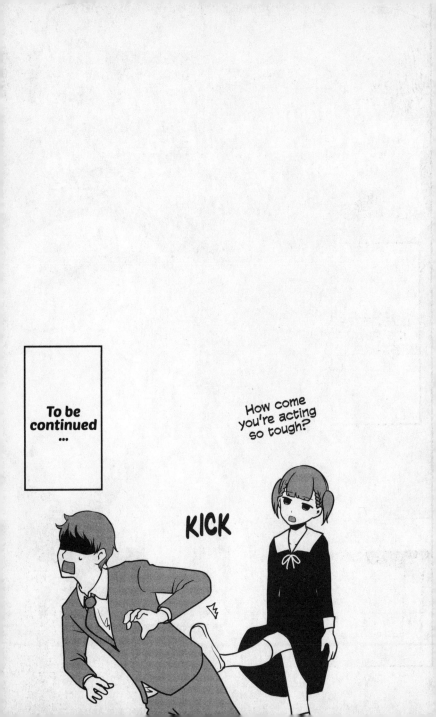

THE DESIRE TO BE LOVED AND THE DESIRE TO NOT BE DISLIKED ARE NOT THE SAME.

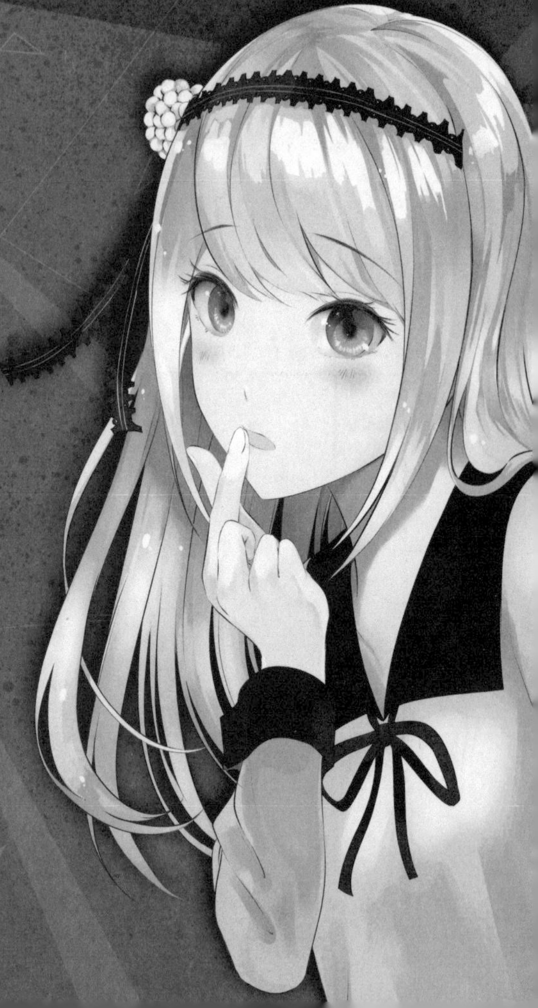

Aka Akasaka

Aka Akasaka got his start as an assistant to Jinsei Kataoka and Kazuma Kondou, the creators of *Deadman Wonderland*. His first serialized manga was an adaptation of the light novel series *Sayonara Piano Sonata*, published by Kadokawa in 2011. *Kaguya-sama: Love Is War* began serialization in *Miracle Jump* in 2015 but was later moved to *Weekly Young Jump* in 2016 due to its popularity.

To my assistants: I'm sorry, I have no time. Please come up with something for the under-cover pages.

Assistant U

Akasaka Studio Random Rankings

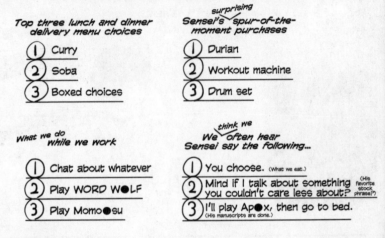

Top three lunch and dinner delivery menu choices

1. Curry
2. Soba
3. Boxed choices

Sensei's surprising spur-of-the-moment purchases

1. Durian
2. Workout machine
3. Drum set

What we do while we work

1. Chat about whatever
2. Play WORD W●LF
3. Play Momo●su

We think we often hear Sensei say the following...

1. You choose. (What we eat.)
2. Mind if I talk about something you couldn't care less about? (His favorite stock phrase?)
3. I'll play Ap●x, then go to bed. (His manuscripts are done.)

<<Color this picture.>>

Assistant O

Park

This is Akasaka Sensei's storyboard. Color the picture and create a great work of art!

Assistant N

WHEN I PLAY A CERTAIN GAME (APOX) WITH AKASAKA SENSEI, I SOMETIMES MEET AMAZING PEOPLE!

"WHAT?! YOU'RE OOSENSEI, THE CREATOR OF ▲▲WA KYO MO USO WO~?!"

"I LOVE YOUR WORK! I'M SO HONORED TO PLAY WITH YOU. OH, THANKS! YOU'RE SO GOOD."

THESE ARE MOMENTS WHEN I'M GLAD I KEPT PLAYING GAMES INSTEAD OF WORKING.

THAT GAME (APOX) IS REALLY GREAT!

LET'S ALL PLAY THAT GAME (APOX)!

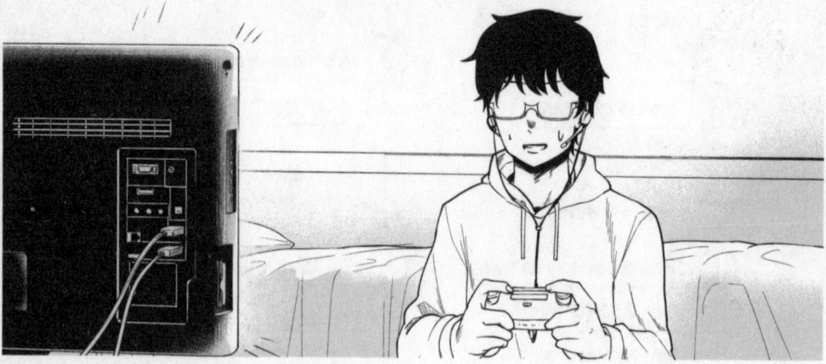

Assistant D

DEAR AKASAKA SENSEI,

THIS MUST BE THE ONLY WORKPLACE IN JAPAN WHERE YOU CAN WORK WHILE PLAYING GAMES EVERY WEEK.

WE HAD SO MUCH FUN PLAYING A CERTAIN RAILWAY COMPANY MANAGEMENT GAME.

WHEN I FINALLY GOT TO USE THE "GYUHO CARD," ANOTHER PLAYER SENT ME NORTH!

THE TEAMWORK AT THIS WORKPLACE IS AMAZING!

I WON'T MENTION WHAT GAME WE WERE PLAYING, BUT WHEN I WAS PLAYING SEASON 7 AND SAID I'D QUIT AKASAKA STUDIO IF I COULDN'T MAKE IT TO DIAMOND RANK, YOU SAID, "NO PROBLEM..."

THINGS AREN'T LOOKING GOOD. YOU'D BETTER START LOOKING FOR A NEW ASSISTANT.

SINCERELY,

ASSISTANT D

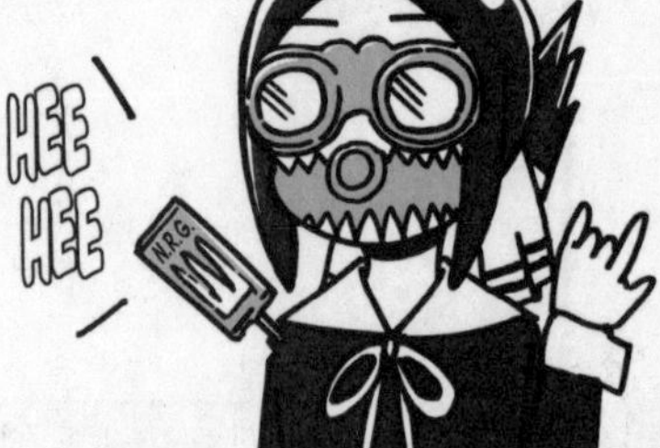
HEE
HEE
N.R.G.

KAGUYA-SAMA
LOVE IS WAR

SHONEN JUMP MANGA EDITION

21

STORY AND ART BY
AKA AKASAKA

Translation/Tomo Kimura
English Adaptation/Annette Roman
Touch-Up Art & Lettering/Steve Dutro
Cover & Interior Design/Alice Lewis
Editor/Annette Roman

KAGUYA-SAMA WA KOKURASETAI~TENSAITACHI NO REN'AI ZUNO SEN~
© 2015 by Aka Akasaka
All rights reserved.
First published in Japan in 2015 by SHUEISHA Inc., Tokyo.
English translation rights arranged by SHUEISHA Inc.

The stories, characters, and incidents mentioned in this publication
are entirely fictional.

No portion of this book may be reproduced or transmitted in any form or by any
means without written permission from the copyright holders.

Printed in Canada

Published by VIZ Media, LLC
P.O. Box 77010
San Francisco, CA 94107

10 9 8 7 6 5 4 3 2 1
First printing, December 2021

PARENTAL ADVISORY
KAGUYA-SAMA: LOVE IS WAR is rated T for Teen
and is recommended for ages 13 and up. It contains
mild language and first-love shenanigans.

SACRAMENTO PUBLIC LIBRARY
828 "I" Street
Sacramento, CA 95814
01/22

COMING NEXT VOLUME

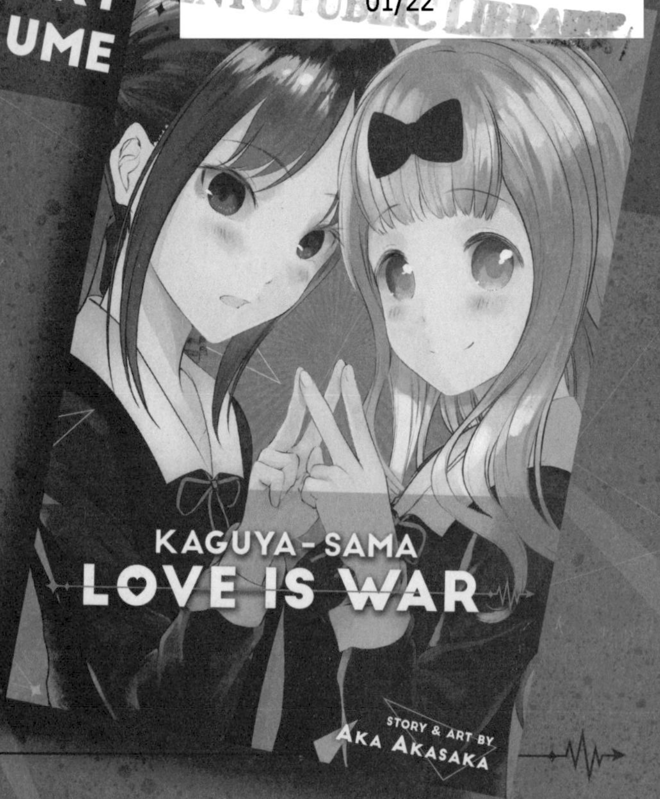

KAGUYA-SAMA
LOVE IS WAR

22

STORY & ART BY
AKA AKASAKA

Will Miko's budding closeness with Miyuki make other interested parties jealous? Entertaining a cat in the student council chambers leads to complications. And as the war between the Shinomiyas and the Shijos heats up, Kaguya's new assistant and Mikado both fall under suspicion. Finally, Kaguya spends the night at Miyuki's place—alone!

How do you know when you're ready?